ATHENS, PARIS, ST. LOUIS, LONDON,
STOCKHOLM, ANTWERP, AMSTERDAM,
LOS ANGELES, BERLIN, HELSINKI,
MELBOURNE, ROME, TOKYO,
MEXICO CITY, MUNICH, MONTREAL

AND NOW IN 1980, MOSCOW

It is a striking record of accomplishment and adventure.

This is the story General Grombach tells. From 1263 B.C. down through history he traces the Olympic pageantry, the rivalries, the triumphs, the color and excitement of the world's greatest athletic contests. The development of each sport is traced from its origins to its present-day stars: from Coroebus of Elis to Kipshoge Keino of Kenya and Lasse Viren of Finland.

Here is a complete history of the Olympic Games; fascinating reading for every follower of every sport.

The 1980 Olympic Guide

John V. Grombach

Complete sport by sport history
with records of every event

Times
BOOKS

CONTENTS

I   Origin of the Ancient Olympics and First
Efforts to Revive Them in Modern Times   7

II   Origin, Management, and Spirit of the
Modern Olympic Games   14

III   Archery   33

IV   Boxing   35

V   Canoeing   54

VI   Cycling   60

VII   Equestrian Events   68

VIII   Fencing   82

IX   Gymnastics   98

X   The Modern Pentathlon   106

XI   Rowing and Sculling   116

XII   Shooting   129

XIII   Swimming and Diving   136

XIV   Team Games   149

XV   Track and Field   163

XVI   Weight Lifting   193

XVII   Winter Sports   198

XVIII   Wrestling   226

XIX   Yachting   239

XX   The 1972 Games   246

XXI   The 1976 Games   266

XXII   The Future and its Problems   274

Complete Appendix (Statistics)   283

Game Winners and Records   313

Daily Schedule, 1980 Games   352

CHAPTER I

Origin of the Ancient Olympics
and First Efforts to Revive Them in Modern Times

THE CAVALCADE of Olympic games is the oldest show on earth. Although revived by popular request in modern times, in 1896, the Olympics ran continuously every four years for at least 1,200 years in ancient Greece. The first recorded Olympic games were in 776 B.C. and the last recorded Olympics were in 394 A.D., at which time Roman Emperor Theodosius suspended the games. According to modern historical research, however, the games actually began long before 776 B.C.—began, in fact, sometime between 1253 B.C. and 884 B.C.

The Olympic pageant of sports (which according to the surviving records started with one foot race, a sprint) therefore probably covers more than 3,000 years and 314 definitely recorded Olympiads, and has encompassed practically every competitive sport known to man. In fact, the Olympics is the greatest single factor behind the development of every one of the sports which form part of the current daily peaceful fare of activity, interest, conversation and entertainment of the peoples of the world. The 21st modern Olympic games at Montreal, Canada, in 1976 were actually the 315th recorded Olympic games in the history of competitive athletics.

Let us go back to the earliest times among the green-wooded slopes and grassy plains through which flowed two rivers in ancient Hellas, now Greece. The banks of the Alpheus and the Cladeus were overshadowed by willow trees, mirrored in the clear sparkling waters. As the first settlement of Olympia, the ancient site of the Olympics, belongs to mythical times and legend, so do the fables which historians and poets tell of the origin of the greatest and oldest series of athletic competitions on earth.

According to one version, Heracles, as a penance for his misdeeds, was given the difficult problem and unpleasant chore of quickly cleaning the stables in which Augeas, King of Elis, maintained a great herd. Heracles accomplished his job with the greatest of ease simply by turning the river Alpheus from its course through the stables, but not before making a friendly bet with the King that if he accomplished his task he would be due, as a commission, a ten per cent cut of the herd. Augeas refused to pay up, claiming that Heracles' method was all wet. Heracles then killed

Augeas and took over the herd, the property, and the throne of Augeas. To salve his guilty conscience and at the same time to celebrate his accomplishments and the acquisition of his new properties, Heracles then instituted the first Olympic games—*circa* 1253 B.C.

Another version would have us believe that Lycurgus, the great Spartan formulator of law, joined with Iphitus of Elis on the alleged bidding of the oracle to "restore" the festival in 820 B.C. This at least would indicate that the games had been run before, as there is some historical basis for this story and definite evidence points to the word "restore."

Greek mythology seems to claim that the Olympics began as religious celebrations and games in commemoration of Zeus' having defeated Kronos in a mighty wrestling match of the gods for possession of the earth.

Another rather stubborn story is given by the natives of Greece interested in the Olympics—the legend of Pelops. Here the river Alpheus is again the background for a story, this time of a King of Elis, Oenomaus, with a beautiful daughter named Hippodamia. The girl was offered to any suitor who could successfully kidnap her in a chariot. The catch, of course, was that the King gave pursuit, had light chariots, fast horses, and was handy with the spear or javelin. According to legend, thirteen young men got away with Hippodamia, but all were caught up with and promptly transfixed with a royal spear. This may be the origin of our modern superstition about the number thirteen. At any rate, one day a young man named Pelops showed up, studied the situation carefully, took certain precautions, and made certain preparations. Shortly thereafter Pelops left his amiable royal host, taking the daughter with him. Oenomaus gave chase, but Pelops had bribed the King's charioteer to tamper with the kingly car's axle, and the result was the ancient counterpart of a blowout. Thus Pelops won a bride and a throne with a bribe and instituted the games and religious ceremonies on the hallowed ground of Olympia in Elis. The date generally ascribed to this episode is 884 B.C.

No matter which one of these uncertain legends or dates we accept, one thing is certain—that the first recorded Olympics occurred in 776 B.C., and that thereafter the Greeks began to reckon time by Olympiads, the four-year intervals at which the games were held. From the first Olympiad to the 315th is history, and what came before is legend. However, archeologists assert that the ruins of Olympia reveal the fact that many of the great buildings within the enclosure for games and religious celebrations of the Olympics were built about five hundred years before the first recorded Olympiad in 776 B.C.

The games were conducted on the highest plane—almost a religious one. At first only pure Greeks could compete, and for centuries the moral standards were carefully upheld. No one with a police record, or even related to anyone with a police record, could be a contestant.

At first, only the sprint or foot race—one length of the stadium (approximately 200 yards)—was involved. At the games of the 14th Olympiad, a second race of two times around the stadium (less than one-half mile) was added; at the 15th, a long-distance race of twelve times around the stadium (approximately 2½ miles). In the 18th, a five-event pentathlon (broad jumping, javelin throw, 200-yard dash, discus throw, and wrestling), obviously for the soldier-athlete, was added. This was the first appearance of wrestling in the Olympics, although it was later added as a separate event. Boxing began at the 23rd Olympics; equestrian events came in with the four-horse chariot in the nearby hippodrome at the 25th games; and the pancratium, a combination of boxing, wrestling, and modern waterfront brawling, was added in the 33rd Olympics. Running with full military equipment, including shields, and jumping were also added in the earlier games.

Many field events closely resembling our modern events, such as javelin and discus throwing, were added to the ever-increasing cavalcade of Olympic sports. However, the jumping events differed from our modern jumping in using weights which contestants carried in their hands and tossed backward at the moment of take-off. Even the tug of war, football, gymnastics and weight lifting can be traced back to the ancient Olympics. From the earliest Olympics, separate but similar events for boys were added.

Interest in all forms of athletics made the Olympics the greatest event in the known world. The Olympic athletic program was expanded from one morning to five days, with two additional days for religious ceremonies. Tourists and sports fans as far back as the fifth century B.C. trooped to Olympia from communities along all shores of the Mediterranean— France, Spain, Africa, Sicily, Italy, Asia Minor. These regions also sent their athletes and representatives to compete and erect sanctuaries and treasure houses at Olympia. The world looked to peace and cooperation and "good will to man" through the Olympic games. In fact the Olympic game

9

movement is the earliest people-to-people peace program.

Although wars did occur, it was evident that the Olympic games had achieved an importance far above that of any other institution or idea of the period. Today, in the twentieth century and in the atomic age, the Olympics once again present a hope to all nations and races that friendly competition hand in hand with freedom and tolerance can make a better world.

Olympia, the center of the ancient Olympics, where the Alpheus and the Cladeus converged, must be described. The reports of contemporary writers and poets, together with the comparatively recent excavation of its ruins, make it possible to visualize the setting. The Altis, or sacred grove of Zeus, was in the shape of a rectangle. Hills surrounded Olympia on the north, the rivers were on the south and the west. The eastern side was formed by the tremendous hippodrome, or race track, site of the equestrian events. The marble stadium was fairly well centered but against the sloping hillsides of the north. The sides or spectator part of the stadium had a capacity of approximately 60,000 and the field was approximately 214 yards long and 32 yards wide. (Yankee Stadium is approximately 180 yards long and 98 yards wide with a seating capacity of 67,000.) No spectators were ever allowed on the field, nor were bleachers ever built to increase the paid attendance. Only judges, competitors and announcers were allowed in the field or enclosure.

The hippodrome was a marble edifice, large even by modern standards. The field or ampitheatre where equestrian events—chariot and mounted races—were run off was 806 yards in length by 405 yards in width. (Delaware Park in Wilmington, Delaware, the largest mile-track race course in the United States, measures 720 yards in length and 280 yards in width, and could neatly fit into the ancient Olympic hippodrome with a little left over.) No Hollywood set ever built could compare with the actual marble splendor of Olympia.

There were numerous treasure houses, temples, and religious buildings in Olympia. The most important building was the Olympium, which housed one of the seven wonders of the world—a huge ivory statue of Zeus with robes of solid gold. The figure of the Greek god was over forty feet high.

The most important building for the athletes was the gymnasium with its long colonnade-covered track. The main floor of the gymnasium, called the palaestra, was about 250 feet square and was like our present-day gyms except that it

10

had sand as flooring. Here the wrestlers, boxers, gymnasts, and pancratium contestants, practiced under the supervision of trainers and judges for the month preceding the actual games.

The Greek thoroughness in athletics in antiquity may have surpassed even that in England in the early part of the twentieth century or that in the United States from 1918 to 1942. According to written records which have come down to us, all the athletes followed a strict regimen which began early and ended late. After a breakfast of fermented bread and grape juice, a morning of punishing exercises was followed, with no stop for lunch, by more training in the afternoon and a mighty dinner. In the earlier Olympics, vegetables, fruits and plenty of cheese was the menu. Later, fish and meat appeared. According to some original sources, Milo of Crotona and Theagenes of Thasos, the greatest wrestler and boxer of antiquity, respectively, each ate a broiled ox at one sitting. Although there may be some exaggeration in this story, there is evidence that the Olympic athletes of ancient Greece averaged over six pounds of meat per man per dinner. From the earliest days, alcoholic beverages and cold drinks were taboo.

The ancient Olympics started, according to the records that have come down to us, with the Olympic Oath taken by the athletes and judges before the statue of the god Zeus. The athletes swore to observe the rules, the judges swore to be fair, and all prayed for personal success and the success of the games. Then came the parade around the stadium, the contestants grouped by city or country. Trumpets were blown at the beginning and at the end of each event. A branch from a palm tree was placed in the hands of the winner and a wreath made from the leaves of the wild olive tree was put on his head. A closing ceremony at the end of the games always featured prayers of thanks.

Although Olympic athletes had their expenses paid and winners received great favors from their communities and rich neighbors and were marked, if not favored, for life and certainly aided if they desired to train for another Olympics, the spirit behind the ancient Olympics was basically one of amateurism. In other words, various types of dispensations were provided to enable qualified athletes to compete, just as they are today. The crux of the problem was then, as it is today, whether the athlete was basically an amateur at heart or whether he was a professional performing solely for actual payment. Some countries today that are advanced economi-

11

cally can, like the United States, send Olympic teams and maintain the apparatus to operate competitive athletics by voluntary contributions from educational, athletic and recreational organizations. Other nations less fortunate must support their Olympic teams by government subsidy.

The question of professionalism is a serious one and that is why the Olympic Committee and the AAU in the United States have leaned over backward to be strict on any issues involving excessive expenses. Every country, according to the Olympic spirit in both the ancient and modern games, should satisfy itself on athletic purity and adhere to the moral principle that two wrongs never make one right. Each must keep its own amateur sports clean. It was the issue of professionalism of the Romans that caused the discord, scandal and free-for-all fighting that made the ancient Olympics a public nuisance and resulted in their suspension. Control of sports and athletes by governments for national, political or ideological propaganda purposes ended the sportsmanship, the purpose and the usefulness of the games.

While it is admitted the ancient Olympic games deteriorated after a thousand years or so and the real Olympic spirit was lost after some sixteen centuries (eleven supported by records) the disintegration may be laid to human frailty and the decline of civilization and morals rather than to any weakness in the ideals or in the organization of the Olympic games. As long as the high moral and religious nature of the participants continued, the games were both successful and popular. When bribery, corruption, and dishonesty crept in, the games lost both their success and their popularity. They became a battlefront instead of a gathering for peaceful competition to bind peoples together.

Shortly after the suspension of the games in 394 A.D., Olympia was sacked and looted by barbaric invaders from the north, and the Romans further destroyed the Greek temples. Thereafter, two earthquakes not only completed the destruction of Olympia but, by changing the course of the Alpheus and Cladeus rivers, soon buried the city beneath hundreds of feet of sand and silt.

Over 1400 years later, in 1829, the French government and later, in 1875, the German government, began to dig Olympia out. In 1881 the ruins, still projecting a golden era in history, were completely uncovered, and there is no doubt that the scientists and historians dug up not only the secrets of

12

the site of the ancient Olympics but their spirit and glory as well, and that the renewal of this spirit led to the many efforts toward a renaissance of the Olympics, first by the Greeks in 1859, 1870, 1875 and 1889—which failed—and then by the French in 1892.

Notwithstanding the full credit usually given the French and the French father of the modern Olympics, Baron de Coubertin, for reviving the games (described in Chapter II), the real story is that the Greeks and a man named Zappas began working toward the revival of the Olympics long before Coubertin and the French succeeded. The four modern Olympics forgotten in history as efforts which did not restore the glory or the existence of the games occurred in Greece on November 15, 1859, November 15, 1870, May 18, 1875, and May 18, 1889.

They failed essentially because the world was not quite ready and because Greece was not a powerful enough country or a rich enough country at the time to put over the idea. Another even more important reason was that the individual sponsor involved was naive and inexperienced in both promotion and amateur athletics. Unlike Baron de Coubertin, he did not first seek out the leaders of school, college, and amateur athletic organizations throughout the world and solicit their help.

Thrilled by the romance and glory of old Greece and by the Olympic spirit of drawing people together through sports, Evangelios Zappas, a Greek living in Rumania, first contributed and, on his death, following the failure of his first Olympics, willed his entire fortune to re-establish the Olympic games in Greece. The Greek government supported Zappas and accepted the money, but organized the games ineffectively. The resulting games were good examples of what not to do. The 1859 games were held in a square—Place Louis—and in the streets of Athens, as no stadium was available. Confusion and chaos resulted. Although the king and queen and many dignitaries attended, spectators were trampled on and injured by mounted police trying to keep the streets open for contestants, and athletes were arrested for acting like spectators. Boys and old men entered the competitions at the last minute and actually ran in some of the preliminary heats in order to get through the police lines. A blind man presented himself to the officials for one of the events, using the opportunity to sing a song to the multitude, for which he was not unrecompensed. One of the runners dropped dead in a race. Events in the 1859 Olympics were the running broad jump, two unusual types of jumps involving ditches and leather bags, 200-meter and 400-meter dashes, 1500-meter run, discus throw, javelin and rope climbing. Hop, step and jump wrestling, pole vault and tug-of-war were added in 1870. Shot put, running high jump and weight lifting were added in 1889. The last three of these Olympics were held in the ancient Athens stadium renovated at a cost of over $500,000. It must be remembered that the 1859 Olympics were held thirty-seven years before the first official recognized modern Olympiad. Though unsuccessful, these recorded but unofficial games were a logical connection between the dim past and the uncertain future.

CHAPTER II

Origin, Management, and Spirit of the Modern Olympic Games

AT THE BEGINNING of the twentieth century, when the rebirth of the Olympics and the Olympic spirit took place, the world was again particularly conscious of the principles of freedom and peace and appreciative of the equality and dignity of man as a result of so many unsuccessful centuries of dictators, wars, and despotism.

"Olympia and the Olympics symbolize an entire civilization, superior to countries, cities, military heroes or even the ancient religions." So wrote a young French nobleman, Baron Pierre de Coubertin. A cadet at St. Cyr, the French West Point, Coubertin resigned to study political science and later became interested in education and sociology. He traveled all over the world and was particularly impressed by the "Anglo-Saxon" (British and American) interest in sports. Alerted by the discoveries at Olympia and more especially by the abortive efforts to re-create the Olympics from 1859 to 1889 and believing that friendly international athletic competitions might teach youth international understanding as it had done once before, he became obsessed with the ambition of reviving the Olympics on a world basis.

"The Olympics—the entire planet is its domain—all sports —all nations," he wrote. French soldiers had found and restored the temple of Zeus at Olympia. Germans had uncovered the entire site of the ancient games after six years of work. Greece retained and glorified every single piece of marble recovered from her Olympic glory. European youth was stirred and demanding athletic competition. Throughout the British Empire, known for its sports and games, and in

14

the United States, a young nation, there was widespread participation in competitive athletics.

Coubertin presented his plan to the Athletic Sports Union in Paris, late in 1892, after a sound public relations preparation. "Let us export oarsmen, runners, fencers; this is the free trade of the future—and on the day when it shall take its place among the customs of Europe, the cause of peace will have received a new and powerful support . . . so please help me re-establish the Olympic games," begged Coubertin.

Coubertin was persistent and soon had the opportunity to sound out other countries for support when the French Sports Union held an International Congress on Amateurism. Mr. C. Herbert, representing the Amateur Athletic Association of the British Empire; Professor William Sloane of Princeton, representing amateur athletics in the United States; and Baron de Coubertin, representing France and the rest of Europe made the original preparations not only to present the amateur issue but also to propose re-creating the Olympic Games. In 1894 the Congress was held and Coubertin obtained surprising and strong support from the United States, Great Britain, and Sweden, and from prominent people such as the Duke of Sparta, the Prince of Wales, the Crown Prince of Sweden, the King of Belgium, and the Prime Minister of the British Empire. Delegates from France, England, the United States, Greece, Russia, Sweden, Belgium, Italy, and Spain were present. Interest was indicated in official letters from Hungary, Germany, Bohemia, Holland, and Austria. The enthusiastic delegates decided not to wait for 1900, heretofore considered a likely basic year to start recomputing Olympiads, but to have the first modern Olympics in 1896 and to hold it in Athens, near the site of the ancient Olympics. It was decided that the games would move every four years to a new major city of the world and that an International Olympic Committee should be selected to have full authority over the games. The dream of Zappas—and later de Coubertin—had become a reality. A Greek, D. Vikelas, a holdover of the unsuccessful games, was the first president of the International Olympic Committee.

Another Frenchman with another idea based on history was responsible for the modern Olympics' most dramatic and spectacular event—the marathon. Michel Bréal, one of the French delegates, wanted to do much more than help the Congress initiate the modern Olympics. He wanted to contribute toward a trophy to top all others and to inspire help and enthusiasm. Shortly after the Congress, he wrote to

15

Coubertin announcing his trophy for a foot race to outdo all others—a race based on the legendary feat and feet of Pheidippides.

About 490 B.C. Darius of Persia had sent Hippias, former tyrant of Athens, and an army to overrun and enslave Athens and its ally Eretria. Eretria was captured after a long siege, and Hippias then landed at Marathon, a plain approximately twenty-six miles from Athens. Pheidippides, an Olympic champion, was sent as a courier to try to get help from Sparta. According to the story, he ran, swam rivers, climbed mountains for days without rest and succeeded in persuading the Spartans to come to the aid of Athens. He later got back as fast as he could to deliver the good news and join the Athenian Army. As the Persians tried to take Athens by a surprise sea attack, the Greeks, under their great general, Miltiades, marched down from the mountain upon a large force left by Hippias at Marathon and killed approximately 20,000 warriors, discouraged Hippias and Darius, and saved Athens.

With the victory won, the Athenian general again sent his Olympic champion, exhausted from his trip to Sparta and his participation in the great battle, to bring the good news to the worried city. The legend goes on to tell how Pheidippides ran the twenty-six miles between Marathon and Athens and on arriving home cried, "Rejoice—we conquer," then fell dead. To Mr. Bréal this was a great reminder of the glory and spirit of the Olympic games, so he proposed the marathon race in the modern Olympics to commemorate this historical event. Today most people believe the marathon was part of the ancient Olympics, and the name and contribution of Michel Bréal are universally unknown. Often nations, races, and large segments of people go mad with pride when one of their contestants wins this, the greatest event in the track and field competitions or perhaps in the entire schedule of the Olympics. An indication of the spread and influence of the marathon is the fact that eighty-six countries at some time have adopted this event temporarily or permanently. Some years ago American G.I.'s in Korea contributed enough money to pay the expenses of a trip by several Koreans to the United States to participate in an American marathon runoff in Boston, Massachusetts. Later a Finn visited the United States from another direction, was welcomed by the people of Boston and won the 1956 Boston marathon. In 1960, against the ancient backdrop of Rome, Abebe Bikila, a barefooted Royal courier of Ethiopia, won

16

the Olympic Marathon for his king, a direct descendent of Solomon. The same man wearing shoes won again at Tokyo in 1964. He tried to win again at Mexico City in 1968 but failed. A younger protege of his, Mamo Wolde turned in a third win for Ethiopia.

The marathon had another and far-reaching contribution to make to the modern Olympics which had been neglected by both sportsmen and historians. Just before and even during the first Olympics in 1896 in Athens, the usual jealousies and nationalism crept in to make Greece and the Greeks antagonistic to the games. The unexpected regularity with which championships were won by Americans discouraged other countries and was particularly galling to Greece, the host nation, with its ancient Olympic memories. However, when a Greek peasant named Spiridion Loues, after fasting and prayers, won the marathon, the Crown Prince of Greece and his brother carried Loues on their shoulders to the royal box to receive the Bréal trophy. This was not only a fitting climax to the first modern Olympics but also swept away all jealousy of foreign victories in other events. Loues was overwhelmed with presents, from money and rare jewels to the offer of a shoe-shine boy to take care of his shoes for life. The Greeks, and in fact all nations present, became enthusiastic supporters of the Olympic idea and Bréal had scored a valuable assist in making Baron de Coubertin's revival of the modern Olympics possible.

Unfortunately, although the Athens 1896 Olympics was successful and the Olympic idea had been sold to the world, there was trouble ahead. The Greek government and the Zappas brothers (the inheritance of Zappas had been used to help sponsor the Athens games) were adamant on taking over from Coubertin and his Olympic committee. Had not the Greek government spent $100,000 in addition to the Zappas money to make possible the first Olympics? George Averoff, a rich Greek merchant in Alexandria, had been the donor of $390,000 with which to complete the restoration of the Panathenaic Stadium in which the 1896 games had been held. Had not the ancient Olympics been celebrated at Olympia for over a thousand years? In the words of the King of Greece: "May Greece be destined to become the peaceful meeting ground of all nationalities, and may Athens become the permanent seat of the Olympic games." At the King's dinner after the games, America's athletes, not knowing they were undermining the plans of de Coubertin and the C.I.O. (International Olympic Committee) responsible for it all, unwittingly helped the Greeks by circulating a petition to hold the games permanently in Athens.

Coubertin, however, was firm in keeping the Olympic games strictly international. The next Olympic Congress met at Le Havre, with France, Russia, and Hungary officially represented and Sweden, the United States, England, Italy, and Germany represented by individuals from educational institutions or athletic organizations. Félix Faure, President of France, acted as President. Greece, involved in a war with Turkey, had to abandon her ideas of taking over the management of the Olympics and retaining them permanently in Athens. A well-thought-out and detailed plan for the future of the modern games was submitted and approved. Competitions were to be in three categories: 1) Ancient sports of Egypt, India, Greece, and Rome; 2) Sports of the Age of Chivalry; and 3) Sports of the modern period.

The Olympics were on the march everywhere and Henri Desgranges offered the use of his seven-acre Parc des Princes and 666-meter track in Paris to the Olympic Committee headed by Coubertin. Desgranges stated, "It is only the Seine that I cannot give you." Newspapers all over the world offered free space for promotion, and the Scotch and the Irish rushed representatives to Paris in a wild dash to be the first to enter. Everything seemed in fine shape when suddenly the French government stepped in and took over and, just as all governments and politicians do, appointed a whole host of committees and groups of politicians, most of whom knew nothing about the Olympics or athletics. The result was that the take-over by government bureaucrats almost ruined the 1900 Olympics and almost ended the modern Olympics.

The Olympic Committee's control over the Olympics was actually strengthened as a result of the many difficulties and disappointments of the "bureaucratic" Paris 1900 games. Coubertin had no difficulty regaining the wheel and helping the United States and the St. Louis Exposition of 1904 to get the III Olympiad.

The 1904 Olympics, while generally successful, were not too well attended by athletes because of the difficulty of traveling great distances. In pre-jet airplane days, an athlete might have to travel three weeks to compete for one day. The outstanding feature of the actual competition was the great number of wins by American college athletes. The Olympics suffered, as the 1900 Olympics had, by being staged as part of a World's Fair. The side-shows and extraordinary events presented may have succeeded as entertainment, but they certainly did not stimulate any great progress in competitive sports, and the St. Louis games featured the worst hoax and the most curious cramp story of any Olympics. The hoax was perpetrated by Fred Lorz, who dashed into the stadium looking as fresh as when he had started, and appeared to be the winner of the classic marathon. After he had been applauded and photographed with Alice Roosevelt, the daughter of the President, it was discovered that he had traversed most of the course in a newfangled affair called an autotruck.

Another story about the marathon deals with cramps. Felix Caravajal of Cuba, who led after eighteen miles, was so far ahead that he stopped along the road and picked and ate a few apples. The apples were green. Felix got violent cramps which cost him the race and Cuba her first and only marathon victory.

At the end of 1905 King Leopold of Belgium, one of the original supporters of Baron de Coubertin, agreed to accept the honorary presidency of the next Olympic Congress. Cities now battled for the award. Rome was originally selected for 1908, but Greece and her claim for the Olympics—or for Panhellenic Olympics every four years between the world Olympics—had to be satisfied. Athens insisted on holding "Olympic Panhellenic" games in 1906.

About this time another great organizer, Olympic diplomat, and leader stepped into a more important position to aid Baron de Coubertin—Count Henri de Baillet-Latour of Belgium. The first Panhellenic games in 1906 in Athens, although officially not a modern Olympiad, nevertheless have come to be accorded a listing with the modern Olympics. The 1906 games resolved many problems raised by the Greeks and sort of packed down everyone and helped make possible the truly international Olympics that had originally been planned. The Greeks were happy to have the 1906 games, but since demands for facilities, services, and money increased as the Olympics expanded, they afterward abandoned—as de Coubertin had expected—their insistence that the Olympics be held every four years at Athens. During this period the Italians lost some of their enthusiasm and fell down in their preparations, and London was awarded the 1908 games. This incidentally is the only case in the 72 years since the modern Olympics began that a city awarded the games was forced to abandon being host to them.

By a strange coincidence the unrecorded games prior to 776 B.C., the unrecognized games from 1859 to 1889 and the extra and sometimes unlisted games of 1906 played major parts in giving us the modern games of today.

The London or IV Olympics were highly successful and settled the question of which events and sports to include in the future—as many sports as practicable, but only those that were genuinely international. It was a happy compromise between the restrictions of the French in 1900 and the honky-tonk additions of the St. Louis World's Fair in 1904.

King Edward VII was the patron and the games were held in a huge bowl at Shepherd's Bush near London, which had a capacity of 70,000. Despite the King's enthusiasm the British government declined to contribute any of the expenses of the games. The Franco-Britain Exposition built the stadium and financed the games to the tune of $250,000. Another $50,000 was raised by popular subscription. The games marked the height of the British Empire, based on the victories of Wellington and Clive, which held world ascendancy from Waterloo to World War I. This influenced the London games adversely, for the British, determined to win at all costs, created incidents and squabbles rather than friendships. They even required all their subjects to represent them, including athletes from India and Ireland. This turned out to be all important to the development of the games. No longer were host nations and their organizing committees to have complete control. This led to the present situation where the C.I.O. and the various world sports bodies or federations direct and officiate the games while the hosts supply the facilities, the welcome and the housekeeping.

The Fifth Olympiad held in Stockholm in 1912 was referred to by contemporaries as "the Swedish Masterpiece." Once more a king—Gustavus V—dominated the arrangements and the hosting of the games. Much of the success was due to a great Swedish sportsman, J. Sigfrid Edstrom, who was in 1941 to become the fourth President of the C.I.O. $665,000 was raised by the Swedish government by a public lottery. To show the ever-growing financial side of the Olympics, the cost of assembling and sending the 176 competitors constituting the U.S. team alone cost over $123,000. One of the features of the opening ceremony was the singing of the 5,000-member Swedish Choral Association in the stadium. The Fifth could be referred to as the "Royal Olympiad" for many medals and trophies were presented or donated by royalty, including the King and Crown Prince of Sweden, the King of Greece, the Czar of Russia, the Emperor of Germany, the Emperor of Austria, and the King of Italy.

World War I prevented the 1916 Olympiad but did not end the Olympic idea.

The 1920 Antwerp games proved that not even a world war could stop the Olympic spirit or the games. The decision to hold the games in Belgium was reached in April 1919 mainly as a gesture to the hero nation of World War I. Count Henri de Baillet-Latour accomplished miracles together with King Albert, individual hero of the war. The latter opened the games which featured two innovations which are now customary. The first was the Olympic oath taken by a prominent athlete of the host nation's team, and the second the first appearance of the now familiar Olympic flag.

The VIII Olympic games were held in Paris in 1924 at the special request of Baron de Coubertin who planned immediately thereafter to retire as President of the C.I.O. Further procedural matters were determined during this Olympiad. These games for the first time indicated the importance of the various federations which had more or less been brought into being to control the various sports throughout the world. The first to assert its power was the International Athletic Union which controlled track and field and several other sports and was led by Sigfrid Edstrom. This Olympiad also more or less crystallized (especially in the United States) the importance and organization of the National Olympic Committees in selecting, training and sending teams and handling all national Olympic matters. Solemn religious services by most of the athletes were held at the Cathedral of Notre Dame before the opening ceremony at the Columbe Stadium in the afternoon. President Domergue of France opened the games before 40,000 spectators, including the Prince of Wales, who was later to abdicate as King of England; the crown princes of Sweden, Prince Carol of Rumania, the Regent of Abyssinia, Marshal Foch, General Pershing, General Gouraud, Marie Dressler, Nora Bayes, Douglas Fairbanks, Sr. and Mary Pickford. Forty-five countries, almost double the record until then—participated. Even Kuomintang China was represented by a team of two athletes.

The outstanding contribution or innovation of this Olympiad was the beginning of the winter Olympic games, also held in France that year in Chamonix, separate games which properly expanded the Olympics to include winter sports.

The 1928 games were held in Amsterdam, Holland, and

21

were opened by Prince Consort Hendrik. A German team participated for the first time since World War I. On opening day there were 40,000 persons filling the stadium and another 75,000 milling around outside who could not get in. Needless to say, the efficient and commercial-minded Dutch did a great job and did better than break even financially, even though costs totalled $1,200,000.

After many previous efforts Los Angeles finally secured the Olympic games in 1932. Following the Hollywood tradition of the "firstest" and the "mostest," some $3,000,000 was immediately supplied by the city and state. A stadium was built costing $1,700,000 with over 30 miles of seats capable of accommodating 105,000 spectators. All of the facilities for all of the events were the best that could be provided. An Olympic Village was built overlooking the Pacific Ocean, covering 521 acres. Over $60,000,000 was spent in Los Angeles by visitors to these games. Over a million spectators paid $1,500,000 at the gate. The games were opened in a ceremony more glamorous than any movie by the Vice President of the United States, Charles Curtis. Count Henri de Baillet-Latour, the C.I.O. president, was on hand as was practically every movie star.

If the Los Angeles Olympiad was "colossal," then the Berlin games in 1936 were "stupendous." The games were awarded to Berlin in 1931, but later unforeseen political events occurred so that before opening day in 1936 Adolf Hitler and the Nazis had taken over Germany. No stone was left unturned, therefore. no money or effort spared by the Nazi government to prove German efficiency in staging the XIII Olympiad and to develop a winning team to prove "Teutonic" racial superiority. The Berlin Games and the German Olympic team which won the Olympics cost the Nazi government well over $30,000,000. The "Reichssportfeld" measured 325 acres and contained four stadiums, a theater, swimming pools, basketball courts, polo field and gymnasium. The stadium, with a fast red clay track, accommodated 110,-000 spectators. The Olympic Village covered 140 acres of great pictorial beauty. To indicate the ever-rising costs and financial figures of the games, the U.S. team at Berlin in 1936 represented an investment of over $325,000. It was en route to this Olympiad that Mr. Avery Brundage, heading the U.S. team, gained world publicity by expelling Eleanor Holm, the popular and attractive backstroke swimming champion, a sure gold medalist, for drinking champagne. Shortly thereafter the C.I.O. appointed Mr. Brundage to fill the vacancy caused by the elimination of his fellow American, Commodore and former Assistant Secretary of the Navy, Lee Jahncke of New Orleans, who bitterly opposed American participation in the Berlin Games.

Under threatening skies the opening ceremonies were dominated by Hitler, Richard Strauss, who conducted an orchestra of over 100 pieces, and old Spiridion Loues of Greece, the first modern marathon champion (1896) who handed Hitler an olive branch from the Sacred Grove of Zeus at Olympia. The total gate receipts were over $2,800,000 reflecting an attendance of over 5,000,000.

The Olympiads resumed in 1948 after World War II cancelled out the 1940 and 1944 games. In 1939 de Coubertin had died. Count Henri de Baillet-Latour died in 1942. Mr. Edstrom of Sweden succeeded to the Presidency of the C.I.O. and Avery Brundage became Vice President, retaining also the presidency of the U.S. Olympic Committee—an office he had held since 1929.

The XIV or 1948 Olympiad was awarded to London and the opening was at Empire Stadium at Wembley. King George VI formally opened the games with the usual British pageantry before a crowd of 84,000, but with typical English weather—mist, fog and rain. Notwithstanding the weather, paid admissions were approximately $1,250,000. These games were not only well run but devoid of any unpleasant incidents.

The 1952 games, both winter and summer, were in northern countries, the regular games at Helsinki, Finland, and the winter games at Oslo, Norway. Germany and Japan appeared for the first time since World War II. As is usual some little time after a war, a splendid spirit of harmony and sportsmanship dominated these games. The Helsinki stadium seemed a throwback to the Grecian sites of the ancient Olympics, because of the severely classic style of Finnish modern architecture. The opening ceremony, held in perfect weather, surrounded by the beautiful scenery of Helsinki, was as impressive as any theretofore, with President Passikivi of Finland officiating. The Finns as hosts left nothing to be desired. Probably the most exciting part of the opening ceremony was the appearance of the incomparable Paavo Nurmi who ran with his smooth strides around the track bearing the Olympic flame to the Peristyle. Of course the sensation of this Olympiad was the appearance of a very strong team from Soviet Russia which was second to the United States in medals, points and accomplishments. Unfortunately, this team, like others from communist countries, raised the specter of national, governmental, political and ideological propaganda rather than the Olympic ideal of sports for sport's sake only. This Olympiad also marked an election which brought in the fifth C.I.O. President in sixty-eight years, Mr. Avery Brundage, who defeated David Lord Burghley, the Marquis of Exeter, 30 to 17. Most of his Lordship's backing, oddly enough, came from communist countries.

The 1956 or XVI modern Olympic games broke previous precedents and records. The Olympiad was the first to be celebrated in the southern hemisphere. Never before had Olympic games been held south of the Tropic of Cancer, much less south of the Equator. The fact that teams had to travel from 8,000 to 18,000 miles to Melbourne, Australia, the site for the games, showed to what great length the Olympics had developed into a world event. The sport-loving island continent of Australia, referred to as "Down Under," held a strange fascination for all. Because of the reversal of seasons in the southern hemisphere, the 1956 Olympics were held from November 22 to December 8, whereas generally they had been held during the northern summer in June, July or August.

Many facts contributed to additional departures from precedent besides the site and the season. Before the opening ceremony the original number of nations entering broke all records—despite the exceptional distance. Then international incidents and actual military conflicts in Hungary and in Egypt introduced an element of tension which threatened the games and reduced the entries. Some half dozen countries withdrew, including Holland, Switzerland, Spain, Egypt, and Lebanon. But overcoming all handicaps, the Olympic spirit won out and the XVI modern Olympic games were held with great success. Eleven world records and thirty-six Olympic records were broken.

The formal opening at the Melbourne Cricket Grounds on November 22, 1956 will long be remembered by the people at Melbourne. A crowd of 50,000 surrounded the stadium during the entire night before the games began in an attempt to get standing-room tickets. Finally, the games were opened on a warm sunny day before a capacity crowd of over 102,-000 with all the pomp and splendor of the British Empire. The historic moment occurred at 10:30 A.M. on Thursday, November 22—but in New York, where the actual ceremony was heard on the radio a fraction of a second later, it was actually, because of the International Date Line, 7:30

P.M. on Wednesday, November 21st. The Duke of Edinburgh, in a British admiral's uniform, officially opened the games. He entered the stadium in a convertible as a massed band of the three Australian Armed Forces played. After the stirring strains of "God Save The Queen" Prime Minister F.F. Menzies presented the Duke with a commemorative medal from the Australian government. Then, pursuant to age-old custom, the athletes of the various countries paraded country by country in alphabetical order so that Australia, which should have been among the first countries to enter, entered last as the host nation.

Just prior to the opening of the games, a controversy almost split the International Olympic Committee. Avery Brundage had tried to change the Olympic Amateur Oath by adding a controversial clause involving a commitment by every Olympic athlete to swear that he or she would never become a professional, as well as swearing that he or she had never been a professional. Naturally this clause was politically and ideologically controversial, since countries enjoying the free enterprise system have professional athletics, while the communist countries have no private enterprise, therefore, no professional athletes. Finally, on November 21, the day before the games, the proposed oath was rejected almost unanimously. Certainly the pledge of intention to remain an amateur has no place in the Olympic games. Every Olympic athlete, like every other human being, should have the right, the privilege and the freedom to select his own way of life and the way he is to make a living in the future. If an Olympic boxer, skater or track star decides to perform professionally, teach, coach or sell breakfast cereals, that should be his inalienable right.

The bringing of teams and their equipment over thousands of miles to Australia proved the tremendous progress of the modern Olympic movement. The U.S. Olympic Committee, for example, successfully transported a large team with its equipment over 8,000 miles to Melbourne, at a cost of over $1,500,000. All problems were solved and the money collected—in fact, even oversubscribed—from private funds contributed by the citizens of the United States.

The XVII modern Olympic games were awarded to Rome, a city as old as the ancient Olympics and probably the most famous city in the world. The International Olympic Committee in 1960 actually recognized 95 National Olympic Committees throughout the world. Of these, 84 sent athletes to Rome. The official bulletin of the International Olympic

25

Committee, No. 73, lists 84 "nations" that participated, although this same committee insisted on labelling one of these, the "Republic of China," recognized by 44 nations and the United Nations as a "sovereign state," as "the Territory of Taiwan." However, the Olympic spirit overrode the Committee's amateur efforts at diplomacy. All agree that sports is the only and proper domain of the International Olympic Committee and that they have done a splendid job in sports, and that world politics is not part of their job. The Committee should be as disinterested in ideology or politics as it is in questions of creed or race.

The Rome games continued to break records, precedents and standards of all kinds. It had more nations participating than any other Olympics, ancient or modern—and more spectators both physically at the competitions and absent but listening to, or seeing, through the great mass media of radio and television. The Rome games and the winter games at Squaw Valley, California, in 1960, were the furthest apart of any pairing of games in one Olympiad. Originally the Committee had envisaged the regular and winter Olympics being awarded to the same country. In 1956 and 1960, however, precedent was broken by separating the regular and winter games geographically by great distances.

Gate receipts at Rome were well over $5,000,000. The daily arrival of tourists during the games was estimated as high as 1,200,000. Over $30,000,000 was spent on the most beautiful stadium the Olympics has ever known and the renovation of the Baths of Caracalla, the Basilica of Maxentius, the Arch of Constantine and the Appian Way, which outdid ancient Rome in its greatest glory. These new Olympic installations will certainly last another 2,000 years.

The opening ceremony featured the Hon. Giovanni Gronchi, the President of Italy. While tremendously impressive because of the backdrop and imperial splendor of ancient Rome and the pageantry of teams from 84 countries parading in attractive, specially designed uniforms, the most extraordinary moment of the entire games to the spectators was the revival of an ancient Roman custom for the last day's closing ceremony. At the end of the final equestrian competition and the closing ceremony as the sun went down and the dusk descended over the stadium, 100,000 spectators waved flaming torches (in this case made of rolls of newspapers, programs or magazines lit with matches) and risked burning themselves and their neighbors alive. This brought to the huge darkened stadium a bright and colorful close to the 1960 version of the greatest show on earth—an extraordinary sight that will never dim in the memory of all those present.

But if the glory of Rome and the Italian-hosted games constituted another high in the Olympic story, they proved merely a build-up for the Tokyo games in faraway Japan. From its eleven different kinds of cooking in eleven different dining rooms, where some competitors sat on chairs with their shoes on and others sat cross-legged on the floor with shoes removed; to the cathedral of swimming, a huge pagoda with the largest and highest suspension roof in the world (capacity: 25,000 spectators); with two swimming pools on the main floor and another Olympic size practice pool in the basement; the Tokyo games outdid all others. Not only in facilities, buildings, operations, decor and surroundings (at a cost of over 500 million dollars) was it the best, but also in the efficiency and graciousness of the hosts. Not a single incident marred the competitions. How could there be any arguments with hosts that used for the first time such innovations of their own as the Fate-Fully-Automatic Electronic Timer? Several seconds after each swimming race a small piece of paper slid out of this shining aluminum machine. On it was the lane number of the eight contestants of the heat or final of each swimming race, their place in finishing and their time to 1/100th of a second (from the starter's gun to the contact of each swimmer's hand with the end of the pool). Also written on the slip was the title of the race, such as "400 meter free-style final." In fact, all the results of the Tokyo games, in every detail, were computed and printed by computers, making statisticians practically unnecessary. The four volume official publication of these results made reporting errors on the Tokyo games pretty unlikely.

Notwithstanding the calculating and timing machines and the judging of events by electronic computers, the Tokyo games maintained all the pomp of past Olympics. The Orient is famous for its symbols. On October 24, Emperor Hirohito, the 124th ruler of Japan, and his Empress and grandson, to the accompaniment of electronic music and bells over loudspeakers, saw some 8,000 athletes from 94 countries parade before representatives of 118 member countries of the Olympic movement and 74,534 spectators. When the parade ended, 5,002 doves were released and five jet planes of the "Japanese Air Self-Defense Force" formed the five colored interlocking circles of the Olympic symbol. On the last day of the games, after the closing parade, the

27

national flags of Greece (birthplace of the games), Japan (1964 host), and Mexico (host of the 1968 Games) were lowered as the national anthems were played, the stadium lights were dimmed, and Avery Brundage declared the games closed. The Olympic flame far above the highest rim of the stadium cast an eerie light in the complete darkness. Another recorded Olympiad had become history. Eighty world and Olympic records were tied or broken. The United States won 36 gold medals, Russia 30. The only incident considered controversial was the election of Brundage to a second four-year term (after serving an original eight years and an additional term of four years by a previous reelection). This caused some bitter feelings, for the election was unprecedented—it was by mail and illegal according to many, for the 1964 Olympic rules in French definitely stated that the President could only be reelected for one extra term of four years. According to Olympic rule, the French text not the English (which was not clear on this point) had seniority. The Marquess of Exeter, again the choice of the Communist countries, resigned his candidacy and graciously requested that the reelection of Brundage be recorded as unanimous. Many people believe this was to assure his election in 1972. The I.O.C. and its reelected President almost immediately and wisely passed a new rule. A great competition and a great show—like the Tokyo games—is a miracle with only four years of preparation. Miracles can hardly be expected every four years. Therefore, from now on (according to the new rule) the sites of both the summer and winter games will be chosen six or more years in advance.

In 1968 the Olympic cavalcade continued at Mexico City in Mexico. Once more precedents and records were broken. Just as in 1964 and 1968, the games were in a part of the world where they had never been held before—this time in Latin America. The distance from Terra Del Fuego to the Rio Grande encompasses more than half of the Western Hemisphere. Because of the geographic location, the games usually referred to as the summer games (as in the case of the Australian and Japanese games) were again held in the Fall.

The XIX modern games in Mexico City were held from the Olympian heights of 7,415 feet above sea level. (Mount Olympus, the home of the gods, according to Greek mythology has an elevation of 9,570 feet.) The Olympic games had never before been held at a higher altitude than some 700 feet above sea level. Notwithstanding the altitude, 111 countries sent 6,082 athletes, and 27 Olympic records were equalled or broken in 36 of the track and field events. More phenomenal in the face of the altitude—14 new world records were broken and two world records equalled. Five new world swimming records were established.

The Mexico games were favored with a minimum of problems and incidents, due no doubt to the Mexican government's resolute and courageous stand against permissiveness. A pre-Olympic college disturbance was handled by the Mexican Regular Army, and student rebels bent on destruction and arson were killed or imprisoned. This show of strength against disturbances and rioting discouraged prospective rioters and disturbers of the peace. Following the example of the Japanese, the Mexican Olympic organizing committee held a games rehearsal a year before to which many countries were invited. This afforded an opportunity to study local conditions and the high altitude, and particularly to learn how to guard against "Montezuma's Revenge"—a short but violent diarrhea. President Ortez of Mexico and Mr. Avery Brundage opened the preliminary games on a beautiful sunny day before a capacity crowd in the new Mexican Olympic stadium.

Today in every country in the world amateur sports organizations are again holding a series of elimination events and competitions in each sport category so they can send their best athletes to the 1976 Olympics. All expenses will be paid by voluntary contributions to the Olympic funds or by government subsidies.

Even the Olympics are subject to human errors and weaknesses, and the interest in sports and particularly in the games has made both dictatorships and democracies based on collectivism want to subsidize athletes for propaganda purposes. The objective is to win and thereby prove superiority, or prove the decadence of countries with different political and economic systems. In many cases people who were never athletes or followers of any sport, and know nothing about sports, try to use sports to gain power or popularity. In the Soviet Union and in some of the other Communist countries, the Government has initiated extraordinary sports programs and subsidized athletes.

The Soviets made an impressive start in the 1952 Olympics and overwhelmed other countries in 1956 and 1960. However, when they ceased giving subsidies to ex-athletes and the bureaucratic control of political management wore thin, dedicated athletes and management based on sports for sports' sake began to close the gap. Russia had led the United States in 1956 by 129 points and in 1960 by 230 points, but barely squeezed by it in 1964 by 10 points. In 1968, communism, which has failed to establish itself as a superior system in science, economics, industry or agriculture, lost out in sports also.

In the winter games, little Norway beat the giant USSR by 118-2/3 points to 109, with Austria third with 93 points. Norway won six gold medals to Russia's five. In the summer games, the United States won with 896.83 points to Russia's 776.0 points. East Germany was third with 348.0 points and West Germany fourth with 243 points. However, this turn-about, like others in the past has been excellent for the Olympic spirit, and may have taught the athletes from the Communist countries true sportsmanship and that chauvinism and propaganda have no real place in the Olympic games. On the basis of Olympic points per million population, Norway was first.

Sports and the Olympic games, like every other field of human endeavor, attract opportunists. For instance, a military man from the United States who had formerly held a high office as a political appointee once tried to become commissioner or director of amateur sports in the United States —supposedly because the United States had made a poor showing in the 1956 and 1960 games, and because of a disagreement between the AAU (Amateur Athletic Union) and the NCAA (National Collegiate Athletic Association). The would-be sports czar had never been on a varsity squad in college or shown any prior interest in sports.

The NCAA-AAU conflict has of course had an impact on U.S. Olympic performance. It is a power struggle by college athletic directors who want to establish a control extending beyond college competition, to dominate the more glamorous and in some cases more profitable international areas of certain sports. For instance, the NCAA wants no part of the many problems involved in amateur boxing and its present drop in popularity. On the other hand, it wants to take over track and field and swimming from the AAU after the AAU's tremendous success in international and Olympic competition, and because the AAU has been recognized by and cooperated with international groups for over 75 years. Another item not generally known is that while the athletic directors of colleges and the NCAA officials are paid sports managers working to improve their colleges' prestige in sports and the physical condition of their students, the AAU management is mainly made up of sports-men who contribute their time and experience in international athletics. How can such management be replaced or under-mined after its unequalled record in track, field, swimming and other sports, including some that the NCAA is not even interested in? The head of a large university privately stated that as far as he was concerned his athletic director better stick to what he was being paid for and let international and Olympic affairs and the activities of graduate athletes alone.

A former government employee on the United States Olympic Committee, now deceased, was responsible for the hiring of a business consultant firm with absolutely no knowl-edge of sports, paid by funds contributed to the Olympic Committee by the public, allegedly to find out what was wrong with the U.S. Olympic effort. The 1964 summer games proved that there was very little wrong (gold medals: U.S.—36, Russia—30). In 1968 it was proved that there was noth-ing wrong at all (gold medals: U.S.—45, Russia—29). The consultants and their reports have not been heard from since. But government interference with sports and the Olym-pic games is nothing new and has been successfully over-come except during the dictatorships of the Dark Ages when the games and most sports disappeared. The International Olympic Committee and the concept of its organization has frequently been put to the test on this issue, and while it sometimes seems complacent, it usually overcomes improper influence in the end. Here Mr. Brundage deserved an Olym-pian accolade.

A few errors are the exceptions that prove the golden rule, and indicate that human error can be made . . . even on Mount Olympus. For instance, in 1896 with the French in a controlling position, the International Olympic Com-mittee was "convinced" that it should place on the program four bicycle races so similar that one Frenchman, Emile Masson, could win all four. (Actually he won three but al-lowed a friend and teammate to win the fourth by taking the Silver Medal.) Sixty-eight years later, in the 1964 winter games the IOC was "persuaded" to schedule four women's speed skating events similar in nature when Russia had the same reasons for influencing the schedule as the French had had in 1896. The result was Lydia Skoblikova of Russia won all four events. In 1964 the Swimming Committee became overenthusiastic and the swimming competitions were in-creased from 19 in 1960 to 33 in 1968. Audiences can be bored by scores of preliminary, quarter and semifinal heats and added and unnecessary events. Scores of heats have resulted in two or three finals with five or more finalists repeating. Again, one contestant—Don Schollender—won four gold medals in similar events. Such instances are usually prompted by ulterior motives and planned by the management—not by the athletes.

There are many who believe that the entire Olympic program may be undermined if there are too many events—both from the viewpoint of the spectator and the athlete. There are over 200 events in the summer and winter games. Let us assume that at the current rate of expansion of the swimming program and other sports that there will be over 400 events. How will either athletes or spectators be able to spare the time to attend the entire games? The increased number of events in each sport will be an all-out test of stamina, perhaps with the finalists badly worn down. It would be ridiculous to have a 60-meter, 100-meter, 200-meter and 300-meter run! The same man if properly rested could win three or four of these. Yet in swimming there are now 100-, 200- and 400-meter contests in various styles, won by the same person in many cases. Added to this are a number of relays involving the same distances. No one knows if this is due to over-enthusiasm of the swimming community or an effort by the United States to pack the score with more wins or to build up some very beautiful competitors by seeing that they win several gold medals in the same Games. Such an over-emphasis is *not* in the best interests of the Olympic games. It may even hurt the swimming program in the long run.

If anyone in the United States wants to argue about the communist bloc's unusual influence over the IOC, which hopefully will adjust itself, then the barring of Nationalist China from the 1960 winter Olympics at Squaw Valley, California is another sad example of a human mistake. The games were allotted public funds by the Congress of the United States and held with the help of U.S. Army personnel and facilities, and Mr. Brundage denied that a U.S. military ally duly invited would be barred. However, Nationalist China was barred. But incidents like this prove rather than disprove the lasting power of the Olympic spirit over occasional errors of management and the pressures caused by the ambitions of groups or countries. The Olympic games are the oldest people-to-people peace program. The only eligibility requirement is that participants be citizens of the countries they represent, that they have no commercial or professional association or past connection (the word "amateur" is now being conscientiously avoided), and that a sufficient length of time has elapsed if an athlete represented another country in the Olympics prior to changing his or her nationality. (This to prevent international proselyting of athletes.)

Up to 1964 anyone who had competed in the Olympic games for one country could never compete for another. Now even this rule has been changed. A new rule for women participants in recent games is that they may be subjected to medical examination. This is because team managers have changed the sex of some of their women athletes with hormones.

A full account of the 1972 summer Games at Munich, West Germany, and the 1972 winter Games at Sappora, Japan, is presented in Chapter XX. Chapter XX will also add to the story of each of the various sports covered up to 1972 in Chapters III to XIX.

The 1976 Montreal, or XXI Summer Games, together with the XII Winter Games at Innsbruck and the story of all sports at these Games are covered in Chapter XXI.

CHAPTER III

Archery

ARCHERY IS perhaps the oldest sport in the world. There are records to indicate that cavemen competed with the bow and arrow besides using them to kill animals and fight enemies. No historian has been able to place the site or the story associated with the invention of the bow and arrow. According to one of the most avid researchers of the subject, Dr. Robert P. Elmer, many-time U.S. archery champion, the Aurignacions, a race which existed over 15,000 years ago, were probably the first to use the bow and arrow. Experts on the Orient claim bows and arrows were used in China and Japan over 5,000 years ago. Others claim the bow and arrow dates back to the Egyptians and there is no doubt that Egyptians with bows and arrows helped defeat the Persians in a war where the bows and arrows of the Egyptians outranged the sling shots and javelins of the Persians. The original Egyptian bow was five feet tall and the arrows were approximately 30 inches long and sharply tipped with bronze. Later the bow and arrow was developed as an even better weapon in Europe. The Norse invasions of England brought the bow and arrow to the country that soon nurtured the top archers of the world. Archery became a national sport in England in 1673 and was sponsored by King Charles II in 1676. In the United States archery got its start as a sport in 1828 but only became popular in 1878. Its popularity led to the formation of the National Archery Association of the United States which still controls the sport in the United States. (President, Marvin Kleinman of Cincinnati, Ohio; Executive-Secretary, Clayton D. Shenk of Ronks, Pennsylvania).

The sport of archery classified along with fencing, shooting, and wrestling as a combat sport will return to the Olympic games at Munich. It was a popular sport in the modern games in 1900, 1904, 1908 and 1920. In the 1904 Olympic games the United States won all six Archery events: two individual men and two individual women won, and both team events were won as well. The sport is now controlled by the International Archery Federation FITA (Federation International de Tir a l'Arc. President, Mrs. Inger Fritch of England; Secretary-General, D. M. Thomson of England.) The Olympic men's events will be the world's championship course of 72 arrows at 90 meters, 72 arrows at 70 meters both at 122 cm. target face; 72 arrows at 50 meters, 72 arrows at 30 meters both at a 80 cm. target face. The targets consist of ten rings with the center ring counting ten points and the outside ring, one point. The maximum score is therefore 2,880 points, with the current world's championship record held by Hardy Ward, Mount Pleasant, Texas, 2,332 points (1969). The women's event is the same except that the maximum ranges are 60 and 70 meters. The current world's championship record is held by Dorothy Lidstone of Canada, 2,361 points (1969). There have already been 25 world's championships in archery, the 26th (1971) will be in York, England. The 1969 championship was held in Valley Forge State Park, Pennsylvania. World's championships are held every two years on uneven calendar years. From now on there will be a world's Olympic championship every four years. Among past world's champions are Ray Rogers, of the United States, a Cherokee Indian from Muskogee, Oklahoma, and Miss M. Maczynski of Warsaw, Poland.

To the uninitiated, archery records are confusing, for in addition to Olympic world's or world's championship records that are based on two rounds or 2x36 (72) arrows at the various ranges there are world competition records based only on one round or 36 arrows at each range. Here a perfect score is 1,440 (instead of 2,880). The world's record holders on a single round are currently men: Jorma Sandelin, Finland, 1,250 and women: Nancy Myrick, United States, 1,208. There are also world's championship team records. These are based on the three highest scores at a world archery championship for the archers of the country. Record team scores are: Men United States, 7,194, (1969), Hardy Ward, John C. Williams, Ray Rogers. Women Russia, 6,887, (1969), Norma Kozina, Emma Gaptchenko and Tatiana Ovraztsava. A perfect score for a world team competition is 8,640 (2,880x3).

The United States has in recent years pretty well dominated the sport with the aid of American Indians. In the last eight world's championships it won 26 of 48 medals. Another U.S. Indian, Joe Thornton, is a former world's champion. There are currently 46 nations in the FITA and over 40 countries are expected to compete at the first regular Olympic archery competition since 1920. In 1920 there were 32 entries from seven countries with Belgium winning all four events. The archery associations and the entire archery community throughout the world have earned the return of archery to the Munich Olympic games by their patience and finally successful all-out effort.

CHAPTER IV

Boxing

BOXING WAS born before the earliest Olympics. It was probably started when a prehistoric man was surprised in a defile by a saber-toothed tiger, picked up a stone and swung desperately. The first blows of primitive boxing were swings. This is proved by Egyptian hieroglyphics dating back before 4000 B.C. showing soldiers of the Pharaohs boxing with primitive cestus or leather taping, not brass knuckles. To prove the swing of primitive African boxing, these leather, bark, or primitive cloth wrappings covered not only the fists and hands of the Egyptian boxers, but their forearms to the elbows. The clublike punches of these primitive boxers required protection for the whole arm rather than just for the fist. Boxing spread from Egypt, via Crete, to Greece. However, the first development in the art of self-defense and the first golden age of competitive boxing are definitely identified with the Olympics.

Boxing as a competitive sport, like so many others, re-

35

ceived its main impetus from Olympic competition and the tremendous rivalry and training brought on by the greatest ancient or modern objective—an Olympic or World's Championship. Through the Olympics, boxing spread first throughout Greece, then over the Greek Empire and later, with the help of Rome and the Roman legions, to the entire known world.

The early Olympics gave us our present-day sport, and evidence shows that there is hardly anything new in modern boxing. Boxers of the Olympic era had boxing gloves of leather, which they kept in good condition by rubbing animal fat on them. The gloves, generally speaking, were used for the same purpose that gloves are used for today. Even the light striking bag and the heavy punching bag are not new. In the fifth century B.C., Olympic boxers trained in gymnasiums just as they do today and used punching bags made of leather and canvas filled with fig seeds and sand.

Today boxers in training and intercollegiate boxers, for a short period before the colleges abandoned the sport, in actual competition adopted a special headguard of padded leather to protect them against being cut over the eyes, to prevent cauliflower ears and serious head injuries. Even this was not unknown to the Olympic boxers of antiquity, who wore a leather cap called an *amphotide* for the same purpose. Even mouthpieces were used; they were not made of rubber, like those of today, but were made of leather.

There were, nevertheless, some major differences between boxing then and boxing now, both in and out of the Olympics. In those days there were no rounds or regular rest periods, nor were there any weight divisions. Boxing contests lasted until one of the men was knocked so cold he could not continue, or one of the contestants gave up (which was allowed), or until either one or both fighters were too exhausted to stand up.

The Greeks had some unfair rules, too. For instance, if, after hours of fighting, both boxers were too exhausted to continue, each was given a free punch at the other, like a free throw in basketball. Lots were drawn for the privilege of taking the first punch, and naturally the boxer fortunate enough to win the draw had a tremendous advantage. This ancient practice gave us our modern fight term "draw" for an inconclusive decision.

Boxing, although one of the main events in the ancient Olympics for hundreds of years, was not an event in the first recorded Olympics in 776 B.C., but was first introduced

36

as a regular championship event in the XXIII Olympiad (688 B.C.) when a Greek named Onomastus won the first boxing crown and later established the first official Olympic boxing rules. Boxing for boys was added in the XL Olympiad (616 B.C.).

In these early games, the contestants were exclusively Greeks; later they came from all over the Greek Empire. The games continued after the conquest of Greece by the Romans until the Greco-Roman athletic rivalry degenerated into so many brawls, especially in the boxing contests, that Emperor Theodosius abolished the games in 394 A.D. The last recorded winner of an Olympic boxing championship is Varasdates, who later became King of Armenia.

Boxing contests in the ancient Olympics featured the cestus, the Grecian boxing glove. It was not loaded with metal or spikes, as its later Roman gladiatorial counterpart was, but was made of heavy leather strips wrapped around the hand and arm, with a harder, thicker leather surface over the knuckles. In addition to the regular boxing contests, the Greek Olympic games included a rough-and-tumble contest called the pancratium, in which wrestling as well as boxing was allowed. There were similar events for boys, with about the same rules.

The athletic uniform of Olympic contestants in all sports including boxing was complete nudity. No women were allowed at the Olympics even as spectators in the beginning on penalty of being thrown to certain death from a nearby rocky cliff called the Typaean Rock. Later, however, this rule was changed, and eventually girls' events were actually included in the games.

The tradition of fair play and sportsmanship in the Olympics was significantly demonstrated in boxing. Hitting below the waist was a foul and not countenanced by the Greeks. This rule was observed so carefully in Greece that no protectors were ever worn at the Olympics; although they were known and used in Crete. Even accidental fouls were unlikely, since ancient Olympic boxing rules made the head the only target for punches. Body punching was illegal.

The ancient Olympic games (776 B.C. to 394 A.D.) did more for the development of modern boxing technique than any other single factor, with the possible exception of the contributions of fencing and of fencing masters during the so-called English renaissance period of boxing from 1700 to 1800. The Olympic champions of antiquity and the first world heavyweight bare fist or prizefight champions of England, James Figg and John Broughton, who were also fencing masters, made the major contributions toward the development of the modern sport. However, there is no question that the basic development of the so-called "manly art of self-defense" came from the Olympics. Few people realize it, but most sports today owe the same debt to the Olympic games.

Even the straight hitting of the boxers was often not sufficient to win in combination boxing-and-wrestling matches. Kreugas, a great Olympic boxing champion, was killed by the wrestler Deoxenos in the finals of the pancratium championship at the Nemean games. Generally speaking, both in Greek and modern times, wrestlers have beaten boxers in free-for-all contests. In the entire history of the Greek Olympics only two boxing champions, Theagenes and Cleitomachus, are recorded as winning both boxing and the pancratium in the same Olympics, while seven Greek wrestling champions doubled up with Olympic wins in the pancratium.

Although the swing and not straight punching is instinctive to man, there is certain proof that the technique of straight punching was developed by the Greeks in Olympic competition. The proof is found in the evolution of the cestus. The first cestus, originally used in Egypt, Crete, and at the outset in Greece, consisted merely of leather strips or bands wrapped around the hand, fist, thumb, wrist, and arm to the elbow, with no special hitting surface. This was replaced in the Homeric period and the beginning of the Hellenic or Olympic period by what is called the "soft glove" cestus, which was very close to our present-day gauze-and-adhesive-tape wrappings except that leather was used, and the wrapping was continued halfway up the forearm. In the later Olympic period, when boxing became more important and vast crowds saw men fight with their fists for "world" championships, the cestus underwent another change. It became what is referred to as the "hard glove." The wrappings around the thumb, hand, wrist, and forearm became simply protective and defensive bindings to prevent bruises and broken bones. A close-fitting glove covered the hand, leaving the upper joints of the fingers free and the palm open. The modern feature of this "hard glove" was the hitting surface, three thick rings or bands of leather joined together, one alongside of the other over the four fingers and between the second joint and knuckle, giving the appearance of a sort of doughnut, the edge of which was the hitting surface. The fingers, in closing to make a fist, grasped the other side of this leather doughnut.

The rules of the pancratium did not allow the use of gloves or cestus, and boxers, deprived of their hard glove as an offensive adjunct and as a protection for their hands, were generally defeated by wrestlers. With the hard glove and its hitting edge, the boxers would undoubtedly have knocked most of the wrestlers bowlegged. With unprotected hands, the boxers broke their fists on the wrestlers' heads before being dumped on their backs.

The ancient Olympics gave us our modern boxing glove. John Broughton, the English "pro" who was buried in Westminster Abbey and has been called the "father of modern boxing," created the design of our present glove from drawings and photographs of the Olympic hard glove.

With the left hand the boxer in ancient Olympic competition held off his opponent or pushed him "off set" or off balance and thereby broke up his offense and his right-hand punches. Olympic boxers also with the straight left measured their opponents for their own right-hand follow-through or knockout swing. The ancient pugilist, by hitting or pushing his opponent with the left hand at the moment the latter was about to throw a punch, threw him off balance and thereby prevented him either from starting the blow, or, if the blow was already started, prevented it from landing with any great force. Much of our present-day defensive technique comes from experience gained in hundreds of years of Olympic boxing.

The absence of rounds and regular rest periods led to stalling, to lulls in the fighting during which both contestants took it easy. Defensive stalling occurred in both the ancient Greek and the more modern English era. In Greece, even in the Olympics and other great games, contestants could by mutual consent take a rest during the progress of a fight. The most famous statue of an Olympic boxer (now in the National Museum in Rome) is believed to show Cleitomachus sitting down during a rest period in his fight against a handsome Egyptian named Aristonikos in the finals of an Olympic boxing championship. Before the rest period Cleitomachus was behind on points, but after the rest he knocked out his opponent and won the Olympic crown. This extraordinary statue that dates back to the ancient Olympics is larger than life—shows a cauliflower eared, broken nosed boxer similar in physique to Max Baer. It is generally credited to the famous sculptor Apollonius, and was found in 1884 during

39

construction work in Rome where it had been brought from Olympia.

An interesting rule in all early boxing was the one which permitted any boxing competitor to indicate his desire to give up and end the bout by merely holding up his right or left hand with a forefinger pointed upward. In early Greece there were no neutral corners and no rules against hitting a man who was partially down but still showed fight.

The Greeks used their feet as well as their heads and fists. There was continuous maneuvering for position. Hundreds of pictures, statues, and friezes show beyond doubt that the Greeks used a stance approximating our own and requiring the same basic footwork. In addition, there is evidence that Greek boxing developed the human figure to the proportions of the typical boxer of today—early Olympic boxers had thin legs, large shoulders, and long muscles, indicating both speed and hitting power.

The winners of each of the events at the Olympics were announced by a herald who proclaimed the victorious entrant's name, his father's name, and the name of the city or country from which he came, and each victor was then privileged to erect a statue of himself in the sacred Altis.

There were other games during the golden age of boxing in Greece, though none so famous as the Olympics. However, the boxing events were just as popular and just as closely contested at the Pythian, Nemean, and Isthmian games. After 573 B.C., the Olympics were held in July or August of every fourth year, both the Isthmian games and the Nemean games in the summer or spring of every second and fourth year, and the Pythian games in August of every third year, making a total of six championships in the four "great games" every four years. According to the records, the various games, including all preliminaries, semifinals and finals in all events, usually lasted five days.

Since the winners of all contests in all sports were virtually certain to be subsidized or supported in some way by their city-states or countries for the rest of their lives, and since most competitors had their expenses paid by their sponsors or city-states, contestants were attracted from every corner of the Greek and Roman Empires, so that at no time in the world's history was a consistent winner more truly entitled to be called "world's champion."

When one examines the records that have been preserved and sees the startling accomplishments and consistency of championship performance of some of the ancient boxers, one wonders why more has not been written about them. For instance, a boxer named Tisander won four Olympic boxing championships over a span of more than twelve years. Boxing as an art and science has progressed technically to such a degree that a modern pugilist should have an advantage over the boxer of antiquity. However, basing a comparison on cunning, experience, endurance, speed, agility, and strength, it is very questionable if the great Olympic boxers of ancient Greece could have been beaten by the best of today. How, for instance, does any boxer's record today compare with that of the man who in twenty years won 1,400 championships, each representing many fights in series of eliminations, often involving as many as 10 fights in a single day? This is the record of Theagenes of Thasos, the greatest of all ancient Olympic boxers.

Theagenes is believed to have been born in Thrace about 505 B.C. At the age of nine he is said to have carried away a huge bronze statue which stood in a square or agora in his city, simply because he took a childish fancy to it. Instead of being punished, he was made to return it to its place and thereupon became famous for his tremendous strength. Upon coming of age, he began competing in boxing and in the pancratium and, when he was older, in long-distance running. He won 25 or 30 major championships in boxing and as many more in the pancratium, some in the same games, and had about 1,400 olive wreaths placed upon his head during his lifetime.

To prove his championship caliber further, Theagenes defeated another of the great boxers of ancient Greece. This boxer, Euthymus, had won many boxing championships, including the 74th Olympics, and probably would have achieved a greater stature in the history of boxing if he had not been a contemporary of Theagenes. In the 75th Olympics Theagenes decided to enter both the boxing and the pancratium events. The two greats met in the boxing final. Theagenes won, but was so badly cut up by Euthymus that, while he had also qualified for the final in the pancratium, he had to forfeit the final bout in this event and consequently the championship. Euthymus was not entered in the pancratium.

The officials took a very arbitrary view of the situation, probably out of love for Euthymus, who was the older champion. They ruled that if Theagenes had been able to defeat Euthymus and also win the pancratium, he would have been a competitor worthy of the best Greek tradition. However, the judges felt that in depriving Euthymus of his boxing

41

title but in having then to default in the pancratium final, Theagenes had shown a flaw in his character by biting off more than he could chew, so they fined him, claiming he had spoiled the Olympic show and wronged Euthymus by being too greedy in wanting two titles. Part of his fine had to be paid to the Olympic gods and part to Euthymus. Theagenes paid his Olympic fine, but settled his debt to Euthymus by not entering the boxing event in the next, or 76th Olympics. As a result, Euthymus won, although he couldn't really be considered boxing champion. Theagenes won the pancratium and at a later Olympiad, probably the 77th, won the double victory. Only one other boxer—Cleitomachus—ever accomplished this feat. When Theagenes died, he became almost a deity and for centuries his statues were thought to have the power to heal the injuries of athletes.

Next in line for fistic immortality are Glaucus of Carystus, Polydamus of Scotussa and Cleitomachus of Thebes. Although they won their Olympic crowns some 2,100 years before modern boxing got its start in the early eighteenth century, these champions should be classed with the best of the modern era, even among such of our professionals as Figg and Broughton, Sullivan and Jeffries, Dempsey and Louis.

Glaucus of Carystus was a farm boy. One day, according to the legend, while he was working with his father, the ploughshare fell out of the plough. He fitted it into place, using his bare hand as a hammer. His father, on seeing this, decided his son should become a boxer, and entered him in the Olympics. The story goes that in spite of his inexperience and lack of boxing knowledge, Glaucus got through the preliminaries by virtue of sheer strength and his good right hand. However, he took lots of punishment and in the finals was so faint from exhaustion and loss of blood that it looked as though he was through. Fortunately for him, it was not then illegal to coach from the sidelines, and his father shouted from the gallery: "Remember the ploughshare!" and Sonny came through with a quick knockout.

After this, Glaucus made a thorough study of the science of boxing as it was understood in those days and, as a great champion, took very little further punishment for many years. His boxing style was considered so fine that statues of him in sparring or "on guard" positions were made. His acquired science, added to an unusual natural punch, earned him several Olympic, two Pythian, eight Nemean, and eight Isthmian boxing championships, as well as hundreds of minor championships.

Polydamus, who lived about 380 B.C., though certainly not in a class with Theagenes, Glaucus, Cleitomachus, or even Euthymus, was nevertheless very colorful and the subject of great contemporary ballyhoo and publicity. While he was a boxer and pancratic performer who won many championships in addition to several Olympics, he is more famous for his accomplishments outside the realm of boxing.

He was the giant of the Hellenic amphitheatres—an Olympian Primo Carnera, standing 6 feet 8 inches tall and weighing 300 pounds. Our other four champions of that period varied from 6 feet to 6 feet 4 inches and from 190 to 235 pounds. The means by which we have been able to figure out the measurements of these fighters may be of interest. In many cases the victory statues had at their bases the actual imprint of the athlete's foot: a sort of Olympian Grauman's Chinese Theatre. As the imprint of a movie star's hands or feet in Hollywood may tell generations to come their stature in the field of the cinema, the imprints of the Olympic athletes' feet, next to their perfectly proportioned statues, allow us, centuries later, to determine rather closely their height and weight. Also, the Greek measurements of some have come down to us in cubits and fingers: 18.25 inches and 0.7 inches respectively.

Polydamus, with his tremendous size, weight, and strength, did some phenomenal things, if we can believe the original sources. He could stop a chariot drawn by three horses by holding on to the back of it. In a battle royal against three men, he killed all three. In various exhibitions he pulled a bull's leg off and killed a lion with his bare hands. Overconfidence caused Polydamus' death. He and some friends were in a cave when a cave-in started. The others ran out, but Polydamus tried to hold the roof up and perished when the hill fell in on him.

Cleitomachus was neither colorful nor a performer of spectacular stunts, but in the ring or in the stadium he was second only to Theagenes. He was the only other man to win both the boxing and pancratium crowns at the same Olympics—the 141st in 216 B.C. But boxing was his specialty, and, like Theagenes, he was undefeated in hundreds of championship contests over many years. Unfortunately for him, however, his competitive career overlapped that of one of the greatest wrestlers of all time, Caprus, who also competed in the pancratium event. In the 142nd Olympics the two men

43

met in the pancratium finals, but the wrestler won, not the boxer. However, Cleitomachus retained his boxing crown, and his reputation through the ages makes him seem a challenger worthy of any one of our best heavyweights.

With the arrival of the barbarian tribes, wars, dictators, and the Dark Ages, boxing first degenerated into gladiatorial boxing with brass knuckles and the cruel and deadly myrmex, called the "limb piercer," and then disappeared completely. The myrmex was a bronze, spurlike instrument which the gladiatorial boxer strapped to his cestus in order to make the blows from his fist fatal. Although the Roman legions carried the sport of boxing all over the known world, boxing, like most athletics and the Olympics, was doomed and did not reappear until some twelve centuries later, when civilization once more began to recognize the dignity of man and to hope for a world of peace and democracy. As both a means and symbol, man sought out and brought back the Olympics.

The first modern Olympics, in 1896, ought logically to have included boxing, but because boxing had become almost exclusively American and English, it was thought best to omit it in the program for fear of discouraging many nations which would have no entries in this sport. Boxing, therefore, was not featured in the modern Olympics until, mainly through the efforts of the United States, it was included in the third modern Olympiad in 1904 at St. Louis. The individual winners in seven classes are listed in the appendix. O. L. Kirk starred in winning titles in both the bantamweight and featherweight classes. The 1904 games did not attract many foreign entries, and as a result the United States had little or no competition in boxing. Every title was won by an American. However, boxing began to spread fast, as it had once before through the Olympics.

The 1906 unofficial Olympics at Athens did not have boxing competition, but the fourth Olympiad in London in 1908 featured boxing competition in five weights. The British made a clean sweep—H. Thomas winning the bantam title, and 38-year-old R. K. Gunn winning the featherweight title with a perfect exhibition of the old British straight-up boxing with the straight left jab developed by the fencing masters and boxing champions, James Figg and John Broughton. Grace won the lightweight title, and the Great British cricket star, J.W.N.T. Douglas, won the middleweight title. A.L. Oldham, a London policeman, won the heavyweight class. No competition was held in the flyweight class, nor in the welterweight division. The United States did not enter a team, as the British had not decided to add boxing until the last minute.

The 1912 Olympics did not have any boxing because the laws of the host nation, Sweden, did not permit it. Although World War I interrupted the Olympics, it spread the sport of boxing as it was a popular pastime and conditioner in the armed services of all the warring countries.

By 1920 truly world-wide interest in boxing led for the first time to real competition, with entries from many countries. The U.S. boxing team, selected after eliminations and competitions throughout the United States, included the best boxers from the army, navy, the colleges, and the amateurs of AAU competitions. The New York police force was also well represented. Among the Americans who boxed for the United States in 1920 was Joe Cranston of West Point, later to become a combat general in the U.S. Army in World War II. Still another member of the 1920 United States team was Eddie Egan of Colorado and Harvard, who was to become a lieutenant colonel in the U.S. Air Force in World War II and later chairman of the New York State Boxing Commission and still later head of the President's People to People Sports Program. Unfortunately, although the caliber of boxing exhibited at this Olympic championship was quite high indeed, the contestants, and particularly the American team, were handicapped by the fact that the quality of the officiating had not kept pace with the spread of the sport. However, sportsmanship won out, and although there is no question that the United States was deprived of a few victories through the inexperience of the officials, no disagreeable incident marred the competition for long.

The United States won more first places than any other nation, but finished second to Great Britain in the unofficial team score. For the United States, Frank Genaro won the flyweight title. He later went on to become the professional flyweight champion of the world. Samuel Mosberg won the lightweight title and Edward Egan the light-heavyweight Olympic championship. Fred Kolberg, another U.S. entry, was third in the welterweight class. The other champions were L. Walter of South Africa in the bantamweight division, Fritsch of France in the featherweight, Schueider of Canada in the welterweight, H. Mallin of the London police in the middleweight class, and R. R. Rawson, also of Great Britain, in the heavyweight division. The coach of the United States team was Spike Webb, boxing coach of the

45

U.S. Naval Academy. His efficiency and sportsmanship made a deep impression on the entire Olympic fraternity. Jack and Pete Zivic, who later became well-known in professional boxing, were both members of this U.S. boxing team.

Twenty-nine nations had representatives in the boxing competition at the next Olympics in 1924 in Paris. The U.S. boxing team won the unofficial team championship. Again, the competition was marred by inexperience in judging and refereeing, and a novel and unusual experiment particularly handicapped the British and American boxers. The referee, who according to custom in British and American boxing is always in the ring, was stationed outside of the ring, following a custom established in some European countries where boxing had just begun. Sometimes the referee's order to break from a clinch was heard by the contestants in the ring, and sometimes it was not. This system was extremely ineffective and led to at least one very unfair decision.

Joe Lazarus, a bantamweight from Cornell University, knocked out his opponent but lost the fight because the referee ruled that he had hit his opponent on a break. The referee claimed he had yelled "break" from outside the ring a split-second before the K.O. punch, but ringside spectators hadn't seen a clinch or heard the referee. Hector Mendez of Argentina, to become an ambassador in the foreign service of his country, also received an inexcusably bad decision in the finals of the welterweight class. And an outstanding middleweight from France was disqualified, after being awarded a decision, for biting his opponent during one of the clinches. Although the bite mark was in evidence, it went unnoticed until after the contestants had left the ring.

Nevertheless, the general caliber of boxing exhibited in these Olympic championships was superior. Three members of the United States team became professional world's champions, and a number of contestants from other countries later fared well in the professional boxing field.

The particular stars of the 1924 Olympic boxing competition were Fidel La Barba of the United States, who later became the professional flyweight champion of the world, and Jackie Fields of the United States, who later became professional welterweight champion of the world. H. Mallin, a lieutenant in the London police force, was the first and only repeat winner in boxing in the modern Olympics up to this time; he had previously won the Olympic middleweight title in

1920. Hector Mendez of Argentina, even though deprived of an Olympic title by a poor decision, impressed everyone with his boxing, punching power, and sportsmanship.

The most dramatic feature of the 1924 Olympic competition was the story of Jackie Fields and Joe Salas. Joe Salas had won the national amateur featherweight boxing championship of the United States in Boston in 1924 to become a member of the Olympic boxing team. Featherweight Jackie Fields had an off day, and was eliminated by a decision in the same tournament. Both boys came from Los Angeles, went to school together, took up boxing together, boxed for the same club and were coached by the same man. Both had the same ambition—to win an Olympic championship. Jackie Fields, because of his past record, was added to the Olympic team as an extra but official member, as were several others, since in 1924 each nation could enter two men in each weight class. Salas and Fields were chosen by Coach Spike Webb as the two U.S. contestants in the featherweight class. They both fought and won five fights and met in the final. For three rounds in the Olympic ring in Paris, thousands of miles from home, the two fought toe-to-toe. The fact that they were close friends made no difference. At the end both were punched out. After a tense moment the officials awarded the bout and the Olympic championship to Fields. The two friends ran across the ring and fell into each other's arms as the band played "The Star Spangled Banner." As two American flags were hoisted to the first- and second-place flagpoles, two California boys in tears stood locked in each other's arms. Jackie Fields later turned professional and became the world's welterweight champion.

As an indication of the increasing popularity of boxing throughout the world, it is interesting to note that points were made for first, second, or third place in 1924 by eleven countries: the United States, Great Britain, Denmark, Argentina, Holland, Belgium, Norway, Sweden, South Africa, France and Canada. The International Amateur Boxing Association was organized at the 1924 Olympics with Mr. Cuddy, the manager of the U.S. team, as its first president and the writer, who was a member of the 1924 team, as secretary-general.

In the 1928 Olympics, the number of nations competing in boxing increased to thirty. Once again the officiating, although improving, left much to be desired, but the poor decisions were evenly distributed and handicapped all the teams more or less equally. For the third time, the U.S.

coach was Spike Webb, and Benny Levine of the AAU was manager.

The unofficial team title for boxing in 1928 went to Italy. Individual titles were won in the flyweight class by Anton Kocsis of Hungary, in the bantamweight class by Vittorio Tamagnini of Italy, in the lightweight class by Carlo Orlandi of Italy, in the welterweight class by Edward Morgan of New Zealand, in the middleweight class by Piero Toscani of Italy, in the light-heavyweight class by Victoria Angel Pedro Avendano of Argentina, and in the heavyweight class by Jurado Arturo Rodriguez of the Argentine.

Once again the referee sat outside of the ring, which was a great disadvantage to boxers accustomed to having the referee inside the ring. The only places the United States was able to gain were second in the bantamweight class with John L. Daly, second in the lightweight class with Stephen Holaiko, and third in the featherweight class with Harry Devine. Thomas Lawn, a welterweight, and Harry Henderson, intercollegiate middleweight champion from the Naval Academy, did not live up to the advance expectancy of becoming title winners.

Spike Webb, for the fourth time as coach, piloted the boxing team at the tenth Olympiad in Los Angeles in 1932, and for the second time saw the United States win the unofficial team title—the last team title, however, which the United States was to win in this sport until 1952.

The U.S. had one of the top amateur punchers in southpaw Fred Feary of California who ruined many an aspiring young heavyweight but who succumbed to stage fright or to the excellent defense of better boxers for he only won a bronze medal. Carmen Barth won the world middleweight crown for the United States. A well-balanced and superbly coached team won for Spike Webb his second Olympic team victory.

According to most experts, the outstanding boxer of the tournament was Edward Flynn of New Orleans and Loyola University, who is the only man in the history of United States amateur boxing to win a national intercollegiate championship, a National AAU championship, and an Olympic championship. In addition to welterweight titles, he won many middleweight titles, although he was a natural welterweight. The refereeing and judging in this Olympic competition was, for the first time, really satisfactory.

At the next Olympics, in 1936, the host nation, Germany, won the unofficial boxing title. The individual winners are

48

listed in the appendix. Louis Lauria of Cleveland, Ohio, placed third in the flyweight class, and Jack Wilson, also of Cleveland, a boxer 6 feet 2 inches tall who only weighed 117 pounds, placed second in the bantamweight class.

The next Olympics were held in 1948, after an interruption of twelve years caused by World War II. The 1948 boxing teams did the best they could to pick up where Olympic boxing had left off before the war. The competition in London was highly successful from the standpoint of the number of nations entered and the number of spectators attracted. The officiating was not as good as in 1932 or 1936 and a score of judges were relieved early in the tournament, being adjudged incompetent by the International Jury of Appeal. The unofficial team championship was shared by Italy and South Africa. The individual winners are listed in the appendix. Only one American, Horace Herring, a U.S. Navy entry, reached the final round. In fact, his second place in the welterweight class scored the only points made by the United States in the entire tournament. It was one of the worst showings made by a U.S. boxing team in any Olympics.

United States prestige in Olympic boxing bounced back fast in 1952 with coach Peter E. Mello, assisted by Joseph T. Owen, and a resolute management group intent on getting a well-balanced boxing team. The boxing championship at the Helsinki Olympics featured more contestants from more countries than any other modern Olympic games to date. The U.S. team was considered by many to be the finest ever to represent the United States, and won five individual Olympic championships as well as the unofficial team championship. Our Olympic champions were flyweight Nate Brooks of Cleveland, Ohio; light-welterweight Charles Adkins of Gary, Indiana; middleweight Floyd Patterson of Brooklyn, New York; light-heavyweight Norvel Lee of Washington, D.C. and heavyweight Edward Sanders of Los Angeles, California. Archie Slaten of Chattanooga, Tennessee, who was our number-one man in the lightweight class, was not able to compete, due to an attack of appendicitis. Norvel Lee was awarded the "most proficient performer" trophy, and Floyd Patterson won in impressive style.

Many of these winners went on to professional triumphs, especially Floyd Patterson who became the youngest world's professional heavyweight champion and the first to ever lose and regain this title. Patterson was a picture boxer with great punching power in the Olympics but later developed a peek-

49

a-boo style which seemed to freeze his offense. Strangely enough, he lost to and rewon the title from Ingamar Johansson, a Swedish heavyweight disqualified from this same Olympic championship when outclassed by Ed Sanders. Sanders was later accidentally killed in a pro bout.

The quality of Olympic boxing in 1956 followed the unfortunate general downward trend of the sport. Russia was the winner of the unofficial team title. At least two boxers appeared for their third successive Olympic games; Dobrescu Mircea of Rumania, who placed second in the flyweight, and Laszlo Papp of Hungary, a light-middleweight who won his third Olympic championship, were both oldtimers. Papp, a southpaw double for the late Errol Flynn in his younger days, was the first man in the history of the modern Olympics to win three Olympic boxing titles. The United States had two world champions: Pete Rademacher, in the heavyweight class, and James Boyd, in the light-heavyweight class; and one second, Jose Torres in the light-middleweight class. Roger Rouse, the U.S. middleweight, lost a split decision in a rough quarter final bout to Chapron of France. However, the French champion received so much punishment he had to withdraw from the tournament losing the semi-final and placing fourth by default. Weight and weightmaking were against the U.S. team. Choken Maekewa, in the bantamweight class, and Harry Smith, in the featherweight class, were both disqualified for not making the weight limit, while Torres was certainly not helped by having to spend from one to two hours a day in a sweat box and by dieting strenuously during the entire week of competition before he met the two-time Olympic champion Papp. The lesson drawn from this was that alternates should be taken along, (as the Russians did) and more attention should be paid to weight prior to the selection of the team. Olympic boxing in 1956 was in no way equal to that of 1952 and 1948. In the words of an English boxing expert at Melbourne: "Boxing form throughout the world is ebbing fast into mediocrity."

Boxing at Rome in 1960 featured 283 contestants from 54 countries and was somewhat reminiscent of bare fist fighting in England when chancery holds and some wrestling were allowed. The boxing was crude and the officiating was bad. There was too much holding and hitting and too many chancery holds. Rough, crude boxers nullified and wore down the few skillful boxers with punching combinations that were in the tournament. This was especially true in the lighter classes where bantamweight Grigoryev of Russia, lightweight

Pazdzior of Poland and light welterweight Nemecek of Czechoslovakia bulled their way to victories. Welterweight Benevenuto of Italy won with good boxing. In the heavier classes the sharper punching prevented bulling and wrestling, allowing the better boxers and hitters to win. Light middleweight McClure, middleweight Crook and light heavyweight Cassius Clay of the United States, and heavyweight DePiccoli of Italy all looked good in winning Olympic titles. DePiccoli, a southpaw, looked like a good puncher, while Cassius Clay who has since made good as a hitter in the pro ranks danced on his toes and boxed to an Olympic victory without showing much punching power. There were several very poor decisions by incompetent officials, such as the one that awarded Mitzev of Bulgaria a win over Saduk of Tunisia. This shocked the crowd into a timed twelve minutes of loud disapproval. The boxing was certainly far below the standards shown at Helsinki.

Strangely enough, all boxing experts in Tokyo in 1964 agreed that boxing in the Olympic games was getting worse —not better. This is unusual, for in practically all sports except perhaps the sport closest to boxing there is impressive improvement—besides the startling but continuous and provable improvement in records where time, distance or scores can be definitely compared. Fencing is the other sport that is not improving with time. This has been through no fault of the hosts. A boxing ring and a fencing strip are pretty much the same anywhere, and boxing gloves are not different, although the fists within them are certainly not the same.

Many evenings of preliminary boxing bouts at Tokyo turned up only one top performer who believed that an offense was the best defense. However, even he was worn down and beaten by the crude wrestling, holding and hitting, chancery holds, the clumsy rushing, grabbing and wearing-down style of most of the boxers from behind the Iron Curtain that seem to have taken over Olympic boxing. Strangely enough, even at the last minute a top coach or any professional boxing manager could instruct any fair boxer on the moves by which he could beat the wrestlers turned boxers. This is borne out by the fact that in the heavier weights, where holding, grabbing and chancery holds meant working in close and becoming vulnerable to being hit, the Iron Curtain boxers usually were knocked out or hit so hard they had to quit holding, and once they were reduced to boxing instead of wrestling they were outclassed. In the semifinal of the heavyweight class when Vadim Yemelyanov

51

of the Soviet Union tried to close, grab, pivot and wrestle Joe Frazier of the United States he became a close target. Frazier had his opponent in trouble in the first round and knocked him out in less than two minutes in the second round. Yet in the finals when Frazier met Hans Huber of Germany, who actually was not as tough as the Russian, Frazier only won on points 3-2, handicapped by a broken hand. Frazier, the only U.S. gold medalist, was an alternate with two losses to 293-pound Buster Mathis, who was injured before the games. Later a greatly improved Frazier became a professional champion. The United States has unusual experience in boxing with its many boxing experts and former managers of professional champions who in some cases are businessmen interested in the sport as a hobby. It is only lately that the AAU has been selecting its managers and coaches of Olympic boxing teams from the military services. As proven in a recent case, they may be fine soldiers but they have limited experience in ring generalship. Another related point is that three out of four of all Iron Curtain medalists at Tokyo were southpaws, an advantage to a properly seconded opponent who can be told what to do. Recent Olympics have produced no boxers to compare with Frankie Genaro, Fidel La Barba, Pascual Perez, Jackie Fields, Ed Flynn or Laszlo Papp.

With the growing popularity of boxing in Mexico and Latin America, and the spread of boxing in Asia, the 1968 Olympic Boxing Tournament broke all records for the most countries and the most boxers competing. Seventy nations entered 337 boxers, although only 67 nations actually sent 312 boxers to compete. Unfortunately, the quality of the tournament did not match the quantity of contestants. The officiating probably matched that of the very early modern Olympic boxing championships, including those where there was no referee in the ring. Favoritism, chauvinism, disagreement, and just plain ignorance and ineffective officiating were factors. The record shows that 32 judges and referees were disqualified and dismissed. Frequently, the boxing in the ring and the poor officiating caused gloveless fights in the audience, some of them of a far better quality than those in the ring. A highwater mark in dishonest officiating influenced by national pride, was the disqualification of Albert Robinson, U.S. featherweight, by Russian referee Zybalov for allegedly butting his Mexican opponent, Roldan. Fortunately, fight films indicated no butting whatever. The AIBA (Amateur International Boxing Association), the governing world body of amateur boxing, in a surprising and illogical decision on appeal ruled that the disqualified Robinson be awarded the Silver Medal even though he was leading in the final when disqualified, and if disqualified could hardly claim any medal. A more proper and fairer solution would have been to re match the two men . . . later, if necessary. To experienced followers of boxing, there is no reason for losers of the semifinals to not box each other to determine third and fourth places, as the winners have to fight it out. The three-round bouts in amateur boxing introduce no great problem of a second bout after a reasonable rest period. However, for the past few Olympics the losers of the semifinals both get a Bronze Medal and split the unofficial 4 to 3 points allotted for third and fourth places toward team credits.

Again the Iron Curtain countries, especially the Russians and Poles, continued their holding and hitting, wrestling, chancery holds and clumsy leaning and clinching, tiring-down style of boxing—similar to the English bare fist era—and again the Russians and Poles had a good share of "southpaws". In many cases the Russians and Poles could not have won if prevented from holding and hitting, wrestling, and wearing down their opponent in clinches, but the Olympic referees were not in control of the bouts. In all fairness, the Russians were not the only ones favored by poor officiating. British middleweight Christopher Finnegan won his Gold Medal by several very questionable decisions.

The general quality of the boxing was a slight improvement over that demonstrated in Tokyo. The most impressive winner was U.S. heavyweight Gold Medalist George Foreman, who in the finals had no great difficulty in knocking out his Soviet opponent, Ionis Chepulis. Foreman, incidentally, waved the American flag when he received his award—amid overwhelming applause—the proper reaction of any good American of any color or creed. The U.S. boxers did not have the type of management, advice and help from their corner that had been supplied by Spike Webb, Al Lacey and Benny Levine in the 1920 to 1932 games.

It is unfortunate that intercollegiate boxing in the United States has been completely abandoned because the NCAA did not want to solve safety and other problems. Many people believe that rough contact sports like boxing and football discourage riots, disorders and student disturbances. It is a sad commentary on a great sport, older than even the Olympics, that accident or death and the use of the sport as a political football, has boxing on the ropes. It is a great character and body builder, even though avoided by an advanced and effete society. It is not a sport helped by long hair or beards. More important, like all rough body contact sports, it tests the staying qualities of the participant and makes for the highest type of sportsmanship. Friendly fists can become salesmen for democracy, tolerance and peace throughout the world.

CHAPTER V

Canoeing

CANOEING IS, of course, the sport of paddling a canoe. The word "canoe" is applied to a wide variety of primitive boats, from the hollowed log of the Iroquois Indians of North America to the kayak of the Eskimo. The history of canoeing, like that of rowing, extends back to the dugout boat of the Stone Age. Its modern popularization dates back to 1865, when a British barrister, John MacGregor, developed the Rob Roy type of canoe and wrote extensively of his canoe voyages throughout Europe, Scandinavia, and the Holy Land. That same year, he organized the Royal Canoe Club. Within three years, other types of canoes had been developed, and over three hundred kinds crowded the waterways around London and Oxford. In 1871 a canoeing club was first organized in the United States at what is now St. George, Staten Island. In 1880, the American Canoe Association was formed at Lake George, New York, and the Canadian Canoe Association was formed shortly thereafter. At about the same time, the British Canoe Association, now known as the British Canoe Union, came into being. The canoe is now standardized—sharp at both ends, without counter or transom. Because of the low freeboard a canoe cannot be rowed but must be paddled.

International canoeing competition was practically created by the Olympics which spread the sport, and the standard canoes used in the Olympics, all over the world.

The eighth Olympiad, held at Paris in 1924, featured demonstration events in canoeing, which Canada won, but the first formal competitions in canoeing were not held until 1936. The winner of the first canoeing competition in the Olympic games was Austria, with Germany second and Czechoslovakia third. Although the United States did not win, the very inclusion of canoeing in the Olympics was an event for which an American could take some credit. W.

54

Van B. Claussen of Washington, D. C., who was the manager of the first U.S. Olympic canoe team, had in the early 1920's begun a correspondence with foreign canoe clubs that eventually led to the formation of the I.R.K., or International Canoeing Association. It was through this organization that 19 nations first organized and then participated in the nine events of the Berlin Olympics, at distances ranging from 1,000 to 10,000 meters.

The canoeing events at the Berlin Olympics were conducted at the rowing course at Grünau, a suburb on the River Spree. Canoeists from Austria took three first, three second, one third and two fourth places. The Germans won two firsts, three seconds, two thirds and two fourths. The United States finished in sixth place in the general team rankings, with one third, one fourth and three fifth places. Twenty-one nations were affiliated with the International Canoe Federation and all of them, except Brazil, were represented at the Olympics. Ernest Riedel of Teaneck, New Jersey, made the best showing of the American canoeists, finishing third in the 10,000-meter kayak single and fourth in the 100-meter kayak single. Joseph and Walter Hasenfus of Needham, Massachusetts, paired together to finish in the Canadian 10,000-meter double event. Joseph Hasenfus was fifth in the Canadian single event at 1,000 meters while Clarence R. McNutt and Robert Graf of Philadelphia were fifth in the Canadian double over the 1,000-meter course. The 10,000-meter two-seater folding kayak event was won by a team from Sweden, with Germany second, Holland third, Austria fourth, Czechoslovakia fifth, Switzerland sixth and the United States seventh. The one-seater folding kayak was won by Gregor Hradetzky of Austria, with Henri Eberhardt of France second and Zaver Hormann of Germany third. The first American to finish, Burr Folks, was tenth. The two-seater rigid kayak was won by a team from Germany, followed by Austria, Sweden, Denmark, Holland, Switzerland and the United States. One-seater rigid kayak was won by Ernst Krebs of German, with Fritz Landertinger of Austria second and Ernest Riedel of the United States third. The tandem Canadian canoe was won by a team from Czechoslovakia, with Canada second, Austria third, Germany fourth and the United States fifth. The 1,000-meter two-seater rigid kayak was won by a team from Austria, with Germany second and Holland third. Tandem Canadian canoe was won by a team from Czechoslovakia, with Austria second and Canada third. And the one-man Canadian canoe was won by Francis Amyot of Canada; B. Karlik of Czechoslovakia was second, Eric Koschik of Germany third.

Between 1936 and the postwar 1948 Olympics the I.R.K. was reorganized as the International Canoe Federation, I.C.F., with J. Asschier of the Swedish Kayak Association as president. In 1948, seventeen nations competed in eight events. Olympic competition has brought about a change in the racing equipment of canoeists, especially in the United States. The I.C.F. supplied for the 1948 competitions several types of racing kayaks never used in this country before. The single-seater (K-1) is 17 feet long, with a 20-inch beam, while the K-2 is about 21 feet long and has a 21½-inch beam. The old 16 footer with a 30-inch beam, which was called a "peanut" and was used for one-man and tandem competition, was replaced by an I.C.F. racing canoe 17 feet long and 29½ inches wide. The K-4 is gaining a place in this country. It is a four-man racing kayak about 36 feet by 23½ inches.

The fourteenth Olympiad at London presented canoeing competitions that had more competitors and better performances than those of the preceding Olympiad. The unofficial team championship was won by Sweden, with Czechoslovakia a close second, Denmark third, France fourth, the United States fifth. The American team was again managed and coached by W. Van B. Claussen. Seventeen nations participated in canoeing—Austria, Belgium, Canada, Czechoslovakia, Denmark, Finland, France, Great Britain, Holland, Hungary, Yugoslavia, Luxembourg, Norway, Poland, Sweden, Switzerland, and the United States. Upon arrival at Henley-on-Thames, it was discovered that the C-1 canoes brought by Sweden, Czechoslovakia, Belgium and France were in violation of the I.C.F. building rules. A protest was immediately drawn up by the United States and signed by Britain, Canada and Finland. Although this protest was formally lodged and argued to the bitter end, it was rejected insofar as it applied to the London Olympics. Although the Czech representatives definitely promised that their C-1 canoes would immediately be straightened to meet the United States demands, this promise was only partly kept.

The kayak singles 1,000-meter was won by G. Frederiksson of Sweden; second was J. Andersen of Denmark; third, H. Eberhardt of France. Kayak singles for women, a new event at 500 meters, was won by K. Hoff of Denmark, with A. G. Van de Anker Doedans of Holland second and F. Schwingl of Austria third. The kayak singles 10,000 meter was won by G. Fredriksson of Sweden; second was K. O. Wires of Finland; third, E. Skabo of Norway. Riedel, the first U.S. entrant to finish, was twelfth. Kayak pairs 1,000 meter was won by a team from Sweden, followed by Denmark, Finland and Norway. Kayak pairs 10,000 meter was won by a team from Sweden, with Norway second and Finland third. The United States finished thirteenth. The Canadian singles 1,000 meter was won by J. Holecek of Czechoslovakia, with D. Bennett of Canada second and R. Boutigny of France third. F. Havens of the United States came in fifth. Canadian singles 10,000 meter was won by F. Capek, Czechoslovakia; F. Havens of the United States was second and N. D. Lane of Canada, third. Canadian pairs 1,000 meter was won by a team from Czechoslovakia, with the United States second and France third. The Canadian pairs 10,000 meter was won by the American team of S. Lysak and S. Macknowski; second was Czechoslovakia, third France. The Olympics were spreading interest in this sport all over the world, and American performance was improving.

At the 1952 Olympics at Helsinki, Finland—being an enthusiastic supporter of canoeing—presented an outstanding program. With the help of various associations, clubs, and the U. S. Army, successful trials in the United States produced 69 entries in the finals and an outstanding team. The manager of the team was Walter Hanner, Jr. The canoeing events of these Olympics brought together a number of nations in close cooperation and good fellowship and an unusual amount of fraternization. The nations involved were Belgium, Great Britain, Canada, Italy, Finland, Norway, France, Holland, Germany, Denmark, Luxembourg, Yugoslavia, Hungary, Sweden, Russia, Switzerland, the Saar, Rumania, Austria and Czechoslovakia. It will be noted that for the first time Russia entered the canoeing competitions. The unofficial canoeing team championship was won by Finland, with Sweden, Hungary, Germany and Czechoslovakia in close pursuit.

Just before the Olympics a one-man kayak purchased by the United States from Sweden a month before was found to be one-eighth inch too narrow and was therefore disqualified from competition. With true Olympic sportsmanship seven different countries offered to lend a K-1 to the United States team immediately after the news got out. The Americans accepted the K-1 from Sweden, because it was most like the one in which the men had trained for the past two

57

years. The United States team, incidentally, did better than ever before in the canoeing competition in these Olympics. Kayak singles 1,000 meter was won by G. Fredriksson of Sweden, repeating his previous victory in this event at the 1948 Olympics; second was T. Stromberg of Finland; third, L. Gantois of France. The kayak pairs 1,000 meter was won by a team from Finland, with Sweden second, Austria third, and Germany fourth. The kayak singles 10,000 meter was won by T. Stromberg of Finland; second was G. Fredriksson of Sweden (who narrowly missed repeating the double win he had scored in 1948), and M. Scheuer of Germany was third. Kayak pairs 10,000 meter was won by a team from Finland, with Sweden second and Hungary third. Russia was tenth in this event and the United States fourteenth. Kayak singles for women was won by S. Saimo of Finland; second was G. Liebhart of Austria; third, N. Savina of Russia. Canadian singles 1,000 meter was won by J. Holecek of Czechoslovakia, repeating his 1948 win, with J. Parti of Hungary second and O. Ojanpera of Finland third. F. Havens of the United States finished fourth. Canadian pairs 1,000 meter was won by a team from Denmark, followed by Czechoslovakia and Germany. The United States team came in seventh. Canadian singles 10,000 meter was won by F. Havens of the United States, the first Gold Medal ever won by an American in canoeing; G. Novak of Hungary was second and A. Jindra of Czechoslovakia was third. Canadian pairs 10,000 meter was won by a team from France, followed by Canada, Germany, Russia, and the United States, in that order.

It seems strange indeed that in canoeing, a sport associated with North America, the United States and Canada should be completely outclassed, but that is what happened at the 1956 Olympics in Australia. Like all other sports, canoeing has been spread all over the world by the Olympics and 112 contestants from 17 nations competed in the Olympic canoeing regatta on picturesque Lake Wendouree, 70 miles from Melbourne, in faultless sunshine and calm waters. Overall features of the canoeing contest were the tremendous progress and success of the Russian and Rumanian paddlers and the extraordinary and unexpected performances of the Australians in their first international canoeing competition. In the Canadian pairs 10,000 meter the Russians, P. Kharin and G. Botev, paddled to an unchallenged win by 100 meters or more over the second place France. Hungary was third, while Canada and the United States were ninth and tenth.

The great star of the Olympic canoeing regatta was Sweden's Gert Fredriksson, who rounded out his record by winning five Gold Medals in three Olympics. He won the 10,000 and the 1,000 Meter Kayak Singles. Fredriksson had previously won the Olympic championships in the Kayak singles 1,000 meter in 1948 and 1952 and in the 10,000 meter in 1948. There was considerable interest in the women's kayak singles, especially as the favorites, representatives of Australia and Finland, were eliminated in the first heat. Miss T. Zenz, representing Germany, won this heat in a very close finish over E. Dementieva of Russia. In the finals, the same two girls led all the way to the near finish; but the Russian girl won, although her time was slower than Miss Zenz's winning time in the preliminary heat. The United States had no entry in this event. Russia won the unofficial team championship in canoeing.

The 1960 Rome Olympic canoeing on Lake Albano was proven superior by the fact that every Olympic record on the books was shattered. U.S. entries failed to win a single medal but improved greatly over Melbourne. Hungary won the unofficial men's championship and Russia, the women's events. The great Gert Fredriksson of Sweden in the 1,000 meter kayak pairs won his sixth gold medal in his fourth Olympics, but was beaten by Erik Hansen in the 1,000 meter kayak singles which he won in 1948, 1952 and 1956. Hansen's and Fredriksson's times were both well under the record. Gert brought his total to nine world championships.

Russia and Sweden tied for all-around honors on points in the 1964 men's canoeing (24-24), and Russia only earned a tie with Germany in the women's events (13-13). However, the United States broke into the medal class when Marcia Jones won the Bronze Medal in the kayak single. Fifteen-year old Francine Fox and Glorianna Perrier finished second in the kayak doubles. These were not only the first medals ever won by U.S. women in this sport but it was the first time any U.S. woman had reached the final. Marcia Jones, as a tourist in Rome in 1960, saw canoe events there for the first time. Returning to the United States she became dedicated to the sport. Twenty-two different countries competed in the seven 1964 canoe competitions.

At the 1968 Mexico games—held in a country famous for its Indian canoeing on rivers and lakes and famous for the Aztec boating—contestants from faraway Hungary ran away with top honors. Hungary won 34 points in the men's canoe schedule—namely, two Gold, two Silver and one Bronze Medal in five events. The U.S.'s Marcia Jones, now Mrs. Smoke, was squeezed out of third place and could not repeat her 1964 Bronze Medal triumph. On the other hand, the women's 1964 kayak pair champions, West Germany's Roswitha Esser and Anne Marie Zimmerman, repeated for their second Olympic title. Altogether 171 men and 37 women from 29 countries competed.

Canoeing is receiving greater world recognition with every Olympiad. Although it is interesting to note that both the canoe and the kayak originated in the Western Hemisphere, most if not all the recent winners have been Europeans.

CHAPTER VI

Cycling

CYCLING IS a clipped term for the sport of riding a bicycle, which in the United States is at least a way to get up an appetite. However, in France, where the bicycle is alleged to have been invented by a Parisian, M. de Sivrac, back in 1690, it is still considered a means of transportation. Strangely enough, suggestions for having wheeled vehicles propelled by the effort of the rider or riders date back to earlier times; they have been found in bas-reliefs of Egypt and Babylon and frescoes of Pompeii. Leonardo da Vinci later drew up a plan for a flying bicycle, and recently the French have claimed a modern Parisian has developed a flying bicycle, which may be featured in the 1980 Olympics.

Although the French may have invented the first bicycle, it took a Scottish blacksmith named Kirkpatrick McMillan to evolve pedals with connection rods working on the rear axle of a tricycle with wooden wheels and iron tires in 1834. The first prototype of our present bicycle appeared in both England and France after 1850, and the first two-wheel bicycle was brought to America in 1866 by Pierre Lallement of France.

Amateur and professional bicycle riding was organized in both Europe and America by 1878. The Amateur Bicycle League of America has controlled amateur racing in the United States through some hundred clubs in most states from the early days to the present. The first national bicycle championship of the United States was held in 1883 and marked the beginning of the great era of bicycle riding and touring. In the United States, road contests became popular and then arenas were built so that races could be held indoors. Some of the tracks were built like saucers. It was not long before the bicycle became a menace to the pedestrian, the race driver often using the sidewalks for his training, and laws were passed against the "scorchers," as they were called. Six-day bicycle races were held in the old Madison Square Garden in New York, where pairs of drivers rode continuously day and night and ate while cycling the track.

As the French are noted as a race of people who never throw anything away, there are still more bicycles in France than automobiles. In 1896, equipped with new bicycles and believing they would win, the French persuaded Baron de Coubertin to make a special plea for the inclusion of this sport at the first modern Olympics in 1896. The Olympic games thereafter helped initiate and maintain international and world's championships run by the International Cyclists' Association and also spread the sport throughout the world.

The bicycle matches of the first modern Olympics were held in the velodrome in New Phaleron, a suburb of Athens. Crown Prince Constantine of Greece officiated. Only ten competitors took part in the match, three of them Greeks. The distance of the race was 100 kilometers, or 300 times around the track. While the interest of the public was very great at the start of the match, after a number of laps the spectators grew bored. Flamand, a Frenchman, won the event, completing the course in three hours, eight minutes, nineteen and one-fifth seconds. Coleitis of Greece, who came in second, was eleven laps behind. The French flag was immediately hoisted to honor the first Olympic champion in cycling. Cycling was so popular at that time that the winner received an ovation from the crowd and special congratulations from the King of Greece. The French won the all-around team championship, as they had expected.

The two-kilometer race had four competitors—one from Greece, one from Germany, and two from France. There were six laps in this race—all contestants starting at the same time. Masson of France won. The third event was the ten-kilometer race, which Masson of France also won. The sprint of 1,000 meters was the main attraction. This was also won by Masson of France, with Nicolopoulos of Greece second. The road race from Marathon, which was a cycling equivalent of the famous marathon race in the track and field meet, stirred up great interest. Goedrich of Germany, Battel from England, and Constantinidis from Greece were the three favorites. According to the rules, the riders were to

61

start from the first kilometer stone outside of Athens on the Kethissia Road, then to race as far as the 40th kilometer stone at Marathon, where they were to sign their names on a parchment in the presence of a special commissioner of the Olympic games. They were then to return by the same road to Athens, cycling through the boulevard called Herodes Atticus and finishing at the velodrome. The total length of this course was 87 kilometers. Umpires were stationed at different points along the road to see that the rules were obeyed. Constantinidis arrived at Marathon first, hastily signed his name, turned his bicycle around, and raced back to Athens. However, his trip back was not as successful as his trip out, for he began to have trouble with his bicycle and this gave Battel of England a chance to overtake him. As soon as repairs were made on his bicycle Constantinidis got on and away he went. He managed to catch up with Battel, pass him, and win, even though he ran into a carriage on the streets and fell. Constantinidis' time for the 87 kilometers was 3 hours, 22 minutes, and 31 seconds. He became a hero to his fellow Greeks, second only to the Greek winner of the marathon foot race.

At the 1900 Olympics in Paris, the 1,000-meter scratch race was won by Taillendier of France, and a Frenchman named Sanz was second. Lake of Great Britain was third. For some reason this was the only event recorded, giving the unofficial team championship to France.

The 1904 Olympic games at St. Louis had a new attraction in cycling. Due to the fact that the public in the United States did not seem to be interested in amateur cyclists, there were competitions for professional cyclists in St. Louis. There were, of course, Olympic or amateur competitions too, the 880-yard race being the most popular, with no less than 124 cyclists competing. Marcus Hurley, Teddy Billington, and Burton Down, all of the United States, finished first, second, and third. Practically no foreign entries in cycling appeared at St. Louis. Because there was no real international competition, and because professionals were included in the program, many sources do not record any official cycling in the 1904 games.

Between the 1904 Olympics and the 1908 Olympics great progress was made in bicycle racing and new world's records were established, some by racers paced by motorcycle. There were cycling events in the 1906 "extra" or unofficial games in Athens. An English team of Matthews and Rushen won the 2,000-meter tandem. Francisco Verri of Italy won the short 333⅓-meter sprint and repeated in the 1,000 and 5,000 meter. W. J. Petti of Great Britain won the 20-kilometer paced race. Italy won the unofficial team championship.

While the Olympics were still going on in St. Louis, the Olympic Committee was making preparations for the 1908 Olympics in London. Each sport federation, including the Bicycle Association, was given the opportunity to consolidate its own rules, make up its own program of events, arrange its own methods, and choose its own officials. Booklets containing all this information were then printed in different languages and sent all over the world. Further clarification and standardization of rules and events came out of the 1906 Panhellenic games—a beneficial effect these "extra" games had on many other sports as well.

In 1908, the French team of M. Schilles and A. Auffray won the 2,000-meter tandem race, although the British made a clean sweep of all other events and won the unofficial team championship.

The 1912 Stockholm Olympics were held in an impressive double-deck stadium built of gray-violet Swedish brick. The Swedes had engaged a Mr. Hjertberg, a famous athlete, formerly from Sweden, who was living in the United States, to make his scientific training methods available to the Swedish athletes. He had a great deal to do with arranging and running the cycling events. The individual road race was won by R. Lewis of South Africa, with the team road race going to the Swedes. C. O. Schutte of the United States came in third in the individual road race. The unofficial team championship in the cycling events went to the host nation.

The 1920 Olympic games were held at Antwerp. War-swept Belgium had overcome great handicaps to present a stadium where it was possible to compete. With the tremendous increase in the importance of the automobile in the United States and the resulting disappearance of bicycle racing, the United States had a very poor team with very few experienced riders. The unofficial overall team cycling championship was won by Great Britain. The 1,000-meter race was won by Maurice Peeters of Holland, the 2,000-meter tandem race by Ryan and Lance of England, the 4,000-meter race by Italy. The 50-kilometer race was won by a Belgian, Henry George. In 1920 events and rules were becoming standardized, and there was a great improvement in performance.

The 1924 Olympiad, in Paris, presented one of the greatest

competitions in cycling of any Olympics up until that time. The United States had made considerable effort to field a strong team for this Olympiad. Every state in the Union was combed for cyclists, with the final tryout in New Jersey. The final road race in the United States was held in Paterson, New Jersey, over the full Olympic distance of 188 kilometers, or 116.8 miles. The U.S. team consisted of six cyclists. Ernest Ohrt, the coach, had lived in France and was familiar with the road race course—some of the roads and streets were five hundred years old—and with the French bicycle. He had a French manufacturer build six bicycles, of the latest French model—one for each member of the U.S. team. Each bicycle was made to the measurements of the man who was to ride it. In spite of all this preparation, the tailor-made bicycles and hard training, the Americans did not win.

Lucien Michard of France won the 1,000-meter scratch. The 2,000-meter tandem was won by a French team, J. Cugnot and L. Choury. The 4,000-meter team pursuit was won by Italy, and the individual road race, the event that the Americans had pointed for, was won by a Frenchman, Armand Blanchonnet. The team road race was also won by France. The 4,000-meter team pursuit was won by a team from Italy. The 50-kilometer race was won by Jacobus Willem of Holland. The over-all winner was France.

The 1928 Olympic games were held in Amsterdam, and Holland won the unofficial cycling championship. The Danes, however, captured the most first places. The manager of the U.S. cycling team was Emil Fraysse, and the team consisted of but four cyclists—Henry O'Brien, Chester Nelson, Peter Smessaert, and Charles Westerholm. While the team did not win a single event, it deserves some credit for effort, for part of its training regimen en route to the Olympics on the *S.S. President Roosevelt* was a spin around the deck on bicycles from five until seven in the morning.

The 1932 Olympics, at Los Angeles, again included cycling events. Emil Fraysse, again acting as manager of the U.S. team, was not satisfied with the system that had been used before in selecting the American team, and therefore introduced another method. Entry blanks and invitations to the Olympics were sent to every state where district trials were to be held. Ten per cent of those entered qualified for sectional trials. Then the fastest riders in each section qualified for the finals, which were to be held in San Francisco. In previous trials for previous Olympics there had been fewer than 100 cyclists participating. In 1936, thanks to Mr. Fraysse's idea, 346 contestants competed in the state trials, 63 in the sectional, and 17 in the national finals. As a result, there was considerable improvement in the performance of American cyclists. The U.S. road team finished sixth—a great improvement over 1928. France, a great cycling country, finished fifth. The Italians won the unofficial team championship, with Attilio Pavesi winning the individual road race and an Italian team winning the team road race. Jacobus van Egmond of Holland won the 1,000-meter scratch, Edgar L. Gray of Australia won the 1,000-meter time trial, France won the 2,000-meter tandem, and Italy won the 4,000-meter team pursuit.

At the 1936 Olympiad the cycling competition was extremely close. Toni Merkens of Germany defeated Arie Gerrit van Vliet of Holland in the 1,000-meter scratch race. These two racers were the great favorites, and Merkins won each of the two finals. However, his performance was marred by a very definite foul which should have resulted in his disqualification. Instead, he was fined 1,000 marks but declared the winner. One hundred riders started in the 100-kilometer road race and only half that number finished. The men were started in one group, and the road was narrow; there were many mean spills. The American entrants were familiar with three-speed gears, but the riders from Peru were not and caused a spill in which twenty riders went down at one time. Robert Charpentier of France won the 100-kilometer road race and played an important part in France's triumph in the 100-kilometer team race and 4,000-meter pursuit race. France's representatives captured three championships, two seconds, and two thirds.

The cycling events were held on the specially banked wooden track in the cycling stadium, while the road race started and finished on the Alvis speedway over a practically flat course. Germany had a strong combination in the 2,000-meter tandem race, defeating Holland. Van Vliet of Holland won the 1,000-meter standing stock time trial race. This was a grueling contest, and many of the competitors finished in very bad physical shape. Albert Sellinger of the United States finished tenth. The U.S. team was coached and managed by Walter Grenda.

The 1948 Olympic cycling competitions in London brought together a great many nations and competitors. The unofficial overall championship was again won by France.

Notwithstanding the complaints that had been made after

the 1936 pile-up, the Olympic road race retained its original form—the riders all starting and racing together. The road race at these Olympics was a circuit of roads in Windsor Great Park, by permission of the king. The riders had to cover the course 19 times, for a total of 135 miles.

The classic event is the sprint, a distance of 1,000 meters. The riders are matched in twos, on a knockout basis, from preliminary heat through to the final of two riders. This event was won by Mario Ghela of Italy, and Reg Harris of Great Britain, who had been, before the race, the world's amateur sprint champion, was second. Axel Schandorff of Denmark was third; Charles Bazzano of Australia, fourth. The 1,000-meter unpaced trial from a standing start was won by J. Dupont of France. J. Heid of the United States finished seventh. The 2,000-meter tandem match race for teams was won by Italy, with Great Britain second, France third, and Switzerland fourth. The 4,000-meter team pursuit was won by France, with Italy second, Great Britain third, and Uruguay fourth. The team road race was won by Belgium, followed by Great Britain, France, Italy, Sweden, Switzerland and Argentina. Individual road race winners were: J. Beyaert of France, first; G. Voorting of Holland, second; and L. Wouters of Belgium, third.

The United States team suffered a number of injuries and accidents. In the 1,000-meter tandem event, Marvin Thomson and Alfred Stiller, both from Chicago, reached the top eight in their series of match races, and but for an accident coming down the home stretch might have reached the top four. In the 4,000-meter pursuit four-man team race, Robert Travani of Detroit suffered a broken wrist in a spill, and a substitute for him was not allowed. The three remaining men made a very creditable showing against the Belgian team of four riders, and in losing made better time than some of the other countries that had started four riders.

At the 1952 Olympic games at Helsinki, the team cycling was won by Italy. Six of the ten members of the U.S. team, interestingly enough, were from the armed forces. The Amateur Bicycle League of America, the governing body of amateur bicycle racing in the United States, hopes that even though there are no longer many bicycle tracks in the United States and there are many in almost every foreign city, we can do better in future Olympics.

An indication of the spread of cycling throughout the world was given in the 1952 Olympic games, when European cyclists, who usually have dominated velodrome races, were forced to concede several places to contestants from points outside the European continent. Australian riders and riders from South Africa proved that the Europeans are not invincible, for they won no less than six of the coveted place medals. United States coaches and managers believe that this should prove to U.S. contestants that European riders can be beaten. Herbert Hoffman was the manager of the U.S. cycling team and Raymond Smith the team coach. Again the United States was disappointed. American riders are handicapped by the fact that the United States has not built velodromes similar to those on which the Olympic competitions are run, and will continue to be handicapped until such courses are built. The 100-meter time trial was won by R. Mockridge of Australia, followed by M. Morettini of Italy, R. Robinson of South Africa, and C. Cortoni of Argentina. The 1,000-meter sprint was won by E. Sacchi of Italy, with L. Cox of Australia second and W. Putzernheim of Germany third. The 2,000-meter tandem was won by the Australian team; South Africa was second, Italy third. The 4,000-meter team pursuit was won by Italy, with South Africa second and Great Britain third. The famous road race, this time over 118 miles, was won on an individual basis by A. Noyelle of Belgium, followed by R. Grondelaers of Belgium, E. Ziegler of Germany, and L. H. Victor of Belgium. The teams were ranked in the following order: Belgium, Italy, France, Sweden, Germany, Denmark, Luxembourg, Holland, Switzerland, Norway, Great Britain, Rumania, Uruguay. The Russians, for the first time in a long while, participated in the cycling championships at these Olympics.

The 1956 and 1960 Olympic cycling events proved that a nation like the United States cannot compete successfully with other countries which have fewer express highways and cars and more velodromes and cycling competitions. The United States just could not win a medal. Italy and France dominated this sport at Melbourne although Australia continued its control of the 2,000-meter tandem which they won in 1952. In 1960 Italy made a clean sweep of all events except the individual road race which was won by V. Kapitonov of Russia. This was the first and only Russian victory in this sport in the 64 years of the modern Olympics. It was close, however, for the Russian beat Italy's Livio Trope by an inch as both were timed in 4 hours, 20 minutes, 37 seconds. The upset was the blanking out of such cycle powers as France, Holland and Australia. The tragedy was that two Danish riders collapsed in the Rome preliminary heat, one of them,

67

Knut Jensen, dying. Later the official Italian police report indicated that death was due to an overdose of a supposedly harmless drug.

In 1964 Italy, with Germany second, continued its prominence in what had been a French and British dominated sport from 1896 to 1924. The United States, with no velodrome and little popular interest in the sport, was not able to qualify any men into a final. U.S. entries John Allis and Mike Hiltner were seventy-fifth and one-hundredth in the 121.77-mile road race. Here also, the only path to success is to make proper equipment, coaching and velodromes available to youngsters in the United States. A Junior Olympic cycling program would probably be as effective as the Junior Olympic swimming program has been in giving us championship performances in 1964.

The 1968 Mexican cycling competitions were held in a wooden indoor track velodrome, considered outstanding by experts. It featured 48 countries and 361 contestants. The French came back to dominate the sport they had controlled prior to 1928 by winning four of the five Gold Medals in the indoor competition. The individual star was Pierre Trentin of France who won two Gold Medals and one Bronze, and broke one world's record. There was an unusual incident in the 4,000 meter team pursuit after West Germany's Jurgen Kissner pushed the bicycle of a lagging teammate which the German team reported after winning. At the time the officials disqualified the German team completely, but on appeal after the games, West Germany was awarded second place and the Silver Medal. The best U.S. performance was that of Jack Simes III who placed twelfth in the 1,000 meter individual time trial.

CHAPTER VII

Equestrian Events

EQUITATION, WHICH comes from the Latin word for horse, is the art or sport of riding. It is the only Olympic sport which requires, in addition to the effort of man, the effort of another living animal. That living animal—the horse— antedates man himself. The evolution of the horse from a dog-sized animal is difficult to trace before 5000 B.C., but John Trotwood Moore, in a tribute to the horse, once wrote that "wherever man has left his footprint in the long ascent from barbarism to civilization, we will find the hoofprint of the horse beside it." Strangely, at the present time the country with the greatest number of different species of horse is Russia, a country that is just beginning to make its mark in Olympic equestrian events and in the modern pentathlon, another Olympic event involving riding.

When the horse was originally domesticated, he was the size of a pony. His size was increased by man through selective breeding, for throughout the Dark Ages larger horses were needed to carry knights in full armor. Horsemanship, or equitation as we currently consider it, was founded in the sixteenth century by an Italian named Pignatelli, who started a school at Naples which sent "masters of the horse" to all parts of the known world. Later, the exported art or sport and its finest techniques were further developed and spread by the Austrians of the imperial stables and by the French at their cavalry school at Saumur. Horsemanship formed part of a gentleman's education.

Prehistoric drawings establish the fact that for a long period men did not mount on the back of the horses, but used them as draft animals. Horses were used by the Assyrians about 4000 B.C. as the steeds of war chariots. By 1500 B.C. both man and the horse had progressed greatly, the horse from the dog stage and the man to the gambling stage, and Assyrian kings were maintaining racing stables and making bets on the outcome of mounted races. There is also evidence that the Persians were playing polo with ponies or horses at about the same time.

Although there is every reason to believe that there were competitions involving horses in the earlier unrecorded Olympics, our first recorded equestrian event is the four-horse chariot race introduced in the twenty-fifth Olympics in 680 B.C. The first actual recorded race with mounted horses was in the thirty-third Olympiad, 648 B.C. The jockeys rode bareback, and there is evidence that the horse was sufficiently large to carry a man on his back at considerable speed for reasonable distances. The Grecian or Olympic racehorse was the ancestor of our present-day racing thoroughbreds. We are, therefore, indebted first to the Assyrians and later and more importantly to the ancient Olympic games for our "Sport of Kings" as well as for the current equestrian competitions in the modern Olympics.

We know that on the fourth day of the ancient Olympic games the tremendous crowds moved from the stadium to the hippodrome (from the Greek *hippos,* meaning horse, and *dromos,* meaning course) to witness contests of horses and chariots. Homer, Sophocles, Pindar, and Pausanias have described these races. Pagondas, a Theban, is the first great Olympic equestrian winner whose name has come down to us. He won many chariot races with his own horses in the Olympics and in other games around 408 B.C. In the horse and chariot races, the prize was not awarded to the riders or the drivers, but to the horses and to the owners. That is why women were sometimes crowned with the wild olive of Olympia for owning winning horses.

Notwithstanding the glory of the horse in the ancient Olympics, the organizers of the first modern Olympics in Athens in 1896 could not include him because they had enough difficulties in building a stadium and coping with a thousand details of various other sports. The transportation, care, and feeding of horses was deemed too great an effort on top of all the other problems. As a result, even though there was great pressure by the Greeks and French to include riding and equestrian events, they were passed up. The only horse present at the 1896 Olympics was the one used in gymnastics, which required a minimum of care and no feeding.

While there was great agitation to add equestrian events to the modern Olympic games in 1900, 1904, 1906, and 1908, none were included. The game of polo, generally considered an equestrian event, was picked up by the British Army in India, where it had been played since the days of the Persians, and became an Olympic event in 1900. The British won in 1900 and 1908. Polo was not included in the 1904 or 1906 games because of the expense of transporting polo ponies. In 1908, Prince Carl of Sweden made the suggestion that the world's military equestrian championship, which had been held annually for many years in Brussels, be transferred and made part of the Olympic games. Although a number of people favored the proposal, nothing came of it at that year's Olympics. However, the Olympic organizers and the host nation, Sweden, made certain that equestrian events would be included in the official program at the fifth Olympic games in Stockholm in 1912. (There were some unofficial competitions in riding as well as polo at the 1908 Olympic games in London, which the British claimed as additional victories.)

The first equestrian events in the modern Olympic games in 1912 included as competitors some of the pioneers in the re-creating of the Olympics: Sweden, Germany, Belgium, Denmark, Great Britain, France and Russia. Sweden won the unofficial team title. All of the contestants were officers of the armies of the various countries participating. There was no polo.

The 1920 or seventh Olympiad at Antwerp again presented an equestrian competition, after an interruption caused by World War I. The war, incidentally, in great part eliminated the cavalry as the elite corps of the armies of the world and dealt an indirect but serious blow to equestrian sports. The 1920 competition included Belgium, Denmark, the United States, France, Italy, Finland, and Sweden, with Sweden again winning the unofficial overall title. The events were held over a period of six days. The 50-kilometer cross-country race was won by Lt. Johansen of Norway, with Capt. Vidart of France second and Lt. D'Emars of Belgium third. The 20-kilometer race had twenty-four starters, of whom nine finished within the allotted time, and it was won by Lt. Misonna of Belgium, with Capt. Bert Santigues of France second and Lt. Bonvalet of Belgium third. The show jumping individual competition was won by Lt. Demowner of Sweden, with Lt. Lundstrom of Sweden second and Major Caffarati of Italy third. The team competition in show jumping was won by Sweden, followed by Italy, Belgium, and the United States. The individually trained horse event was won by Capt. Lundblatt's Uno of Sweden, followed by L. Sand-storm's Sabel and Lt. Count de Resen's Running Sister, all four of the leading places in this training event going to Sweden. A vaulting competition, limited to enlisted men of the armies involved, was won by Trooper Bonckaert of Belgium, with Private Field of France second and Trooper Finet of Belgium third. The jumping competition was won by Lt. Lequio of Italy, who took all the jumps with no faults; second was Major Vallerie, with three faults; third was Capt. Lowen-haupp of Sweden, with four faults. The team results for this event were: first, Sweden; second, Belgium; third, Italy; fourth, France; and fifth, the United States. In polo Spain defeated the United States, 18-3, while England defeated Belgium, 8-3. England then defeated Spain for the championship.

The U.S. Olympic riding team in 1920 was actually the U.S. Army riding team, with Colonel W. C. Short as commandant. Officers and men came directly from Fort Riley. Some of them had previously participated in the Inter-Allied games in Paris in 1919, and two of the competitors had represented the United States at Stockholm in 1912. Eight officers and sixteen horses were selected to go to the games. One of the members, realizing the poor quality of the U.S.

71

horses, obtained permission to go to Virginia to buy a horse, which he paid for out of his private funds at a cost of over $3,000. Unfortunately, the horse did not win a medal at the Olympics, nor was he even able to go, as he contracted distemper upon reaching New York. Colonel Short, in his report of the games, makes the interesting statement that "in all the competitions not an American rider was thrown without his horse going down and only one horse refused, the first time that particular horse had ever refused." The most outstanding United States rider at these Olympics was Major H. D. Chamberlin.

The 1924 Olympics at Paris marked the first time that there was no complaint from any participating nation about the selection of events or the officiating or the courses. Eighteen countries participated, a new high. The unofficial team championship went to Sweden, with Holland second, Switzerland third, and Italy fourth. The United States and France tied for tenth place. The U.S. team was managed by Major J. A. Barry, U.S. Cavalry, and consisted of ten U.S. Cavalry officers. Major Sloan Doak was our only medalist, placing third in the individual three-day competition. Holland distinguished herself not only by coming in second on the overall unofficial team championship, but also by winning more first places than any other country and collecting three Gold Medals. The polo was won by Argentina, beating the second-place U.S. team and the third-place British team, which included some of the greatest stars in the game. Supremacy in polo has shifted all over the world—as supremacy in many sports has—in this case from Persia to India, to the British, to the United States, to Argentina.

At the ninth Olympiad, held in 1928 at Amsterdam, twenty-one nations participated in the equestrian events. There were more competitors and more nations, but fewer events—only three. Two of the three events were won by Dutch army officers, and the third by a German. For the first time, there were a number of civilians in this championship; in future Olympics there were to be more. Holland won the unofficial team championship. There was no polo at this Olympiad.

Major General Guy V. Henry, in opening his report on the Olympic equestrian competition, wrote, "The equestrian events differ from all other Olympic events in that they are the only events in which success does not depend solely on human ability or the mastery of inanimate objects, but

72

depends on a combination of the best horses and the most skillful riders." The United States, after so many disappointments in riding, decided that it would, as European countries do, concentrate its riders and horses and train them together over a long period of time, and preparations for the 1932 Olympics were begun early in 1929. In the fall of 1931, after a series of tryouts, twelve riders and forty horses were moved to Fort Rosecrans, California, and training continued until the Olympic games began. The manager of the U.S. team was Lt. Colonel Charles E. Scott, and the finest men and horses that could be turned out by the U.S. Cavalry were on hand. The result was never in doubt.

In 1932, for the first time, the United States equestrian team won the unofficial championship in the modern Olympics. The dressage competition was won by François Lesage of France, with Charles Marion of France second and Capt. Hiram E. Tuttle of the United States third. In the team ratings, France was first, Sweden second, the United States third. In the three-day event, encompassing discipline, endurance, and jumping, the winners were: Charles F. Pahud de Mortanges of Holland, first; First Lt. Earl F. Thomson, U.S. Cavalry, second; Clarence von Rosen, Jr. of Sweden, third; and Major Harry D. Chamberlin of the U.S. Cavalry, fourth. In the team event, the United States was first and Holland was second. It is interesting to note that de Mortanges won six medals in the 1924, 1928, and 1932 Olympic games, four gold and two silver, all in the three-day event indivdual and team, to set an all-time record. The all-around jumping championship was won by Capt. Takeichi Nishi of Japan, with eight faults; second was Major Harry D. Chamberlin, U.S. Cavalry, with twelve faults; third was Clarence von Rosen, Jr. of Sweden, with sixteen faults. In the team competition, no nation had three riders who completed the course, and therefore there were no team awards. The equestrian championships at these Olympics attracted tremendous crowds. There was no polo, because there had already been an international competition between the United States and Argentina in 1932.

The 1936 or eleventh Olympiad in Berlin featured equestrian events. Due to the military nature of the host nation a great deal of importance was placed upon the equestrian event, the reception of the equestrian teams—which consisted in most cases of army officials—and the effective running off of the competition in such a manner as to permit the greatest number of spectators. The host nation, which had apparently concentrated on winning this event, namely, Germany, won the unofficial all-around championship, with Holland second, Portugal third, the United States fourth, Switzerland fifth, Japan sixth, and France seventh. Twelve other nations participated: Italy, Poland, Great Britain, Belgium, Bulgaria, Norway, Sweden, Turkey, Hungary, Rumania, Austria, and Czechoslovakia—a great increase in the number of competitors. Out of a total of six gold, six silver and six bronze medals, Germany won six gold and one silver, with the other eleven medals scattered among eleven different countries. Capt. Earl F. Thomson of the United States won a silver medal in the three-day competition. The team jumping was won by Germany, with Holland second, Portugal third, the United States fourth. The individual results in this event were: first, a tie between Kurt Hasse of Germany, with Tora (four faults) and Henry Rang of Rumania with Delfis (four faults); third, Joseph von Platthy of Hungary, with Sello (eight faults). The team scoring of the three-day test was Germany first, Poland second, Great Britain third. On an individual basis, first was Ludwig Stubbendorff of Germany, on Nurm; second, Earl Thomson, the United States, on Jenny Camp; and third, Hans Lunding of Denmark, on Jason. The dressage team was won by Germany, with France second, Sweden third, Austria fourth, Holland fifth, and Hungary sixth. The United States was ninth. Dressage individual was won by Heinz Pollay of Germany, on Kronos; second was Frederick Gerhard of Germany, on Absinth; third was Alois Podhajsky of Poland, on Nero. The highest-ranking American in this event was Captain C. Stanton Babcock, in 23rd place.

The polo competition was won by Argentina, with Great Britain second, Mexico third, Hungary fourth, and Germany fifth. Once more the superiority of the Argentinians, and more particularly of their ponies, seemed to discourage many countries from entering, as did the tremendous costs involved in breeding, developing, training, caring for, and transporting sufficient animals.

The manager of the United States team for the 1936 Olympics was again Major General Guy V. Henry. After the 1936 Olympic games another world war broke the Olympic sequence and also threatened to destroy the Olympic spirit. As far as the equestrian events were concerned World War II indirectly dealt more damage in that it further de-emphasized the cavalry, particularly in the United States.

In fact, the horse was completely eliminated from the U.S. Army and the U.S. Military Academy, although not necessarily from other armies throughout the world. However, General Eisenhower authorized the temporary reactivation of the U.S. Army equestrian team at the former Cavalry School at Fort Riley, Kansas, in the spring of 1946. From an Olympic standpoint, this was an important step, for U.S. Olympic equestrian teams have always been composed of army personnel—although civilian riders have become more and more interested.

The equestrian competitions in the London Olympics were held at the stadium at Aldershot. Nine nations entered the dressage competition, sixteen the three-day individual and team competition, and fifteen the *Prix des Nations* show jumping.

It might be interesting to describe here the several events which formed part of the Olympics in 1948 and have been standardized and should be the basis for equestrian competition in future Olympics. The three competitions are dressage, the three-day riding test, and show jumping.

The dressage competition is essentially an exhibition of the art of riding, following the principles of the classical school. Each rider has to perform a set of test exercises of an academic character calculated to display balance, suppleness, brilliance, obedience, and ease of control. The test has to be ridden from memory and in thirteen minutes.

The complete riding competition, also known as the military or three-day test event, is a searching series of tests of practical riding. There are three tests to be performed by the same rider on the same horse. A dressage test takes place the first day. Each competitor has to perform a set test to be ridden from memory in twelve minutes. The exercises are designed to show that the horse is balanced, supple, freegoing, and obedient and that the rider possesses the fluency, the ease of control, and the lightness of touch that are expected of an educated horseman. The second day is devoted to the endurance test. This grueling competition consists of five sections to be carried out by each competitor singly and consecutively, without a break and with certain time allowances and time limits. Two sections are over roads and tracks, one over a steeplechase course, one across country with many fixed obstacles, and one on the flat. The total distance is just over twenty miles. The jumping competition comes on the third day, over a course of twelve obstacles to be taken at a speed of 440 yards per minute. The object of this competition is to determine whether the horses still possess, after their previous two days' effort, the necessary reserve of energy.

The third overall competition is a jumping one for the *Prix des Nations* and is show jumping over a course including from sixteen to twenty jumps over obstacles formidable in height or width and arrangement.

Each of these three competitions is open to three riders and three horses from each competing country. All riders must, of course, be amateurs. There are three individual prizes in each competition and three team awards. No team prize is awarded unless all three team members complete the course.

The equestrian events at the London Olympiad of 1948 were won by the United States. The team dressage competition was won by Sweden, with France second, the United States third, Portugal fourth, and Argentina fifth. Unfortunately Sweden was disqualified because of the ineligibility of one of its team members. The individual dressage was won by Captain Moser of Switzerland, with Colonel Jousseaume of France second, Captain Boltenstern of Sweden third, and Lt. Borg of the United States fourth. The three-day competition team award was won by the United States, Sweden was second, Mexico third, Switzerland fourth. The individual three-day test results were: first, Captain Bernard Chevalier of France; second, Lt. Colonel F. S. Henry, the United States; third, Captain J. R. Selfelt of Sweden; fourth, Lt. Charles Howard Anderson of the United States. The show jumping or *Prix des Nations* team event was won by Mexico, Spain was second, Great Britain third, and no other teams finished. The individual placings were: first, Colonel Mariles of Mexico; second, Captain Uriza of Mexico; third, M. D'Orgeix of France; fourth, Colonel Franklin F. Wing, Jr. of the United States.

Notwithstanding the superior performance of the United States in this Olympics, the future of American teams in this sport was clouded by uncertainty. The abandonment by the U.S. Army of polo, equestrian sports, and horses left a large hole to be filled. Unselfishly, a group of sportsmen undertook to correct this deficiency by organizing and incorporating The International Equestrian Competitions Corporation in New York State on June 2, 1950. Colonel John W. Wofford, U.S. Army (Retired), of Milford, Kansas, was elected president. A member of a former Olympic team, he was ready to donate practically all of his time, energy, and equestrian experience to the development, training, and technical management of future Olympic teams. The corporation raised funds as a non-profit organization, and in 1950 selected its first team of six horses and three riders—two men and one woman—which in November represented the United States in equestrian competition at the Pennsylvania Horse Show at Harrisburg, Pennsylvania, the National Horse Show at New York, and the Royal Winter Fair at Toronto. The success of the team provided an incentive and a demand to continue with a view toward the Olympics. The name of the corporation was changed to The United States Equestrian Team, Inc.

The corporation leased from the U.S. Government some of the veteran horses from the defunct U.S. Army Horse Show Team. It also leased premises at Fort Riley and maintained for a while a stable of up to 35 horses. It had the services of Captain Robert J. Borg, of the 1948 Olympic team, in helping train the competitors. This organization finally selected competitors for the 1952 Olympic team— eighteen horses, ten men, and one woman, Miss Marjorie B. Haynes, the first woman member of the U.S. equestrian team. The team manager was Colonel Wofford.

The 1952 Olympic competitions were won on an all-around basis by Sweden. The dressage individual went to Henri St. Cyr of Sweden, on Master Ruffus; second, Mrs. Lis Hartel of Denmark, on Jubilee; third, Colonel A. Jousseaume of France, on Harpagon; fourth, Gosta Boltenstern of Sweden, on Krest. The team competition was won by Sweden, with Switzerland second, Germany third, France fourth, Chile fifth, the United States sixth, Russia seventh, Portugal eighth. The three-day event was won by H. von Blixen-Finecke of Sweden, on Jubal; second, Captain G. Le Frant of France, on Verdun; third, W. Busing of Germany, on Hubertus; and fourth, P. Mercado of Argentina, on Nambinga. The team results in this event were: first, Sweden; second, Germany; third, the United States; fourth, Portugal; fifth, Denmark; sixth, Ireland. No other team of three finished. The *Prix des Nations* was won by Great Britain, with Chile second, the United States third, Brazil fourth, France fifth, Germany sixth, Argentina seventh, Portugal eighth, Mexico ninth, Spain tenth, Sweden eleventh, Egypt twelfth, Rumania thirteenth, and Russia fourteenth. Italy and Finland were eliminated. On an individual basis this competition was won by P. J. D'Oriola of France, on Ali Baba; second, O. Cristi of Chile, on Bambi; third, F. Thiedemann of Germany, on Meteor; fourth, O. de Memezes of Brazil, on Bigua. There was, amazingly, a five-man tie for first place, and a five-man jump-off was held which resulted in the placements above. The man placing fifth in the jump-off was W. White of Great Britain, on Nize Fella. Sixth place went to General H. Mariles of Mexico, on Petrolero—only three-fourths of a fault behind the five who tied for first place. On an overall basis, Sweden won by a very large margin, and France was second. Considering the tremendous reorganization job done by the United States, it did not do badly at all, with two third places, both in team events. Eighty thousand people witnessed these Olympic equestrian events.

The sixteenth Olympiad, in 1956, presented equestrian events for the first time as a separate show. This was done because, while Australian hospitality is extended to all human beings, strict quarantine laws so limit animal visitors that foreign horses are not welcome. The equestrian events were, therefore, held in June in Stockholm, by agreement between the Olympic Committees of all nations, in the old brick stadium especially built for the 1912 games. The reaction of the riding fraternity throughout the world seemed to be that having a separate show along the lines of the Olympic winter games, in a host country enthusiastic about horsemanship, might have great advantages over pooling the riding events in the large Olympic overall program.

Twenty-nine nations sent contestants: Argentina, Australia, Austria, Belgium, Brazil, Bulgaria, Cambodia, Canada, Denmark, Egypt, Finland, France, Germany, Great Britain, Holland, Hungary, Eire, Italy, Japan, Norway, Portugal, Rumania, Russia, Spain, Sweden, Switzerland, Turkey, the United States and Venezuela. Over 25,000 persons, a capacity crowd, were on hand for the impressive opening ceremonies. King Gustaf of Sweden, Queen Elizabeth of England with the Duke of Edinburgh and Princess Margaret, Prince Bernhard of Holland, all enthusiastic and experienced equestrians themselves, opened the competition; there were three military bands and a 260-voice choir. Prince Bertil of Sweden, as President of the Swedish Organizing Committee for these games, was host to Avery Brundage, President of the International Olympic Committee. The competition was outstanding, although because of rain and soggy footing there were many falls and accidents.

The dressage was won by Major Henri St. Cyr of Sweden, on Juli, with Mrs. Lis Hartel of Denmark, on Jubilee, second. These two repeated exactly their placement in the 1952 Olympic games. Third was another woman, Liselott

Linsenhoff of Germany, on Adular. The top six teams in this event were Sweden, Germany, Switzerland, Russia, Denmark, and France, in that order. The higest-placed United States entrant was Major Robert Borg, on Bill Biddle, in 17th place. This horse and rider finished eighth in this event in 1952. Bill Biddle was a 15-year old chestnut gelding who was competing in the Olympics for the third time, and, by the rules, would now be ineligible for further Olympic competition. Although human beings may compete in as many Olympics as nature will allow, horses, who do not live as long as men, are restricted to three Olympics. This is to prevent a nation from taking too great an advantage of a superior animal competitor.

The three-day test was won by Lt. Petrus Kastenman of Sweden, on Illuster; second was August Lütke-Westhues of Germany; on Trux von Kamax; third was Lt. Colonel Frank Weldon of Great Britain, on Kilbarry; fourth was Lev Baklychkine of Russia, on Guimnast. The team results were: first, Great Britain; second, Germany; third, Canada; fourth, Australia. None of the American contestants finished. The *Grand Prix* jumping results were: (Team) 1. Germany, 2. Italy, 3. Great Britain, 4. Argentina, 5. The United States; (Individual) 1. Hans Winkler of Germany, 2. Raimondo D'Inzeo of Italy, 3. Piero D'Inzeo of Italy. Pierre D'Oriola of France, the 1952 winner, came in sixth. The American who finished highest was Seaman Hugh Wiley, of the United States Navy, who tied for eleventh place.

The unofficial over-all equestrian team scoring—which was, of course, together with the winter games points, added to the scoring at Melbourne to determine the overall winner of the sixteenth Olympiad—was as follows: Germany, 42 points; Sweden, 33; Great Britain, 22; Italy, 16; Denmark, 7; Russia, 6. The United States scored 2 points. The final medal tally was: gold—Sweden 3, Germany 2, Great Britain 1; silver—Germany 3, Italy 2, Denmark 1; bronze—Great Britain 2, Canada 1, Switzerland 1, Germany 1, Italy 1.

The modern Olympics have brought lovers of equestrian sports and of the horse together from all over the world; thirty-one nations participated in 1956, as against only seven in 1912, an increase that augurs well for the future. It is to be hoped, however, that the United States—once known for its cowboys, pony express, and wide open spaces, for bluegrass and fast horses—will someday come back to win the Olympic equestrian events as it did in 1932 and 1948.

The 1960 Olympics indicated a start in the right direction by the United States which made its best showing since 1948. However, the Australians who had refused to permit the equestrian competitions in Melbourne in 1956 because of their strict animal (horse) quarantine served notice on the world of their interest in horsemanship. Australia won the unofficial all-around championship. Lawrence Morgan, a 45-year-old Australian rancher, won the 3-day event individual as well as leading his team to the team title in that event. Here, as in cycling, Russia won its first and only gold medal in the sport, in dressage, usually associated with the aristocracy of high society and wealth. Sergey Filatov and his well-trained horse Absinthe ended the eight-year reign of Sweden's Major Henri St. Cyr who finished fourth. The final competition of the entire Olympics in the Stadio Olympico before the closing ceremony was the team jumping with Germany, the United States, Italy, the United Arab Republic and France leading the field in that order.

Germany was the unofficial overall winner on points in this sport in Tokyo in 1964. The U.S. entries performed well, but they only accounted for one silver medal, although that was for the arduous three day team test including dressage, endurance and jumping. The second place U.S. team consisted of Michael Page, Kevin Freeman and Lana DuPont. France won its only gold medal in the "summer" games when Pierre D'Oriola regained the title he won twelve years before in Helsinki. With nine penalty points on his first ride, he rode over the course for the second time without a fault. By coincidence, Christian D'Oriola, a relative, also won two gold medals for France in men's foil fencing in 1952 and 1956. One of the most applauded and popular victories was that of Henry Chamartin of the Swiss Army on his mount Woermann in the individual dressage. The Karuizawa facilities were soaked by heavy rains and on the day of the most demanding of the equestrian events, the endurance test, the 20-mile course looked more suitable in places for the victorious U.S. swimming team than for horses. In the 2-mile steeplechase Michael Bullen of England on Sea Breeze fell at the second jump and dislocated his shoulder. Bullen and Sea Breeze carried on, but in the 4-mile cross-country with its 31 big jumps Bullen, in great pain, was not able to control Sea Breeze and at the twenty-fifth obstacle, an up jump across a ditch, they failed. Three times they tried and three times horse and rider tumbled back into the ditch and were eliminated. Notwithstanding the bad weather there were much higher riding scores than usual and less point difference between the competitors. The Japanese, who could not be faulted for their great effort as hosts, desired perfection, and in trying to avoid accidents and improve performance made the riding courses much too easy. Prince Bernhard of Holland, a top horseman and former head of the International Equestrian Federation, stated: "If the ground would have been hard (no rain) everyone with a good mount would have galloped straight through the course without a fault."

The dinner at the Olympic Village after the final equestrian event was one of the gayest at the Tokyo games. French Bordeaux and Italian Chianti appeared on the tables and Russian vodka, in water glasses. Alexander Sakalob, Soviet substitute and groom, was particularly friendly and sang Russian folk songs to everyone's enjoyment. People learned that the Russian horses are state owned and neither horses nor riders are restricted to Mr. Brundage's maximum three week training and interruption of employment period demanded for men by IOC rule. In fact, the grooms of the Russian Olympic Team still in training were the unsuccessful riders of the Russian Olympic Squad already in training for 1968.

The Equestrian competitions in 1968 were in Mexico, a stronghold of the horse, and consequently the courses were not easy. In fact the grand *Prix des Nations* jumping held at Campo Marte presented one of the toughest courses ever seen in Olympic competition with unusually high fences, difficult turns, and unduly short distances between obstacles. The career of a horseman is longer than that of a cross-country runner since the horse does the running and the jumping, so the Mexico individual and team events featured the top riders of the past 15 years.

Among this seasoned field was d'Oriola of France who won in 1952 and 1964, West Germany's Winkler who won in 1956, the U.S.'s Bill Steinkraus, Italy's D'Inzeo who won in 1960, and many other veterans. Steinkraus won and Canada was a surprise team winner.

The 3-day event held at Avandaro 12 miles from Mexico City was a tragic competition. The course was most difficult to begin with but was made almost impossible by torrential rain on each and every day. The result was a wet nightmare for competitors and spectators alike.

A raging torrent where a brook had once been, added another deadly risk. The result: one Irish horse broke a leg and had to be destroyed, a Russian mount was swept under

81

a bridge and drowned, and 10 of the 48 entries failed to finish. The Russians coped with the situation by placing observers along the course with walkie-talkies, coaching their riders, although this was both illegal and unfair. Told this was a violation they certainly knew about they nevertheless professed complete ignorance, but since they failed to finish anyway no one was disqualified. Jean Jacques Guyon of France won the individual, and Great Britain won the team competition, with the United States second, Australia third, and France fourth.

The dressage competition was popular and closely contested, with the Russian Kozomov winning and Josef Neckermann and Reiner Klimke of West Germany coming in second and third. The West German team won with U.S.S.R. second and Switzerland third in the team competition.

The attendance at all the equestrian events was outstanding, and at the Grand Prix at Campo Marte thousands could not get tickets and thousands were turned away from standing room.

The 1972 and 1976 winter games are covered in Chapters XX, XXI, and appendix.

CHAPTER VIII

Fencing

HISTORIANS HAVE estimated that swords have been used for about 5,000 years. The most treasured—if not the oldest—sword in the world was located in Japan, and according to many, the nearest thing to modern fencing originated in Japan over 4,000 years ago. A sort of Japanese fencing in which contestants whaled away at each other with two-handed bamboo sticks is alleged to be thousands of years old.

No one can prove that spears were not used in the early Olympics, not only in throwing contests similar to the modern javelin event but hand-to-hand in fencing sessions. However, everyone agrees that no matter when the sword was first thrust into man's hand, the development of the button (a soft cover for the point of a sword), the foil (a thin harmless practice sword), and the fencing mask were necessary before competition in swordsmanship was practicable as a part of religious ceremonies or peaceful sports gatherings.

Therefore, fencing is one of the very few sports that cannot be proved to be directly tied in with the ancient Olympics, although it owes much of its present popularity and spread throughout the world and its technical development in a major part to the modern Olympics and to the world's fencing championships contested annually between Olympics and inspired by them.

The cruel and dangerous, if not deadly, art of swordsmanship became of vital importance in Europe and later all over the world during the sixteenth, seventeenth and eighteenth centuries. But swordsmanship as a sport became popular in Europe in the first half of the nineteenth century. In the United States there was such great interest in fencing that an independent group, the Amateur Fencers League of America, was formed in 1891 and took over the general supervision of the sport. This same group, incidentally, controls this sport in the United States to this day, and selects and trains U.S. fencing teams and sends them to the Olympic games. While fencing is a major sport in Europe and in many countries in Latin America, U.S. interest in fencing is secondary but not exactly small, for there are today perhaps 400,000 fencers in the United States, and an expanding interest in fencing in schools, colleges, clubs, and in the Air Force and Navy. There is fencing in some 600 colleges in the United States.

Because this sport is not known generally in the United States, an outline description of it is in order. In fencing the object is to touch the opponent with a certain part of the weapon and at the same time prevent him from scoring a touch. Three types of weapons are used. The foil is the direct descendent of the short dress sword, and has a flexible rectangular blade, a blunt point, and a small guard. Touches must be made with the point on a target, which is the trunk of the body from the collar to the groin lines in front and to the hip-bone line. The épée is the modern counterpart and almost exact replica of the duelling sword and has a rigid triangular blade and a large bell guard; the point is covered by a small cone with barbed points. (To reduce fatal accidents the point is now a round flat surface one-fourth inch in diameter with a one-eighth inch plunge to electrically record a touch). A touch can be scored on any part of the body, even a finger or a toe. There are no conventions—the first touch from a standpoint of time is scored whereas in the other weapons an attack has the right of way and should be parried. The saber is a flexible, thin, triangular blade with a dull cutting edge along the entire front and one-third of the back edge, and a blunt point; it has a large guard with one section curved from the end of the pommel to the weapon in front of the hand. It is the counterpart of the deadly sharp-bladed weapon of the same name. Both the point and the cutting edges of the blade are used to score touches. Valid touches must land on the body above the waist, including the arms and head. Masks, gloves and protective clothing are used in all fencing events.

In some sports, such as boxing and the track and field events, the United States has contributed improved techniques, training methods, coaching, teaching, and equipment to other nations all over the world. In fencing, however, Italian and French, and later Hungarian competitors, teachers, and coaches have made the major contribution, and many have come to the United States and have gradually built up great interest and unusual performances in America.

The very first modern Olympic games featured fencing as one of the major events. In fact, contrary to American belief, the fencing in the 1896 Olympic games at Athens was considered every bit as important by the Europeans as any other event, including track and field, where United States interest was concentrated.

The three men's events of the 1896 Olympic games represented the three weapons of the sport. (Women's foil competition, an important fencing event today, was not officially started in the Olympics until 1924, after women had begun to win the right to vote.) E. Gravelotte, one of the greatest earlier fencers of France, won both the foil and épée championships in 1896, while a Greek, I. Georgiadhis, to the great pleasure of the host nation, won the saber title.

In fencing, experience, mental poise, and maturity, together with a delicate sense of timing, are so important that the average age of great competitors is far above that in other sports. Great fencers reach their peak between the ages of 28 and 35, and the average competitive life of a fencer covers a span of almost 25 years. Quite a few fencers have competed in four or five Olympiads. Imagine an all-American college football player or even an amateur boxer actively competing with young men of another generation at the age of 55. Fencers, like old soldiers, fade but never die. Baron de Coubertin, the founder of the modern Olympic games, who was a fencer, went to his *Salle d'Armes* for frequent workouts in his seventies, as did Colonel Graeme Hammond, one-time U.S. Olympic fencer and former president of both the Amateur Fencers League of America and the New York Athletic Club.

The 1900 Olympics saw for the first time one of the great fencers of all time—a man who was to leave a great mark in the annals of modern swordsmanship. Ramon Fonst was a Cuban who lived in Paris and became an ardent and enthusiastic fencer. With great teachers and competition, and great natural skills, he soon became one of the greatest swordsmen in Europe, especially with the épée, and in 1900 won the world's épée championship. E. Coste of France won the foil, and Comte de la Falaise, a dashing French cavalry officer, won the saber. Robert Ayat won the special individual sword event.

The 1904 Olympic fencing, however, was a Cuban and a Fonst show. These were the Olympics which gave Fonst immortality among modern fencers. He won the individual foil, the individual épée and led his teammates to a Cuban win in the first fencing team competition in the Olympics—team foil. There was only one discordant note in the Cuban victory. Most of the European countries did not send their best fencers to the St. Louis Fair in distant Missouri, almost a month's travel away. Few of the best fencers in France and Italy made the trip.

Fonst also won the individual sword championship, an event discontinued thereafter. M. de Diaz, inspired by Fonst, won the saber for Cuba. Only one man—Nedo Nadi of Italy —has come near equaling Fonst's record in the sixty-year history of the modern Olympics. An added event never again contested—the single sticks made famous by Robin Hood and Little John in English legend—was won by V. Z. Post, an American living in Cuba. This is the only Olympic title in any fencing event ever won by the United States of America. Post won five assorted U.S. national championships in foil, épée, or saber between 1896 and 1903.

By 1906 fencing in the Olympics had become so popular that for the first time regular team competitions in all three weapons, in addition to the individual championships, were begun. An Irish-Frenchman named Dillon-Cavanagh won the foil for France. France won the team foil. In épée, Comte de la Falaise won the individual honors and France the team event, while I. Georgiadhis of Greece, winner of the 1896 individual saber, won this event again. Germany won the team saber and Gustav Casimir the three-cornered saber event, never before and never again contested.

The 1908 Olympic fencing produced its quota of fine

85

champions. The épée individual was won by G. Alibert of France, and the épée team by France. Hungary began her grip on saber handles and titles as a result of the work of the great Italo Santelli, an Italian fencing master who started coaching saber in Budapest and created a style to fit the national character and spirit of the Hungarians. His Hungarian pupils and his Hungarian pupils' pupils have pretty well dominated saber fencing throughout the world since then. To show what transplanted and adapted genius in athletic coaching can do, since 1908 Hungary has won eleven out of thirteen Olympic individual saber championships and nine out of thirteen saber team titles. Hungarians have also won national competitions wherever they have emigrated, such as Hungarian-Americans Dr. Tibor Nylas and George Worth in the United States. More recently U.S. fencing has been helped if not dominated by Gene Hamori, Attila Keresztes, Dan Magay, Tom Orley, Alex Orban and Coach Elthes, all originally from Hungary. The Olympics, it is interesting to note, have given the world such an appetite for sports competition that in many international sports, including fencing, world championships are now held separately in the years between the Olympics.

The 1912 Olympics in Stockholm presented the most hotly contested international fencing competition ever held up until that time. During the period between 1908 and 1912, several countries met in international competitions, especially the fencing leaders of the world: France and Italy. Thanks to the Olympics the sport was improving and spreading rapidly, with more and better competition. When 1912 rolled around, top fencing contestants from many nations were ready to do or die for Olympic championships.

Another all-time great appeared on the Olympic fencing strips of Stockholm—Nedo Nadi of Italy. Nadi won the individual foil in 1912, to begin a brilliant career. Paul Anspach of Belgium won the individual épée and helped Belgium win the épée team honors. E. Fuchs of Hungary repeated in individual saber, and Hungary again won the saber team.

World War I interrupted the Olympics, but two sports made great advances notwithstanding the war—in fact, as a result of it. Boxing and fencing competitions were held in the military services of many countries, to provide recreation and build morale. The Inter-Allied games after World War I pitted the great amateurs against the greatest professional athletes in many sports. In fencing the greatest amateurs and professionals crossed swords in friendly competitions, and improved their techniques.

When the Olympics were resumed in 1920, many great fencers with greatly improved techniques and styles competed internationally. Seventeen countries were represented, and the teams of most countries reflected the great interest in fencing by their armed forces. The U.S. team was no exception. Its coaches were George Heintz of the U.S. Naval Academy, and Maitre F. H. Darrieulat, a French fencing master. Ten of the eleven members of the U.S. team were from the armed forces. Ensigns E. G. Fullenweider, R. S. Bowman, F. J. Cunningham, C. J. Walker, and George Calnan represented the Navy, and the Army was represented by Colonel Henry Breckenridge, Lt. Colonel Robert Sears, Major Harold Rayner, Major F. W. Honeycutt, and Sgt. John Dimond. The American team surprised everyone by coming up with some real fencing, in a sport in which theretofore the United States had not been much of a contestant. The foil team placed third, the épée team sixth, and the saber team seventh. George Calnan, one of the greatest fencers developed in the United States, began to show his great talent in these Olympics. First honors went to Italy, which won the individual foil with Nedo Nadi— who repeated the victory he had won eight years before at the 1912 Olympics. Italy also won the team foil. André Massard of France won the individual épée, but Italy won the team event in this weapon. Nedo Nadi surprised everyone by overcoming the Hungarians at their own game and winning the individual saber, and helped the Italian team upset the Hungarians in the team saber. Nadi established himself as one of the greatest fencers of the world and of the modern Olympics. He was, however, to be seriously challenged by a man whose career was just beginning and who may be properly considered another of the three greatest swordsmen of modern times—Lucien Gaudin of France, who first appeared in the 1920 Olympics. Fonst, the French-trained Cuban, had he been in his prime in this period of top competition, might be more highly rated in any evaluation of all-time greatness, but he was handicapped by the limited nature of his competition at the 1900 and 1904 Olympics. Still Ramon Fonst is the only fencer in the 76 years of modern Olympic history to win two successive Olympic gold medals in épée and also win an Olympic title in foil and one in swords.

U.S. fencing, like Hungarian fencing, owes its real

start to imported teaching. An Italian master is the founder of Hungarian fencing, while a French coach, Louis Vauthier, was responsible for America's earliest interest and later improved performance. Vauthier was an honor graduate of Joinville-le-Pont, the great French physical training school for fencing masters. He came to the United States in 1893 and coached at the New York Fencers Club and then went to West Point, where he remained over thirty years, twenty as fencing coach. Vauthier's West Point teams dominated the intercollegiates in the United States, winning the all-around championship for ten years and placing second for four years out of fourteen years of competition. Vauthier developed or coached many U.S. national champions, including the Olympic fencers Breckenridge, Sears, F. W. Honeycutt, H. M. Rayner, L. Castner, and Jack Dimond. Dimond succeeded him as West Point coach and developed U.S. national champions and Olympic fencers R. W. Mayo, T. G. Sands, F. R. Weber and G. M. Heiss, between world wars. West Point discontinued intercollegiate fencing in 1955 although a Cadet Fencing Club sent greatly handicapped but enthusiastic teams into a few competitions for many years. It now fields a regular team with a part-time coach but U.S. intercollegiate fencing is now dominated by N.Y.U., Columbia and Navy which have professional fencing masters.

In the years between 1920 and 1924, many international games were held, bringing to all sports great technical development, so that by the time the 1924 Olympics came along, not only were there more contestants and more countries entered in fencing (19), but also the quality of the competition was greatly improved.

The 1924 Olympic fencing was won by France, with the help of Lucien Gaudin in the team competitions. Roger Ducret of France won the individual foil, and France won the team foil. H. Delporte of Belgium won the individual épée, and France won the team épée. Alexander Posta of Hungary won the individual saber, with Italy nosing out Hungary for the team saber title. Women began to compete in fencing in the individual foil in these Olympics, with Mrs. E. O. Osiier of Denmark winning the first women's Olympic title.

The American team was coached by F. M. Costello and Darrieulat, both Europeans. As in 1920, the armed services contributed most of the team—Breckenridge, Castner, Jeter, Allison, and Walker from the Army, and Fullenweider and

88

George Calnan of the Navy. Calnan, in foil, was the first American ever to reach a semifinal round in fencing. Two American women did quite well in the women's foil—Mrs. Irma Hopper and Adeline Gehrig, sister of Lou Gehrig. In the team épée, Portugal and the United States tied in bouts, and when it came time to count touches, mistakes were discovered in the running of the match, so it was agreed to run the entire match off again from scratch. In this exciting contest, Portugal finally eliminated the United States by 10 to 6.

Further progress was made in international fencing competition between the 1924 and 1928 Olympics. Twenty-two nations competed for Olympic medals in 1928 in one of the most hard-fought Olympic competitions of all time. Lucien Gaudin of France established himself as, probably next to Nadi, one of the three greatest swordsmen in modern times. He won the individual foil, although Italy won the team foil, and he also doubled up, a rare accomplishment, by winning the individual épée, although here also Italy nosed out France for the team title. The Hungarians took over in saber and have been hard to beat since. E. Tercztyansky won the individual saber, and Hungary won the team.

Helene Mayer of Germany won the women's foil. She was one of the greatest women fencers of modern times and probably could have beaten all but a very few male contestants in her specialty. She later came to the United States and became an American citizen, winning the U.S. National women's foil championship in 1934, 1935, 1937, 1938, 1939, 1941, 1942, and 1946. She was second in the 1936 Olympics, and won the world's title in 1937—both for Germany before she became an American citizen. She could never represent the United States, however, for a rule then in effect made it impossible for anyone who had represented one nation in the Olympics to represent another later. On a Hollywood set, Helene Mayer, introduced as an unknown extra, was asked to fence against Cornel Wilde, a motion picture star with fencing experience and ability, by a fencing coach directing some fencing scenes in a movie. She beat Wilde with great ease. He felt better after finding out her true identity. (Incidentally, whenever you see a duel or sword combat in a Hollywood movie from the Errol Flynn era to the present you can be fairly certain the scene was directed and supervised by Ralph Faulkner, a member of the 1928 U.S. team).

The U.S. team in 1928 was coached by Georgio

Santelli, son of the great Italo Santelli of Hungary, and René Pinchart, a Belgian master. Neither of these great instructors was afraid to compete against his pupils. Pinchart won, after a tie with the author, the first Masters or Open Championship (amateurs and professionals) ever held in the United States in épée or in any fencing event. Georgio Santelli was third and George Calnan fourth. Open competitions in fencing did not become annual affairs in the United States, however, until the épée "Masters" in 1950 (won by the author). However "Masters" competitions in fencing were abandoned in the United States in the early 1960s. In all countries competitions between top amateurs and professionals have helped many sports.

The U.S. fencing team of 1928 was up with the leaders for the first time. Joe Levis, of M.I.T., the Boston A.A., and the New York Fencers Club, was the first American ever to make the finals in any weapon in Olympic fencing, placing eleventh in foil. Calnan was great in both foil and épée, and became the second American to make the finals in Olympic fencing and the first U.S. Olympic medalist, placing third in the world in épée. Calnan later went on to win 21 out of 28 bouts in team épée.

With regular official world fencing championships in 1929, 1930, and 1931 and open championships between amateurs and professionals, in addition to national championships in most countries, fencing made great strides. Interest in the sport increased throughout the world.

In 1932 the Olympics were held at Los Angeles, in a country where fencing is not considered even an important minor sport. Nevertheless the occasion produced many records. As if inspired by being the host nation and by the unexpectedly large crowds of Americans who turned out to see the fencing, the U.S. team made its greatest record in the modern Olympics. Levis won the silver medal in the individual foil, with the United States winning third in the team foil. Calnan was seventh in the épée, with the United States winning third in épée team. In saber, Santelli's coaching began to show, as the United States qualified its first two sabermen to the finals in that weapon—Dr. John R. Huffman of Yale and the N.Y.A.C. and Norman Armitage of Columbia and the New York Fencers Club. Huffman placed sixth, and the United States placed fourth in the saber team. Marion Lloyd also made the finals, scoring ninth place in the women's foil. These Olympics were the high-water mark of U.S. fencing. Thereafter the efforts of Italy,

France, and Hungary to retain their leadership and the explosive progress of fencing in Russia, Poland and Rumania proved too much for the United States, and the United States has never again scored as well—three medals, one fourth, and finalists in six of seven events—as in 1932.

Another European who made an important contribution to American fencing was Leo Nunes, a great sportsman and amateur fencer who came to New York City from Italy and later became a U.S. citizen. Nunes won a second at the 1919 Inter-Allied games against the best amateurs and professionals in the world and was appointed a member of the 1924 Italian Olympic team. In the United States he won sixteen foil, épée, saber, and three-weapon national championships between 1917 and 1932.

A great loss to U.S. fencing came with the death of George Calnan, who took the opening Olympic oath at the Los Angeles 1932 Olympics as a fourth-time member of a U.S. Olympic team. He and another Navy Olympic fencer, Lt. Calloway, lost their lives in the catastrophe of the dirigible *Akron*. An indication of the friendships that grow out of competitive athletics and the Olympics is the fact that condolences from the governments, athletes, and athletic officials of twenty-two countries were received by Calnan's widow.

At the 1936 Olympics in Berlin many fencing records were broken; there were more contestants, longer fencing sessions and competitions (contestants fenced in morning, afternoon, and evening sessions), and more spectators than ever before. Two large gymnasiums, as well as hard clay tennis courts, on which épée competitions were held, were crowded day and night with spectators. Stamina and youth became very important, for the long fencing sessions wore down even the greatest among the older veterans.

The 1936 Olympics mark a new era in fencing, for electrical judging equipment, officially adopted by the *Fédération Internationale d'Escrime* (F.I.E.), was used for the first time at any Olympics. An electrical machine, developed in Geneva by L. Pagan, was capable of measuring a difference of 1/25 of a second between touches in the épée (where the fencer to hit the other first scores). From the 1936 Olympics on, very little was left to chance or to the officials' eyesight or judgment of time in épée competition, as the machine positively identified the winner. Later an electric machine was developed for foil which only registers touches on a metallic plastron covering the limited target in this technical and basic weapon.

Italy almost made a clean sweep, with firsts in both épée and foil teams and a very close second in saber team. In ten individual events, Italy placed first, second, and third in individual épée, first and third in individual foil, and second in individual saber. Andre Kabos of Hungary, World Saber Champion in 1933 and 1934, won the world or Olympic title; Franco Riccardi of Italy won the épée, and Giulio Gaudini the foil. The 1932 winner of the women's foil is probably the greatest woman fencer of modern times. Ilona Elek of Hungary won the World Championship in 1934 and 1935, repeated in the 1936 Olympics, defeating Helene Mayer, and then, just to prove her class, came back after World War II to win in the Olympics again in 1948 and win another World Championship in 1951. In 1936 not a single U.S. individual or team reached the finals.

West Point's swan song as a contributor to Olympic fencing in the United States was sung in the 1936 Olympics, when it contributed John Dimond as épée coach and the three top men in épée—Weber, Heiss, and Sands. Heiss and Sands were both U.S. national épée champions. After 1940, with Vauthier and Dimond gone, West Point lost interest in fencing, but intercollegiate fencing in the United States rose to an all-time high in 1963 when 41 colleges participated in a national tournament won by Columbia with Navy and the Air Force second and third. N.Y.U., with all three men of its first team out, still managed to come in fourth. Most of these colleges have contributed many fencers to U.S. Olympic teams.

An unpleasant incident marred the 1936 games, but showed how new nations were learning the game and threatening the leaders although some of these leaders sometimes used unsportsmanlike tactics to try to maintain their leadership. Major Haro Oliva, Mexican army officer, like Ramond Fonst of Cuba years before, lived in Paris for many years and became interested in fencing. As Mexico's Junior Military Attaché, as a student at the French War College, and as Mexico's Military Attaché, he learned fencing from French masters and gained experience in European international competitions. He became the Western Hemisphere's greatest fencer since Fonst. In fact, in one World's Championship he made the finals in both épée and saber, finishing sixth in épée and eighth in saber in the world. Making the finals in a world championship in two weapons is unusual. The 1936

Olympics was the time he had pointed for and had trained for during all his adult life. His target was the world's épée title, which only one man from the Western Hemisphere had ever won before—Fonst, in 1900 and 1904. In fact, no one from the Western Hemisphere but Fonst of Cuba has ever won any regular fencing title in 80 years.

Oliva qualified through the preliminary strips (equivalent to heats), the quarterfinals, the semifinals, and reached the finals. Oliva won his first bouts in the finals and seemed headed for the championship, to the obvious concern and annoyance of some Europeans. There was a lot of whispering and finally a group of European officials came over and began examining, testing, and measuring Oliva's weapons— his electrical épées. These had been tested and measured as normally provided for before the opening of the fencing competitions by official technical personnel. The Italian and German officials now found that one of his épées, the one they maintained he had been using, was about one-fifth of an inch too long. The directors of the competition ruled that Oliva would have to fence all his bouts over again, from the first preliminary round, with other épées of regulation length, to be checked before each bout. Oliva started to fence his bouts over again, although there was insufficient time to complete them before the final started. Mexican officials appealed that Oliva be permitted to fence in the final, subject to some later ruling, but the German officials supported the Italians to exclude him completely.

At the 1948 Olympic games, twenty-two countries competed in the fencing tournament. The coaches of the 1948 U.S. team were again René Pinchart and Georgio Santelli, who had been with U.S. fencing since 1928. Levis placed seventh in foil, Lewis ninth in épée, Worth fifth and Dr. Nyilas seventh in saber, with the United States coming in third in saber team. Maria Cerra was fourth in women's foil. The French won the individual foil (Jean Buhan) and the foil team. Italy, with Luigi Cantone, won the individual épée but was edged out by France in the épée team, and Hungary performed as usual, winning the saber team and the individual saber with Aladar Gerevich.

The progress of fencing between 1952 and 1956 was great. With the war over, world championships were held and were well attended in 1949, 1950, and 1951. For the first time fencers from the United States and other Western Hemisphere nations began to participate in these competitions. Interest increased throughout the world, and thirty-two nations sent fencers to the 1952 Olympics in Helsinki. The countries where fencing is a major national sport—Italy, Hungary, and France—won all the firsts, all but one of the seconds, and all but three of the thirds. Switzerland won the all-around fourth place. The winners are listed in the appendix. The Russians returned to Olympic fencing for the first time since 1912, when the Czar and his Imperial Guard officers had been interested in the sport. A Russian team and a U.S. team met in the first preliminary round in épée. The result was eight wins for Russia and eight wins for the United States; but the United States won by having been hit only 29 times, as against 32 hits scored against the Russians.

The U.S. team, coached again by Georgio Santelli and René Pinchart, obtained some new training blood in Stanley Sieja, a phenomenal developer of new national and international épée talent at Princeton University. Norman C. Armitage, saber member of five Olympic fencing teams from 1928 through 1952 and ten times national champion, was chosen to carry the U.S. flag at the opening ceremonies in Helsinki. Janice Lee York won fourth place in the women's foil, and the U.S. saber team placed fourth.

Much to the surprise of many Americans, the quality of the teams and the tremendous popular appeal in Russia, Poland, Rumania, Czechoslovakia, Yugoslavia, as well as in Hungary, would indicate that fencing is considered a sport for the people in these countries, and not for the privileged. Perhaps competitive athletics not only overcome differences of nationality, race, and religion, but also of classes and ideologies. Fencing and riding, behind the Iron Curtain as on this side of it, are sports like any others, and victory in these sports, as in others, goes to the best man.

The 1956 Olympic fencing competition, held at St. Kilda Town Hall in Melbourne brought together the 170 greatest fencers from 22 nations. Although the entries, especially in the team events were smaller than usual, the standard of competition was unusually high. Particularly in foil fencing, this Olympic competition was a turning point. In recent years, due to the introduction of the electrical foil—with an altered balance caused by the increased weight of the point limiting the finger and wrist play upon which the classic fencer relies —foil fencing changed to a more robust dueling sword game based on speed, opportunism and athletic agility rather than on the higher techniques and form of the classic French and Italian schools. Finer and more technically competent fencers were replaced by younger fencers of the new school. This same change also occurred in women's foil. However, between 1952 and 1956, leading foil fencers in the world finally adapted their game to the requirements of the new electrical weapon with the result that foil fencers of the classic school at Melbourne imposed their superiority through the application of better form and technique.

Nine nations competed in the foil team competition. Once again, Italy and France met in the final match, which the better balanced Italian team won 9-7 despite four victories by the French ace, d'Oriola. Hungary defeated the United States for third place. The men's foil individual featured 32 competitors and resulted in a clear victory for Christian d'Oriola. This phenomenal French foil man, who won his first world championship in 1947 at the age of 18, seemed to have at last mastered the electrical foil which had handicapped him for several years. Two classic Italian foil men, Bergamini and Spallino, took second and third places after a fence-off. Twenty-three women participated in the women's foil individual. To indicate the severity of the very first preliminary round, the champions of the British Empire, Hungary, Italy, France and Russia were all eliminated. Miss Gillian Sheen, champion of Great Britain, achieved an unexpected victory, and became the first British fencer ever to win an Olympic gold medal. Janice Lee Romary of the United States came in fourth, a further tribute to the progress of fencing in the United States. To indicate how long a fencer lasts competitively, Ellen Muller-Preiss of Austria, who had won an Olympic championship in 1932, made the finals. There were eleven countries with dueling sword teams and many upsets in the very first round when the U.S.'s very strong team was eliminated by the British and the Swedes defeated by Russia. Italy won the world championship with Hungary second, France third, and Great Britain fourth. Forty top dueling sword men competed in the individual épée championship, with many famous fencers eliminated in the first round. The final round produced the following results: 1) Carlo Pavesi of Italy; 2) Delfino of Italy; 3) E. Mangiarotti of Italy; 4) Richard Pew of the U.S.A.

The saber competitions were not up to the standard of the competitions in other weapons. Only eight countries competed, and with the elimination of Italy in the semifinal round, Hungary, which has controlled saber since 1928, had little difficulty retaining the team title. The young and fast-improving Polish team was second, with the Russians third,

95

and France in fourth place. In the individual saber, there were 34 contestants. Rudolph Karpati of Hungary won with calmness and ease. Second went to Pawloski of Poland, while Kuznetsof of Russia beat Lefevre of France in a tie for third place.

Russia, Italy, Hungary and Germany shared top honors in the 1960 Olympic tournament which involved a record field of 43 countries. Russia won the unofficial all-around title in this sport. The tremendous changes in fencing were dramatized in the individual foil event where Christian D'Oriola of France, two-time Olympic champion, finished eighth with 22-year-old Viktor Zhdanovich of Russia as the new titleholder. Italy retained both the individual and team épée and Hungary held on to both saber championships. André Deladrier of the U.S. Naval Academy was coach of a U.S. team which distinguished itself. Albert Axelrod of New York City, aged 39, a three-time Olympian, won third place in the individual foil and the United States placed fourth in the saber team competition, the best ever, except for a third in 1948. The United States placed eighth in the foil team event.

Fencing at Tokyo was epoch-making in many ways, although the caliber of the fencing was not above standard. A world fencing competition returned to Japan where, according to the most reliable sources, the sport began over 4,000 years ago. Exhibitions of Kendo, a sort of Japanese fencing thousands of years old in which contestants whale away at each other with two-handled bamboo sticks, were held at the Imperial Palace for the Olympic fencing teams visiting Tokyo for the games. Next, for the first time a top team of excellent modern fencers with experience as well as technique represented the host nation, Japan. The competition also proved unusual in many ways. For the first time since 1928 when a Frenchman, the incomparable Lucien Gaudin, won the Olympic crown, a non-Italian won the épée world title. Grigory Kriss of Russia won all but one of his bouts in the final round robin, losing that one to his teammate who finished third. Next, after nine épée team Olympic wins by France or Italy (one exception, Belgium in 1912) the épée team event was won by Hungary with Italy and France close behind. Egan Franke won Poland's first gold medal in the individual foil—another precedent breaker. Last but certainly not least, the team saber championship was won for the first time by Russia after nine Hungarian and two Italian wins in eleven previous Olympic games. However, Hungary,

This series of pictures shows one of the most dramatic episodes in the modern Olympic Games, the finish of the marathon in 1908. (1) The Italian entry Durando Peitri collapsing in his final sprint in the stadium. (2) Peitri being helped to his feet by spectators and pushed over the finish line as apparent winner, although disqualified because of the help given him. (3) The gold medal went to Johnny Hayes, U.S.A., shown finishing unaided a half-minute later.   *(UPI)*

The all-time all-American Jim Thorpe, 1912 Decathlon and Pentathlon Olympic champion. Also intercollegiate and professional baseball and football star.
(Reportagebild)

Duke Kahanamoku at his first Olympic Games in Stockholm in 1912. Winner of 3 gold and 2 silver medals in 3 Games. If it had not been for World War I he would have won 5 gold and 2 silver.
(Wide World)

U.S.A.'s top combination runner, swimmer, swordsman, pistol shot and horseman in the Modern Pentathlon event at the 1912 Olympic Games, Lt. George Patton. *(UPI)*

Sweden's Gillis Grafstrom, only 3-time men's figure skating Olympic champion, and Norway's Sonja Henie, only 3-time Olympic women's champion, at St. Moritz in 1924. *(Wide World)*

"Tarzan" Johnny Weismuller, winner of 4 Olympic gold medals in 2 games, with Andrew Charlton of Australia, winner of 1500-meter swim, in 1924 at Colombe, France. *(UPI)*

U.S.A. Charlie Paddock, the "Human Bullet," explodes to win the 1924 100-meter Olympic final. *(UPI)*

Finland's contribution to long-distance running—the greatest—"Flying Finn" Paavo Nurmi and Willie Ritola (dual total 7 Olympic gold medals and 5 silver). *(UPI)*

Four-time gold medalist Pahud de Mortanges (center) of Holland with teammates and horses that put Holland on top in the "3 Day" riding event from 1924 to 1932. *(UPI)*

One of the greatest all-time Western Hemisphere riding teams, 1948 Olympic "Prix des Nations" gold medalists Mexico's Colonel Mariles, Captains Valdez, Carielo and Uriza. Mariles also won the individual event. *(UPI)*

Floyd Patterson after winning Olympic middleweight boxing title at Helsinki in 1952; later to become world's professional heavyweight champion. *(Wide World)*

Swedish winners of the 1960 Olympic double kayak event. Gert Fredricksson (left) is the only 7-time Olympic gold and 1 bronze medalist (canoeing 1948-60). *(UPI)*

Tokyo's Komazawa Park, site of the 1964 Olympics. *(Wide World)*

The "fastest humans" of their times—Bob Hayes, 1964, and Jesse Owens, 1936. *(UPI)*

U.S. Marine Corps Lt. Billy Mills wins only 10,000-meter Olympic run ever won by the U.S.A. at Tokyo in record time (1964). *(UPI)*

V. Ivanov of Russia, only 3-time single sculls Olympic winner (1956-60-64), wearing a U.S. Olympic pin. *(Wide World)*

Al Oerter, 3-time discus winner, favorite for 1968, shows his throwing form. *(UPI)*

Abebe Bikila, bodyguard and messenger for H.I.M. Haile Selassie of Ethiopia, only 2-time winner of the Olympic marathon. *(UPI)*

Peggy Fleming winning at Grenoble, France. *(UPI)*

Russian in orbit? Olga Karaseva-Kharlova, Gymnastics. *(UPI)*

not to be outdone, continued its monopoly of the individual saber honors. Tibor Pezsa won the eleventh saber title out of the last twelve games for Hungary. Hungary made a clean sweep of the women's events. The United States had one of its worst showings in this sport, with not a single one of its contestants even reaching the quarter-finals. U.S. fencers that looked so good in competitions at home—such as Paul Pesthy in épée, Alfonso Morales in saber, and Albert Axelrod, a mature Olympic bronze medalist in 1960—all faded out fast before the more aggressive and more versatile game of the foreign fencers. Most experts agree that lack of competitors and competitions, especially contact with more experienced fencers and a variety of games (i.e. strategy and tactics and techniques), has atrophied U.S. progress. We are simply not following the new school of fencing practiced by the Russians, Poles and Hungarians and now copied by the widely experienced French and Italians—namely more offense, less defense; more games and tricks, less form; more fight, less finesse. With these changes and longer competitions also came the need for stamina and condition. A psychological factor in a sport so dependent on mental processes is the complicated and controversial method used to select U.S. Olympic fencing teams. Few people can argue against the time-honored method of taking the result of one competition, whether it be the national championship or a special Olympic tryout open to all. Such a contest has the same pressures and element of chance that occur in the Olympic games. Point systems involving competitions weighted and evaluated by amateur statisticians over a period of more than a year are highly controversial and do not take into account the fact that an Olympic performer must deliver when the chips are down, irrespective of any overall performance in many contests over a considerable period of time.

The Mexican Olympic fencing tournament showed a number of basic shifts in national superiority. For the first time in 60 years, Hungary did not win either the individual or the team gold medal in saber after twenty wins out of twenty-four. Captain Jerzy Pawlowski of the Polish Army was the first non-Hungarian saber champion since Nedo Nadi of Italy won in 1920. France made a strong comeback at Mexico, winning the foil team for men over Russia, Poland, Rumania and Hungary. France won fourth in team saber, a third, fourth and fifth in individual foils, a sixth in épée individual. Overall, Russia nosed out Hungary by a single point—36 to 35. Russia won both women's events. The United States continued its hopeless ineffectiveness and inexperience, making a single point with a sixth in team saber, but the most effective competitor on this team was Hungarian-trained. Many persons close to fencing in the United States believe a complete change of management and approach, and a reorganization of the Amateur Fencers League of America, are in order. Fencing is certainly growing on a worldwide basis: 34 countries sent 278 contestants (220 men, 58 women) to Mexico. But once more the U.S. fencing team sent to the 1971 world's championships in Vienna were selected by amateur statisticians, with poor results. If the United States wants to even qualify a single fencer to the first six places at an Olympic Games, it will have to determine its team on the national championship or a single competition instead of by computers fed by amateur evaluators.

CHAPTER IX

Gymnastics

ONE OF the world's least publicized sports is gymnastics. Yet gymnasts perform in a single evening acts of greater daring and greater difficulty than most baseball and football players or track and field men are called upon to equal in a whole season. Unfortunately, however, gymnastics has no great crowd appeal and the greatest gymnasts in America cannot draw the crowds that gather regularly in baseball parks and football stadiums. Similarly, gymnastics are an almost unnoticed part of the modern Olympic games.

But gymnastics as a sport has proved itself by having outlived many other sports and is today a feature of the modern Olympics. The sport dates from the ancient Greeks, and the words "gymnastics" and "gymnasium" come from the Greek *gymnazein,* meaning to exercise (naked). Gymnastics, weight lifting, and track and field were, in the days of the ancient Greeks, coupled together as the proper regimen for young men. Students in ancient Greece were required to learn to run, jump, lift and throw weights, wrestle, and perform disciplinary gymnastics. Every city of ancient Greece had a gymnasium or many gymnasiums in which gymnastics were practiced.

In the early years of gymnastics in the United States, the sport was engaged in chiefly by European-Americans from countries where such exercises were extremely popular. In

1897 the Amateur Athletic Union assumed national control of the sport. Shortly thereafter, the colleges began to take an interest in gymnastics, and forty-three years later, in 1940, the University of Illinois, a college team, captured the national championship. In more recent years, high schools and junior high schools have taken an interest in gymnastics and have developed performers who will compete and compare favorably with the greatest in any other country.

In modern gymnastics, the all-around championship is won by the contestant making the best showing in free calisthenics, long horse, side horse, horizontal bar, parallel bar, and flying rings. One compulsory and one optional exercise are required for the horizontal bar, parallel bar, side horse, and long horse. Each contestant must execute the compulsory exercises, and the optional is some exercise of his own choosing in which he feels he will appear at his best. The judges base their decisions on the degree of difficulty in performing the exercise, the execution of the movement, and the form displayed. On the flying ring, one still and one brisk-swinging exercise are demanded. In rope climbing, each contestant receives three chances, and speed alone determines the winner. The rope is twenty feet long. In tumbling, the contestant performs one optional routine. The judging is on the basis of the amount of tumbling performed and the degree of difficulty. In club swinging, the contestant is allowed one trial of four minutes. The club must weigh one pound, and the dropping of a club ends the exercise. In free calisthenics, one optional exercise is performed in one and a half to two minutes, without hand apparatus.

Probably the greatest gymnast ever developed in the United States was Alfred Jochim, and the most famous club was the Swiss Turnverein of Hudson County, New Jersey, of which Jochim was a member. Jochim was the all-around winner in all national AAU championships from 1925 to 1930, and then came back in 1933 to win his seventh crown. The Swiss Turnverein won its first team championship in 1926, then repeated in every year from 1928 to 1934. Another extraordinary performer was Edward A. Hennig of Cleveland, who won the first AAU national championship in Indian club swinging in 1904 and then repeated in 1911, 1933, 1936, 1937, 1939, 1940, 1942, 1945, 1946, 1947, 1950, and 1951, besides winning the 1904 world's championship or Olympic gold medal in that event.

Women's gymnastics first appeared as an AAU championship event in 1931. Probably the greatest American performer among women gymnasts was Clara M. Schroth Lomady of Philadelphia, who won the all-around title in 1945, 1946, 1949, 1950, 1951, and 1952.

At the first modern Olympics at Athens in 1896, eight events were contested by competitors from some half-dozen countries. The unofficial team title in this sport was won by Germany. There was no all-around competition, either individual or team, but only individual events. If there had been an all-around individual championship, Zutter of Switzerland probably would have won it; he excelled in several different events.

The gymnastics at the 1900 Olympics in Paris was won by the host nation. These were the first Olympic games to hold an all-around gymnastics individual competition, which was won by Sandras of France; there was still no all-around team championship. In 1904, according to the report by the committee running the Olympics in St. Louis, there were official gymnastic events and the all-around championship was won by the United States. According to other sources, there is considerable doubt that the gymnastic events were recognized as official. However, the United States won practically every event except the all-around team, which was won by Germany. The greatest individual stars were Anton Heida of the United States, who won the all-around individual, tied for the long horse, and won the side horse and tied for the horizontal bar, and George Eyser, also of the United States, who tied for first in the long horse and horizontal bar and won the parallel bars and rope climb.

In the 1906 games in Athens, generally counted as one of the modern Olympics, France won the unofficial gymnastic championship, although Denmark and Norway tied in the all-around gymnastic team event. A Frenchman, Payssee, won the all-around gymnastic individual title, and a Greek, G. Aliprantis, won the rope climb in an astonishingly slow time. A prince of the royal family of Greece officiated at this Olympic gymnastic meet.

There is considerable argument about who won the all-around championship in the London games of 1908. Italy, Great Britain, and Sweden claimed the top honors, each basing its claim on its own method of scoring. Sweden won the gymnastic team event. Italy served notice of her future strength in this sport, uncovering a new star, Alberto Braglia, who won the all-around individual event.

The 1912 Olympic games emphasized gymnastics, and the host nation, Sweden, one of the greatest supporters of the gymnastics schedule and winner or co-winner in 1908, contributed to making the gymnastic competitions more interesting than they had been in any previous Olympics. Many new events were added, such as calisthenics, team exercise, both free system and Swedish system, and a special team competition. Italy was a close second to Sweden, and Alberto Braglia repeated his 1908 victory as the best all-around gymnast. Italy also won the team gymnastics event.

When the 1920 Olympics came around, an even larger program of gymnastic events was scheduled. Fourteen countries participated, and Italy made good her earlier promise by taking the gymnastic team championship and winning the unofficial all-around team. Sweden won one and Denmark won two of the calisthenics competitions. The United States sent only four men. The American who finished highest in the rankings was Frank Kriz, who was tenth. Roy E. Moore was manager of the team and came back to the United States certain that, with proper organization and proper selection and training, Americans could do well in future gymnastic events in the Olympics.

Thanks to the enthusiasm and dedication of Mr. Moore, who also managed the 1924 team, the United States broke into the winning column in the 1924 Paris Olympics, although the Italians won the unofficial all-around championship. The U.S. Olympic team in 1924 was selected after many tryouts and a very thrilling final tryout held at Madison Square Garden in New York City, on May 27, 1924. Nine nations competed in the all-around event, finishing in the following order: Italy, France, Switzerland, Yugoslavia, the United States, Great Britain, Finland, Luxembourg, Czechoslovakia. In the individual events, Frank J. Kriz was first in the long horse, with Max H. Wandrer of the United States placing fifth in this event. Kriz also placed sixth in the rope climb. For the first time since 1904, the system of giving gold medals and awarding places in the individual events as well as for the all-around scoring was used. Switzerland made the greatest improvement of any country, and came out second from an all-around standpoint. At these Olympics, it was proposed the gymnastic events for women be added to the program, and it was decided that beginning in 1928 there would be a women's gymnastics team event and later, perhaps, an individual all-around competition.

The gymnastic competition at the ninth Olympiad in Amsterdam covered a period of three days. Switzerland won, with Czechoslovakia second, Yugoslavia third, France fourth, Finland fifth, Italy sixth, the United States seventh, Holland eighth, Luxembourg ninth, Hungary tenth, and England eleventh. No member of the U.S. team was able to place in any event. Alfred Jochim, who had also been a member of the 1924 team, was high man of the U.S. entries. Roy E. Moore was again manager and coach of the team. Switzerland made almost a clean sweep, winning the gymnastic team, the gymnastic all-around individual, the long horse, the side horse, the horizontal bar, and the side horse vaults, the last an event held only in 1924 and 1928. The remaining two titles went to Czechoslovakia and Yugoslavia. The women's gymnastic team event, held for the first time, was won by the host nation, Holland. The addition of individual events for women was postponed.

Only seven countries brought gymnastic teams to the tenth Olympiad at Los Angeles in 1932, but there were more competitors than at any gymnastic meet of the Olympics up until that time and the level of performance was high. There were eleven events, extending over a period of five days, and attendance at the Olympic stadium ranged from 3,000 to 27,-000. The United States won the unofficial championship, with Italy second, Hungary third, and Finland fourth. The United States took the first three places in the rope climb; the first three places in tumbling; a third and fourth in the side horse; first, second, and fourth in flying rings; sixth in the parallel bars; first in the horizontal bars; first, second, and third in the Indian clubs; second and third in the long horse vaulting; second in the team all-around; and sixth in the individual all-around. It was the high-water mark of American effort in gymnastics. Alfred Jochim was an important member of the 1932 team, as he had been in the 1924 and 1928 teams. Roy E. Moore, the manager and coach of the team, played a major role in the United States' climb from last to first place.

The 1936 Olympic gymnastic championships in Berlin brought back one of Germany's oldest traditions in competitive athletics. In 1896, at the first gymnastic championship of the first modern Olympics, Germany had been the winner. Germany was also the winner at Berlin, winning five Olympic titles, including the individual men's all-around and the men's team all-around. The United States finished tenth among the fourteen countries competing, each of which was represented by a team of eight men. The gymnastic competition took place at the Reichssportfeld in the Dietrich Eckart

Stadium. Crowds of 25,000 to 30,000 enthusiastic spectators attested to the great popular interest in this sport in Germany.

After Germany, the thirteen other countries finished in the following order: Switzerland, Finland, Czechoslovakia, Italy, Yugoslavia, Hungary, France, Japan, the United States, Austria, Luxembourg, Bulgaria, and Rumania. There were some complaints about the judging, based on the fact that the Germans, after agreeing to name three judges from every country, allowed only one judge from the United States. Whatever the validity of these complaints, the United States fared very badly in the individual competition, our highest-ranked contestant coming in 38th. Alfred Jochim was for the fourth time a member of the U.S. team.

There had been no women's gymnastic events in 1932, but the 1936 Olympics in Germany featured a regular schedule of gymnastic events for women and the United States was represented by a women's gymnastic team for the first time. Eight nations entered teams of eight women each. They finished in the following order: Germany, Czechoslovakia, Hungary, Yugoslavia, the United States, Poland, Italy, Great Britain. Miss Conseppa Caruccio was the United States' high scorer.

The 1948 Olympiad saw outstanding competitions in both the men's and women's gymnastic championships. Sixteen countries entered teams in the men's competition, eleven in the women's. The outcome of the men's championships was so close that different methods of scoring give different winners—Finland according to one and Switzerland according to another, although Finland did take the men's all-around gymnastic team championship and a Finn won the all-around men's individual. The Swiss, however, won three individual gold medals, as against two for Finland, and scored many points in the individual events. The team events for the men were: free exercises, pommeled horse, rings, parallel bars, horizontal bars, and vaults. The final standing in the men's team was: Finland, Switzerland, Hungary, France, Italy, Czechoslovakia, the United States, Denmark, Austria, Yugoslavia, Luxembourg, Great Britain, Egypt, Cuba, Argentina, and Mexico, in that order. In the all-around men's individual, Finns placed first and third and the Swiss captured second, fourth, fifth, and sixth places.

In the women's team championship, consisting of free exercises, beam, vault, rings, and hand apparatus, the results were as follows: Czechoslovakia, Hungary, the United States,

Sweden, Holland, Austria, Yugoslavia, Italy, Great Britain, France and Belgium.

The U.S. men's team was coached by Eugene Wettstone and George Miele, with the women's coached by Joseph Salzman. The women's team showed to great advantage and, according to many, did not get the breaks in judging. The U.S. officials and experts in gymnastics were surprised by the showing of their women's team, but very disappointed in the men's team. On the other hand, they pointed out that the United States, by adopting better training policies and stimulating competition, could achieve prominence in gymnastics, and gave as an example the experience of the Finns, who had first entered a team at Amsterdam in 1928, where they placed a poor fifth. At Los Angeles in 1932 and at Berlin in 1936, the Finns placed third, and at London in 1948 they came into their own and were first or tied for first—depending on whose scoring you accept.

The fifteenth Olympiad at Helsinki in 1952 attracted an even greater number of competitors than any earlier modern Olympics had. These games also featured the arrival of a nation new to Olympic gymnastic competition—Russia. The Russians, who won with ease, were impressive because of their superb condition, their consistency, and their strength. Their optionals on horizontal bar and parallel bar were very short and may not have been the fluent longer combination work expected at international tournaments, but their exactitude and perfection on the compulsory routines showed the effect of long and excellent training. The United States, coached by Thomas E. Maloney, finished eighth in the 29-nation competition. The 1952 games produced a new world star, E. V. Tchoukarine, of Russia, who won the all-around men's individual competition of twelve events, and also won gold medals in the side horse and long horse, and a silver medal in the parallel bars.

The men's team championship placed the nations in the following order: Russia, Switzerland, Finland, Germany, Japan, Hungary and Czechoslovakia (tied), the United States, Bulgaria, France, Italy, Austria, Poland, Denmark, Norway, Egypt, Sweden, Luxembourg, Rumania, Yugoslavia, Great Britain, the Saar, Portugal, Belgium, Cuba, South Africa, Argentina, Spain and India.

In the women's gymnastics, eighteen nations participated, and finished in the following order: Russia, Hungary, Czechoslovakia, Sweden, Bulgaria, Germany, Italy, Poland,

Rumania, France, Yugoslavia, Austria, Finland, Holland, the United States, Great Britain, Norway and Portugal.

The women's gymnastics enjoyed great popularity at Helsinki; the spectators saw some very glamorous performers. The program of women's events was greatly expanded because of the great popular interest, and it now includes not only an all-round individual competition of eight events, but also beam, parallel bars, long horse, free standing exercise, and—a new event—team calisthenics.

As expected, the Olympic gymnastics events in Melbourne produced some very close competition. While Russia managed to retain both team and combined individual championships, her margin over the runners-up was extremely small. The all-around standard of performance was improved over the Helsinki Games. There were no revolutionary changes, although the tendency toward "balletic" movements in floor exercises and on the beam made the skill, grace and daring of the competitors more apparent. Although Miss Keleti of Hungary was first in three of the four individual events, she failed to win the combined exercises championship because of a lapse in the compulsory vault; therefore, Latynina of Russia became the new champion, with Muratova (whose husband Valentine won two gold medals in gymnastics) third. The Muratovs won two gold, one silver and two bronze medals.

Japan upset Russia's eighth year domination at Rome in 1960. Nippon won the team championship and three other gold medals. Russia, although it lost the team title, earned five individual gold medals, four of them by world champion Boris Shakhlin. Finland was the only other nation to win a gold medal—Eugen Ekman tying Shakhlin for first in the long horse. Twenty nations entered full teams, with another 28 nations sending individual competitors. The United States made its best record since 1932 and its overall score was the best ever made by an American team.

Japan again won all-around honors in the men's gymnastics at Tokyo, while the Russians retained top honors in the ladies' gymnastics. Boris Shakhlin of Russia won his sixth gold medal (one in 1956, four—two shared—in 1960, and one in 1964) and Larissa Senyonovna Latynina of Russia won her sixth gold medal (three in 1956, two in 1960, one in 1964). Yukio Endo of Japan, with two gold medals and one silver medal, was the male star, while Vera Caslavska of Czechoslovakia was the leading lady, winning three gold

105

medals. The United States was seventh in the all-around men's team, while the U.S. women's team placed ninth. The best U.S. individual contestant was Douglas Sakamoto, a 17-year-old Los Angeles schoolboy, who finished twentieth in the men's all-around. Twenty-four nations entered full teams at Tokyo, with 34 nations represented by team or individual competitors.

Although Mexico City was very far from the eastern European countries and Japan, where gymnastics is a major sport, 254 gymnasts (139 men, 115 women) from 26 countries participated in the 1968 gymnastic events before capacity crowds. It was actually a battle between two countries—as the dedicated, exact, but unimaginative robot-like Russians competed against the individuality, imagination and sometimes unrehearsed innovations and skills of the Japanese. Japan won, with Russia a close second. In the women's competition it was between Czechoslovakia's beauty queen of gymnastics, Vera Caslavska, and the Russian women's team. The real winner was Caslavska, although the USSR team won nine gold medals while Miss Caslavska won six and a husband. She was married in an Olympic Village ceremony to a member of the Czechoslovakian track and field team. Of course, she successfully defended her 1964 all-around gymnastic championship and was the brightest and most attractive personality in the nineteenth Olympic games. The only other gold medal winners were Yugoslavia and Finland in the men's events, and East Germany won a couple of silver and bronze medals in the women's events. The United States made a giant although limited stride when its women's team came in sixth, with Linda Metheny fourth in the balanced beam. Linda was the first U.S. entry to ever qualify for a final in a gymnastic event in the Olympic games.

CHAPTER X

The Modern Pentathlon

AFTER THE seventeenth Olympic games in ancient Greece, the war-like Spartans complained that the Olympics did not have an all-around athletic competition for warriors, and as a result the pentathlon, a contest consisting of five events, was initiated in the eighteenth Olympics (708 B.C.). The pentathlon was designed purely for the soldier athlete. It was an elimination contest in which all entrants first took part in a broad-jumping contest. Those who cleared a certain distance qualified for a second event, or spear- or javelin-throwing contest. At this time the spear or javelin was the major equipment of the Greek soldier, from private to general. Only the four best in this military event were qualified to participate in the third event, a sprint of one length of the stadium, or approximately 200 yards. One more athlete was eliminated here. The fourth challenge for the remaining contestants was the discus throw, and in this event one more contestant was eliminated. Then the two surviving athletes, in the grand finale of this grueling competition, wrestled each other to a finish. The winner was the Olympic pentathlon winner. Later the pentathlon, and perhaps the decathlon (ten events), were restricted to competitions testing track and field prowess only, and wrestling became a separate event.

When the modern Olympic games were inaugurated in 1896 there was too much confusion, and too much scrambling by partisans of various sports, for the sponsors to worry about a pentathlon or decathlon. Efforts were made, after the modern Olympics began, to add a pentathlon and, later, a decathlon, but both were all-around tests involving track and field events only. These efforts led to the inclusion of a pentathlon, which was discontinued after 1924, and the regular decathlon, which is still contested in the track and field program of the modern Olympics.

Before the 1912 Olympics, the organizers of the Olympic games felt that there was room for a dramatic event with a military background that would appeal to the armed forces of the various nations of the world. It is even said that the idea was first suggested in a conversation between Latour and de Coubertin. Some even claim that de Coubertin said that to stimulate better international relations and to insure peace, the armies of the world should be made to meet in friendly competition in some event that would particularly attract army personnel. In any case, the modern pentathlon, personally sponsored by Baron de Coubertin, was added to the Olympic program in 1912.

The modern pentathlon, which should have been called the "military pentathlon," was based on the function of the dramatic military courier or aide-de-camp who in the glorious Napoleonic days or even as late as 1912 was often called upon to deliver on the battlefield a message or an order that might mean victory for his country. The aide-de-camp or courier, before the advent of radio, had to be able to ride a strange horse over hill and dale and over obstacles of every kind and, when his horse became exhausted or was shot from under him, had to proceed on foot by running cross-country; and when he came to a stream or river he had to cross it by swimming, and if he encountered an enemy he had to shoot his way through with his pistol; and then, at close quarters, he had to fight any remaining enemy with his sword, if he was finally to deliver the message. This might well be called the swashbuckling or motion-picture event, if it were considered literally; as a sports competition it was an excellent test of athletic versatility.

The modern pentathlon requires each contestant to run 4,000 meters cross-country, to ride a strange horse over a 5,000-meter steeplechase course with some 30 jumps, (recently changed to a 1,500-meter *Prix de Nation* type course) to compete in rapid-fire pistol shooting at a silhouette target, to fence with a dueling sword, and to swim 300 meters free style. With the exception of the fencing bouts or tests, contestants do not compete against each other but against time, just as a courier would in riding, running, or swimming to deliver his message. There are many people who believe that this is the most interesting event in the entire Olympic program. Certainly it is the greatest test of all around athletic ability. There is, fortunately or unfortunately, one big element of luck in this event; the drawing of horses by lot. A contestant can draw a good, average, or bad horse, and the horse's performance will definitely affect his placement in the riding event.

The 1912 Olympics were the first in which the modern pentathlon was an official event. It was considered an individual event and only unofficially a team event of three contestants per nation until 1952, when it became a team event with an official team scoring system. Olympic medals, however, are still awarded to the first three individuals to finish, as well as the first three teams.

Americans have traditionally excelled in riding, shooting, swimming, and running, yet no American has ever placed first in the individual standings, and the United States has never won the unofficial or official team championship in the 60-year history of this event. The military forces of many countries throughout the world became so enthusiastic about the event that an International Modern Pentathlon Union was formed, and for some twenty-five years, except during the last war, there have been annual world championships in the modern pentathlon. This has improved training techniques and performance. The author has been associated with most of the U.S. Olympic and world's championship teams from 1924 to 1968, generally as advisory coach.

In the 1912 Olympics a slim young American cavalry lieutenant named George Patton, the first U.S. entrant in this event—who was to be known later, when he was a combat general in World War II, as "Old Blood and Guts" —finished fifth. Although Patton was a great shot, his use of a U.S. Army revolver while the Swedes used target pistols was too great a handicap in the competition. The Swedes practically monopolized the first modern pentathlon competition in Stockholm, winning first, second, third, and fourth places. Patton was twenty-first in shooting, seventh in swimming, fourth in fencing, sixth in riding, and third in running, for a general standing of fifth.

In 1920 the Swedes again won both the individual and the team titles, again taking the first four places. A Dane was fifth; and the American to finish best, Harold Rayner, was sixth. The other American competing, Robert Sears, placed eighth. By 1920 the pentathlon pistol shooting had been standardized and consisted of 20 timed-fire shots, in four series of five, fired at turning silhouette targets at 25 meters with any type of .22-caliber pistol. As far back as the 1920 Olympics the U.S. entrants were falling behind, mainly because of their poor showing in riding. Major Rayner, for instance, who placed sixth in 1920, was fourth in running, fifth in shooting, twelfth in swimming, thirteenth in fencing —but fourteenth in riding.

The 1924 modern pentathlon was again won by the Swedes, who took the first three places. The first American entrant to finish, Lt. George Bare of the U.S. Army, was tenth. The French sent one of the most improved modern pentathlon teams to these Olympics, placing three men in the first twelve. A great many U.S. Olympic and world's championship contestants in this event became generals. Major Gen. William C. Rose controlled all U.S. efforts for 40 years with Manchu policies, but Major General Pete Haines has been in charge for the past twelve years.

Next to riding, fencing was the greatest obstacle to most American contestants in these Olympics, as was demonstrated by the fact that Lt. Bare, who placed first of the U.S. entrants and tenth in the competition, was fourteenth in shooting, fifteenth in swimming, sixth in riding, thirteenth in running, but twenty-seventh in fencing. All of the contestants were either officers or noncommissioned officers in the various armies of the countries participating.

In the 1928 Olympics the modern pentathlon was again won by the Swedes, with a first, second, and fourth; but Germany showed tremendous improvement with a third, fifth, and eighth. There were entries from many countries that had not competed before. Sweden, Germany, Great Britain, Holland, Denmark, Italy, Poland, Finland, the United States, Hungary, Belgium, France, Czechoslovakia and Portugal were represented by teams. Again the United States did poorly, finishing fifteenth, nineteenth, and twentieth. The winner was Sven Thofelt, now a general in the Swedish Army and president of the International Modern Pentathlon Union. Major Harold Rayner, a pentathlon contestant and fencer in previous Olympics, was the manager of the U.S. team, and the team members were Richard W. Mayo, Peter C. Haines, and Aubrey S. Newman—later all generals in the United States Army.

The 1932 Olympic games brought together contestants from ten nations and, as if by habit, Sweden again captured the team honors with a first, second, and fourth. The fourth, incidentally, was Sven Thofelt, Sweden's winner in 1928. Richard Mayo was the first American ever to win an Olympic medal in the modern pentathlon, placing third. Mayo's background combined perfectly the elements of the modern pentathlon: He was a field artilleryman, an expert horseman, and had been an intercollegiate fencing champion and an Olympic fencer; he was also a crack shot and winner of many shooting competitions. His weakness lay in the two events in which most of the Americans had been good in the past. Although he placed second in riding, fourth in fencing, and first in shooting, he was fourteenth in swimming and seventeenth in running. General Guy V. Henry of the U.S. Army was in charge of the team.

In 1936 the Army and the U.S. Military Academy made an all-out effort to break the grip of the Swedes on this event. Twelve officers and fifteen cadets trained for months at the U.S. Military Academy. Several civilians had competed in the tryouts in 1932 and one competed in 1936—C. B. Smith of Los Angeles. Warrant Officer Jack Dimond of West Point was selected as coach, and Captain Mayo was manager. All three of the representatives of the United States placed in the first ten. According to the unofficial scoring system used in all Olympic sports at that time, the Germans properly laid claim to the team championship, since they had a first and a sixth. Sixteen nations participated. According to the point system later adopted as one of the methods of scoring this event as a team competition, the Germans won by 160 to 186. By using another method of arriving at a team

110

score, based on the relative placings of all three team members, the United States could claim a win by 18 to 19 (low score indicating the winner). Lt. Charles Leonard, who scored an unprecedented 200 out of a possible 200 in the shooting event, won the silver medal for second place. Leonard got his second place by coming in first in shooting, sixth in swimming, seventh in running, tenth in fencing, but—as so often Americans do in this event—fell down to fifteenth in riding. Lt. Gotthardt Handrick of the German Army finished some eight points ahead of Leonard and won first place. Captain Silvano Abba of the Italian Army was third and our old friend Sven Thofelt was fourth. This was his third Olympiad. Lt. Alfred Starbird was seventh and Lt. Frederick Weber was ninth. Weber was considered the iron man of the U.S. team, participating in the five events of the modern pentathlon and also in both épée individual and épée team in the fencing events at the same Olympics. He was first in fencing in this modern pentathlon competition and second in shooting; but twenty-second in riding, thirty-fourth in swimming, and twentieth in running.

The 1948 competition was won by a Swede, as usual. Finland, however, won the unofficial team title, although the Finns were given a close race by Sweden, which scored a first and a third. The third member of the Swedish team, however, was seventeenth, whereas the Finns placed fourth, fifth, and tenth. The individual championship was won by Capt. W. O. Grut of the Swedish cavalry. Colonel Grut is now secretary general of the International Modern Pentathlon Union. Second was Major George Moore of the United States, third Lt. Gardin of Sweden, fourth Lt. Vilkko of Finland, fifth Major Larkas of Finland, six Lt. Reim of Switzerland. The other American contestants, Lts. R. L. Gruenther and H. Baugh, finished eighth and thirteenth respectively. This pentathlon competition included, for the first time, a great many teams from Latin America—Argentina (first in the team riding), Brazil, Chile, Mexico, Cuba, and Uruguay. Lt. Col. Weber was the manager-coach of the U.S. team.

Competitors from Sweden, Hungary, Russia, Finland, the United States, Brazil, Great Britain, Argentina, Chile, Switzerland, France, Uruguay, Italy, Germany, Portugal, Belgium, and South Africa entered the modern pentathlon event in 1952. Hungary won the team championship—the first official team championship awarded on the basis of an official Olympic scoring system. Lt. L. Hall of Sweden won first in the individual; second was G. Benedek of Hungary, third I. Szondi of Hungary, and fourth I. K. Novikov of Russia. In fifth place was O. A. Mannonen, an unusually old contestant who improved so much in the succeeding three years that he was a very close second in the 1955 world championship in Switzerland. The Russians served notice in the 1952 Olympics and in the annual world championships in 1955 that they were going to go all-out and someday win this event. Constatin Szalnikov, of Kasachstan, Russia, a former riding instructor in the Soviet Army, won the world's individual championship in 1955, although Novikov, his compatriot, dropped to seventeenth.

The highest-ranking American in the 1952 Olympics was Capt. F. L. Denman, who placed sixth. The other entries, Pvt. W. T. McArthur and Capt. Guy Troy, placed eighth and fourteenth respectively. The first ten teams were Hungary, Sweden, Finland, the United States, Russia, Brazil, Chile, Argentina, Switzerland, and Great Britain, in that order.

The 1956 Melbourne Olympic pentathlon, the greatest test of all-around athletic ability and the most grueling competition ever seen in Australia, numbered 40 starters, representing twelve full national teams as well as individuals from four other countries. On the first day, the riding event was held at the Oaklands Country Club, 15 miles north of Melbourne. None of the jumps was very difficult, with the possible exception of No. 25—a pond which proved a trap for tired horses at the end of the course. The Australian horses provided were unusually young and short of training, and therefore required careful handling. The fact that 13 riders scored less than 200 points, with four riders so severely injured they were hospitalized and withdrawn from the competition—all on an easy course—indicated poor horses rather than incompetent riders. The U.S. team (all civilians, William André, Jack Daniels and George Lambert) won, giving it a lead it did not lose until the last day, with George Lambert of the N.Y.A.C. first in the individual riding.

The fencing on the second day was held on seven strips, with the competition lasting over ten hours. C. Vena of Rumania was the winner, with 29 victories out of 36. The shooting event was held on the Williamstown range some miles southwest of Melbourne by the sea. Unfortunately, this range proved to be one of the windiest places ever encountered by pentathlon shooters. However, expert shots can not be disturbed, as was proven by Almada of the Mexican Army, who won with a score of 193 out of 200. Lambert of

112

the United States was fourth with 190. The swimming was the only event held in the main Olympic area in the Melbourne pool. The Russian I. Derivgoin broke the pentathlon record in the swim by negotiating 300 meters in 3 minutes 46 seconds. After this event the United States still retained the team lead, with Russia in second place.

The last day, which as usual featured cross-country running, was at the Oaklands Hunt Club. Sgt. V. Cobley of the British Army was the winner of this event. However, the running of the entire Russian team in this final event was not only impressive but sufficient to allow it to pass the U.S. team, which had led for four days. In the final team standing, the United States was second, Finland third, and Hungary fourth. In the individual: Lars Hall, for the first time in the history of the modern Olympics, won his second Olympic championship; O. Mannonen of Finland was second; V. Korhonen of Finland third; I. Novikov of Russia fourth; George Lambert of the N.Y.A.C. was fifth. The U.S. champion, Robert Miller. had been injured in training and could not compete.

The Hungarians surprised and upset the Russians in the modern pentathlon at Rome in 1960, which featured Hungary's Ferenc Nemeth (5,024) who came in first as an individual, Imre Nagy (4,988) second and Andreas Balczo (4,973) fourth, a young team making a record score of 14,985. A 15,000 total would mean par in every event or the equivalent of a perfect score. The Russian veterans of Novikov, Tatarino and Selg ran up 14,408 points for second place against the United States' 14,238 for third place. George Lambert, fifth in 1956 and U.S. National Champion, had a bad week and placed eighteenth while Robert Beck turned in inspiring performances and placed third individually. The third man on the U.S. team was Jack Daniels from Oklahoma. Beck won the Pan Am games modern pentathlon in Sao Paulo in May 1963.

The world's championships in Mexico City in October 1962 featured a Japanese modern pentathlon team and the 1963 Pan Am games further expanded this event to many Latin American countries. The world's championships for 1963 in Bern, Switzerland featured some of the greatest performances, records, improvements and innovations. Twenty nations competed with Hungary, Russia, the United States, East Germany, Sweden and Australia finishing in that order. The Hungarian team broke all records with a score of 15,316. The individual medalists were (1) Balczo, Hungary,

113

5,267, (2) Török, Hungary, 5,185, (3) Novikov, Russia, 5,060. The U.S. team was made up of Captain James Moore, U.S.A. World's (CISM) 1963 Military Champion, Robert Miller of Seattle and Paul Pesthy of the New York Athletic Club, who placed tenth, eighth and twenty-fourth. The Japanese team showed great improvement. Practically all records were broken by the winners in each event. Last but not least, to solve a problem threatening this event in the Olympics, a short but difficult jumping course of approximately 1,500 meters of a horse show type was substituted for the long steeplechase riding course. This enabled the horses to be used twice, once in the morning and after a rest again in the afternoon, with any injured or fractious horse withdrawn for a substitute in the afternoon session. This practically cuts the organizers' costs and problems in half and will no longer limit the number of Olympic contestants. The short course can be seen by more spectators and is a far greater attraction, reducing accidents occasioned by very tired horses on the longer course. It was unanimously adopted for Tokyo. The 1963 world's championships were the first to be televised both to Europe and North America.

The 1964 Olympic hosts gave the modern pentathlon one hundred per cent support and perfect facilities—in fact too good insofar as the riding. Although some doubt had been expressed about the horses to be supplied by the Japanese, the mounts provided were excellent and well trained. The course was too easy. As a result, what has traditionally been the most colorful and decisive event of the most romantic five-sport combination played almost no role in determining team and individual placings. There were too many perfect scores in riding. The U.S. team, consisting of Army Captain James Moore and Lt. David Kirkwood and Paul Pesthy of the New York Athletic Club, placed second to Russia. Hungary was third, followed by Sweden, Australia and Germany in that order. The future of the modern pentathlon in the United States depends in one way on the continued support of the U.S. Regular Army, which has exercised absolute control of this Olympic event for 60 years, since its beginning in 1912 at Stockholm. The Army operates a Training Center at Fort Sam Houston. Yet paradoxically the continued military control discourages, to some degree, civilian participation by clubs, colleges and individuals. The future prospects for U.S. Olympic teams are no longer West Point cadets and young Army officers. From 1912 to 1952 (40 years) U.S. Olympic teams in the pentathlon were ex-

114

clusively Army officers, almost always West Point graduates except for the 1952 team that included a private first class. Then West Point eliminated riding, replacing its horses and its great riding hall with calculating machines and closed circuit T.V. studios. It also withdrew from intercollegiate fencing and de-emphasized pistol shooting. Today an Army officer should be more interested in nuclear physics and rocketry, and few are required to know how to fence, ride or shoot a pistol.

As a result, the U.S. Army makes an all-out effort to find athletes among its enlisted and drafted personnel and make pentathletes out of them in order to maintain a tight control on this Olympic event. However, a pentathlete is best developed when in high school or as a freshman in college. The Army method either comes too late, or by the time the new pentathlon prospect becomes proficient he is ready to leave the Army. The present hopes of the United States rest principally on several civilian juniors and several former or temporary Army candidates, but top training facilities with top competition in each of the five separate sports is restricted to major centers of population, notably New York and Los Angeles. It is difficult to correlate with the military who insist on maintaining a training center at Fort Sam Houston. As a result of many factors, the Army control has become outdated, although its continued support and contributions are important. The showing of the United States at the 1967 world's championship in Stockholm, fifteenth out of 20 national teams, indicated that new blood and new ideas are needed.

Yet nothing was done about it, although at various times clubs have fielded modern pentathlon teams or athletes, supplying needed facilities or arranging for training in all five events. The New York Athletic Club contributed in the development, training and performance of our top man in the 1956 games, and that of one member of the team of the 1960 games and two of the team at Tokyo, one at Mexico, and the present U.S. national champion, but became discouraged by the tight Army control and particularly by the controversial selection of the 1968 team. It is apparent that this has handicapped U.S. efforts, for at Mexico the United States could have had the same, or a better team than its silver medal-winning team at Tokyo. Yet the U.S. team came in fifth at Mexico, later advancing to fourth because of the disqualification of Sweden from third place. Sixty-one

115

competitors representing 19 countries were entered, with 15 countries entering full teams.

For the first time in the Olympic games an athlete and his team were disqualified as a result of an alcohol test. A Swedish competitor reportedly drank a few glasses of beer to dull his nerves prior to his shooting, and reportedly exceeded the alcohol test limit fixed by a newly appointed Olympic medical board. However, police and medical experts agree that the test was actually inconclusive because the Olympic medics had held the blood sample too long. As the advantages of drinking before the shooting competition are well known to all modern pentathletes, and blood tests had been instituted by the International Modern Pentathlon Union prior to the 1968 games, there is grave question of the legitimacy of the ruling. However the Swedes accepted the ruling in a superior show of sportsmanship, especially considering that they are currently the principals of the world body governing this sport. In contrast, the Russians, who came in second in the team competition, violated written rules by having men spotted over the riding (jumping) course with stopwatches, signalling information on the jumps and the time to their riders. Although they were challenged and a number of witnesses gave testimony about an individual Russian rider, neither he nor the team was disqualified. The Hungarian team, composed of A. Balczo, Istvam Mona and Ferenc Tork, won, with the Soviet Union, France, the United States, Finland and East Germany coming in next in that order. The individual gold medal was won by Bjorn Ferm of Sweden. With the exception of Charles Richards, formerly of Indiana University and the NYAC, who came in seventh in the 1970 world's championships, the United States has no pentathlete of international caliber. On the other hand if Richards had trained in New York City to improve his fencing, he might have been a medalist in 1972.

CHAPTER XI

Rowing and Sculling

EDGAR THE PEACEFUL, King of England from 944 to 975 A.D., wrote an unusual page in the history of rowing when in 973 he launched an eight-man crew consisting of eight kings —including the King of Scotland—all of whom had sworn submission and allegiance to him. Edgar, as coxswain, sat at the stern, while the crew of kings rowed him down the Dee River from his palace in Chester to the nearby church of St. John. Because he was racing to his own coronation, the river banks were crowded with spectators.

The story of rowing, however, goes much further back, and to another corner of the world. The Chinese were the first to engage in the sport of longboat racing on rivers and tidal waters and to this day Chinese festivals include races of dragon boats, great shallow-draft boats seventy-three feet long propelled by twenty-seven oarsmen. Paddle and oar racing in Siam and Burma go back to the dawn of history, and there are records of races between state barges in Egypt in 6000 B.C.

The ancient Greek author Thucydides refers to a sculling boat, as do the Romans Cicero and Livy, and although crew racing and sculling were not recorded events in the ancient Olympics, boat races probably did constitute part of the Panathenaic and Isthmian festivals. Vergil describes a boat race in vivid detail.

However, 2,000 years later racing in oared craft had yet to be organized. Then, on August 1, 1715, a well-known comedian of the day, Thomas Doggett, posted a notice at London Bridge. This notice proposed a six-crew boat race from London Bridge to Chelsea for a prize and announced that the race would be held annually.

Since there were about ten thousand watermen on the reaches of the Thames River, it was more of a problem to select than to solicit contestants. The race was held, and has continued to the present day, supported by the proceeds of a sum which Thomas Doggett left in trust at his death to be administered by the Fishmongers' Company.

Thereafter river races were organized all over England— mostly on an informal basis. In America interest in crew racing resulted in the formation of several rowing clubs, and in 1834 the various clubs combined to form the Castle Garden Boat Club Association in New York, which sponsored the first organized boat races for six-oared shells on the Hudson River at Poughkeepsie in 1837. From this beginning crew races spread to the colleges, and the first intercollegiate Poughkeepsie Regatta was held in 1875.

However, it was not until rowing appeared in the Olympic games that the sport began to become popular all over the world. But if there was to be successful international competition, many obstacles had to be surmounted. In rowing there was not only the problem of standardizing the events to be contested—pairs, fours, sixes, eights—but also the problem of standardizing the equipment. Probably in no other

117

sport has there been greater progress in equipment, and it has been extremely difficult to keep competition athletic rather than technological.

First came Clasper, an Oxford inventor who, in 1845, designed an oarlock which was suspended out over the water from light iron brackets. This changed the position of the fulcrum; and the oar, being essentially a lever of the second class, could be more effectively stroked by the rower. This principle was immediately seized on by all crews in England and America and, later, throughout the world. Then came Matt Taylor, in 1856, with the first keel-less boat in England, an innovation that changed rowing style to its present form. In 1856 smooth sides to boats were introduced, and in 1869 the greatest improvement of all, that of Walter Brown—the sliding seat. It was used for the first time in 1872, at Henley in England, the center of modern oared-craft racing. The sliding seat was almost immediately credited with taking half-minutes to minutes off the time records of various courses.

The history of sculling, which goes hand in hand with rowing, took a different turn in the United States, Canada, England, and Australia, where sculling first attained popularity in the latter part of the nineteenth century. The sport took an almost exclusively professional direction. Professional scullers raced locally for purses ranging from fifty to a hundred dollars, with side bets many times higher, and some international match purses are said to have been more than $60,000. However, due to excesses and corruption growing out of its tremendous popularity, professional sculling disappeared after 1900, except for a mild revival in the 1920's.

The Olympics revived interest in amateur sculling and rowing, and spread the sport to countries in which it had not been known before. Not counting the regatta involving only boats of the Greek Navy and Greek rowing and sculling clubs at the 1896 Olympics, by the time the first Olympic crew races were held in 1900, all the improvements and features of today's shells had been generally adopted. After a period of experimentation with varying lengths, oarsmen of eight-man boats had settled on a length of about 60 feet and a width of about two feet or a little less. Sliding seats with a slide of fifteen to seventeen inches are the only kind ever used in modern competition.

The effect of the sliding seat in increasing efficiency cannot be minimized. Before the introduction of the slide, the oarsman's legs were used only to provide him with a means of

118

bracing his feet for the application of the back and arm pull. Now, however, by sliding his seat nearer to the foot brace, the oarsman is in a position to gain a greater amount of leverage on the oar and also shift the burden of the pull to his greatest source of power, the legs. In all other respects the technique of the stroke remains the same.

The first modern Olympics, the Athens games of 1896, presented rowing and sculling exhibitions, but no contests; but in 1900 the sport was represented by four competitive events on the program, including single sculls and pair oars, and fours and eights with coxswain. In the twenty years preceding this Olympic competition, rowing had caught the fancy of many European nations, and, in fact, it was the newcomers to the sport who took three of the first places. Nine nations participated. In the race for fours with coxswain, Germany triumphed, while Holland, represented by Brandt and Klein, won the pair-oar championship. Barrelet of France won the single sculls. The venerable United States Vespers Club won the eight-oar title. France won the unofficial all-around title.

The roster of victors in the 1904 Olympics was not very international, with the United States winning three events. The Atlanta Boat Club of New York rowed a double sculls demonstration, while the Sewanhaka Boat Club captured the pair oar without coxswain title against competition. In the eights, the powerful and consistent Vespers crew was without competition, and rowed a demonstration event. In the fours without coxswain, the Century Boat Club was victorious. The single sculls championship was won by Frank Greer, also of the United States.

At the 1906 Olympiad at Athens, the rowing was won by Italy, with Greece second, France third, and Belgium fourth. There were five events.

In 1908 Great Britain won the eight-oar race, the double sculls, the four-oar shell with coxswain, the pair oar shell without coxswain, and the single sculls—won, in fact, all of the four events included in that year's Olympics. Few points were made by anyone except the all-winning British, but the United States and Belgium tied for second and Canada and Holland tied for fourth in all-around rowing and sculling. H. T. Blackstaffe of Britain won the most popular event of the time—the single sculls.

In 1912 there were twelve nations in the rowing and sculling events. The all-around point scoring shows Great Britain as the world's champion in rowing and sculling, followed by

Germany, Denmark, Norway, Belgium, Sweden, Canada and Russia. The eight-oared shell event and the single sculls were both won by the British.

Following the World War I hiatus, the Olympics were resumed in 1920 at Antwerp, with competition for eights, fours with coxswain, pairs with coxswain, double sculls, and single sculls. The Naval Academy crew, because of its outstanding record during the 1920 intercollegiate season, was chosen to represent the United States, and embarked for Belgium with twenty-five men and their boat. On the same ship, the cruiser *Frederick,* were also the members of the Pennsylvania Barge Club, who were to seek the fours-with-coxswain title. John Kelly, the national rowing champion, entered in the single sculls, and Paul Costello, also a member of the Vespers Boat Club, were on hand in Antwerp for the double sculls competition.

The races that year were rowed on the main canal between Antwerp and Brussels. In the preliminaries of the eights, the United States defeated Belgium, Norway defeated Czechoslovakia, England beat Switzerland, and France won over Holland. The French team was drawn for the semifinals by the United States, and was defeated by eight lengths. England won her semifinal match with Norway, and so, for the championship, it was once again a contest between the two oldest rivals.

The English crew was the Leander Club crew, and the race started off with a furious pace of 42 for Leander and 40 for Navy. Navy soon dropped the stroke to a long, powerful 38, but England maintained a relentless 40 and soon had her shell three-quarters of a length in front of the United States. After about 1,600 meters of the 2,000-meter course, Navy picked up some distance on Leander, and at about the 1,850-meter mark the U.S. crew upped its 38 to match England's never-varying 40. The Leander Club had set itself too big a task, and the Americans won the race by a good half-length, shooting ahead of their opponents by about four feet every stroke at the finish. The time—6 minutes, 2 3/5 seconds—was a new world's record for 2,000 meters.

In the four-oar with coxswain, the Swiss team navigated the 2,000-meter course on the canal in 6 minutes, 54 seconds, establishing a new European record. The Pennsylvania Barge Club from the United States finished second, with Norway third.

There has probably never been a championship sculler more consistent than John B. Kelly was during those years immediately before and after the war, and the combination of Kelly and Paul V. Costello was invincible in the double scull championship. Despite the fact that Kelly had just rowed and won his single sculls championship thirty minutes before the race, he and Costello won over Italy, which was second, and France, which was third. When Kelly, father of Princess Grace of Monaco, won the single sculls, the Englishman in second place was J. Beresford, a popular oarsman who was to go on to make amateur and professional sculling and rowing history. The unofficial scoring on an all-around basis put the United States first, Italy second, Switzerland third, Great Britain fourth. In the finals of the other race, pair oar with coxswain, Italy held on to win after her two opponents had collapsed, after all three had been neck-and-neck 50 yards from the finish line.

Possibly the most romantic river in the world was the site of the 1924 Olympic crew races, for they were held on the Seine at the Argenteuil Basin, only several minutes from the Olympic stadium at Colombes, France. The 2,000-meter course was a straight line, and the French went to considerable effort to transmit standings during each race to a master scoreboard at the main stands a hundred meters from the Paris-Rouen railroad bridge.

John B. Kelly and Paul V. Costello of the United States again won the double sculls. The race was close and exciting, as the French combination of Stock and Detton led all the way in the final four-contestant match, yielding only at the very finish. Switzerland was third, Brazil fourth. In the pair oared shell, Holland won by defeating France in the finals by a half yard. England was third. Switzerland and Italy, finishing one-two, showed their mastery of the pair oars with coxswain, with the United States third. Brazil forfeited, and France came in fourth. Belgium was eliminated in the preliminaries. This event had not been held before 1924. Four oars without coxswain was won by Great Britain, with Canada second and Switzerland third. In the fours with coxswain, no less than twelve nations were entered. Switzerland won the final, France was second, the United States third, and Italy fourth. Thirteen nations registered for the eight-oar race, with ten actually showing up. England, Canada, the United States, and Italy qualified for the finals. The United States eight, the Yale University crew undefeated in two years, was a sensation, having won its preliminary heat in the fabulous time of 5 minutes, 51 1/5 seconds. Although, in the final, because of wind and roughness, the time of the winning U.S. team was slowed to 6 minutes, 33 2/5 seconds, the exceptional class of the crew was obvious. Canada, which came in second, was 16 seconds slower than the United States eight. Italy was third and England a disappointing fourth. Beresford of England won the single sculls, with W. Gilmore of the United States second and J. Schneider of Switzerland third.

The ninth Olympiad featured eighteen nations in rowing and sculling. Holland, the site of the 1928 Olympics, provided a course only 105 feet wide. This necessitated many heats and an extended period of tension for the record number of contestants in the various events. Nevertheless, the performances at this Olympiad were outstanding. The University of California crew, representing the United States, won the eight oar championships, but was forced to win five separate races to do so. The English eight was defeated in the finals, and Canada was awarded third place. The single sculls was won by an Australian, Bobby Pearce, whose father and grandfather were rowing champions of Australia, with Kenneth Myers of the United States second. Paul V. Costello raced without his two-time Olympic teammate, John Kelly, in the double sculls. However, Charles McIlvaine, a 24-year-old Philadelphia undertaker, showed himself a superb oarsman in Kelly's stead, and this event also went to the United States, with Canada and Austria second and third in that order. Italy, Switzerland, and Poland came in one-two-three in the four oars with coxswain, while England, the United States, and Italy finished in that order in the fours without coxswain. In the pair without coxswain, Germany beat England and the United States. Switzerland took the pair with coxswain, with France and Belgium next. The overall unofficial title went to the United States, with Great Britain, Germany, Italy, and Switzerland close behind.

In 1932 Los Angeles brought good luck to the United States team, which scored its most resounding unofficial rowing championship since 1904. There was plenty of competition, with thirteen nations represented. The British were second, with the Germans and Italians tied for third. The site of the competitions was the Long Beach Marine Stadium, about 30 miles from Los Angeles, and the final eight-oared race was like a page straight from a home-town movie script, for it was the University of California crew which represented the United States. Over 130,000 people were on hand for the final in this event, a titanic competition of great crews in superb physical condition. The California

122

crew, accustomed to the California sun, nosed out the Italians by a fraction of a boat length. Canada and Great Britain followed in order. Germany was successful in the four with coxswain, once again bringing despair to the desperate Italian rowers, who were beaten only in the last hundred yards, to lose by a foot. Philadelphia, which has produced many sculling champions, came through again for the United States with the double-scull team of Kenneth Myers and W. E. Garrett Gilmore. They defeated Germany, Canada, and Italy, who finished in that order, in the final heat. For the first time, Japan entered a crew.

Bobby Pearce of Australia won the single sculls again; he had not been defeated in almost six years. W. G. Miller of the United States and G. R. Doublas of Uruguay were second and third.

Another Philadelphia crew—Shauers, Kieffer, and Jennings (coxswain) won the first place for the United States in the pair oars with coxswain, Poland, France, and Brazil earning the next places. Jack Beresford (four-time winner of the Diamond sculls, single sculls, Olympic champion in 1924 and four-time Olympic regatta competitor) was one of the crew of the British four without coxswain which won in that event, defeating Germany, Italy, and the United States. Great Britain also won the pair without coxswain.

The eleventh Olympiad featured twenty-three nations in rowing, with Germany winning in a startling and impressive manner. Writing in the official 1936 United States Olympic Report, United States manager Henry Penn Burke reports: "Our previous opinion of German oarsmen was that the majority were mediocre and inclined to be overweight, but their oarsmen now are trained down like greyhounds. They don't look like the same breed at all." And they weren't. In the double sculls, they were second only to Great Britain, followed by Poland, France, the United States and Australia. Jack Beresford, one of the greatest oarsmen of modern times, competing in his fifth Olympiad, was one of the gold medalists in Britain's win in double sculls. Germany won the pair-oared shell without coxswain, beating out Denmark, Argentina, Hungary, Switzerland and Poland. Then they proved they could also win the same race *with* coxswain. This time, Germany set down Italy (fast becoming the perennial second crew of Olympic matches), France, Denmark, Switzerland and Yugoslavia. It was the same story in four-oar shells, both with and without coxswain. Germany was almost unbeatable, taking first in both these races. In fact,

123

with Pearce of Australia no longer an amateur and therefore not competing. Germany even won the single scull championship. It was the first time in 36 years that this race was not won by a sculler from the United States, Great Britain or Australia.

The finish of the eight-oar race in 1936 at Grünau remains the most exciting in the history of the games. The U.S. eight-oared crew was from the University of Washington, and eager to gain the fifth straight eight-oar title for the United States. And Italy was eager to avenge her heartbreaking loss at Long Beach in 1932, where she lost by a fraction of a boat length. Germany was on the verge of sweeping all the rowing events. When these three leading crews in the final flashed across the finish line, the thousands of spectators along the banks could not tell which of the three had won. Then the order of finish was posted: the United States first, Italy second, Germany third. Less than one second separated the first and third crews.

It was 1948 before the world was ready for the fourteenth Olympiad. London was the site, and for the crew and rowing events, this meant the most famous rowing course in the world—Henley. The games drew a record number of crews, with 27 countries represented. Racing had never been more international. The Italians overcame their old second-place jinx in many events, winning the unofficial overall championship for the first time since 1906. Italy won the four without coxswain, defeating Denmark and the United States in the finals. She came in third in the pair without coxswain, behind Great Britain and Switzerland, and second in the pair with coxswain, beating Hungary but losing to Denmark. Indeed, it was Denmark which showed the greatest improvement in these Olympics, taking one first place, two seconds, and a third. The University of Washington crew represented the United States in the four with coxswain, and beat Switzerland and Denmark. Another West Coast crew, the University of California, repeated the United States' win in the eight-oar shell for the sixth time. Great Britain was second and Norway third. Denmark's other second place was in the double sculls, won this time by Great Britain, with Uruguay third. The single-scull title went back to Australia, with Uruguay second.

The fifteenth Olympiad indicated the general growth of rowing and sculling in many ways. The number of nations entered in the rowing events in 1952 was a record—there were thirty-three nations competing for seven titles. Russia

124

made her first appearance on the water in Olympic competition since 1912 and, although she won only one event, showed great promise in many events. In the eight-oar shells, the United States took its seventh consecutive Olympic championship, with the Naval Academy crew as its representative. However, it was the Russian eight which doggedly hung on to come in second, 5 2/5 seconds behind the winner, a splendid effort in this first year of Olympic competition for the USSR. Australia was third, with Great Britain and Germany fourth and fifth. In the double sculls, Russia was also second, this time to Argentina. Uruguay placed third. France took first place in the coxed pairs, winning over Germany, Denmark, Italy and Sweden.

For the first time, the United States won the coxswainless pairs, beating Belgium, Switzerland, Great Britain, and France in the finals. Czechoslovakia took the coxed fours, with Switzerland second, the United States third, and Great Britain and Finland next. The 1952 Olympiad saw Great Britain fall into an uncharacteristic rowing slump, failing to place once, but coming in fourth in four races. Yugoslavia won the coxswainless fours, with Yuri Tyukalov of Russia, to the great surprise of the rowing world, winning the single sculls crown after two grueling races with Wood of Australia and John B. Kelly, Jr. of the United States. Wood came in second, but Kocerka of Poland was third. Thus Russia and Poland, using the experience and techniques of the British, Americans, and Australians, developed outstanding athletes to win, in their turn, single scull Olympic honors. Denmark was a disappointment in these Olympics, after such a promising showing four years before, gaining only one third place.

The United States won the over-all point score in rowing and sculling in 1952, with Russia second, France third, and Argentina and Czechoslovakia tied for fourth. Although the competition was unusually keen, there was great sportsmanship and unusual friendship shown by the contestants in rowing and sculling at these Olympics, especially between the Russians and the Americans.

The rowing events of the 1956 games, in which 249 oarsmen from 24 countries competed, were held on Lake Wendouree. Unfortunately, the regatta was held in unusually strong head winds for the first three days, which made conditions unpleasant and record-breaking impossible. The final day, however, was a perfect one, and a crowd of over 40,000 thronged the tree-lined shores of the lake. The U.S. team scored its greatest victory in the history of the modern

Olympic games, with three firsts, in the eight and both pairs; two seconds, in the four without and double; and a third in the single sculls. Canada won a first and a second place out of only two entries—the four without and the eight. In other words, North America won four gold medals with Russia taking the single and double, and Italy the four with coxswain.

As usual, the single sculls provided great excitement. With two new young champions, both barely out of school, 19-year-old MacKenzie of Australia and 18-year-old Ivanov of Russia, the final result was in doubt to the very last second. The Russian, per his usual custom, won the race from behind. With but 300 meters to go, the Soviet sculler sprinted past everyone, but could not pass MacKenzie. It was stroke for stroke, when suddenly MacKenzie weakened and Ivanov crossed the finish line. John B. Kelly of the United States, who competed in this event for the third time, was third, and Kocerka, the Polish champion and twice Diamond Sculls winner, was fourth. The Russians (Yuri Tyukalov and A. Berkutov) repeated in the double sculls.

Several innovations were noticed at the games as Italy rowed a weird combination of bow and stroke on the port-side, and Germany's second-place pair had its coxswain in the bow of the shell lying on his back.

In the eights, the United States was represented by the crew from Yale University. On the first day they were decisively defeated by both Australia and Canada, and as a result had to race in the repechage—a humiliation for a country that had won the Olympic "eights" seven times in succession. Because of this experience, they became desperate and did not lose again. In the final, a hot one, the United States won with Canada second and Australia third. The Japanese rode in an unusual boat which was about 12′ shorter than the normal 62′ shell. This reduced the overall skin friction on the water without losing anything in stability. A quick short stroke characterized their technique. While they raced well, with the lightest crew by 25 pounds per man, they had no chance in the head winds prevalent on Lake Wendouree.

The 1960 Olympic rowing on Lake Albano near Rome featured Germany's vaunted oarsmen and strong European crews. The four-oared crew without coxswain was the only winner for the United States. The Germans won three of the seven championships and an unexpected second in the single sculls while Russia won two gold medals, two silver and one bronze. The single scull super contest of MacKenzie of

Australia and Ivanov of Russia did not come off as the Australian was forced to withdraw because of illness. The highlight of the program was the victory of the German eight and the failure of the United States to win the finals of the eights—the climax race of the regatta. Canada, Czechoslovakia, France, the United States and Italy finished behind Germany in that order. The winning German crew broke the Olympic record set by a U.S. Naval Academy crew in 1920. This German crew was developed and coached by one of sports' wonder men, Karl Adams, a high-school teacher of Physics and former boxer of Ratzeburg. Shorter spoon-like oars and a new "interval" training method, both created by Adams, were used by this crew. Mr. Adams, who seems to be revolutionizing the sport and given half a chance may well be responsible for many years of German prominence in this sport and new records, explained to the author that:

(1) Oarsmen should be started very early and in skiffs.
(2) Oarsmen should practice in short practice distances controlled by the stopwatch.
(3) The back swing should be eliminated.
(4) The forward roll should be accelerated up to the turning point.
(5) The number of strokes per minute increased—over 40.
(6) Rowing equipment should be re-examined by arranging the outrigger along the pattern proposed by Angelo Alippi, changing the forms of the blades of the oars, trying to find the most favorable lever action (adjustable row locks).

Adams' coaching is purely an extracurricular activity from his teaching and he has had very limited backing and money. His story is one of very many that has contributed to the saga of Olympic progress. Will he be sought after by the United States, Canada or Australia and immigrate to some country to give it rowing supremacy for many years as the Italian fencing coach, Santelli, gave Hungary supremacy in saber for almost fifty years? Or will the sports-loving Germans appreciate the prophet in their midst and give him the opportunities and support he rightly deserves? If given a free hand and proper support, this man may give Germany many more Olympic gold medals. In any case his coaching, techniques and innovations contributed three gold medals and an "eight" to Germany's overall supremacy in rowing at the 1960 Olympic games and broke the U.S. string of eight victories since 1920.

In 1964 at Tokyo there were no new technical innovations, but some surprises. An upset victory by the U.S. eight-oared shell over the favorite Olympic defending German championship crew brought back to the United States a win in an event involving ten previous victories out of thirteen. The nine prized gold medals went to the crew of the Philadelphia's Vesper Boat Club, which has the unusual record of having never been beaten in Olympic competition from the time of its first gold medal in Paris in 1900. Only three members of the 1964 winning crew ever rowed in college; all the others learned as club members. Another U.S. win in the coaxed pair included F. Conn Findlay, rowing in his third Olympics, and his teammates Ed Ferry and Kent Mitchell. V. Ivanov of the Soviet Union won his third Olympic single scull gold medal. The United States outscored the Germans in points (30-27) for all-around supremacy in rowing, and the Russians also scored 27 points.

The 1968 rowing regatta was on the Xochimilco Cuemanco Canal, a beautiful basin that reflected the sunshine with enervating effects which, added to the high altitude, produced breathlessness and exhaustion. There were many surprises—for instance, the Harvard crew petered out, and for the first time in the modern Olympics the United States did not qualify for the finals. In fact, with the exception of 1960 the United States had won the eight at every Olympics from 1920 to 1964. The eight with coxswain wound up as follows: (1) West Germany, (2) Australia, (3) Soviet Union, (4) New Zealand, (5) Czechoslovakia, (6) United States.

Two gold medals in the rowing events went to East Germany, one to West Germany, one each to New Zealand, U.S.S.R., and Italy. The all-around winner was East Germany with 31 points. Three hundred ninety-four contestants were entered from 28 countries, according to the U.S. Olympic Committee records, although 350 competitors from 30 countries with 102 boats was the local official count, showing the difficulty in getting Olympic statistics. All that can be guaranteed, whichever figures are correct, is that there will be very little change at future games, notwithstanding innovations and new records, but the races described will be similar to the races described by Virgil almost two thousand years ago:

"Their bent arms churn the waters into foam,
The sea gapes open, by the oars uptorn.
With shouts and cheers of eager partisans

128

The woodlands ring, the shelter'd beach rolls up
The sound, the hills re-echo with the din."

CHAPTER XII

Shooting

SHOOTING IS the sport of marksmanship with small firearms.
It includes bulls-eye or silhouette-target shooting with the
pistol and rifle and shooting with hunting weapons at trap,
skeet, or running-deer targets. The shooting competition in
the Olympics has varied a great deal. Marksmanship is the
direct descendent and the modern counterpart of archery,
an earlier and less lethal form of warfare. Archery played a
major part in early human history, from the ancient
Pharaohs to the Spanish Armada in 1588. The English, although the greatest bowmen in the world, discarded archery
as obsolete in their defense preparations against the Spanish
invasion. Archery has just returned to the modern Olympics,
after being discontinued.

In the United States, competitive shooting dates from a
period shortly after the Civil War. The National Rifle Association, which grew out of competitions between various
units of the National Guard throughout the states, was organized in 1871. The first act of the organization was to try
to standardize the targets and distances. The N.R.A. is still
in control of the sport in the United States, governing competition in both rifle and pistol. An indication of the great
early interest in the sport can be found in the fact that a
championship held in 1872 at Creedmoor, Long Island, in
which a team of crack shots from Ireland participated, attracted 100,000 spectators, most of whom were taken from
New York to the ranges in special trains.

An even greater interest resulted from another international
match between the U.S. and the Irish teams, labelled the
greatest in the British Empire. This match was to be held in
England. This was also in 1871, and the United States
again won by a score of 957 to 921. Great rifle shooters at
the end of the nineteenth century enjoyed the same popularity
as top pugilists, baseball or football players of a later year.
Then a President's Annual Match was instituted in the United
States in 1901 and Congress, aware of the value of this sport
both for warfare and for keeping the peace, appropriated
funds and encouraged shooting competitions and marksmanship. The National Rifle Association continued in complete
control and conducted all national championships. The stand-

129

ard ranges for the small bore rifle were 50 feet, 50 yards or meters, and 100 and 200 yards. For high-powered rifle shooting the standard ranges were 200, 300, 500, 600, 800, 900 and 1,000 yards. For pistol and revolver the standard ranges were 50 feet or meters, 25 and 50 yards (outdoor). Our first official U.S. champions were: high-power, 1904, George Sayer; and small-bore, 1919, G.L. Watkins. As a result of this early interest in the United States in rifle and pistol shooting, when the modern Olympics began in 1896 the United States had some experience in competitive marksmanship.

Eight countries sent contestants to compete in this sport at the 1896 games in Athens. Twenty-eight years later, in 1924, 20 nations sent contestants to compete in the various shooting events at Paris, and fifty-six years later, in 1952, there were contestants from 38 countries—ten from the Western Hemisphere, twenty-two from Europe (including Russia and such smaller powers as Monaco), and six from Asia, Africa, or Oceania. Shooting with hunting weapons is popular in many countries widely separated, and is—partly for that reason—a difficult sport to standardize.

Shooting is one of the most complicated Olympic sports to follow. When one considers the pistol, one must think of revolvers, pistols, and target pistols, and one must also think of bulls-eye targets and silhouette targets, slow fire and rapid fire, as well as various distances or ranges. When one considers rifle marksmanship, one has to think of a wide variety of "free" rifles, military rifles, and sporting or hunting rifles and shotguns, miniature or small-bore rifles, slow fire or rapid fire (as well as slow-fire or rapid-fire types of targets and moving targets), not to mention distances or ranges. This very wealth of possible tests of skill has caused confusion in the sport for many years.

In the 1896 Olympics there were four shooting events: any-rifle individual, which was won by Orphanidhis of Greece; any target revolver, 30 meters, which was won by S. Paine of the United States; automatic pistol (25 meters) individual, which was won by Phrangoudhis of Greece; and revolver individual (25 meters), which was won by J. Paine, the brother of S. Paine, of the United States. In all-around rankings, the Greeks won the unofficial team championship.

In 1900 increased interest in the sport led to the inclusion of seven events: automatic pistol or revolver individual; pistol or revolver team; any target pistol, 50 meters; clay-bird shooting individual; running-deer shooting, single shot, individual; army rifle individual; and army rifle team. Although the Swiss won more titles, the French scored enough points to win the unofficial championship in shooting. There was no shooting at the 1904 Olympics.

In 1906 pretty much the same events were run off, but one more of them was doubled up as both an individual and team competition, making a total of eight events. The French won again.

By 1908, when Great Britain won the all-around championship, the number of events had been increased to fourteen, with clay-bird shooting individual and team, running-deer shooting individual and team, pistol or revolver individual and team, and rifle individual and team, army rifle individual and team, miniature rifle (or, as it is now called, small-bore rifle) individual and team, free rifle 50 meters, and rifle at odd distances.

The 1912 Olympic shooting events were won by Sweden, and in these competitions at Stockholm the number of events was increased to sixteen, pretty evenly distributed between the non-sporting and the sporting.

In 1920, for the first time, the United States won the all-around championship, although determining the winner was almost a job for an adding machine. There were nineteen events, and contestants from nineteen countries. There were both individual and team matches with rifle, pistol, and shotgun at various ranges.

At the 1924 Olympic games the military events were dropped and there were only ten events. This simplification indicated a tendency to standardize the shooting events. Twenty nations sent competitors, with the United States repeating its 1920 victory. Sergeant Morris Fisher of the United States won the any-rifle individual event in 1920 (and again in 1924) and he was the 1923 international world's champion in shooting. As in other sports, the Olympics had led to international competitions and world's championships between Olympics. A running-deer-shooting expert from Norway, Lilloe-Olsen, won the running-deer-shooting double-shot individual in both 1920 and 1924, and also helped Norway win the team championship in 1920—although the Norwegians were nosed out in 1924 by Great Britain. On the U.S. team was a 17-year-old named Dinwiddie, from Washington, D.C., who broke the Olympic record in the miniature rifle individual, only to come in second to Charles DeLisle of France, who shot 398 out of a possible 400.

There were no shooting competitions in the 1928 Olympics

because there was a conflict in the International Olympic Committee about the definition of an amateur in shooting. The committee members could not resolve their disagreements in time for the Olympic games and cancelled the shooting event. But at a meeting of the International Olympic Committee at Oslo in February of 1935, it was agreed to admit as eligible for competition any marksman who had not received a money prize for shooting since August 1, 1934.

The matter of amateur status again came up to plague the various committees in the Olympic competition, not only in 1928 but also in 1932 and 1948, the crux of this conflict being that since shooting is not a spectator sport there is no reason for any competitive shot to turn "pro" except as an exhibition shot for arms or ammunition manufacturers. It had been the custom in the United States, and in many other countries, to offer small cash prizes in shooting tournaments, but these prizes were not valuable enough to reimburse the winner for his expenses or his equipment and could scarcely place him in the class of a professional. However, the acceptance of even one dollar is sufficient, under normal Olympic rules, to make any marksman accepting cash prizes a professional. The Olympic rules, it was believed by the United States and certain other countries, should be interpreted to mean that any country could enter its best marksmen if it excluded exhibition marksmen actually employed by the munitions industry. Certainly most people agreed that the hundreds of competitive sharpshooters who had accepted past cash prizes as amateurs instead of medals, hams, or turkeys should not be banned from future competition. Most people also agreed that cash prizes should be banned in the future.

In 1932 shooting was back on the Olympic schedule, but in a very restricted way. Only small-bore or miniature rifle individual at 50 meters and figure shooting at six targets with a pistol were included. This abbreviated schedule of two events brought complaints from nearly every country, including the United States, that had competed in this sport in earlier Olympics. The influence of the military in the Axis countries was quite evident in the 1932 Olympics— Italy and Germany capturing the first four places in the pistol shoot, although the honors in the rifle competition, which wound up in a number of ties, were fairly well spread. Competitors from Sweden and Hungary tied for first, with the Swede winning the shoot-off; a Hungarian and an Italian

132

tied for second place, actually third, with the Hungarian winning the shoot-off. Italy won the unofficial team championship.

In the 1936 Olympic games a number of events that had been contested in earlier Olympics were reinstated. The unofficial team championship was won by Germany, with Sweden second, Denmark third, and France and Hungary following. The performance of the competitors in these Olympics was exceptionally good. The target pistol event, at 50 meters, was won by Torsten Ullman of Sweden, who broke the Olympic and world record (his record is still the world's record), making a score of 559 out of a possible 600. Erich Krempel of Germany was second and Charles de Jammonnières of France was third. The American who finished highest in the scoring, Elliott Jones, was sixth. The automatic pistol or revolver 25-meter event was won by two Germans; Torsten Ullman of Sweden, who placed first and broke the world's record in the other pistol event, was third. The miniature rifle at 50 meters was won by Willie Rogeberg of Norway, who established an Olympic and world's record by shooting 300 out of a possible 300; in second place was Dr. Ralf Berzsenyi of Hungary; Wladyslaw Karas of Poland was third.

There was general dissatisfaction expressed by many of the countries with the events chosen for championship competition. It was pointed out that, with the greatest shots of the world gathered for competition, it was ridiculous to have only two events in pistol and one in small-bore rifle, and that something like the old schedule should be brought back—so that the test for the Olympic championship would include a variety of events with all types of weapons.

The 1948 Olympic games, after a hiatus of twelve years, brought many nations together in the shooting competitions. Sweden won the unofficial all-around championship, with the United States second, Switzerland third, Finland fourth, Czechoslovakia and Norway tied for fifth, Peru (a newcomer) sixth, and Hungary seventh. Colonel Roy D. Jones was in charge of the U.S. Olympic pistol team for the third time, and Major General Milton A. Reckord was in charge of the U.S. rifle team committee, as he had been in 1932 and 1936. Teams from 22 nations participated in the shooting events in the 1948 Olympics. The free pistol was won by a Peruvian, with H. L. Benner of the United States tying for third. In the small-bore rifle competition at 50 meters, the United States placed first and second, A. E.

133

Cook and W. Tomsen being tied with 599 out of 600. In the rapid-fire pistol a Hungarian, K. Takacs, won, with Diaz Valiente of Argentina second and Lundquist of Sweden third. Torsten Ullman of Sweden, who won the 50-meter pistol in the 1936 Olympics, not only came in third in that event in 1948 but also scored fourth in the rapid-fire pistol. The free-rifle 300-meter competition was won by E. Grunig of Switzerland; second was Janhonen of Finland; third, Rogeberg of Norway. Swanson, the American who ranked highest, came in tenth.

In the 1952 Olympic games there was a better rounded program that included more events than had been included in many years. As a result of the better rounded program there was more interest, more competitors from more countries, and better performance. The events were: free pistol, 50 meters; silhouette, or rapid-fire pistol, 25 meters; free rifle, 300 meters; small-bore rifle, 50 meters; small-bore rifle, prone, 50 meters; clay pigeons; and running deer. The unofficial team championship was won by Norway, with Russia second, Hungary third, the United States fourth, Rumania fifth, and Canada sixth. Thirty-one nations—more than ever before—entered the Olympic shooting competitions. H. Benner of the United States won the free pistol 50 meters, the first win in pistol shooting for the United States in 32 years. He made a higher score than any other American had ever made. A. Jackson of the United States came in third in the small-bore rifle prone event. A nation new to the shooting competition—Russia—showed great promise. Norway was the only country to have two winners in 1952, the winners of single championships being the United States, Hungary, Russia, Rumania and Canada. Two Olympic records and one world's record were broken.

The shooting events in the sixteenth Olympiad produced many records despite unfavorable conditions throughout the entire competitions. Six of the seven events took place on a military rifle range at Williamstown, the seashore of a strip of land which juts out into Port Philip Bay on the southwestern outskirts of Melbourne. Despite a wind blowing in from the sea, only one record remained intact—the free pistol. Incidentally, this record was established in 1936 in Berlin by T. L. Ullman of Sweden, who was sixth in this competition and was still one of the world's greatest pistol marksmen. He has competed in three postwar Olympiads, placing in the first six each time.

As was expected, the Russians won. They captured three

134

gold medals, four silver and one bronze from the seven events in which only two entries per nation are permitted. In only one event—the clay pigeon—did they fail to gain at least one medal. Despite the overwhelming strength of the U.S.S.R., it is interesting to note that three of the seven events were dominated by marksmen of other countries. In the clay pigeon, the Italians took first and third; in the small bore rifle the Canadians took first and third; and in the silhouette pistol the Rumanians took first and third. G. R. Ouellette of Canada was the individual star of the meet. Although Ouellette broke the 1948 Olympic record of A. Cooke of the United States of 599 points, his score of 600 points was not accepted because when the range was measured the distance was found to be short.

The 1960 Olympic shooting was won by Russia which retained its supremacy in this sport, first gained in 1956. Russians won two gold, two silver and three bronze medals in six events. The United States won a gold medal—its first since 1952—in the rapid fire pistol with Captain William McMillan, USMC; also a silver medal and a fourth place. Sixty nations participated and three Olympic records were set. One interesting event, the running deer, was not held in Rome.

After two overall Olympic wins in 1956 and 1960, Russia was edged out of general supremacy in shooting by the United States in Tokyo in 1964. Two U.S. marksmen, two Finns, one Italian and one Hungarian won gold medals for shooting and set two world records and one Olympic mark. Lones Wigger, leading U.S. marksman from Carter, Montana, with a world record 1,164 out of a possible 1,200 won the three position small bore rifle event and came in second in the small bore rifle after tying Hungarian Laszlo Hammerl, the ultimate winner. Gary Anderson of the United States won the free rifle event with a world record score, while P. Linnosvuop of Finland set an Olympic record in winning the rapid fire pistol event. There was no running deer competition in 1964, although it is hoped that this event will be reinstated. In the meantime, the world record in this event is held by a Russian (1968). The 1968 Olympic shooting in Mexico resulted in a record number of competing nations and marksmen and many world's records, for Mexico is a country where the rifle, the pistol and the shotgun are regular equipment of the sportsman. In Mexico free men are allowed legitimate possession of firearms. Unfortunately illegitimate possession of firearms will always

135

be a problem, particularly since few if any honest people will be armed for self-defense if anti-firearm legislation becomes too difficult while criminals will carry firearms illegally. City police pistol permits in the United States currently handicap U.S. Olympic effort, although appeals usually result in leniency in the application of existing rules.

The shooting facilities at the Mexico Games in 1968 were superior in every way—both for the competitor, the organizer, the officials, and the spectators. The United States' showing was a disappointment, for after winning seven out of eighteen medals and the overall team title in 1964, the United States was out-shot and out-scored by Russia and Mexico. The U.S. divinity student, Gary Anderson, won another gold medal in the free rifle event, completing a seven-time world championship and winning a second Olympic gold medal, and also breaking his own world's record. The 21 medals in seven events were divided among 12 countries, four world's records were broken or equalled. Sixty-five countries entered 377 competitors (374 men, 3 women).

CHAPTER XIII

Swimming and Diving

MAN FIRST learned to swim either by instinct or by watching animals go into a swimming motion in the water in order not to drown. Just how far back swimming goes as a recreational or competitive sport is not known. Early mosaics and drawings in the Middle East show men swimming and using the "dog" stroke. The Greeks and Romans were able swimmers and divers. Plato stated that the man who did not know how to swim or dive was uneducated. History tells us that Caesar was a great swimmer, that Charlemagne was noted for his swimming stroke—which might have been the forerunner of the crawl—and Louis XI of France often swam in the Seine. It remained for the English, however, according to the records, to take up swimming as a competitive sport.

In 1837, in London, there were competitive swimming exhibitions and six swimming pools located in the city. In 1844 some North American Indians were brought over to London to swim in competition and they beat everyone, with an Indian named Flying Gull allegedly swimming the length of a 130-foot pool in 30 seconds. These Indians, it was remarked, swam in an "uncivilized" or "different" manner, while the "civilized" British swam the breast stroke. In the late nineteenth century, two great swimmers, Captain Matthew Webb, the first man to swim the English Channel, in 1875, and J. Arthur Trudgen, began to make swimming history. Trudgen, who had gone to South America in 1860, learned a stroke there from the natives which was a double overhand and which he made so famous it was named after him. However, Trudgen had failed to observe that the South American Indians kicked their legs, and therefore taught his pupils the double overhand but had them retain the scissor-like movement of the legs.

Although Trudgen should be credited with a great advance in the technique of swimming, the greatest step forward in the sport was wrought by the remarkable Cavill family, who introduced the Australian Crawl to the world. In 1878, Frederick Cavill, a competitive swimmer, left England for Australia, where he had six sons and built and operated swimming "tanks" and taught swimming. The Cavills studied the natives and finally found that their leg action involved a "kick" generating extra speed. The Cavills introduced this new method of swimming to the English in Australia and it became known as the Australian Crawl. Richard Cavill, the eldest son, went to England and used the crawl to win championships. He coached the British to many wins in international competitions. Another son, Sydney, came to the United States as a swimming coach and taught the crawl to America. He was swimming coach of San Francisco's Olympic Club for 25 years. In the United States, a man named Daniels, of the New York Athletic Club, had been using the Trudgen stroke, but on seeing the style brought to the States by Sydney Cavill, began to experiment with a kick timed to the stroking of the arms, with the result that he developed the American crawl of today.

This history of the early development of swimming is part of the saga of the earliest swimming competitions of the Olympics. The Olympic games, more than any other factor, accelerated the technical advancement and popularity of swimming as a competitive sport throughout the world.

The same Daniels represented the United States in the 1904 Olympic games, where he was third in the 50-yard dash, second in the 100-meter free style, first in the 220-yard free style, and first in the 440-yard free style. He broke all existing records and won thirty-three National AAU Championships, from 50 yards to the mile, and won four Olympic titles, reaching his peak in 1910, when he lowered his world's record for 100 yards to 54.8 seconds.

Before Daniels' time, the British had dominated swimming, with a slight interruption by Hungary. The 1896 unofficial swimming team championship of the Olympics went to Hungary, but by 1900 the English were in command again. In 1904, with the assistance of Daniels, English coaching, and the Australian crawl, the United States won the aquatic title, if diving events are included in the scoring. The 1906 and 1908 unofficial championships were won by Hungary and Great Britain respectively. In 1911 a Hawaiian, Duke Kahanamoku, arrived in San Francisco from Honolulu with a great reputation as a swimmer, and was eligible for membership on the United States Olympic team. It was immediately noticed that he was using the latest crawl stroke, and upon being asked who had taught it to him, he said that he had no teacher but that his people had been using this stroke for many generations, if not centuries.

The 1912 Olympic aquatic events were won by Germany. Many nations competed, and drew capacity crowds. The Hawaiian, Duke Kahanamoku, was the central attraction and individual star of the meet—breaking the 100-meter record of the famous Daniels, who had won this event in 1906 and 1908. G. R. Hodgson of Canada was the surprise winner of both the 400 meters and the 1,500 meters. An American won the backstroke, and Germany won the 200-meter and 400-meter breast stroke and the springboard dive. Australia won the 800 meter. The Swedes won the high dive and Great Britain repeated her 1908 victory in water polo. For the first time, women's swimming events were featured: the 100-meter, which was won by Fanny Durack of Australia; the 100-meter relay team, which was won by Great Britain; and the high dive, which was won by Greta Johansson of Sweden.

In 1920, for the first time, the actual swimming competitions were won by the United States. Our 1904 unofficial team victory had been due to two firsts, one second, and two thirds in diving. In 1920, however, eleven of the sixteen aquatic events were won by the United States, which in addition succeeded in winning seven second, six third, and eight fourth places. In five events the United States won the first three places. The most successful individual competitors were Norman Ross of Chicago and Ethelda Bleibtrey of New York, with three gold medals each, and Duke Kahanamoku of Hawaii, with two. The victory of the United States was overwhelming and unique. Sweden was second, England third, Australia fourth, followed by Belgium and Finland.

138

Despite the terrifically cold water—around 55 degrees—representatives of the United States established four world's records and six Olympic records. The American team included seven Hawaiians. In water polo, the temperature of the water was so low that many of the regular U.S. team could not play in successive games. Great Britain won, the United States taking fourth place.

The eighth Olympiad, held in Paris in July of 1924, presented to the world the greatest swimming and water polo teams ever formed in the history of American swimming. Duke Kahanamoku was elected captain of the swimming team, which won the team championship, and Hal Vollmer of the New York Athletic Club was chosen as captain of the water polo team. Evidences of the spread of swimming competition were seen at the 1924 Olympics, for a number of countries sent swimming teams for the first time—including Japan. The star of the American team was Johnny Weissmuller of the Illinois A. C. He succeeded in winning the 100-meter and the 400-meter free-style events, breaking the records in both. He also was anchor man on the victorious relay team, which also established a world's record, and played the final game of water polo, in which the Americans finished in third place. Al White of Stanford University won both the springboard and high fancy diving events. Warren Kealoha of Hawaii repeated his victory in the Antwerp games by winning the backstroke event in world's record time. Robert Skelton of the Illinois A. C. broke the world's record in winning the 200-meter breast stroke. The Misses Ethel Lackie of the Illinois A. C., Martha Norelius of New York, Sybil Bauer of the Illinois A. C., Elizabeth Becker of Atlantic City, and Carolyn Smith of Cairo, Illinois, won the 100-meter free style, 400-meter free style, 100-meter backstroke, fancy diving, and high plain diving, respectively. The head swimming coach of this successful aggregation was William Bachrach of the Illinois A. C.

The 1928 swimming competition brought together more nations and more contestants and produced better competition. The American team won. It was again coached by William Bachrach, ably assisted by Robert Kiphuth, who went on to achieve one of the greatest coaching records in America in any sport, leading Yale University to 445 dual swimming meet victories out of 457, from 1918 to 1953. The stars of the American team were Johnny Weissmuller, George Kojac, Buster Crabbe, and Ray Ruddy. Another great diving star was presented by the United States in the person of Peter Des Jardins of Miami Beach, who won both the springboard diving and the high diving. One of the greatest threats to American supremacy in diving was Simaika of Egypt, who placed second in high fancy diving and third in springboard diving. Simaika, although an Egyptian, owed much of his prowess in his sport to American diving experience and coaching; he had received all of his training and acquired all of his competitive experience in the United States. (The winners of the various events can be found in the appendix.)

In 1932 Robert Kiphuth became head coach of the swimming team, and took twenty-seven men swimmers and divers, eleven water polo players, and twenty women swimmers and divers to Los Angeles. The Olympic competition lasted eight days, with contests every morning and every afternoon. The seating capacity of the swimming stadium was 10,000, but there was a sellout for every session every day. The final point score, which was very close until the very last day, was Japan 87, United States 71. Japan won five firsts, four seconds, and two thirds. The outstanding individual performance in swimming was Buster Crabbe's winning of the 400-meter race. Jean Taris of France, the world's record holder at this distance, led by over ten yards at the halfway mark. Crabbe won in the last stroke by 1/10 of a second, in a new Olympic record. Crabbe now ranks with Daniels, Kahanamoku, Ross and Weissmuller in the history of American swimming. In the diving, the United States asserted its supremacy, with Mickey Riley and Dutch Smith winning first and second in both diving events and contributing 30 of the United States' 71 points.

The United States won the first points in water polo it had scored since 1904, finishing a very close third behind the German team. Hungary was first. One of the outstanding features of the swimming meet in Los Angeles was the extraordinary work of one of the officials. Captain Roy E. Davis of Chicago did not make one false start during the entire competition, an accomplishment believed unequaled in the history of Olympic swimming.

The American women swimmers did better than the men, in winning six of the seven events, losing only the breast stroke (to Australia). The U.S. women also won first, second and third places in both dives, and the women's final point total was 96. Australia and Great Britain tied for second place. The individual star of the women's swimming was Miss Helene Madison, who won two events, and was the only double winner for either men or women. It was a fitting climax to a short but remarkable swimming career in which she established new records for every free-style swimming event from 50 yards to a mile. It would be improper to omit mention of Miss Eleanor Holm, who won the 100-meter backstroke in 1932 but was prevented from representing the United States at Berlin in 1936, even though she was a member of the team, because she engaged in some champagne drinking on the boat en route to Europe. She later became a star in the entertainment world.

Great advances in swimming technique were made during the period 1932-1936 because there was a great deal of international championship competition. The United States accepted Japanese invitations for some of our star swimmers to visit Japan in 1934 and for fourteen American champion swimmers and divers to visit Japan in 1935. Japan, after its swimming victory in 1932, had made swimming a national sport, and the experience gained by the American groups in Japan was of great value.

Kiphuth was again head coach of the U.S. Olympic team in 1936. The swimming events were held in a magnificent swimming stadium, with a seating capacity of 20,000 and standing room for 5,000 more. The popularity of swimming was indicated by the fact that the stadium was sold out for all of the swimming competitions. According to the host nation, over 100,000 persons had to be turned away. There were some difficulties in the officiating, due to the fact that not enough persons could stand in a line facing the finish line, so that there was considerable confusion and the judges' placement rulings were not always in agreement with the photograph of the finish.

At this meet there was tremendous anxiety and nervousness on the part of Japanese and American swimmers, for both countries expected to win the overall championship. They had raced against each other so often that they watched each other carefully and did not perform up to their standards. This enabled, for instance, the Hungarian, Csik, who was in the outside lane in the 100-meter final, to swim his own race and win in very slow time, much slower than the record set by Peter Fick, who finished fourth. Jack Medica won the 400-meter race, establishing a new Olympic record and beating two great competitors, Uto and Makino of Japan. Flanagan of Miami, who had beaten Medica several times in the United States, swam a nervous and disappoint-

141

ing race. The Japanese were too much for the Americans in the 1,500-meter, and although Medica was able to win second place, the Japanese won first, third, and fourth. The Japanese also won the relay. The 200-meter breast stroke was another disappointment for the United States. Higgins of the United States, the American record holder, was beaten by two Japanese and a German.

In diving the United States again showed world superiority.

The swimming competition in the 1936 Olympics demonstrated a new high in world interest in competitive swimming, with thirty-six countries represented.

In swimming and diving combined, the United States nosed out Japan by a score of 43 to 41, with Hungary third and Germany fourth. However, if, as the Japanese claim, a swimming championship involves only points scored in swimming, with diving and water polo left out, then the Japanese repeated their 1932 win in 1936.

In water polo the United States was again disappointed, although it must be said that the caliber of water polo had been improving by leaps and bounds. The American team just could not compare with the Hungarian teams that had been winning this event. Hungary won again in 1936.

In the women's swimming the United States, by the slimmest of margins, continued its 16-year reign as top nation in this event. Holland was second, only 2½ points behind. The Dutch figured in every final and won all but one— the 20-meter breast stroke taken by Miss Maehata of Japan. The Dutch claim, quite reasonably, to have won in the women's swimming, for without counting the diving events, in which the United States won five out of six places, the Dutch women's team far outscored the United States. The number of wins scored by Holland's women swimmers was quite unexpected, although four members of the Dutch team held a total of eleven world's records. Willie den Ouden, who held seven world's records, placed only fourth in the 100-meter free-style, but was a member of the winning relay team. She did not swim up to her best form at Berlin.

After twelve years without any Olympics, the swimming competition at the fourteenth Olympics in London in 1948 showed a drop in the number of nations engaged in the sport —only twenty-one. The United States won, with plenty to spare, the overall aquatic competition, with 145 points for the men and 82 points for the women. The nearest nation in points for men was Hungary, with 30, and on the women's side Denmark, with 46. The men won all six championships, and only three of the eighteen men on the swimming team failed to reach the finals in their events. Of the eighteen swimming medals, the United States won eleven—six firsts, four seconds, and one third. In diving the United States won first, second, and third in the 3-meter springboard, and first and second in the high board. Robert Kiphuth was again coach of the U.S. team.

Notwithstanding this great showing in both swimming and diving, the United States' showing in water polo was, as usual, disappointing, and it was eliminated. The final placings in water polo were: first, Italy; second, Hungary; third, Holland; fourth, Belgium; fifth, Sweden; sixth, France; seventh, Egypt; and eighth, Spain.

In the women's diving the star was Vicky Draves, who won both diving events. Many people believe, however, that equally deserving of stardom was Ann Curtis, who won the 400-meter free-style after losing a very close decision in the 100 meter. Miss Curtis was credited with a great performance when she swam anchor in the 400-meter relay, overcoming a seemingly insurmountable lead and bringing the U.S. team an Olympic title.

At the fifteenth Olympic games in 1952 in Helsinki, forty-four countries, a new high, competed in the swimming, with the United States again winning the overall title. The coach of the U.S. team was Matt Mann of Michigan. The competition was keen, the number of competitors large, and the attendance a sellout. Every Olympic record was shattered during the meet. The U.S. men won six out of eight swimming and diving events and lost the other two by a whisker. France, with contestants in every one of the finals, was always a great threat. Japan qualified many men, but failed to win any gold medals for the first time in many years. Hungary, South Africa, Australia, England, Russia, Czechoslovakia, and Brazil—a newcomer—all showed capable performances, with their contestants reaching the finals.

The greatest thrill of the swimming competition at the 1952 Olympics, from the standpoint of the United States, was the 800-meter relay. The United States team—Moore, Woolsey, Konno, and McLane—did a tremendous job in beating a crack Japanese team which used the unusual strategy of swimming its men in reverse order of ability. McLane's anchor leg put the eventual winner, the United States, in the lead for the first time.

The impression of all who witnessed the meet was that

swimming technique, coaching, and performance outside of the United States were improving rapidly. The facilities of other nations are consistently getting better and their interest is increasing. It is not just one nation, like Japan, to whom we must look for our keenest competition. We must now take cognizance of tremendously growing strength in all the Scandinavian countries, as well as in France, England, Australia, South Africa, Italy, the Soviet Union and Brazil.

Major Sammy Lee of the U.S. Army broke an all-time Olympic record in diving by repeating with a championship in the highboard diving in 1952, having won the same event in the 1948 Olympics. This is the only double in this event in the history of the modern Olympics. In water polo a number of new nations participated, but Hungary, as usual, won. The order of finish after the winning Hungarians was: Yugoslavia, Italy, the United States, Netherlands, Belgium, the Soviet Union and Spain. There was an entertaining diversion in the swimming competition: The first act of France's Jean Boiteux after he had won the 400-meter freestyle was to assist his father out of the pool, into which the old man had impetuously leaped to tender his son prompt and effusive Parisian congratulations.

The women's team starred Pat McCormick, who won two gold medals in the two diving events, but in general the American women did not do as well as usual. The 100-meter freestyle was won by K. Szoke of Hungary; second was J. Termeulen of Netherlands, third J. Temes of Hungary. In the 200-meter breast stroke, E. Szekely of Hungary was first, E. Novak of Hungary second, H. Gordon of Great Britain third. The winners in the 100-meter backstroke were: first, J. Harrison of South Africa; second, G. Wielema of Netherlands; third, J. Stewart of New Zealand. In the 400-meter freestyle, first was V. Gyenge of Hungary, second E. Novak of Hungary, third E. Kawamoto of the United States. In the 400-meter relay, Hungary was first, Netherlands second, the United States third. In the diving events, as usual, the United States did well, taking five of the six places. Only M. Moreau of France, who took second place in springboard diving, kept the United States from scoring a clean sweep. But—except in diving—this was the worst showing of any U.S. women's swimming team in many Olympics.

Only thirty-eight nations competed in the 1956 Olympic games swimming tournament; but against this small entry the spectator interest was so great that the limited 5,500 seats in the swimming stadium were sold out months before the opening of the games, and capacity crowds attended even the practice sessions. Tremendous improvement in performance was shown by thirty-four swimmers who beat former Olympic records. The meet also featured the addition of two events: the 200-meter butterfly stroke for men and the 100-meter butterfly for women. George Breen of the United States broke both the Olympic and the world record in one of his heats, but could not reproduce his form in the highlight of the meet—the final of the 1,500 meter—and placed third to Murray Rose of Australia and Takashi Yamanaka of Japan. The United States won two gold, four silver and five bronze medals.

In the women's swimming, Australia took top honors. Dawn Fraser and Lorraine Crapp, both world record holders, alternated in first and second positions in the 100 and 200 meters free-style and participated in Australia's world record win in the 400-meter relay. Shelley Mann of the United States won the new 100-meter butterfly while Ursula Happe of Germany won the 200-meter breaststroke. Faith Leech, an Australian swimmer, age 15, won one gold (relay) and one bronze medal.

The men's diving was dominated by Mexico's Joaquin Capilla, who finally won the high board event after seven American wins in that number of Olympics. He was runner-up in this event in Helsinki. Capilla almost scored a double by winning the springboard championship, but an unfortunate slip during the first dive in the finals of this event spoiled his chances of gaining a gold medal and dropped him to third place. Pat McCormick of the United States, coached by her husband, Glen McCormick, repeated her Helsinki golden double; namely, winning for the second time both the springboard and high board Olympic women's diving championships.

The water polo competition was particularly excellent from a technical standpoint, although the final result was a foregone conclusion—Hungary successfully defended its title won in 1952. The Italian and the U.S. teams showed great promise for the future.

The 1960 Olympic swimming competitions were held in Rome's Stadio del Nuato, a new $1,500,000 aquatic stadium. Inspired by Jeff Farrell who left a hospital bed to make the team, the United States won six gold, four silver and three bronze medals and regained supremacy of this sport from the 1956 victor, Australia. Every Olympic record and three world's records were broken. A very controversial decision caused a furor in the 100-meter free style where John Devitt of Australia was awarded a protested but confirmed win over Lance Larson of the United States in the finals. Both men were credited with 55.2, an Olympic record. The three electronic machines in Devitt's lane all registered 55.2 while the three in Larson's registered 55.0, 55.1 and 55.1. While the first place judges may have not had good eyesight, the total votes of the first place and second place judges split evenly. Probably the most exciting race was the 1,500 meter free style where John Konrads of Australia outlasted his teammate, Murray Rose, in a thrilling finish. George Breen of the United States was third with Yamanaka of Japan next. Six men in the finals broke Breen's former Olympic record. The United States won both diving titles.

The women's swim competition matched the men's. Every Olympic record and four world records were smashed. The U.S. team was the best since 1932. Miss Chris Von Saltza, a teenager, was the star. She won three gold and one silver medal. A shapely girl from East Germany, Fraulein Kramer, broke a 40-year U.S. monopoly in the three-meter springboard dive. Americans had won this event eight times since the event was added to the Olympic program in 1920. Then to prove it was no accident, Miss Ingrid Kramer also won the 10-meter platform dive breaking a string of seven U.S. wins. Mrs. Juno Stover Irwin, a 31-year-old mother of four competing in her fourth Olympics, was fourth for the United States.

A wonderfully conditioned Italian water polo team, helped by cheering local fans, won the water polo championship. They upset the favored Hungarians who were further surprised by being nosed out of second place by the Russians. Yugoslavia was fourth. The U.S. team with an all-Californian squad finished seventh, the best American performance because the Rome competition was considered the best in Olympic history.

With the impetus of the Olympics, international competition has made for such tremendous strides in technique and performance that the times of the great swimmers of yesterday, whose marks stood for years, seem slow to us now. Robert Kiphuth has made an interesting tabulation to show the march of progress in swimming. It shows that in 1897 the 100-yard free style world's record was 60 seconds, set by J. H. Derbyshire of Manchester, England. Ten years later, in 1907, the world's record was 55.4, set by Charles M.

146

Daniels of the United States. Daniels, in 1910, lowered it to 54.8. In 1917 the world's record was 53.0, made by Duke Kahanamoku of the United States; in 1927 it was 51.0, set by Johnny Weissmuller of the United States; and the world's record made in 1952 by Richard Cleveland of the United States is 49.2 seconds. Official world's records of 100 yards were terminated in 1957 but U.S. Steven Jackman swam the distance in 1963 to an unofficial world's record of 46.5. In 66 years the record has been improved by 13½ seconds out of 60.

It is safe to predict that contestants in the near future, perhaps from countries still unheard from in swimming, may lower the 100-yard record to 42 seconds flat. Perhaps when this happens there will be fifty or more nations competing, with 100,000 people present and millions more witnessing the great event on television.

The Tokyo Olympic swimming and diving competitions in 1964 were held in a dreamlike installation called by many newspapermen "The Cathedral of Swimming." The National Gymnasium, constructed for swimming and diving, is like no other building in the entire world. Viewed from an airplane, it has the shape of a huge seashell. Viewed from one side it looks like a big bow, while a general look gives the impression of a huge pagoda. Inside it looks like a huge aluminum and concrete circus tent—large enough for a small airplane to fly in. There is not a single beam or column. The largest and highest suspension roof in the world is far above the audience and the swimmers and divers. In this surrounding, new world records were common. Australia's Dawn Fraser established a new record winning her third gold medal in her third Olympics in the 100-meter free-style. The United States won nine out of twelve men's events and seven out of ten women's events. The reason for this phenomenal performance is simple—start youngsters out in sports early. Give kids the facilities, the coaching and the incentive and they will enjoy themselves and become great.

Don Schollander of Lake Oswego, Oregon, aided by the expansion of the swimming program and closely similar events won four gold medals—a record in one Olympics. He broke a record every time he got into the pool in the Tokyo Cathedral of Swimming. The U.S. swimming team, 27 men (oldest 23) and 22 girls (oldest 19) set eleven world's records and won thirteen gold, eight silver and eight bronze medals in thirteen swimming events. Australia's Robert Windle won the 1,500-meter free-style in record Olympic

147

time while another Australian, Ian O'Brien, broke the world's record winning the 200-meter breaststroke in 2:27.8. Still another Australian, Kevin Berry, set a world's record to win the 200-meter butterfly. The U.S.'s Jed Graef also broke a world's record in the 200-meter backstroke.

Hungary reversed things at Tokyo by winning the water polo in the final which featured four Rome finalists. Yugoslavia was second, Russia third, with Italy, the Rome winner, finishing fourth. Dezso Gyarmerti was a member of the winning Hungarian team and in his fifth Olympic water polo final. This brought him his fifth medal: 3 gold (1964, 1956, 1952), 1 silver (1948) and 1 bronze (1960).

The women's swimming competitions at Tokyo were exciting, with the most popular swimmer, 15-year-old Sharon Stouder, who broke one world's record in winning one gold medal and was on two winning U.S. relay teams. Sharon finished one stroke behind Dawn Fraser's world record 100 meter. A U.S. 14-year-old, Claudia Kolb, was the first American ever to win a medal in the 400-meter free-style when she came in second to Russia's Galina Prozumenschikova.

The diving by both men and women was closely contested, with the final order being decided only on the very last performance of every contestant in each of the four events. The U.S. representatives won the two men's events and one of the women's, and Germany's Ingrid Engel won the springboard dive. Among the most enthusiastic spectators, special guest of the Japanese Organizing Committee, was one of the greatest swimmers of yesteryear—Duke Kahanamoku of Hawaii—since deceased.

The 1968 swimming and diving competitions expanded to 34 events from 16 in 1952—it more than doubled in four Olympiads—and was held in the Alberca, a specially built swim center in Mexico City. The women's free-style events were all won by U.S. girls who won four silver medals as well. After a 36-year wait, Jan Henne of the United States won the 100-meter free-style although Dawn Fraser's 1964 world's record was not equalled. The U.S.'s Debbie Meyer won three gold medals and could have won four. The ladies' diving produced some of the greatest performances ever seen in the Olympic games with the U.S.'s Sue Gossick fourth at Tokyo, winning the springboard event, while Milena Duchkova of Czechoslovakia took the platform diving honors. As a nation the United States, with the sudden expansion of events, won twenty-three gold medals, fifteen silver,

148

and twenty bronze in the water, taking advantage of the great increase in swimming events. However, progress was noted especially in the countries who have found that in swimming, training should start almost in childhood. The Australians, South Africans (kept out of the Olympics for political reasons since they had affirmed any and all races would be eligible and welcome on their team), Canadians, Russians, French and Mexicans showed great improvement in swimming. Michael Wenden of Australia, Mike Burton of the United States, Roland Mathes of East Germany and Charles Hickcox of the United States won two gold medals each, Hickcox adding another gold medal in a relay. Don Schollander although on one gold medal relay team failed to live up to his great name in swimming but wrote a book after the Mexico games in Yale tradition claiming they almost did not come off "because of many errors in management." Fortunately, the Olympic games were never threatened by anything that occurred at Mexico notwithstanding Don Schollander's disappointment.

In the men's relay races the United States made a clean sweep and continued its tight hold on springboard diving as Bernie Wrightson was the eleventh U.S. gold medal winner in this event in the last eleven games (1920-1968). But the platform diving was won by Klaus Dibiasi of Italy.

The water polo tournament although not well attended was worthy of more attention as the games were closely fought and exciting. The key game of the tournament produced a startling upset when Yugoslavia defeated Russia, matching the last-minute Yugoslav triumph over the Russians in basketball. The final rankings in water polo were: 1—Yugoslavia, 2—Russia, 3—Hungary, 4—Italy, 5—United States, 6—East Germany.

CHAPTER XIV

Team Games

1. BASEBALL

ALTHOUGH BASEBALL is known as the "great American game," it had its roots in England and is said to have been played there as early as 1744. This was probably a form of the game of rounders, which was popular in West England at the time. Early British settlers in America brought this pastime with them, and there is evidence that soldiers and Princeton students played a form of the game in New Jersey long before Abner Doubleday first set up teams to play at Cooperstown, New York, in 1839. However, the first formal teams organized were formed by the Knickerbocker Baseball Club of New York. At this time, Alexander Cartwright, Jr., set up standard rules of play and the first game with the new rules was played at Hoboken, New Jersey, in 1846 between the Knickerbockers and the New York Nine. By 1858 there were so many baseball teams in New York that they grouped together into the National Association of Baseball Players, and by 1860 the game had spread all along the Atlantic seaboard. The Civil War then carried it further and by 1869 the first professional team was organized—the Cincinnati Red Stockings—and the game was on its way. It spread to practically every town in the country. Sunday afternoon games between local teams provided recreation for the community and soon became a symbol of the American way of life.

The movement to develop the sport in other countries began when other athletic teams participating in the Olympics were asked to demonstrate this American game which was gaining so much popularity and was being enjoyed by so many people. In 1928, at Amsterdam, the American soccer team played an exhibition game of baseball, which excited the interest of many Europeans, but it was not until the 1936 games that baseball got its real international push. The baseball demonstration that year was no spur-of-the-moment affair. Germany had requested that the United States present a baseball game as a demonstration and the United States Baseball Congress had asked all colleges and baseball commissioners to select the outstanding players in their territories.

More than 125,000 people came to see the Berlin game— the largest attendance of any professional or amateur baseball game. Leslie Mann, the manager of the team, gave a series of lectures on the technique of the game for teachers and athletic coaches of other nations. So much enthusiasm was generated that the lectures were printed overnight in various languages. The Japanese introduced the game on a wide scale in their country so that they could participate in a baseball tournament at the next Olympics. The sport spread so rapidly in Japan that it is now practically the Japanese national sport.

Perhaps the most important result of the Berlin exhibition was the organization of an International Baseball Congress, with no less than twenty-one countries represented. These countries agreed to hold a baseball tournament at the next Olympics, scheduled for 1940. These Olympics were, of course, never held.

During the war years baseball did not have much chance to spread throughout the world—though armed services teams did compete overseas and excited a good deal of interest—but in 1952 the United States was again asked to demonstrate the game at the fifteenth Olympiad. The games that year were held at Helsinki, and the Finns were most enthusiastic. They and other Scandinavians had developed their own version of baseball called "pesapallo," which they also demonstrated, but baseball leagues of the American version were growing and functioning on a wider scale throughout the world. Foreign countries were impressed at hearing about the physical and recreational good resulting from the interest of youth in baseball. In the United States alone four youth leagues enrolled over one million players between the ages of eight and seventeen in one year, and championship games among their teams drew crowds of over 40,000.

The Pan-American games, another outgrowth of the Olympics, held by the nations of the Western Hemisphere every four years between Olympics, featured baseball as its most important team game. In addition, baseball drew more interest and spectators at the first two Pan-American games—the first in Buenos Aires in 1951 and the second in Mexico City in 1955—than any other event. Cuba defeated the United States in the final game to win in 1951, and the Dominican Republic won in 1955. Cuba also won in 1959 and 1963. Then finally in 1967 at Winnipeg for the first time a U.S. baseball team was crowned as the Pan-Am champs.

Baseball was on exhibition again at Melbourne, but not at Tokyo, notwithstanding its great popularity in Japan. But someday it may become the great team game of the Olympics, and arrangements for the use of the main stadium before or after the track and field events will be in order. The future may well bring hotly contested, well-attended intra-continental eliminations with a final of four teams in a sudden death tourney of four games to determine first, second, third and fourth places, witnessed by over 200,000 fans per game. Perhaps these Olympic baseball games will be broadcast around the world by television as sports, gaining strength everywhere, will be on the march in the direction of common understanding and world peace.

151

2. BASKETBALL

Basketball is probably the only game in Olympic competition that has strictly American roots, and differs from most sports in that it was deliberately "invented." Credit for the game is given to Dr. James Naismith, who, as an instructor at the famous YMCA College in Springfield, Massachusetts, tried to think of some kind of competitive game that could be played indoors, still be exciting for the players, and afford practice in teamwork. He had some form of soccer in mind and in 1891 brought a group together to try out his new game. When it came to deciding what kind of goal to use, into which the ball could be thrown, he thought of an elevated box and asked the superintendent of buildings for some old crates. Crates not being available, he was given two peach baskets, which were fastened to the gymnasium balcony—and the game of basketball was born. The problem of dislodging the ball when a goal was made from the floor was solved by knocking out the bottom of the basket. The sport caught on immediately. Twelve of the thirteen rules that Naismith laid down are still basic, although the game itself has vastly improved. It was picked up in schools and colleges in the United States, particularly along the Eastern seaboard, and by 1940 was popular in over seventy-five countries of the world.

Although there was a demonstration game of basketball in the 1904 Olympic games in St. Louis, there was no formal Olympic competition until 1936. In the Berlin games, twenty-two nations entered the basketball competition, more than competed in any other team event that year. The American team won, with Canada placing second and Mexico third. Poland was fourth, the only European country to place among the top six teams. The American team members averaged over 6′ 3″ in height (two members even towering 6′ 8″), which must have had an overpowering psychological effect on the other teams. The U.S. team was composed mostly of members of teams that had competed in the AAU national championships. Dr. Naismith, the originator of the game, attended the Berlin Olympics.

The next Olympic games were held in 1948 in London, and basketball was again part of the program, with twenty-three nations represented. The sport had spread rapidly throughout the world, and before World War II there were twenty million players and official rule books had been printed in over thirty languages. By 1948, basketball in the

United States had achieved such popularity that as a result of a series of exhibition games the Olympic team, after paying all training expenses, was able to contribute $75,000 to the Olympic Committee. In the actual Olympic games in London, the team from the United States was composed of five members from the Phillips 66 team and five from the University of Kentucky. The United States again showed its basketball supremacy.

At Helsinki in 1952 the United States maintained its undefeated record in basketball against the teams of twenty-two other countries. However, it was obvious that the competition was going to become increasingly strong. The international rules were different from the American rules. Even the ball was different. It was not perfectly round, but was made of eighteen pieces of leather put together in a rather lopsided fashion, which made it less suitable for dribbling and long shooting. Because of the undefeated position of the United States in this sport, everyone was out to try to beat the American team. The tournament in 1952 attracted great crowds, with the United States having its first really tough game, against Uruguay. However, Bob Kurland—a 7' 1" player, who had also been on the 1948 team— scored 21 points and the United States won, 57-44.

The U.S. team played the team from Russia twice, and so many people wanted to see these two games that they had to be moved to a larger hall, and even then thousands of people were turned away. The Russian team had been undefeated in 900 games with various local teams in Russia and Europe prior to the Olympics, and expected to win. The first game was not a close contest, the United States winning by a score of 86-58. In the second game, the Russians imitated Brazil, which had given the United States a tough game by purely defensive playing and held the U.S. team to a score of 26-24, which was much closer. At half-time the United States' lead was only two points, 17-15, but the Americans finally won, 36-25. The final standing of the teams was: United States first, Russia second, Uruguay third, and then Argentina, Chile, Brazil, Bulgaria and France.

It is believed that the 1956 Olympics has popularized basketball in Oceania, Asia and Africa, so that future tournaments will include teams from all over the world.

The Olympic basketball tournament at Melbourne established one outstanding fact; namely, tremendous progress has been made in basketball all over the world and American superiority in this game will be severely tested from now on. Fifteen teams from fifteen countries were entered. The final rankings were: first, United States; second, U.S.S.R.; third, Uruguay; fourth, France; fifth, Bulgaria; sixth, Brazil.

The basketball tournament at Rome in 1960 broke all past records in interest, number of spectators and the quality of the competition. Probably the greatest basketball team in Olympic, if not world, history swept through eight games by margins of 24 points or more to maintain the United States' all-time Olympic supremacy in the U.S.-originated sport. Of the twelve men there were two at 6′ 11″ and three at 6′ 8″. In the three final games the United States defeated the Soviet Union 81-57, Italy 112-81 and Brazil 90-63. The Russians were second, Brazil third. All basketball experts seemed unanimous in labelling the U.S. team the best, the most explosive, the most terrific team ever assembled. Every man on the squad was a star.

The U.S. basketball teams at the Olympic games had the record of never having lost a game in what, of course, is an American game recently developed in the United States. At Tokyo the U.S. team won again. Only the Yugoslav team, which was defeated 69-61, gave the U.S. team any trouble. In the final contest the Soviet Union was defeated 73-59 by a U.S. team (squad of 12) that averaged 6 ft. 5½ inches in height and 204 pounds in weight. The U.S.S.R. was second, Brazil third, and Puerto Rico fourth. The stars for the winning team were: Lucius Jackson, Pan Am University; Jim Barnes, Texas Western; Bill Bradley, Princeton; and Jerry Shipp of the Phillips Oilers. Once more experts evaluated this team as the best ever, but could not prove it.

The Mexico basketball tournament was, as is usual in the case of the Olympic games the best, the most successful and had the greatest attendance ever. Large crowds packed all 72 games in a round robin competition. The Palacio de los Deportes was jammed mornings, afternoons and evenings with 25,000 persons per session. Although the U.S. team could have been stronger if it hadn't been for the absence of such great college stars as Lew Alcindor, who became a pro before the games, it was as usual a well-balanced and smooth machine with players that were tall in size and ability. Coach Henry Iba in four weeks moulded a faultless aggregation. Captain Mike Silliman from West Point was a great leader, and together with Joseph White of Kansas University and Spencer Maywood of Detroit, he welded together a well-motivated and irresistible force. The surprise of the

154

tournament was the defeat of the Russian team by Yugoslavia in the last four seconds of their game. The final standing: first, the United States; second, Yugoslavia; third, Russia; fourth, Brazil; fifth, Mexico; sixth, Poland.

3. FIELD HOCKEY

Field hockey is said to be the oldest game in the world played with a ball and stick, and according to most historians had its roots in Persia around 2000 B.C. It is further known that the ancient Greeks played a game with a ball and a stick which resembled hockey.

Centuries later the game appeared in France under the name of "hoquet" (which was the French word for a shepherd's stick) and was played from time to time during the Middle Ages. Eventually it made its way across the Channel to Great Britain, and the word was anglicized to "hockey." At one time the game was outlawed in England, along with practically every other sport except archery; archery seemed to the English to be the only practical means of training young men to be soldiers.

The present game of field hockey was developed in England around 1850 from the crude French game. The rules varied from time to time and underwent many changes until 1883, when the Wimbledon Hockey Club of London formulated new rules which made field hockey the fast, exciting game that it is today. Interest spread very quickly throughout England, especially by means of school and college competition. Because it was a game that was not dangerous and could be played only as fast and as roughly as the individual teams desired, women took it up, and as early as 1887 it was considered England's national sport for women, and has retained that status ever since.

In fact, the game was introduced in the United States by an English hockey enthusiast for women. Louise Robert, in 1926, was an English teacher at a girls' school in Connecticut, and she interested Henry Greer of Rye, New York, in the sport. Greer, in the years to come, was to coach every American Olympic team, and at that time he tried to arrange hockey matches among men. He wasn't successful at first, but persevered until, in 1928, formal matches were arranged and the sport began to catch on in various schools.

In the meantime, due largely to British enthusiasm for the sport, field hockey received a tremendous spark from Olympic competition. As early as 1900 it was played in the Paris

155

Olympics, but each visiting team was matched against one from the host country and no official champion was determined. It was played at the Olympics in 1908 and again in 1920 on a championship basis, and both times the teams from Great Britain won. During the latter part of the nineteenth century and the first part of the twentieth century British Army officers and British Army teams had introduced the sport in India and it soon became the national sport of that country, with thousands of teams and matches. In 1928, in the next Olympic hockey tournament, India won the field hockey championship and held the title until 1960, consistently producing the greatest hockey teams in the world. Their fast, sure playing is partly due to a development of their own: they shortened the toe of the stick, so the player can turn it over for reverse play without relaxing his grip. This slight refinement in equipment brought greater flexibility to the play, and eventually it was adopted by most European countries in the hope of wresting the championship from India.

In 1932, for the first time, the United States sent a team to compete in Olympic hockey. Although it came in third and actually managed to score a goal against the great Indian team, they were, of course, as green as the grass they played on. The Indian team, on the other hand, was so good that Los Angeles sportswriters voted the showing they made in the Olympics the most outstanding exhibition of skill in any sport.

In the 1936 games at Berlin, although India easily retained her supremacy, the German team put up a very good fight. The Germans had developed a hockey game combining the best features of the English and Indian methods of play. The U.S. team, with many players back from 1932, showed great improvement. Japan, Hungary, Afghanistan, Denmark, Holland, France, Belgium and Switzerland also participated.

At the Olympic games in 1948, in London, hockey teams of seventeen countries competed for the world's championship. India defeated Great Britain in the final match, 4-0. While the U.S. team did not fare well, it toured Europe and gained valuable experience.

Although field hockey has been played by men in the United States for about thirty years, at the present time the competition is limited to only nine clubs along the Atlantic Seaboard. The United States started competing in this event in the 1932 games, but dropped out in 1952. Unfortunately, in the 1956 competition the United States had the bad luck of drawing a very tough first pool and was eliminated early. The final result was never in doubt with India winning its sixth successive Olympic title. Pakistan was second, Germany third, and Great Britain fourth.

After six straight Olympic victories India was defeated by Pakistan in a close final game 1-0 at the 1960 games in Rome. Pakistan had been edged out 1-0 by India at Melbourne four years before. Spain, Great Britain, Australia and New Zealand finished in that order behind India.

At Tokyo, India blanked Pakistan 1-0 in the final game and regained the Olympic title it lost to Pakistan in 1960. Australia was third, Spain fourth, Germany fifth, and Kenya sixth.

The Mexico City games of 1968 marked an unusual termination of a country's almost habitual supremacy in a sport. India, which had won seven Olympic titles and many second place awards failed for the first time in more than forty years to reach the finals. Australia, on the other hand, had come up in this sport and earned a second place, improving on its third position at Tokyo. Pakistan had a team accustomed to playing at high altitudes, a combination of Asian techniques and European tactics, and a great all-time star in Abdul Rashid. It won nine games out of nine, with twenty-six goals as against only five scored against it during the entire tournament. One incident reportedly resulting from the players' getting younger and the officials' getting older was the Japanese team's walkout and abandonment of the tournament in protest over a decision by a British official. There is no question that Olympic hockey bears no similarity to the original schoolgirl's game, but has developed into a tough, ruthless, all-out contact game with an almost professional type of packed defense, and man-to-man coverage. The final top rankings were: first, Pakistan; second, Australia; third, India; fourth, West Germany; fifth, Holland; sixth, Spain.

4. SOCCER

Soccer is one of the many offshoots of ancient football, a game as old as history itself; there is evidence that football games were played in both Babylon and early Egypt. In the Sixth Book of Homer's *Odyssey* is a specific allusion to football. The early Greeks referred to the game as "harpaston" and from all indications it was very similar to modern Rugby football. The game of harpaston was the

157

prime means of training the Spartan warriors, and with the growth of Spartan culture the game was widely played in Greece and later spread to the Romans. Many detailed descriptions of the Roman game of football, startlingly like our own game, can be found in the works of Julius Pollux, an Egyptian sophist of the second century.

With the advent of the barbarians and the fall of Rome, football almost disappeared in the confusion and chaos of the troubled Dark Ages. However, the Augustan game was played throughout Italy until the Middle Ages, and was revised in Florence as late as 1898. It was one of the few games which lived through the Middle Ages.

Throughout the Middle Ages, a new Italian form of the game was played, called "calcio." This game was very similar to the Greek harpaston. However, the most fertile field for the development of football was England. The Roman legionnaire brought the game of football with him fairly early, and the Anglo-Saxon took to the game and developed it rapidly. Towns and even countries played against each other.

When Edward II was king, football was popular in London —but unpopular with merchants whose windows were broken, and with parents of sons who were hurt playing the game. It was a primitive, rough, and almost brutal game, and in 1314 things were so bad that Edward II forbade its being played.

In the next century, its tremendous popularity among the people kept the game alive, and it survived the edicts of a series of kings and queens and remained the favorite sport of both the people and soldiers of England to the beginning of the seventeenth century. Several new types of football games were played, which were not as rough as the original game. These developed into Rugby and, about 1870, association football, which is also known as soccer. Largely through the influence of the military, the standardization and development of the game was accomplished during the Crimean and Colonial wars of the early nineteenth century. Soccer had a small following in the United States as a result of English influence, but it wasn't until Olympic competition drew international attention to the sport that it reached any great height of popularity throughout the world.

In the early years of Olympic soccer, beginning in 1900, the competition was mostly between European countries, with Great Britain usually the winner—except in the 1906 Olympics, when Great Britain did not send a team and the Olympic championship was won by Denmark. In 1912,

Denmark still showed great strength, but finished second to Great Britain.

In the 1920 games at Antwerp, two comparative newcomers at the game took over the star roles. Belgium defeated Czechoslovakia in the finals.

In 1924, the United States sent its first soccer team to compete in the Paris Olympiad. The United States defeated Estonia, 1-0, in its first match, but was eliminated by Uruguay, 0-3, in the next round. Uruguay went on to win the world's championship, with Switzerland second, Sweden third, and Holland fourth.

George Burford, who trained the U.S. team in 1924, took over the job of preparing for the 1928 games in Amsterdam. There the United States drew Argentina as its first opponent—an Argentine team which had recently defeated Uruguay in the South American championships. It is to be noted that even in team sports the Olympics inspired international competition and continental and world's championships between the years of the games. The increase in the popularity of soccer is attested to by the fact that there were twenty-one teams from twenty-one nations present to compete for the Olympic title. Uruguay won, with Argentina second and Germany third. After the Olympics, the U.S. team toured Europe and gained valuable experience, and spread the message of friendly competition and sportsmanship far more than if the United States had paraded its superiority in its own specialties.

In 1932 the Olympic games were held at Los Angeles. Unfortunately, soccer was not included in the program. This was not because the United States desired to exclude it, but because most of the countries could not afford to send the large groups necessary to field soccer teams on such a long voyage.

In the 1936 games in Berlin, the Italian soccer team, which had recently won the world's championship, won the Olympic title, defeating Austria in an exciting overtime match, 2-1. Austria was second, Norway third, and Poland fourth. A total of sixteen nations had teams in this championship, including China. The United States, for the first time, showed definite class. It was eliminated by Italy, but in a very close game which ended with the score 1-0. Experts agreed that the Americans might have been the second or third strongest team but were unlucky in drawing the winner in the first round.

In 1948, American interest in soccer had spread widely

159

and there was considerable competition within the United States. Over 5,000 soccer players participated in the pre-Olympic trials, and it was believed that the United States had a chance to win its first Olympic medal in this sport.

The 1948 Olympiad at London included a soccer tournament of eighteen nations, and for the first time the soccer championship was won by Sweden, with Yugoslavia second, Denmark third, and Great Britain fourth. The United States team, perhaps because of overconfidence, was eliminated by Italy in an early round. The team made a post-Olympic tour of Ireland and Norway and, returning to New York, played the national team of Israel, defeating it twice.

Between the 1948 and 1952 Olympics, soccer seemed to make greater progress throughout the world than ever before, particularly in Latin America. World's championships and international meets, which had grown up as a result of the Olympics, became so important, especially to Latin America, that the world's largest stadium was built in Rio de Janeiro in time for the 1950 world's championship in soccer. This stadium, one-half mile in circumference, held the record-breaking crowd of 199,855 people for the final game of the championships. This showed to what extent the Olympics had spread soccer and an interest in the game throughout the world. This stadium should be impressive even to Americans, who seem to believe that they have the greatest audiences in the world for sports events. Brazil is bidding for the Olympic games, and this stadium may well be the site of an Olympiad in the future.

The 1952 Olympics at Helsinki featured twenty-five nations in the soccer tournament. Russia entered a team for the first time. Italy, as usual, proved a jinx for the U.S. team in the early rounds, although in exhibition games after the regular competition the United States scored wins over Finland, India, and Brazil, and the national champions of Finland, the Kotka Workers Club. Experts commented that the individual American players were now very definitely up to the standard of those in other countries, but that team coordination and strategy were still not up to the international level. The results of the 1952 games were as follows: first, Hungary; second, Yugoslavia; third, Sweden; fourth, Germany.

The future of soccer as a team game on the Olympic program is secure and within the next few Olympiads every one of the Latin American countries will send strong soccer teams to the games to compete against teams from the rest

160

of the world. With improved, faster, and cheaper means of transportation, team competitions will be able to spread common understanding and friendship.

Because soccer football teams require a considerable number of men—players, substitutes, trainers, coach (totalling 20 to 25)—they represent great expense. This therefore is one event of the Olympics where costly competition has been recently overcome by holding preliminary rounds on a "continental" basis before the Olympic games. This saves many teams the necessity of making long journeys. In the Melbourne Olympics eleven finalists appeared. The championship game staged on the day of the closing ceremony was seen by a huge audience of over 102,000. The Russians won and their giant goal keeper, Yashin, was the best player in the tournament. He was a third back and commanded the penalty area. Bulgaria had an excellent team, while Yugoslavia, as usual, produced a well-balanced organization which was the runner-up for the third consecutive Olympics. The final standings were: first, Russia; second, Yugoslavia; third, Bulgaria; fourth, India; fifth, Great Britain; sixth, Australia.

"If at first you don't succeed, then try again" was the lead in the Olympic soccer story of Yugoslavia in 1960. The final sixteen teams at Rome did not include the United States, which was eliminated by Mexico in the North American eliminations. Yugoslavia, defeated in three straight previous Olympic final games, finally took the title by defeating Denmark 3-1 in the finals in the Stadio Flaminio. Hungary was third, and Italy fourth.

At Tokyo in 1964 both Russia and the United States were eliminated in the so-called preliminary intra-continental competitions. Soccer football, now known overseas as football rather than soccer, was very popular in Japan. Such great crowds turned out in Tokyo that thirty-two games were well attended for nine days in the National Stadium, the Prince Chichibu Field, the Komazawa Stadium, the Mitsuzawa Field, and the Omiya Field. Hungary won, followed in order by Czechoslovakia, Germany, and the United Arab Republic. The losers of the quarter finals (Yugoslavia, Japan, Rumania and Ghana) did not meet each other to determine fifth and sixth place.

Mexico City, Latin blood and soccer produced more brawls, cushions thrown by spectators, disqualifications, bad officiating, and tumultuous fights in the stands than most any other sport or series of events in the 1968 games. Notwithstanding the great support afforded the Mexican team from the stands, it did not make the finals. The final result: first, Hungary; second, Bulgaria; third, Japan; fourth, Mexico. No matches were held to determine the rankings of Guatemala, Israel, Spain and France, the quarterfinal losers. The audience was too exhausted and worn down to concern itself with the fifth and sixth scrolls or in any further consolation games.

5. VOLLEYBALL

Men's and women's volleyball was added to the Olympic Team games for Tokyo in 1964.

This game, like basketball, was invented in the United States and by a YMCA physical director. It was created by William G. Morgan in 1895 at Holyoke, Massachusetts. Its original name was minonette. It grew out of the popularity of basketball and the idea that more people could have as much fun knocking a ball over a net as throwing it into a basket. The first net was a lawn tennis net spread across the middle of a gymnasium floor. The first ball was the inside of a basketball, which could easily be batted with the hands. The current standard 8-foot net divides a 60 x 30 foot court.

After spreading from Holyoke through Massachusetts and New England, it only became really popular when the game was taken out of doors and its name changed to volleyball. The first U.S. national championship was in 1922. During World War II American G.I.'s spread the game all over the world. The U.S. Volleyball Association was formed in 1928, and the international body in 1947, which now includes over forty countries.

The U.S. men's teams have been highly successful in Pan Am competitions, closely followed by the U.S. women's teams. The center of top volleyball playing so far in the United States is in the state of California. Various YMCA's have continued this organization's traditional interest in the game by winning many U.S. national championships.

The first volleyball Olympic competition in Tokyo exhibited such great precision and strategic team play executed with all-out effort that many people did not recognize the well-known playground pastime. The standards of play of most of the foreign countries far exceeded those of the United States, which won only a few matches. The men's competition results were: first, Russia; second, Czechoslovakia; third, Japan; fourth, Rumania; fifth, Bulgaria; sixth, Hungary. The women's results were: first, Japan; second, Russia; third,

Poland; fourth, Rumania; fifth, United States; sixth, Korea.

The second Olympic volleyball competitions—those in Mexico City—were so exciting that their elimination from the Olympic schedule for long is very doubtful. The U.S. volleyball team, an outsider and seventh in the tournament, nevertheless beat the Russian gold medalists 3-1 in a great upset. The final 1968 results were: first, Russia; second, Japan; third, Czechoslovakia; fourth, East Germany; fifth, Poland; sixth, Bulgaria. In the women's teams: first, Russia, second, Japan; third, Poland; fourth, Peru; fifth, South Korea; sixth, Czechoslovakia. The skill, speed, technique and excitement of volleyball competition captured the enthusiastic popularity of large crowds in Mexico.

CHAPTER XV

Track and Field

SINCE THE ancient Olympics began 3,100 years ago with foot racing, to which later were added jumping and throwing, the Greeks gave us the track and field events, which are often thought of as the main course in the Olympic diet, probably because the events in track and field competition involve the first athletic gestures of man. Another reason for the great popularity of track and field is that it is held in great open spaces and, as a result, can be witnessed by a practically unlimited audience. Because certain events in track and field are at various periods specialties of different countries throughout the world, the entire track and field program has great international appeal. It also includes events for women, which further increase its appeal. Track and field, however, has been overemphasized in connection with the Olympic games. While there is no question of its importance, it should not overshadow the other sports within the Olympic competition. Unfortunately, there is a tendency in the United States to regard the Olympics as purely an international track and field meet, with the other sports as side shows. Naturally the United States should be proud of having won men's track and field in every Olympiad, but someday, with American methods, techniques, equipment and contributions, following the Olympic tradition, other countries may well take over for a while.

The events in track and field are the normal athletic motions of any man, woman, or child. They consist primarily of walking, running, jumping, and throwing, or combinations of these actions. To prehistoric man, these basic actions

163

were more important than they are to us; walking was the only way of going from one place to another. Running and jumping sometimes saved him from becoming a meal for some man-eating prehistoric animal, and throwing enabled him to kill animals for food. It was natural that skill in these vital activities became the basis of the earliest athletic competitions.

Running was the first event in the ancient Olympic games. Just as in boxing, there is very little today that is completely new in track and field. From the sprint of one length of the stadium (200 yards), a middle-distance race of twice around the stadium (less than one-half mile), and a race of twelve times around the stadium (about two and one-half miles), the number of events contested in the ancient Olympics has been increased to include all kinds of distances in walking and running. The original standing broad jump, usually from a marble step into a loose sand pit, has led to the running jump, the triple jump—now called the hop, step, and jump—the high jump, and later, with the help of a pole, to the pole vault. Since primitive man had to hurdle stones and bushes as he ran away from a mammoth, hurdle races were also added. In the throwing, the objects thrown were the javelin, the discus, the "stone" or shot, and the hammer. According to the Irish, the last-named weight throwing event can be traced to the Tailtean games in County Meath, Ireland, in 1829 B.C.

From the earliest days, great stars were developed in track and field. The first victor at the first Olympic games in 776 B.C. was the winner of the 200-yard dash, an Elian—that is, a native of Elis—named Coroebos. A man named Hermogenes of Xanthos won eight crowns in the foot races during three very early Olympiads. As a result, he received the nickname of "Hippos," which was not the Greek word for a hippopotamus but for a race horse. Argeus was a great long-distance runner and when he won his Olympic victory he ran home to Argos from Olympia, a distance of thirty-four miles, to tell his girl friend about it. Two other great runners in the ancient Olympics were Dandes, also of Argos, and Ladas of Lacedaemon. Later the foot races were dominated for some considerable time by contestants from a Greek city in Italy named Crotona, where a great running coach evidently resided.

After the ancient Olympics were broken up, there was a lapse of eight centuries in sports. This absence of competitive athletics, except for horse racing, jousting, and wrestling, is one of the great mysteries of history. However, it is interesting to note that this same period was one of wars, dictators, chaos, and cruel injustices and inhumanities. We do not find the beginnings of track and field competition in England until the thirteenth century, and finally we find track and field gaining a firm grip in England by 1834, when the first amateur athletic organizations began to make formal rules and to organize competitions in running, jumping and throwing. The first college track and field meet in the world, as far as can be ascertained, took place in 1864, when Oxford competed against Cambridge. The first national meet to determine the champions of England occurred shortly thereafter. In 1868 the New York Athletic Club arranged for the first amateur track and field meet in the history of the United States. All during the nineteenth century there was a great interest in track and field events in many countries throughout the world—in Scandanavia, led by Sweden and Finland; in Russia; in Central Europe, especially in Hungary. In France, too, there was an upsurge of interest in track and field. When the first modern Olympics rolled around in 1896, the flags of France, Russia, the United States, Germany, Sweden, England, Hungary, Australia, Holland, Bohemia, Italy, Belgium, and Spain were waving over the re-created stadium to usher in another golden age of athletics. These flags were those of the original pioneers and originators of the modern Olympics. The participating nations at the first Olympiad were: Great Britain (including Australia), Denmark, France, Germany, Greece, Hungary, Sweden, Switzerland and the United States.

The silhouette of the Grecian temple had never been lost, but the stadium had disappeared with the athletes and their audiences. A living stadium had not been seen for centuries. And now the restored stadium was alive with people. There was room for 50,000 spectators. Portions of the stadium were of wood; there had not been time to replace all the marble. After the games this work would be completed, thanks to the generous gift of George Averoff. The track was not the sandy track of the ancient Greeks, but had been replaced by a cinder track built by experts brought from England. Such was the scene at the opening of the track and field competition of the first Olympics in April, 1896, as the King and Queen of Greece, the former in full military uniform and the latter in white, officially opened the ceremony. Athletes, officials, and a choir added color to the scene. A chorus of several hundred voices sang the Olympic hymn. The oldest

165

show on earth had reopened. It was to be an American show. In fact, of the twelve official track and field events, nine were won by Americans. Two events were won by E. H. Flack of Australia, and the marathon, which turned out to be the most dramatic race of the show, was won by S. Loues of Greece. Baron de Coubertin, to whom this Olympics owed so much, was all but ignored by the Greeks and the Greek government, but he was there nevertheless, helping in a major way to prepare for the future.

The United States Expeditionary Forces to Greece in the first Olympic games were volunteers. Baron de Coubertin had, at a very early stage in the preparation of the Olympics, enlisted the help of the American professor, William Sloane, to represent the United States in the preliminary Olympic Congress. Unfortunately, few Americans paid much attention to Sloane when he returned, but the Boston Athletic Association finally decided that it should send a team to Athens. The athletes selected were Tom Burke, sprinter; E. H. Clark, Harvard all-around athlete; Thomas P. Curtis, hurdler; Arthur Blake, middle- and long-distance runner; John and Sumner Paine, revolver shots; W. W. Hoyt, pole vaulter; C. B. Wiliams, swimmer; and John Graham, the coach of the Boston Athletic Association. This team, after various difficulties en route, arrived in Athens in the nick of time, and was joined by other Americans. Robert S. Garrett, captain of the Princeton track and field team, had decided he would like to go to Athens. Although he had never seen a discus, he had heard about the modern discus competition; he dug up the dimensions of a discus somewhere and had a steel one made. He practiced throwing the discus at Princeton for a while and then set forth for Athens. James B. Connelly, later to become a well-known author, was a student at Harvard with an interest in athletics. He became interested in going to Athens and applied to Harvard for a leave of absence, which was refused. He quit school and went to Athens anyway. The Americans, who went to Athens informally on a catch-as-catch-can basis, were just too good and won practically all the events.

By far the most exciting event was the marathon. The contest was run over the exact course that Pheidippides had taken in bringing the news of the Greek victory at Marathon to anxious Athens. There were twenty-five starters.

Spiridion Loues was a Greek shepherd. He had heard on the hills, as he watched over his sheep, that athletes from all over the world were coming to Athens and that his country would have a difficult time upholding the tradition of the past. A tireless runner, although physically a very small, short man, he saw himself as the one hope of Greece to win the marathon. Baron de Coubertin, a great public relations expert, told the world that Loues spent two nights before the race praying and that the day before the race he fasted. In any case, he was one of the starters the next morning. The favorite, Lermusiaux, a Frenchman, led for almost half the race. Then he was passed by Arthur Blake of the Boston Athletic Association, who had never run twenty-six miles before. After nineteen miles, Blake had to quit. Loues, who had kept a steady pace, was the next to take the lead. When three miles remained to go, Loues was still in the lead position. Word was sent ahead to the Royal Box and to the crowd—a Greek crowd—who were waiting in a frenzy of enthusiasm. An uproar burst as Loues trotted into the stadium. To make the day even more glorious for Greece, a Greek was second and a Greek was third.

The second modern Olympic games, in Paris in 1900, listed the track and field championships merely as an international meet at the World's Fair. The United States entered fifty-five athletes as their official track and field team, although actually this team consisted of many groups from various colleges—Yale, Princeton, Pennsylvania, Syracuse, Georgetown, Michigan, and Chicago—and some club representatives. Each college financed its own group. The New York Athletic Club also financed a team. The unattached entrants reached into their own pockets for their expenses.

The site of the track meet was bad, and the facilities almost non-existent. There wasn't even a cinder path for running. The sprint course was on turf and was not level. The discus had to be thrown into trees. There was much confusion in the running off of the meet. Just as at Athens, it was an American show. The star was Alvin Kraenzlein of Pennsylvania, who won four Olympic championships—the 60-meter sprint, the 110-meter hurdles, the 200-meter hurdles, and the running broad jump. One of the most interesting features of the second Olympic games was the fact that, notwithstanding the confusion, bad management, the horrible site, and the lack of proper facilities, every record made at Athens in 1896 was broken. Although all of the events that he was in have been discontinued, Ray Ewry of the United States was in a class by himself in the standing jump events, capturing all three of them. Sheldon of the United States broke the 16-pound shot record by no less than ten feet. Great Britain showed up quite well in this track meet, winning four gold medals, including the relay. Hungary, one of the original sponsors of the Olympic games, won its first track and field victory in the classical discus event. One other Olympic pioneer nation scored a victory in the stadium—France in the classic marathon race, when Teato defeated a great field. The great originator of the Olympics, Baron de Coubertin, was ignored by his own government in the running of the 1900 games, just as he had been by the Greek government in the 1896 games. However, he was not one to be discouraged, and he continued to be present to help in any way he could, and to lay proper plans for the next Olympics and the continuation of his great idea and ideals.

The track and field competition in the third Olympiad at St. Louis, in 1904, was again won by the United States and almost exclusively by college athletes, who broke records in almost every event. The competition included a large number of competitors, although there were comparativey few Europeans. There were a number of athletes who captured more than one first place. Archie Hahn won the 60-, the 100-, and the 200-meter sprints. Ray Ewry took first place in the standing broad jump, the standing high jump, and the standing hop, step and jump, repeating the victories he had scored at the second Olympiad. Harry Hillman won the 200- and the 400-meter hurdles and the 400-meter flat. J. B. Lightbody took first in the 800-meter and 1,500-meter runs and the 2,500-meter steeplechase, and Myer Prinstein won the broad jump and the hop, step and jump. Martin Sheridan, a New York policeman, won his first Olympic discus throw.

Although there were big crowds and a lot of enthusiasm at the St. Louis game, the track and field events were so badly mixed up with the St. Louis Fair and there was so much confusion and so many side-shows that it is doubtful if it could be called any improvement on the very poorly run Paris Olympiad of four years before. Baron de Coubertin, as usual, weaved with the punches and took advantage of every opportunity to keep improving and advancing the Olympic games.

The 1906 Olympic games, usually referred to as the "unofficial" Olympics, were actually the first to which many countries sent large teams. The United States, which had won in St. Louis more or less by default, was determined to demonstrate its strength against real competition, and did win the unofficial all-around honors in the track and field events, paced by stars such as Paul Pilgrim, the New York

Athletic Club surprise winner of the 400- and 800-meter run.
Pilgrim became director of athletics at the New York Athletic
Club, which still contributes many track and field stars to
U.S. Olympic teams. The Greeks received a sad disappointment in having Sherring, a Canadian, win the marathon and Jarvinen, a Finn, win the Greek-style discus. However, as usual, there was something to swell Greek pride, for
their representative in the shotput—or, as it was then called,
the "stone throw"—George Georgantus, won this event.

One of the outstanding features of the games was the
actual, active, and effective participation of the Greek royal
family. The Crown Prince presided at the games and the
Princes George, Nicholas, and Andrew all actively officiated
and did so with skill. The King and Queen of Greece were
present at the games every day, and the King of Servia and
the Prince of Wales also attended the games as guests of
Greece. It was a great show in the finally completed marble
stadium. 1906 was a turning point between the experiments,
the uncertainties, the petty jealousies, and the grabbing of
management of the Olympics by various local organizations,
governments, and fairs, and the smooth-running modern
Olympics managed and controlled by the International Olympic Committee and the various national Olympic Committees
together with the Olympic Organizing Committee of the host
nation.

The 1908 or fourth Olympiad in London is said, according
to many, to have supplied more drama than any other
Olympics up to that time. The stadium for the track and field
events—the Olympia—was overflowing with 80,000 people.
The stadium had a 660-yard concrete cycling track, and inside of that was a five-laps-to-the-mile cinder track. In front
of the main stands, within the oval, was a swimming pool
100 meters in length, with a diving tower that could be collapsed to disappear from sight when not in use. King Edward VII and Queen Alexandra of England formally opened
the games.

The track and field competition was undoubtedly the greatest in athletic history up to that time. Many unusual happenings added to the excitement. Reggie Walker, a 19-year-old
South African not originally picked to represent his country, outsprinted a great field to win the 100 meters. Lt. Halswelle of Great Britain, who had run the fastest 400-meter
semifinal, ran against three Americans in the final. As two
of the three had been accused of technical fouls—namely,
cutting in front of Halswelle—the officials declared the race

169

null and void. Only one of the Americans was officially disqualified, and the officials ordered the race re-run by Halswelle and the other two Americans. However, the U.S. representatives refused to start again, and as a result the Englishman was allowed to trot alone around the track to win the event. The British fared better than ever, winning most of the long-distance events and most of the places in the steeplechase. Ray Ewry of the United States brought his total of Olympic gold medals to ten, a record which has never been surpassed. Martin Sheridan repeated his Olympic discus win at St. Louis, and John Flanagan won the hammer throw for the third time in succession.

Great Britain had expected to win the track and field. While the British did win the unofficial all-around championship of the fourth Olympiad, they were not able to head off the Americans in the unofficial track and field team championship. As in the case of the first three Olympiads, there was great interest in the running of the marathon. At the start of the race, two English distance runners named Lord and Jack ran the first four miles in record time, with J. Price, a third Englishman, following closely behind, trailed by Hefferon of South Africa and Dorando Pietri of Italy. Jack was soon exhausted and eliminated, but the others continued at an unbelieveable pace for about 15 miles. Then Price and Lord both dropped back, while Hefferon, followed by Dorando Pietri, kept pushing ahead until they were about three miles from the stadium. Dorando started to gain on Hefferon, and, coming in sight of him at the twenty-fifth mile, sprinted after the tired South African and passed him within sight of the stadium. Dorando's sprint having worn him down, he had to slow up. When he entered the stadium he was greeted by a mighty roar from the crowd but he became confused and at first started running in the wrong direction and then collapsed on the track. In the meantime, Johnny Hayes, Joe Forshaw, and A. R. Welton, all Americans, were approaching the stadium. Doctors and officials, in the meantime, had rushed to the Italian and, humanely but illegally, dragged him to his feet and pushed him in the proper direction, not knowing that by so doing they had disqualified him. Dorando, with rubber legs, weaved around the track. A roar from the crowd signalled the fact that Hayes had just entered the stadium. Hayes, in very good shape, swung around the track with a sprint finish and finished a bare half-minute after the Italian runner, who fell unconscious after he had been pushed and dragged over the line. Hayes, of course, was declared the winner of the marathon, and Dorando was disqualified. Hefferon, the big South African, was second, while Forshaw and Welton scored third and fourth honors for the United States. Twenty-seven of the original seventy-five starters finished in what is generally considered the most dramatic race in the annals of the modern Olympics.

South Africa, Canada, and Australia began to take a tremendous interest in international athletics in the Olympics and were represented by some very strong, as well as courageous, contestants.

The fifth Olympiad was awarded to Stockholm, in recognition of the Swedes' enthusiastic support of the Olympic games from the very beginning. The Stockholm games presented a number of new problems in connection with track and field. Finland wished to compete as an independent nation, but was forced to participate as representing Russia. Similarly, Bohemia desired to send a team of its own, but was forced to represent Austria. The organizing committee in Sweden had to build a stadium, swimming pool, and other facilities from scratch.

Silver trumpets heralded the opening of the track and field competition in the new and imposing stadium. For the first time, electrical timing devices were used to assure accuracy in track events. While the United States, as usual, won the unofficial overall track and field competition, the Stockholm games were replete with unexpected and unusual performances by nations new to the Olympics and by unknown athletes. While the sprints were fairly easy for the United States, the competition in the middle-distance events was rough. As a result of the Halswelle incident in 1908 at London, the Swedes hit upon the idea of using lanes for the final of the 400 meter. Hans Braun, a great German runner; Ted Meredith, an 18-year-old schoolboy from the United States; and Charles Reidpath and E. F. J. Lindberg, also of the United States, were the finalists. Although Ted Meredith led for the first half of the final, it ended practically in a dead heat between Reidpath, Lindberg, and Braun. The officials picked Reidpath as first, Braun as second, and Lindberg as third. The final of the 800 meter was just as exciting, with Braun again representing Germany and running against six Americans and a Canadian. Mel Sheppard, the 1908 winner, was the favorite and he quickly opened quite a gap. But as the runners reached the final straightaway, they became closely bunched. Again it was almost a dead heat. The decision went to Meredith for first, Sheppard second, Davenport third, Braun fourth, and Caldwell fifth, with the official timing of two-fifths of a second difference between the first man and the fifth.

The 1,500 meter, or the "metric mile," was, of course, the special target of many. The only trouble was that too many Americans coveted this particular gold medal, with the result that the Americans in the finals—John Paul Jones of Cornell; Mel Sheppard, the 1908 winner; Norman Taber; Abel Kiviat; and three other Americans—became so intent on out-maneuvering each other, having run against each other often, that they not only allowed Arnaud of France to set the pace for more than half the distance but at the finish permitted A. Jackson of England and Oxford to stage a last minute sprint to win the event. A dramatic race was also presented in the 5,000 meters, in which two great runners, Hannes Kolehmainen of Finland and Jean Bouin of France, ran neck and neck for almost 5,000 meters and hit the tape together, with Kolehmainen winning by a whisper to set a new record. Kolehmainen went on to win the 10,000-meter flat and the 8,000-meter cross country, for three long-distance gold medals. However, possibly his greatest performance was in another event which he did not win, although he broke the existing world's record. The explanation of this unusual occurrence is that he was also entered in the 3,000-meter team race, which was run in heats, the winning team alone qualifying for the final. Finland was eliminated by the United States and therefore Kolehmainen did not qualify for the final, although he set a new world's record in winning his heat. Kolehmainen and a teammate of his named Stenroos were each to win a future Olympic marathon. As usual, the marathon was looked on by almost everyone as the climax of the track and field events. Two South Africans, K. K. McArthur and C. W. Gitsham, finished first and second, with Gaston Strobino of the United States third.

However, the greatest performance at Stockholm in track and field was one that is not in the record books. Jim Thorpe won both the pentathlon and decathlon, the all-around track and field events, but was later disqualified. Before his disqualification Thorpe's records in fifteen events attracted the attention of the world, and on his return he was greeted as the hero of the fifth Olympiad. An American Indian and probably the greatest all-around track and field athlete of all time, Jim Thorpe is also generally considered the greatest natural football player of all time, and was a good enough baseball player to make the big leagues. (A town in Pennsylvania, formerly an Indian town and until 1955 known as Mauch Chunk, where Jim is buried, is now named Jim Thorpe in memory of America's greatest athlete.) Yet F. R. Bie of Norway was officially given the pentathlon title and Hugo Wieslander of Sweden the decathlon crown of the fifth Olympiad after Jim Thorpe had been disqualified.

Because of his prominence, Thorpe was found to have accepted a small amount of money for playing baseball in a semi-pro league preceding the Olympic games. This fact was not discovered until 1913. The officials of the American Olympic Committee decided it was their duty to award to the men who had won second place in the two events the official victories, to have Thorpe's records eliminated, and to reclaim Thorpe's two gold medals.

The Swedes' handling of technical facilities was great at Stockholm. Not only was an electrical timing device used for the first time in any Olympics, but also the first photo-finish camera, and the first public-address system, and in addition there were charts and other methods of projecting the progress of many events to the great crowd all through the games. Baron de Coubertin expressed the admiration of the Olympic world in a letter to the Swedish Olympic Committee. Great progress was being made in the Olympic games, but it was interrupted, of course, by the world war.

The first announcement that the Olympic games were to be revived after the close of hostilities filled the athletic world with delight, but very little time was left for preparation. The choice of Antwerp was almost unbelievable; it was astounding that the brave Belgians should have been able to gather their resources and get organized at all, as they had suffered so cruelly in the war. Before the games began, a religious service was conducted by a Cardinal Mercier, in the imposing cathedral at Antwerp, for the athletes killed in World War I. Following the religious services at the cathedral, the regular Olympic ceremony was held at the stadium, with King Albert of Belgium opening the games. The Olympic flag with the five rings made its first official appearance at these Olympics, although it had made its unofficial debut in 1916 at Paris, when the twentieth anniversary of the revival of the games was celebrated. The stadium had been hastily put together, and the track suffered from continuous rains, which influenced performances adversely, but the games were smoothly run.

There were more surprises at Antwerp than usual, for no

one knew the relative abilities of the contestants. A. G. Hill, an Englishman well past the usual age of competitive runners, surprised everyone by winning both the 800 and the 1,500 meter. American sprinters, as usual, dominated the short distances. The long-distance races presented to the Olympic games a new star who was to become the greatest runner of modern times. Paavo Nurmi of Finland, then unknown, opposed in the 5,000 meters the great Guillemot, who had a world reputation and was beyond doubt the greatest French runner of all time. The Finn stayed with the Frenchman all the way and lost by a stride. However, Nurmi won the 10,000-meter run and the 10,000-meter cross-country. Hannes Kolehmainen, the outstanding distance runner in the 1912 Olympics eight years before, won the classic marathon race in new record time. Finland surprised the United States by winning most of the field events—the shotput, the discus, the javelin throw, and the hop, step and jump. A Swede won the broad jump. Although the United States won the track and field section of the seventh Olympiad, the Finns, considering the size of their country and the number of their entries, scored even more impressively.

Amsterdam was scheduled to be the site of the next Olympic games, as the Dutch had applied for the 1916 games and in 1920 had voluntarily retired in favor of Antwerp. However, the Dutch withdrew again, with great generosity, this time at the request of the founder of the games, Baron de Coubertin, who wished to have the 1924 games held in Paris.

The eighth Olympiad in Paris was distinguished by the all-out effort of the French government, which was determined that the thirtieth anniversary of the rebirth of the Olympic games would not be the fiasco of 1900. The great hero of the track and field competition was Paavo Nurmi of Finland. While Nurmi had first shown great exhibitions of long-distance running at Antwerp, his appearance in Paris marked him as a finished performer with a veteran's poise. Nurmi's four gold medals in a single Olympiad surpassed the performance of Alvin Kraenzlein at Paris in 1900. The Finnish runner won the 1,500 meter, 5,000 meter, 3,000-meter steeplechase, and 10,000-meter cross-country.

The United States was set back on its haunches by the surprising wins of the British in short-distance events. Great performances were turned in by contestants from countries new to track and field; for instance, a young Swiss named Paul Martin, now a distinguished doctor, provided a great thrill by taking second in the 800 meter, a second that

174

many observers believed would have been a first if he had had more experience and had properly timed his closing sprint to the tape. Records fell every day. Probably one of the most interesting feats was the world's broad jump record set by Robert Legendre, an American, with a jump of 25 feet 6 inches while he was performing in the pentathlon. Legendre was not even a competitor in the Olympic broad jumping contest, but on hearing that another American, whom he didn't like, had won this event with a record jump, he announced to everyone that he would break the world's record and beat his teammate when he got around to the broad jump event in the pentathlon, and he made good his promise. To complete this human interest story, Robert Legendre, along with Johnny Weismuller, the swimmer, and Nat Pendleton, the wrestler, was tapped by Hollywood for stardom. While Weismuller became Tarzan on the screen and Nat Pendleton became a leading tough guy and a character who wrestled lions, Robert Legendre, the most photogenic and the greatest prospect for Hollywood stardom, was cut down by pneumonia in three days after several years as a United States naval officer and Navy track coach.

Two 18-year-old Americans, Lee Barnes and Glen'Graham, tied for the pole vault title, Barnes winning in a jump-off, and Clarence Houser, another American college star, was a double winner in the shot and the discus. U.S. relay teams broke two world records and helped to establish the 1924 Paris games as the greatest producer, up to that time, of Olympic and world's records.

The ninth Olympiad at Amsterdam produced another great track and field competition, this time handicapped to some degree by cold and rainy weather, but with a very fine track. The track and field program embraced some 760 male competitors and 121 women representing 40 nations. The competition started out with an unknown Canadian sprinter, Percy Williams, winning both the 100- and 200-meters, with Great Britain providing a surprise runner-up. The United States was in for an even greater surprise, for up until the final track event of the 1928 program, none of the American runners or hurdlers had been able to win a single first place. Ray Barbuti therefore won great fame by winning, at the very finish, the 400-meter final from Ball of Canada. The United States didn't do much better in the middle distances, with Douglas Lowe, Great Britain's 1924 winner, repeating in the 800 meter; and Finland's runners Larva Loukola and Ritola and a great French runner, Ladoumegue, dominated

175

the distance events. Nurmi was unable to repeat his past victories and had to be satisfied with two second places in the 5,000 meter and 3,000-meter steeplechase and a first in the 10,000 meter. Another great surprise was furnished by Lord David Burghley of Great Britain, who scored an upset over the Americans in the 400-meter hurdle event. In track the United States had to be satisfied with Barbuti's 400-meter victory and with wins in the 400- and 1,600-meter relay events. In the field events, however, the United States made up for its deficiency in the track events, winning almost all of the events and making up sufficient points to win the unofficial all-around track and field championship. One of the great showings of the track and field meet was that provided by the Germans, who had been turned away from Olympic competition in 1920 and 1924, and had not participated since 1912. These Olympics also marked the beginning of women's track and field competition. Of the five track events for women, Canada won two and the United States, Germany, and Poland one each.

The tenth Olympiad in Los Angeles in 1932 brought track and field to one of the largest and finest stadiums in the world. With the selection of the host nation and city years ahead of time, the site and facilities for the games, and particularly for the track and field competition, could be properly prepared. Los Angeles outdid itself in providing facilities that could not be improved upon. Over 100,000 people, with thousands of disappointed latecomers thronging the nearby streets, witnessed the opening of the Olympics on July 30, 1932. Trumpets blared while Lt. George Calnan of the U.S. Navy, four-time American Olympic fencer, took the Olympic oath. Because of the excellence of the track, the great improvements in technique and performance, the number and quality of competitors, and the enthusiasm of the tremendous crowd, practically every existing record in track and field was broken during the dramatic competition between the greatest athletes from all over the world.

Eddie Tolan of the United States was the only double winner, with record-breaking performances in both the sprints, while the only 1928 champion to defend his title successfully was Dr. Patrick O'Callaghan of Ireland, in the hammer throw. The most sensational and most controversial race of the track events was the 5,000-meter run, in which Ralph Hill, a comparatively unknown American, stayed with the world record holder, Finnish runner Lehtenin, to the head of the stretch. Hill attempted to pass the Finn on the outside, but Lehtenin swung out and cut him off. Then Hill tried to pass him on the inside, only to have the Finn close him off again. As a result of these maneuvers, Hill was beaten by a half yard. The audience of 100,000, believing that the Finn had fouled Hill, broke into such booing that it looked as though a serious incident was imminent. However, a fast-thinking announcer silenced the outburst and brought on immediate applause by cautioning the crowd: "Remember, please, these people are our guests." Outstanding records in the hurdles and in the field events followed. The marathon, as usual, was thrilling, with the four leading contestants all finishing within less than 400 yards. An Argentinian, Juan Zabala, won the gold medal. U.S. relay teams broke all records. In the women's track and field competition, Mildred Didrikson was the star, winning two gold medals and one silver. At the closing ceremony attended by 110,000 people, the great chorus sang the plaintive Hawaiian farewell "Aloha" while the banners of all of the nations participating in the tenth Olympiad were lowered.

The eleventh Olympic games in Berlin, although beset with many problems caused by the Nazi government and Nazi control, were nevertheless successful and their technical direction, with German thoroughness, was nearly perfect. Every possible electrical timing and photo-finish device was improved at Berlin. Devices smoothed the announcing systems for the judges, for the officials, and for the public. Press and radio service was excellent and there is no question that technical arrangements were handled in an outstanding fashion. The athletes were housed in very fine style in the Olympic Village and were extended every comfort so that they might be at their best for the competition. These Olympics rang up a record at the box office, for the greatest income the games had yet known—over $2,800,000. The opening ceremony was heightened by the arrival in the stadium of the last of a team of more than 3,000 relay runners of many nationalities who had carried a torch lighted on the ancient site of Olympia in Greece across Europe to the games. There was an audience of close to 125,000 people (133,000 at eight other arenas and events), and approximately 5,000 athletes from 52 nations were drawn up on the field in uniforms of every color. Spiridion Loues, the Greek shepherd who had won the first Olympic marathon in 1896 at Athens, was on hand. Members of the International Olympic Committee, headed by President Baillet Latour, were there. The ceremonies finished, the oath taken, and the huge Olympic torch

177

blazing at the open end of the stadium, thousands of doors were released and the games and the track and field competition had begun.

However, the great star of the 1936 Olympiad was not the crowds or Adolf Hitler, but Jesse Owens. The accomplishments of Jesse Owens are without parallel in modern Olympic history. Owens won three individual events and ran a decisive lap on a winning relay team, thus winning four gold medals and four of the tiny potted German oak trees that the organizing committee had provided the winners as living memorials of their victories. More startling, Owens broke both the Olympic and world record in the 100 meter, although it was disallowed because of a wind behind his back. He set a new Olympic and world record for 200 meters, he broad-jumped over 26 feet for the first time in Olympic history —another record—and the 400-meter relay team, of which he was a member, set a new Olympic world record. Another spectacular performance was the 1,500 meter win of Dr. Jack Lovelock of New Zealand, who smashed both the Olympic and world records with a great sprint of almost a full lap of a 400-meter track as a climax. Glenn Cunningham, one of America's greatest milers, was second. The Finns continued their dominance of long-distance races, and the historic and dramatic marathon was won by a representative of Japan, who was actually a Korean, as was his teammate, who finished in third place. Helen Stephens was the star of the women's track and field competition, winning the 100 meters and anchoring the winning 400-meter relay team. In the twenty-nine events, fifteen of the track and field records set four years before at Los Angeles were surpassed and three were equaled.

The track and field part of the fourteenth Olympiad in London in 1948 was impressive. Six thousand athletes from fifty-nine countries were present, as was a capacity crowd of over 82,000 people. Trumpeters of the Household Cavalry filed into the stadium and sounded their fanfare. Then came the massed bands and the Scottish Highlanders, and then the King. The parade of athletes began soon after, with Greece traditionally number one in the order of nations. After that they were in alphabetical order from Afghanistan to Yugoslavia, with Britain as the host nation at the end of the line. The Olympic flame, which had been lighted in the temple of Zeus at Olympia almost a fortnight before, was carried into the stadium on the last leg of a 1,600-man relay.

The first dramatic moment of these Olympics was the 10,-

178

000-meter run, considered a Finnish property, with Heino, the Finnish world's record holder, running in a field that included several other strong contenders. However, there was a dark horse named Emil Zatopek, of Czechoslovakia. This race had been won at five out of the last six Olympics by Finns, including Hannes Kolehmainen and Paavo Nurmi. Heino led as a slight drizzle of rain fell, while Emil Zatopek, a Czech Army officer, followed. The grimacing Czech, in a faded red jersey, took over the lead from Heino at the tenth lap of the 25-lap race. For six more laps the two men stayed fairly close together, and then Zatopek in a dozen strides pulled away. In less than a lap the margin was getting bigger and then, to the great surprise of everyone, Heino ran off the track and quit. This seemed, however, to be a signal to Zatopek, who actually sprinted for the last two miles. The second Finn was run into the ground and had to be escorted off the track. The third Finn, Konenen, was so worn out that he was even beaten by two Americans, Eddie O'Toole and Fred Wilt. Zatopek won and broke the Olympic record. About 350 yards behind, in second place, was the Algerian Alain Mimoun-o-Kacha, representing France.

One of the most impressive and interesting victories in the London Olympics in 1948 was that of Harrison Dillard in the classic 100-meter flat. Dillard, a world's record hurdler, fell in the finals of the American Olympic tryout in the hurdles, and was therefore eliminated under the ironbound rules of the AAU. Dillard then turned around and entered the 100-meter flat race and qualified for a position on the Olympic team. In winning the 100-meter dash, he certainly gave an example of great ability and great will-power, for his normal event was the hurdles.

The 1,500 meter, which has become one of the greatest and one of the most popular races in the Olympics, presented thirty-six starters. The Swedish Strand, Eriksson, and Bergkvist had all run faster than existing Olympic records. Only one U.S. contestant, Don Gehrmann, reached the finals. There was also the great Dutch runner, Slijkhuis; and Hansenne, the Frenchman, also had never been beaten at the distance. For the first time in thirty-six years in this event, Sweden placed three men in the first six to finish: Eriksson winning, with Strand second and Slijkhuis third, while Bergkvist took fifth. Eriksson's time, however, was slower than Strand's world record. In the 5,000 meters all eyes were on Emil Zatopek, the Czech who had previously set the new Olympic record in winning the 10,000 meters,

179

but at the finish Zatopek was some 30 yards behind Slijk-huis, who in turn was led by Gaston Reiff of Belgium. Zato-pek started a sprint at the finish and although he was able to pass Slijkhuis, he could not catch Reiff, who won and established a new Olympic record.

There was one controversial incident in the meet and that was in the 400-meter relay, in which the U.S. team of Barney Ewell, Lorenzo Wright, Harrison Dillard, and Mel Patton finished comfortably in front of the second-place British quartet. However, the U.S. team was disqualified for allegedly passing the baton outside of the limits of the passing zone. Later a formal protest was entered by the United States and the Jury of Appeals, after reviewing the motion pictures, ruled that the hand-over from Ewell to Wright, which had been questioned, was entirely within the prescribed limits and so the U.S. team was re-designated as the winner.

The marathon provided the usual thrills, with Gailly of Belgium sprinting into the stadium first but staggering and weaving and almost collapsing. Before he could finish he was passed, in the crowded stadium, by D. Cabrera, an Argentinian running smoothly and effortlessly, and by T. Richards of Great Britain. The first American to finish was Theodore Vogel, who finished fourteenth. One of the greatest individual performances in the 1948 Olympics was that of Robert Mathias, a 17-year-old high-school boy from Tulare, California, who broke a world's record, scored more than 7,000 points, and defeated twenty-seven other contestants from all over the world in the all-around or decathlon chamionship. In men's track and field, the United States won, of course, but Sweden was a good second, with France a poor third, England a poor fourth, and little Jamaica a surprisingly strong fifth.

In the women's track and field the fabulous Dutch girl, Fannie Blankers-Koen, won four Olympic gold medals by running away from the field in the 100-meter dash (at which she was also the world record holder), winning the 200-meter dash (in which she established a new Olympic record), and the 80-meter hurdles (where she was the world's record holder), and running a tremendous anchor leg that made up a big lead to win the 400-meter relay for Holland. The American women's team did not fare well, winning only one gold medal, in the running high jump, although even here the winner's jump did not equal Fannie Blankers-Koen's world's record. Fannie just could not par-

180

ticipate in many events in which she was the best in the world. She could not enter the running broad jump either, although she also held the world's record. The women's unofficial team championship was won by Holland, if not by Fannie alone.

The 1952 Olympic games in Helsinki, Finland—the fifteenth Olympiad—was an imposing spectacle. The Finns and the Finnish Organizing Committee did everything they could to make this Olympiad a tremendous success, even retaining many foreign specialists to help organize the games, including the author, who made three visits to Helsinki prior to the games. It might be said, even though it is said every four years, that the Olympic flame never burned brighter than in 1952 and that the fifteenth Olympiad presented more nations, more competitors, better competition, and greater world interest than ever before. In the United States, the Olympics received greater support and more attention than ever before, from the President of the United States, who proclaimed an Olympic Week, down to the humblest of sports followers. The Olympic telethon arranged by Bob Hope and Bing Crosby to raise funds by contributions from the television audience was undoubtedly the greatest event of its kind ever staged, and it is estimated that over 50 million people in the United States witnessed it. Over one million dollars was pledged on the telethon, but unfortunately only $353,000 was actually collected.

More than ever before, it was evident to all that the Olympic games are a great idealistic enterprise. Those who participate, being amateurs, contribute to it and do not seek to take from it. It is free from dollar signs and from political intrigue. Amateur sports were not designed to be used by any individual or nation for selfish or propaganda purposes. That is why the Olympic movement has spread throughout the world without large funds or huge endowments. From an original start of nine nations, in less than seventy-six years it has spread to every corner of the globe. Today over one hundred and twenty-seven national Olympic committees are recognized by the International Olympic Committee. History records nothing to compare with this amazing march of amateur sports despite distances, and differences in language, race, color, religion and ideology.

The 1952 track and field competition involved 995 individual entries from 57 countries. Thirty-nine countries entered contestants in the women's track and field events. Even Bermuda and Singapore were represented.

The men's unofficial track and field championship was won by the United States with a total of thirty-one medalists; second was Russia with seventeen medalists. Russia served notice to the track and field world that, with the techniques, form, equipment and the training methods learned from the United States, it would be a candidate for the track and field championship in the very near future.

The U.S. track and field team won fourteen gold medals, two more than ever before, as well as numerous silver and bronze medals. Robert J. King, the team manager, said in his report: "The games were impeccably conducted and all were impressed by the quietly efficient Finnish people, their graciousness and warm hospitality." Arrangements for track and field in particular set a new high in organization, and the track was in extraordinarily good shape. Seven Olympic records were broken, two tied, and one world's record was surpassed.

The 100-meter dash supplied one of the greatest finishes of any Olympics. Several photos at several angles were necessary to establish the winner. Four men finished under the proverbial blanket in a near dead heat, and although Remigino of the United States was declared the winner, there is still some doubt to this day whether McKenley of Jamaica did not deserve a tie. The metric mile of 1,500 meters, as usual, provided tremendous thrills for the crowd of some 74,000 people. Bannister of England, who was later to become the first man ever to break the four-minute barrier for the mile, was fourth. The surprise winner was J. Barthel of Luxembourg. This was no fluke, however, because Barthel's time was an Olympic record and only 2.2 seconds off the world's record. It was, incidentally, the first time that little Luxembourg had won an Olympic gold medal. Emil Zatopek, considered by many to be past his prime, nevertheless won the 5,000 meter, the 10,000 meter, and the marathon, and may well go down in history as the greatest long-distance runner of modern times. It is interesting to note that Zatopek had never run the marathon distance and yet won with plenty to spare and was quite fresh at the finish. According to many, he looked fresher and more relaxed than he had appeared in any of his other races during the week. The time of all of the first six men to finish was faster than any marathon ever run in past Olympics. R. Gorno, an Argentinian, finished second, then G. Jansson of Sweden, Yoon Chil Choi of Korea, V. Karvonen of Finland, and in sixth place, D. Cabrera of Argentina, the winner of the marathon at the 1948 London Olympiad.

Harrison Dillard, appearing in his regular specialty—the 110-meter high hurdles—won and established a new Olympic record. Parry O'Brien won the shotput with an Olympic record throw and showed the form which was later to enable him to break the world's record many times. The Rev. Robert E. Richards of LaVerne, California, a standout in the pole vault, won that event with the greatest of ease. Brazil's hop-step-and-jumper, Adehamar Ferreira da Silva, was an outstanding star of the show, breaking the Olympic and world's record; in fact, he exceeded the former world's record many times during the competition. Robert Mathias became the first man in history to win an all-around modern Olympic championship, or decathlon, for a second time. This established him as the greatest all-around track and field athlete in the world. He also broke his own world's record. Strangely enough, however, he was pushed by a new sensation, Milton Campbell, an 18-year-old high-school junior from Plainfield, New Jersey, who came in second. The leading European threat and runner-up in 1948, Heinrich of France, was forced to withdraw after the first day when he aggravated an old injury. The versatility of Mathias, like that of Jim Thorpe, might be commented on here, for Mathias was also an all-American football player.

In the women's track and field, the all-around women's unofficial track championship was won by Russia, with Australia second. The most interesting performances were the winning of the relay by the U.S. team and the winning of the javelin throw by D. Zatopekova of Czechoslovakia, the wife of Emil Zatopek. Mrs. Zatopek, by the way, broke the Olympic record. Czech and double Czech!

The track and field competition in Melbourne, Australia in 1956 again broke records for the greatest number of countries participating. The United States again won the unofficial team championship with 15 individual championships against three for Russia—the nearest competitor. The track events were dominated by Bobby Morrow of Texas who won both the 100- and the 200-meter dash; by Charlie Jenkins, who won the 400 meter; by Glenn Davis, who won the 400 meter hurdles; by S. Calhoun, who won the 110 meter hurdles; and by Tom Courtney of the New York Athletic Club, who came in first for the United States in the 800-meter run, breaking the Olympic mark. Courtney's win was by superhuman effort, for it took him nearly an hour before he could recover and take the victory stand. The U.S. team in the 400-meter relay (Ira Murchison, Leamon King, Thane Baker and Bobby Morrow) not only won but also established a new world and Olympic record.

The popular metric mile, or 1,500-meter run, was won by Ron Delany of Villanova, representing Ireland. To show the progress in competition, out of the twelve men in the finals of this event, eight broke the old Olympic mark. The 5,000 and 10,000-meter runs were both won by Vladimir Kuts of Russia, who broke both Olympic marks.

The famous marathon was replete with unusual angles. To begin with, there was actually a false start in this grueling race of over 26 miles run on a day with the temperature over 80 degrees. The ultimate winner, Alain Mimoun of France, was running his first marathon. In addition, Mimoun, who wore number 13, was informed before the race started that he had just become a father. He knew that France had won the marathon in 1900 and 1928, and therefore was scheduled to win in 1956 (although no one else knew it, for the favorite was Emil Zatopek—the 1952 winner). Notwithstanding all the pre-race facts, Mimoun came home a solitary winner with Zatopek in sixth place.

The 3,000-meter steeplechase was won in a startling surprise by a dark horse, Christopher Brasher of Great Britain, but it featured a disqualification and a reversal of the disqualification. Almost ignored as a possible winner, Brasher finished well ahead of the runner-up, Sandor Rozsnyoi of Hungary, who had set a world record in Hungary sometime before. Then, to the amazement of over 100,000 cheering spectators, the announcer told the crowd that Brasher had been disqualified for "interference in the last lap." Rozsnyoi was declared the winner. It transpired that a judge had ruled that Brasher had bumped Ernst Larsen of Norway, third place winner, at the fourth jump from the finish line. The British immediately lodged a protest. After Larsen stated he had felt a slight bump on the shoulder going over the hurdle, but made no complaint, and after Rozsnyoi also refused to make any protest, the jury voted unanimously to uphold the British appeal.

In lieu of a 10,000-meter walk, Olympic officials for the first time experimented with a 20,000-meter walk. The Russians won first, second and third in this event, while Henry Laskow, the perennial U.S. walker, placed twelfth. In the discus throw, hard luck continued to bother Fortune Gordien notwithstanding his first name. This great athlete and amateur magician, who held the world mark of 194' 6", placed third in 1948 and fourth in 1952. Despite his world mark and his unknown ability, he could only throw the discus 179' 9", taking second to Al Oerter's 184' 10½". The United States took all three medals in this event.

In the hammer throw, Harold Connolly of the United States and Mikhail Krivonosov of Russia continued their duel, in which first one and then the other got off throws to win and to raise the record. This time, however, Connolly won with a new Olympic mark of 207' 3¾". This mark would be unbelievable to sportsmen of the pre-Olympic period, when the world record was under 165'. The javelin throw produced a new world and Olympic record of 281' 2¼". The winner, Egil Danielsen, won the first gold medal for Norway in thirty-six years of Olympic track and field competition. Janusz Sidlo of Poland, who had held the world mark, was second, and Victor Tsibulenko of Russia was third. Strangely enough, Cy Young, the 1952 Olympic champion and former world record holder from the United States, qualified for the final competition with a toss of 245' 3"—sufficient to place him fourth—but the rules did not permit qualifying performances to count in the final competition.

In the high jump, to show the general improvement of performance, the qualifying height had been established at 6' 3½"—normally a pretty rough criterion. Nevertheless, 22 competitors cleared it and reported for the final competition, which lasted more than five hours and undoubtedly prevented Dumas from equaling or exceeding his world record of 7' ⅝". Dumas won, however, with a new Olympic record of 6' 11¼", with Charles Porter of Australia and Igor Kashkarov of Russia taking second and third. Bob Richards of the United States and A. Ferreira da Silva of Brazil were repeaters from 1952 in the pole vault and hop, step and jump respectively. The decathlon, the most grueling of all events in the Olympic track and field, was won by Milton Campbell, with Rafer Johnson second and Vasiliy Kouznetsov of Russia third.

The women's track and field was a runaway for Australia, with Betty Cuthbert winning both the 100- and 200-meter dash and running in the Australian 400-meter relay team that not only won but also broke the world and Olympic records. Australia also won the 80-meter hurdles. Mildred McDaniel of the United States won the high jump, while the javelin, discus and shotput were dominated by Russia and Czechoslovakia.

185

The 1960 Rome Olympics resulted in four world records, the tying of two others, the posting of the world's fastest time in the marathon, nine Olympic records, the tying of one and the greatest number of spectators of any past games. Two of the world and nine of the Olympic records were set by the United States which won nine gold, eight silver and five bronze medals. Russia, Germany, New Zealand and Poland were next in medal-winning in that order.

The United States no longer has a monopoly on experience, know-how or track and field athletes. The entire world is learning fast and catching up. There were many surprises at Rome, such as Hary of Germany's win in the men's 100-meter dash—the first non-U.S. victory in this event in 32 years. To compound this surprise, Livio Berutti of Italy won the 200 meter, again the first non-U.S. victory in the event in 32 years and the third non-U.S. victory out of 13 Olympics.

Lee Calhoun in the 110-meter hurdles, Glen Davis in the 400-meter hurdles and Al Oerter in the discus repeated their 1956 Olympic wins. A Russian win over the U.S.'s John Thomas in the high jump was unexpected. The marathon was won by Abebe Bikila, a 28-year-old, 126-pound Ethiopian, who ran the 26-mile 385-yard course barefooted faster than this distance has ever been run before. Another U.S. string of victories was broken in the 400-meter relay after eight straight Olympic wins. Although the U.S. team finished first, it was disqualified in favor of the German team when Ray Norton, running second for the United States, grabbed the baton from Frank Budd some three yards beyond the passing zone. Dave Sime, the anchorman, started three yards behind Germany's Martin Lauer but overhauled him to win by two feet—but to no avail. The U.S.'s Bill Nieder, Parry O'Brien and Dallas Long took 1-2-3 in the shotput.

In the women's track and field, the competition was completely dominated by wondrous Wilma Rudolph, somewhat as Betty Cuthbert of Australia had starred in 1956. In spectacular fashion, the tall Tennessee State University co-ed won three gold medals. She, together with the Russian women, broke every Olympic mark in the women's track and field book. She tied the world's record and in fact broke it (not allowed because of wind) in the 100-meter dash, then won the 200 meter in Olympic record time and helped break a world's record in the 400-meter relay won by the U.S. team. Strangely enough, Wilma, although unknown, was a 16-year-old member of the U.S. team at Melbourne. Betty Cuthbert's luck was out at Rome as she pulled up lame in the second heat of the 100 and had to withdraw from the 200. Nothwithstanding very strict qualifying standards, the United States nevertheless managed to send 18 girls to Rome. Eight of these were from Tennessee State University which also supplied the head coach, Ed Temple, who has developed great girl track stars for many years.

Track and field events, known throughout the world except in the United States as "athletics," were held at the Tokyo games from Wednesday, October 14 through Wednesday October 21 and from the start of the first heat of the men's 100-meter dash to the finish of the marathon. All were contested or finished in the National Stadium in the Komazawa complex. Unlike the situation at past games, all contestants were likely winners because of the extraordinary qualification performance required of them. The Games were officially opened by the Japanese Emperor and Ryotaro Azuma, Mayor or Governor of Tokyo. The stadium contained an eight-lane 400-meter track and a bright green grass field within it. Over 75,000 persons watched the games on practically every one of the eight days. It is estimated, however, that over 500,000 persons saw the 1964 marathon race through Tokyo—a highlight of the games because for the first time an Olympic marathon runner won two in a row. Abebe Bikila of Ethiopia won in Tokyo as he had at Rome—with ease. His time, perhaps because of an easier course, perhaps because he wore shoes at Tokyo but ran barefoot at Rome, was the fastest run in any Olympics. After finishing with no visible strain, Abebe ran half way around the stadium, then proceeded to perform calisthenics to loosen himself up. He competed again in Mexico's 1969 marathon and because he was experienced in running at the high altitude of Addis Ababa (9,950 feet) was an early favorite, but he was forced out by too fast an early pace, a cramp, a cold and perhaps age.

The great surprise of the meet was the winning of both the 5,000- and 10,000-meter races by U.S. runners. Neither race had ever previously been won by an American. Bob Schul, in a final drenched by rain, zoomed ahead of Ron Clarke of Australia and Michael Jazy of France with his final kick for an unexpected win. In the 10,000 meter, 1st. Lt. William M. Mills, U.S. Marine Corps, an American Indian who first started running as roadwork for his training as a boxer, was the winner—also coming from behind to set a new Olympic record. A mid-distance king of runners established his class when Peter Snell of New Zealand won both the 800

187

meter and the metric mile—the 1,500 meter run. To evaluate Snell's performance, Bill Crothers, who placed second, ran the fastest 800 ever run by any man in the Western Hemisphere, 1:45.6, Wilson Kaprugut of Kenya, who placed third, ran the fastest ever run by an African or Asiatic, while Snell won in 1:45.1 after many heats. This was better than his winning time in Rome in 1960 of 1:46.3, and almost as fast as his world's record of 1:44.3. In the 1,500, Snell's winning time was 3:38.1 after lots of previous running, but still the equivalent of a 3:55 mile.

The pole vault Olympic record, which had heretofore edged up by ¼″ to 1′, suddenly went from 15′ 5⅛″ to 16′ 9″ in one Olympiad, but was merely an omen of things to come, for John Pennel of the United States, world record holder, who re-injured his back and had to quit, could have easily vaulted 17′ 4″ with his plexiglass pole. In the long (previously called broad) jump both Ralph Boston of the United States and Igor Ter-Ovanesyan of Russia were surprised and out-jumped by Welsh teacher Lynn Davies with 26′ 5¾″—a man-size improvement over the jump by the U.S.'s Ellery Clark, at the 1898 games, of 20′ 9¾″ and that of Chionis *circa.* 820 B.C. (twelfth Olympiad) of 23′ 1½″. Al Orter of the New York Athletic Club won his third gold medal in the discus, repeating his 1956 and 1960 successes. In the decathlon the United States gave up its 32-year monoply when Willi Holdorf of Germany, a physical education student, edged the field that included Rein Aun of Russia and the favorite and world record holder C. K. Yang of Taiwan.

In the women's track and field at Tokyo, all-around honors went to Russia. Top performances were those of Britain's Mary Rand in her world's record win in the broad (long) jump of 22′ 2¼″, with no U.S. competitors in the first ten, and the win of Ann Packer of Australia in the 800 meter with a new world record of 2:01.1. Miss Rand, not satisfied with her gold medal, won a silver medal in the new ladies' pentathlon and Miss Packer won a second in the 400. Probably the most unusual incident in the women's competitions was a javelin throw of Elena Gorchakova of Russia in the qualifying rounds. It set a new world's record and would have won the competition with plenty to spare. However, it did not count in the regular competition, which was won by Michaela Penes of Rumania with a throw of over six feet less. Miss Gorchakova actually was lucky to finish third on her throws in the final.

Nothwithstanding the altitude of Mexico City (7,533 ft.

above sea level) athletics *ie* track and field, proved the most popular sport at the 1968 games based on: the largest audience or cumulative number of spectators, the most athletes or entries 1,122 (864 men, 258 women) from 89 countries according to one official source (1,459 from 91 countries according to another), with Olympic records equaled or broken in 18 of the 24 events for men and nine of the 12 events for women.

Outstanding performances were many. First came Oerter's fourth gold medal over four Olympiads in the discus with his greatest throw in 13 years of world competition—212' 6½". In the first modern games in 1896 the winning throw was 95' 7½". In the ancient Olympics a slightly different discus was thrown 150' for an Olympic olive wreath. In setting a new Olympic record in the decathlon Bill Toomey was outstanding. In the women's events Wyomia Tyus was the first woman in Olympic history to retain the 100-meter title and also won for the United States the 400-meter relay crown. Dick Fosbury of Oregon State with his new Fosbury flop in which he goes over the bar flat on his back established a new high jumping Olympic record of 7' 4½". Bob Beamon probably topped all the rest by winning the broad jump with a world's record 29' 2½", almost 2 feet over the previous record.

Another phenomenal performer was Kipchoge Keino of Kenya, who had trained by running up steep hills at high altitude and broke the metric mile (1,500 meters). The competitions also featured two victories by crafty or strategic generalship where the mind as well as muscle determined the winner. Bob Seagren out-maneuvered his two top opponents, West Germany's Schiprowski and East Germany's Nordwig, when he passed 17' 6¾", although both Seagren and Schiprowski cleared 17' 8¼" on their second attempts and both missed all three attempts at 17' 10¼". Seagren won on the basis of one miss less than Schiprowski. Aftali Temu of Kenya beat the field in the 10,000 meter by shrewdly never taking the lead for the first 9,080 meters. Another world's record was broken by Dave Hemery of Britain in the 400-meter hurdles. The finest performance in the women's events was West Germany's Ingrid Becker who won the pentathlon. Madeline Manners of the United States broke the world's record in winning the 800-meter race.

Man's latest inventions greatly widen the number of spectators. Worldwide TV coverage to an extent probably never achieved before brought track and field to literally millions with the help of super and colored cameras, satellites, relays

189

and videotape. Tomorrow, no matter where the Olympics may be held, its competitions, particularly those in track and field, will be seen from Terra del Feugo to Hudson Bay and from Lapland to the Cape of Good Hope.

The Munich Olympics, July 22 to August 6, 1972, were not a success because the Munich Organizing Committee tried, in their own words, to "humanize" the Games and limit them to "proper proportions" so that all spectators could enjoy a "more intimate or close view of the spectacle." In other words, Munich did not provide a stadium of 100,000 or more persons, even though Munich was more readily available to large population centers than Mexico City, Tokyo or Melbourne. No one knows why Munich believed its enlarged stadium of 65,000 seats would do for the world games when Rio could seat 200,000. Also, Munich's welcome was not very warm. A 100% advance payment, not recoverable, was demanded, with rates at $40 per day for a double room (in 1972) and no guarantee of a bath or even of a location any closer than 75 miles from the city's center. These were the rules of the Munich Organizing Committee. Further, early applicants from the United States could not purchase a seat at the opening ceremony of the Games. In fact, U.S. applicants, even with Olympic credentials, could not reserve rooms with bath two years before the Games. This resulted in an article, in a U.S. magazine, entitled "Yankee Stay Home!". Notwithstanding all this, while not a success, the 1972 Games broke all records for number of athletes, number of countries participating and total number of spectators.

In conclusion, due to the improvement of everything connected with the Olympics and better methods of training, finer equipment, coaching, etc., the progress in track and field, unlike that of other sports, can be measured and compared by the records in the events from 1896 to the present. A table in the appendix shows the percentage of improvement. These figures of competitive athletic improvement in the realm of amateur sports show that man should be able to break any barrier and accomplish almost anything for his own progress and betterment.

IMPORTANT FACTS ABOUT TRACK AND FIELD EQUIPMENT, DISTANCES AND NEW RULES LIMITING THE NUMBER OF CONTESTANTS

Here is a collection of facts and figures relating to some of the events in the Olympic games.

First, the marathon race. The distance is 26 miles and 385 yards, or 42 kilometers and 195 meters; it takes about two and a half hours to run.

An early Olympic test was the throwing of rocks and weapons. These events have their counterparts today in four throwing events: the discus, hammer, shot and javelin.

The first discus was of stone. Now it is a circular wooden plate with a smooth metal ring around its edge and brass plates set flush into the sides. It weighs 2 kilograms, or 4 lbs. 6.4 oz.

The shot or weight is spherical, weighs 16 lbs., and is of solid iron, brass, or any metal not softer than brass; or it can be a shell of such a metal filled with lead.

The hammer weighs 16 lbs. overall, including a handle of spring steel wire or No. 36 piano wire looped at one end to provide a grip and connected to the head by a swivel. This head, like the weight, is spherical, and of iron or brass; the whole must not measure more than 4 ft. in length. It is not, of course, a "hammer," though in the old days a blacksmith's hammer was thrown, and is still used in the Highland games of Scotland.

The javelin is a wooden spear (made of birch) with a sharp iron or steel point. The space between the foremost point and the center of gravity is between 3 and $3\frac{1}{2}$ ft.; at the center is a grip formed of whipcord without thongs or notches in the shaft. It is circular in section throughout. The length of a javelin is not less than 8 ft. 6 in., and the weight is not less than 1 lb. 12 oz. The women's javelin weighs 1 lb. 5 oz.

By contrast, the pole with which the pole vaulter propels himself upward may be of any material, length or diameter. It was in the past made of aluminum, bamboo, or other wood, and may terminate in a single metal spike. Each competitor brought his own to the meet; in recent years the poles have been made of plexiglass with considerably more whip. This with better timing and form and vaulters will ultimately bring the record to 20 feet or more.

Now for the running track. It is the inner edge that counts; cinder tracks are marked by a border of wood 2 inches high, and grass tracks (for hurdles and steeplechase) by a chalk line. Races of 120 yards or less must be run on a straight course, in lanes not less than 4 feet wide. In long-distance races, held on an oval track, the distance a runner has to run is calculated from a point measured 12 inches to the outside of this inside edge. In measuring lanes for distances up to and including 440 yards, the inner lane is measured first, and the others 8 inches from their inside borders.

The relay baton is a smooth, hollow, wooden or metal tube circular in section, a little less than 12 inches in length, and weighing 1¾ oz.

Hurdle races are over ten obstacles; for the 110-meter or 120-yard race these are at 10-yard intervals with a 15-yard run-up from the start to the first hurdle. For this distance the hurdles are 3 ft. 6 in. high, with level top rails, 3 ft. 11 in. wide, weight 22 lb. 3½ oz., and designed so that a force of 8 lbs. applied to the center or the top bar is needed to knock one over.

For the 400-meter or 440-yard race, hurdles are 6 inches lower, the first is 49¼ yards from the start, and the rest 38¼ yards apart.

In steeplechases a water jump is included, and there must be five jumps in each lap. The hurdles used in this case are 3 feet high; each obstacle must have a total width of 12 feet. Every competitor must go over or through the water.

The finish in track races is not the tape, but a white line on the ground. The tape is stretched 4 feet above it for the purpose of assisting the judges only. The finishing order is judged by the order in which any part of the competitor's body (the torso, as distinct from the head, arms, hands or feet) reaches the line. In the event a competitor falls, he is held not to have finished until head, body, and feet are all over the line.

So long as certain countries do not use the metric system, there must be some difficulty in comparing times and distances. In the Olympic games all weights and measures must be in accordance with the metric system.

The 100-meter race is, by U.S. and British equivalent, 109 yards, 1 foot, 1 inch. The 800 meter is not an exact half-mile (880 yards) but 874 yards, 2 feet, 8 inches. The nearest event to the mile (1,760 yards) is the 1,500 meter equivalent to 1,640 yards 1 foot, 2¾ inches.

We are indebted to the International Athletic Federation (IAAF) for a great improvement in Olympic track and field competition. According to a new rule each country is allowed one entry in each of the track and field events but in order to enter two, or the maximum of three competitors in any event, a certain standard has to be officially met by these additional candidates at any time during a fixed (about ten months') period prior to the games. These standards are difficult, as the criteria is to establish the potential of the extra entries for winning the event.

1976 qualification standards in men's athletics were:

100 m run	0:10.2	Long jump	7.8	meters
200 m run	0:20.8	Pole vault	5.2	meters
400 m run	0:46.4	Triple jump	16.4	meters
110 m hurdles	0:13.8	High jump	2.18	meters
400 m hurdles	0:50.5	16 lb. hammer	69.0	meters
800 m run	1:47.4	Javelin	80.0	meters
1500 m run	3:40.6	Discus	60.0	meters
Decathlon	7,650 pts.	Shot	19.4	meters

The 1980 qualifications are improved.

CHAPTER XVI

Weight Lifting

MAN OUT of necessity has always been a weight lifter, from the days when our cave man ancestors lifted great rocks to block cave entrances for protection, through the days of ancient Egypt, when the greatest collection of weight lifters in the world was assembled to heave mighty stones into pyramids as monuments to dead kings. There is some evidence that weight lifting and weight throwing were practiced by the ancient Greeks in connection with gymnastics and track and field. There is also positive evidence that weight lifting and weight throwing were part of the ancient Irish Tailtean games almost four thousand years ago.

However, weight lifting as we know the modern sport originated with the Europeans. Most likely some village youth, in an effort to make a show of his superior muscular prowess to some fair lady, bragged to a rival swain that he was the stronger and could lift a greater weight to prove it. The challenge made and accepted, a new sport and means of diversion was born. In its early years the sport was popular in central Europe and then spread to the Scandinavian countries, Egypt, Turkey, and even to Japan, and about a hundred years ago European settlers brought the sport to America. However, it still had limited appeal, and not until weight lifting had been introduced in the Olympic games did interest in it become widespread in America and all over the world.

In the 1896 Olympic games at Athens, there were only two weight lifting events, the dumbbell and the bar bell. A little byplay which delighted the spectators during this competition was that Prince George of Greece, one of the judges, who stood six feet five and had quite a reputation as a strong man himself, when he saw that an attendant ordered to remove the weights was having trouble doing so, couldn't resist picking up the heaviest of the weights and throwing it a good distance out of the way. In these early games, weight lifting was included as part of the track and field program and the events were contested in the stadium. A Dane and an Englishman each won one of the two events.

In the dumbbell contest in 1904, Americans won all three places—O. S. Osthoff first, F. Winters second, and F. Kungler third. In bar bell lifting, Pericles Kakousis of Greece, who later became known as one of the greatest strong men of his time, won, with Osthoff placing second and Kungler third. Two years later, at the Athens games of 1906, there were no entrants from the United States, and Josef Steinbach of Austria won the one-hand lift while D. Tofolas of Greece won the two-hand.

There appear to have been no official weight lifting events in the 1908 or 1912 Olympics. In 1920, however, interest in standardized weight lifting with definite procedures and rules had grown and it held its own place in the Olympics instead of as part of the track and field program. In that year the events were divided into five weight classes ranging from featherweight to heavyweight, and individual honors were divided among Europeans. The all-around unofficial championship was won by Belgium, with France almost even. Estonia and Italy produced individual winners.

In modern weight lifting the three important lifts are: the two-hand or military press, in which the contestants must toe a line, not move away from it, and after lifting the weight from the floor to rest on chest, neck or shoulders, then lift it to the limit of their arms without bending but retaining military position; the clean and jerk, or the jerk, in which, with either hand or both, the contestant lifts the weight from floor to rest against chest, then lifts it as high as possible on call from the referee; the snatch, in which, with either hand or both, the contestant picks up the weight and in one continuous movement lifts as high as possible. The contestant must hold the weight for the referee's count of one-two. There are two judges and a referee. Records are figured by adding totals of press, snatch, and clean and jerk. Weight classifications now in use follow approximately the same limits as in wrestling: bantamweight (123½ lbs.), featherweight (132¼ lbs.), lightweight (148¾ lbs.), middleweight (165⅜ lbs.), light heavyweight (181⅞ lbs.), middle heavyweight (198⅜ lbs.), and heavyweight (weight unlimited).

In 1924, when there were only five weight classes, Italy took three gold medals and France the other two. There was no U.S. team in either 1920 or 1924.

In 1928, the honors were again well distributed, with Germany, Egypt, France and Austria all getting gold medals; Germany won the unofficial team championship.

The French took over in 1932 and won three of the five weight lifting titles. The Americans, however, going into weight lifting on a major basis, showed great promise, with Dietrich Wortmann as manager and Mark Berry as coach. Anthony Terlazzo and Henry L. Duey were third-place medal winners for the United States. There were eight countries in the competitions. Germany and Czechoslovakia produced the other two champions.

The 1936 Olympic games saw the United States win its first gold medal in weight lifting and also give promise of eventually attaining supremacy in this sport. Although Americans had won a sort of empty victory at St. Louis in 1904, they had not even entered this sport or any weight lifting events in 1906, 1908, 1912, 1920, or 1924. In 1928 the United States first organized and presented a very creditable team, so the results in 1936 were encouraging. The same manager and the same coach were behind the U.S. team, which met teams of fifteen nations. The unofficial team results were: first, Egypt, followed by Germany, Austria, the United States, and France. Anthony Terlazzo, who had placed third in 1932, won in the featherweight class, breaking the world's record with a total of a fraction under 689 lbs. At these Olympics eight world's records were broken. L. Hostin of France repeated his 1932 win in the light-heavyweight class, a feat never previously accomplished in Olympic weight lifting. The United States took two fifths and one sixth place, in addition to its one win. Mohammed Ahmed Mesbah of Egypt, in the lightweight class, was the star of the entire competition, breaking three world's records —twice in the clean and jerk, and in his total.

During the war years, American interest in weight lifting more than caught up with the head start of other countries, so there were numerous candidates and very tough competitions to select the U.S. team for the 1948 Olympiad. The London games attracted competitors from 35 nations in the weight lifting championships. The United States, entering a full team for only the third time, won the unofficial all-around championship with four firsts, three seconds, and two thirds. One hundred thirty-five weight lifters puffed and huffed to create eighteen new Olympic and four new world's records. Dietrich Wortmann's dream and ambition had come true—in three Olympics he had, as manager, brought the United States from nowhere to first place. Robert Hoffman was coach of the winners. John Davis, U.S. Olympic heavyweight champion, broke one world's record, and U. S. I. Fayad of Egypt, in the featherweight class, broke three. Evidence of the growing popularity of this sport is the fact that there were entries from India and Pakistan, Peru and Argentina, Korea and South Africa, as well as the European nations.

An example of the good sportsmanship shown during these games is the conduct of Stanczyk of the United States. On the third trial he snatched 292 lbs. for a new world record and received the approval of the two judges. However, he reported to the referee that his knee had accidentally grazed the platform, and disqualified himself.

In 1952 the late and honored Dietrich Wortmann was again the manager of the U.S. weight lifting team, and again saw his team win. At his death, the sport suffered a great loss.

The Helsinki 1952 Olympiad surpassed all previous Olympics in the number of contestants and the quality of the performances in weight lifting. Russia was a newcomer to the games but showed great promise, winning three titles to four for the United States (a bantamweight class having been added in 1948 and a middle-heavyweight class in these Olympics). Twenty-one Olympic and six world's records were broken. R. Chimishkyan of Russia broke one world's record; N. Schemansky, U.S. middle heavyweight (199 lbs.), broke three; and T. Kono, U.S. lightweight (148 lbs.), broke two. Of the 28 world's records (press, snatch, jerk, and total in each of seven weight clasifications), American weight lifters then held 13. To demonstrate the awesome accomplishments of weight lifters, T. Kono, weighing under 148 lbs., can press, snatch, and jerk over 798 lbs.

Thirty-six nations entering 122 competitors participated in the weight lifting tournament at the Exhibition Building in Melbourne. Based upon the number of entries this sport was the third most popular in the games. The main rivalry was between Russia and the United States, with the latter springing a surprise by taking four gold medals to the U.S.S.R.'s three. The competition was so superior that Olympic records were equaled or broken 119 times and world records beaten 17 times. Another interesting feature was the sudden advance of weight lifters from all over the world—Iran, Korea, Japan, Burma, British Guiana, China, Trinidad and the Philippines. The standouts were: the Brooklyn teenager I. Berger, a newcomer in international lifting who racked up a new world record in the featherweight class with a total of 776½ lbs.; C. Vinci of the United States in the bantamweight class, who also broke the world and Olympic records with a total of 754½ lbs.; and T. Kono of the United States in the light heavyweight class, with a world record total of 986¼ lbs.

The Rome weight lifting competition was greatly influenced by U.S. complacency as a result of its 1948, 1952 and 1956 Olympic team victories. There was a definite let down with even one of the top U.S. weight lifters electing to compete in a class so he could meet the "toughest" Russian opponent. Russia surprised and upset the U.S. team with five gold medals and one silver out of seven events. U.S. competitors bettered all marks made in 1956 but were only able to win one gold medal (Chuck Vinci, who retained the bantam weight title) four silver and one bronze. The actual margin, involving close differences in four classes, was small.

The Tokyo weight lifting events represented an easy win for Russia, which scored an overall 55 points against Poland, 28; Japan, 25; United States, 20, and Hungary, 18. Three world and four Olympic records were broken. The U.S.'s Isaac Berger of Brooklyn, featherweight winner in 1956, was second to Yoshinobu Miyake of Japan, who established a new world's record with a total of 874½ pounds. In the heavyweight class, two Russians and two representatives of the United States huffed and puffed with 340-pound Leonid Zhabotinsky, 300-pound Yuri Vlasov, both of Russia, the U.S.'s 320-pound Norbert Schemansky and N.Y.U. shotputter 305-pound Gary Gubner, finishing in that order.

The Mexico weight lifting competition was conducted in the picturesque but inadequately small (1,200 capacity) "Teatra de los Insurgentes". On the outside wall of this theater is a famous Rivera mural but during the games it was hardly noticed as the contests inside were close and very colorful. Unfortunately the United States did not recover its post-war supremacy lost at Rome in 1960 and in Tokyo in 1964. Several countries have improved and outclassed Uncle Sam's grunters as weight lifters are often called in the States. There were 160 competitors from 54 countries in the seven weight categories. Russia again won all-around honors, with Poland second and Japan third. John Dube of the United States tied for second in the heavyweight class but because he weighed more than Serge Redding of Belgium, had to be satisfied with the bronze medal, because of the rules. In case of a tie in the weight lifted, the lightest man wins.

CHAPTER XVII

Winter Sports

IT IS not known whether the ski or the snowshoe came first, but both were originally fashioned from animal bones and were used as a means of travel in snow-covered countries thousands of years ago. In fact, a pair of skis said to be 5,000 years old is displayed at a museum in Stockholm. Primarily, skiing was a means of transportation and still is, because of climatic conditions in many countries. Human nature, however, naturally seeks diversion and people began to see that skiing could be converted into a sport of many forms. Today skiing seems to have no bounds of climate, for there are ski enthusiasts performing even on sand in warm desert areas and on water.

The old bone skis, naturally, could not be turned up at the ends, and after the beginning of the Christian era, wood was used which made this innovation possible. The development of the ski is attributed to the Scandinavian countries and even played a part in their history when a more maneuverable, shorter, and better type of ski could mean victory for their soldiers. About 1590, skiing was introduced into central Europe through Austria, famous today for its ideal skiing areas, and has spread to all parts of the world where there is snow.

In the early nineteenth century people began to take notice of little impromptu races held between travelers in Scandinavia. Soon a little jumping was added to the play and by the 1850's, in Norway, carnivals were held for actual competition. Ten years later, the Norwegian royal family took notice of the jumping competitions and the King of Norway became so enthusiastic that he donated a special trophy for the winner. This soon grew to be the greatest sporting event in the country, "The Norwegian Ski Derby."

From Scandinavia, skiing ranged to continental Europe about the middle of the nineteenth century. The first mid-

European ski club was formed in Munich in 1890. The Swiss organized their first ski club in 1893. Chamonix, in France, was established as a winter resort in 1898-99.

The facts about the introduction of skis into North America are uncertain. The Canadian Indians used snowshoes and in all probability constructed skis, or snowshoes with long runners for use down steep mountain sides. There are those who contend that early settlers or visitors from Sweden, Denmark and Norway brought them to Canada. In predominantly Scandinavian settlements in the United States, particularly in the north Midwest, various local clubs were formed. By 1904, these local clubs drew enough attention and support to band together into the National Ski Association, but it wasn't until formal international competition was begun in the modern Olympic games that skiing was brought into the limelight.

Skiing was demonstrated at some of the early Olympic games, but it was not until 1924 that winter sports finally won international recognition and became part of the formal Olympic program. In the games at Chamonix, France, winter sports were an outstanding success. The Norwegians, real masters at skiing, won all four events and in two of them took all of the top four places. Thorleif Haug was a triple gold medal winner, taking first place in the Nordic combined, the 18-kilometer and the 50-kilometer race. In the jumping, the most spectacular of all skiing events, Jacob Thams of Norway won, with Anders Haugen, the only American to place in skiing, in fourth place, which was a good showing considering the limited appeal the sport had in the States in 1924 Norway easily won the all-around winter sports championships, which attracted contestants from sixteen countries. Finland was second, the United States a poor but surprising third, then England, Austria, Sweden, Switzerland, Germany, Canada, Belgium, Czechoslovakia and Italy, in that order.

The 1924 games at Chamonix were so successful that winter sports were firmly established as part of the Olympic program, and the second winter Olympics in 1928 were held at St. Moritz, Switzerland. Twenty-five nations sent representatives. During the preceding years, the United States had developed a strong winter sports team, and in the unofficial overall score they placed second to Norway. However, skiing was their weakest point, and again the Scandinavians proved their complete mastery of the sport. The United States made 1 point in skiing, 10 in speed skating, 10 in figure skating, and 24 in bobsledding. Sweden was the overall third, Finland fourth, and Austria and Canada fifth and sixth.

According to competition rules, forty entries or twenty actual competitors were allowed, but the United States had only three men: Rolf Monsen, Charles Proctor and Anders Haugen. In spite of an injured knee, Monsen placed sixth in the main jumping event to earn the only point won by the American ski team. In the combined ski-jumping event a championship performance almost cost Jacob Thams, 1924 Olympic gold medal winner from Norway, his life. It must be explained that the ski jump at St. Moritz is geared for jumps of about 60 meters and is safe only for jumps measuring up to 65 meters, but the object of ski jumping is to see how far you can go and still maintain perfect form, and Thams jumped an unprecedented 73 meters and suffered a terrible fall—this was impossible to prevent because of the physical conditions of the hill—but he miraculously escaped death. A fellow Norwegian, Johann Grottumsbraaten, won this event and also the 18-kilometer race. Andersen of Norway won the gold medal in the special jumping and Pete Hedlund of Sweden the 50-kilometer race.

In the 1932 games at Lake Placid, New York, though the Americans did well in the overall winter sports competition, they were still green, though game, in skiing. The United States won the overall games but with just 2 points in skiing as against Norway's 47. In skiing, Finland was second with 19 points and Sweden third with 18. The Americans had hoped to gain points in jumping. However, the most hopeful prospect, Casper Oimen, captain of the ski team, had hurt himself during tryouts in the United States before leaving for the games, although he insisted upon participating and took fifth place. Birger Ruud gave Norway the jumping championship and Grottumsbraaten won another medal for Norway in the combined racing and jumping. The 50-kilometer race, won by Saarinen of Finland, was extraordinary in that it was run at all. The weather conditions were almost impossible. In fact, the snow was fast disappearing and part of the race was run on bare ground, with rocks and stumps sticking up. The hardy Finn perserved, however, to win this marathon, and as evidence of the grueling run, when he came across the finish line his face was streaked with blood and his clothes were in shreds.

The coach of the American team, Julius Blegen, after these games reported that, "The third winter Olympic games, as far as skiing is concerned, was the biggest boost the sport has ever had in the United States and should in years to come open the eyes of the American boys and girls to the possibilities in this wonderful health-bringing, clean outdoor pastime." This proved to be true and the Lake Placid winter games proved a stimulant to millions of potential enthusiasts, for skiing was seen by people who had never seen it before. It caught on immediately, with its fascinating combination of danger and grace, and ski groups began mushrooming all over the country. Instructors were brought over from the Scandinavian countries and Austria, France, and Switzerland, and now there are said to be over eight million ski enthusiasts in the United States alone.

The 1936 games at Garmisch-Partenkirchen, Germany, opened in a raging blizzard. The greatest number of contestants so far—almost one thousand, representing twenty-eight nations—participated. Skiing was gaining widespread appeal and was attracting more and more contestants from more countries. The Norwegians again maintained their consistently high standard of performance in skiing and also won the overall winter games championship, with Germany, Sweden, Finland, the United States, and Austria completing the top six. A welcome newcomer to the Olympics was the first of the events for women, the Alpine combined, which Christel Cranz of Germany won. Germany also edged in on the combined downhill and slalom race for men, a combination of the most dangerous and the most graceful of skiing routines. Norway and Sweden took all the other events, and in the 18-kilometer race, in which there were 115 entries, they took the first nine places.

In 1948 there were 942 participants in the winter events, with contestants from twenty-nine nations. Sweden, for the first time, won both the overall skiing events and the unofficial all-around winter games championship. In all winter sports combined, for both men and women, Switzerland was second, the United States third, Norway fourth, Austria fifth, Finland sixth, and France seventh. The United States entered a ski team with thirty members (in contrast to the earlier three-member team), including women. The inclusion of women in winter events was to bring the United States its first gold medal in skiing. The outstanding success of Mrs. Gretchen Fraser of Vancouver, Washington, in the slalom brought applause from all countries. She also placed second in the Alpine combined. The Norwegians upheld their fine jumping tradition, winning the top three places. Birger Ruud, who had previously won two Olympic championships, took

201

second place and made room for Petter Hugsted in first place. In the jumping, Gorden Wren of the United States came in fifth, the only American to place. The French also gave top performances and Henri Oreiller won two gold medals in the downhill and Alpine combination and a bronze medal in the men's slalom. In the slalom, Edi Reinalter of Switzerland won first place and James Couttet of France second place. Couttet also came in third in the Alpine combination. Karl Molitor of Switzerland was second in the Alpine combination and tied for third with Rolf Olinger, also Swiss, in the downhill. In this last event, Franz Gabl of Austria was second.

Thirty nations with almost 1,200 contestants participated in the 1952 games at Oslo. Skiing events drew enormous crowds of spectators and the ranks of competitors were filling up with contestants from as far away as Japan, and in one event there were over eighty contestants. The Nordic events were won mostly by Finland and Norway. An Italian, Zeno Colo, gave a magnificent performance and won the gold medal in the downhill race, and Ol Schneider of Austria won the special slalom for men. The only Americans to place in the men's events were two boys from Dartmouth—William Beck, who came in fifth in the downhill (out of seventy-two contestants), and Joseph Brooks Dodge, sixth in the giant slalom and ninth in the special slalom. However, while the American men gained mostly experience, the women made up for it in honors. Mrs. Andrea Mead Lawrence, a young housewife from Vermont, won two gold medals in skiing in the slalom and the giant slalom. Katy Rodolph and Imogene Upton tied for fifth in the slalom and Catherine Wegeman placed fifth in the giant slalom.

The four-year wait for the 1956 winter Olympics was worthwhile to the skiing world, for there was unprecedented skiing at Cortina that year. A young, handsome Austrian boy, Toni Sailer, with a fast-gained reputation, won not only both slalom events but the downhill race as well, earning three gold medals, a feat never before accomplished in thirty-two years of Olympic skiing. Besides his flawless skiing form, his good looks must have won over more than one woman to the sport. His boyish shyness won him the American nickname of "Li'l Abner of the Tyrol." Stenersen of Norway won the Nordic combined, with Ericsson of Sweden coming in second and Gasienca of Poland placing third. This was the first time Poland had won a medal in a skiing event. The Japanese had been sending skiers to the Olympics for some time and this year Chiharu Igaya won a silver medal in the men's slalom. Hyvarinen and Kallakorpi of Finland took the first two places in the special jump. The Russians made a grand showing, although it was the first time they had ever been represented in skiing, winning the gold medal in the cross-country relay and third place in the other three cross-country events. With points made in the other winter sports, Russia won the all-around winter sports championship. In the women's events, Kozyreva and Erochina won the first two places in the women's cross-country, the first time this event was held in the Olympics. Ossi Reichert of Germany won the women's giant slalom, and Andrea Mead Lawrence of the United States tied for fourth place in this event. The wide geographical distribution of participants, including Russia, Japan, and Great Britain, in addition to the usual strong central European and Scandinavian representation, is an outstanding example of what the Olympics have done to bring people from all corners of the earth together in common interest and proves that skiing is no longer an exclusively Scandinavian sport but one of worldwide importance and interest.

The 1960 winter Olympics at Squaw Valley, California, was the site of many new records in skiing. Led by Penny Pitou and Betsy Snite and their three silver medals (two by Penny) and one fourth by Betsy, the U.S. girls made the best showing since 1952 when Andrea Mead skiied to two gold medals. Miss Pitou's specialties were the Alpine downhill and Giant Slalom, while Miss Snite's was the Alpine Slalom and Giant Slalom. In the men's events, with Toni Sailer, the triple gold medalist of 1956, gone, Austria won only one gold medal—in the last event, the Slalom, where Austrians Ernst Hinterseer and Mathias Leitner finished first and second. The Germans upset a Scandinavian monopoly in the Nordic combined and the jumping, with George Thoma and Helmut Recknagel. Finland, Sweden and Norway, however, dominated the other individual events. Sweden's "King of the Skis," Sixten Jernberg, won the 30 km. race and was second to Norway's Haakon Brusveen in the 15 km. Old, balding Veikko Hakulinen (35) of Finland won his third gold medal in his third Olympics as anchor man of the winning Finns in the 40 km. relay. He made up 20 seconds to nose out Brusveen at the finish. This third gold medal was his seventh Olympic medal—one gold in 1952, one gold and two silver in 1956 and one gold, one silver and one bronze in 1960. In the giant slalom Tommy Corcoran, popular American, came in a close fourth, the high mark of any American in this event. The men's downhill produced two surprises. First Jean Vuarnet of France, a comparative unknown, upset a field of 63 by flashing downward two miles in 2 m. 06 sec. flat and next he did it with metal skis—and no wax, a new French idea. Germany won three gold medals; Sweden, Finland and Switzerland two each; while Norway, Austria, France, Russia and Canada had to be contented with one each. This sport also proved that improvements in equipment as well as form and training methods make for higher, further and faster records. The United States could only collect three silver medals and two fourths but with the increase in the popularity of skiing in America and with better coaching and more competitions—especially with foreign performers—the United States should finally get the momentum to glide over the snow with the best.

Dr. Adolph Schaerf, the president of Austria, opened the ninth Olympic games at Innsbruck, Austria, before a crowd of over 50,000 people. As is usual at all Olympics, this was the best, the biggest, the most successful edition, with the greatest athletes and the greatest performances ever. Thirty-seven nations were entered, but only 36 were reported as having competed. 1,359 athletes participated, and the widely scattered facilities cost over $40,000,000. Everything was ready except the snow. No snow fell for two months before the first day's program, so the Austrian Army was turned out to bring the snow and pack the slopes, the runs and the trails.

As a sort of preliminary climax to the opening ceremony, 51 nations and the International Olympic Committee voted for Grenoble, France, as the site of the Winter Olympics in 1968. The 1972 winter games are scheduled for Sapporo, Japan. While the Innsbruck games and events were well attended, probably a record was established when over 100,000 people witnessed the new 90-meter ski jump contest on the last day. This event actually developed from the fact that ski jumpers became so good they literally jumped out of their original ski jump space.

Five bobsledding and tobogganing events were added to the Innsbruck games, as was a women's 5 kilometer cross-country ski event, for a total of 34 events. This meant that under the unofficial press scoring system the winter version of the games totalled 850 points. This means that the winter Olympics is becoming more important than ever in the overall unofficial scoring of future Olympic games, no matter how it is computed.

There can be no doubt that on a point per million population (the most logical method yet found to evaluate comparative athletic or Olympic accomplishment) Norway with 3.61 million won the 1964 winter games, for Austria has 7.3 million and Russia, the largest point-getter, has a 251 million population.

A 21-year-old Oregon State University coed representing the United States at Innsbruck tried very hard to win a gold medal in skiing. That girl, Jean Saubert, tied for second in the giant slalom and won the slalom. She missed the gold medal in the giant slalom by less than a second.

The U.S.'s William Kidd and James Huega came in second and third in the slalom with Kidd missing the gold medal by fifteen hundredths of a second. Sweden's Sixten Jernberg won the famous 50,000 meter (31 mile) ski marathon, finishing minutes ahead of his Swedish teammate, who came in second. It was his fourth gold medal in skiing in three Games.

Science, however, was perhaps the top star at the 1964 winter games. Every race timed to one-hundredth of a second, distances to fractions of a millimeter, placement of contestants, game scores and judges' points to two decimal places in these Olympic games were fed into a $3,000,000 computing and communications system designed to pour out final results in a fraction of a second. While there was an IBM first at Squaw Valley in 1960, the machines at Innsbruck were more complex, all-encompassing and speedier. In addition, while centered at one spot at Squaw Valley at Innsbruck, the net of robot-like machinery was scattered over 18 miles with 12 feeding points connected with the processing center at Innsbruck University. The center clicked out results and standings and flashed them back to all sites, installations, other receivers and to news agencies. The complicated figure skating calculations, which sometimes took hours and which took twelve minutes at Squaw Valley, took a single minute or less at Innsbruck.

The "winter games" of 1968 in Grenoble, France, matched the grandeur and pomp of any "summer games." Without ancient or Greek background, in only ten games, the winter Olympics were no longer a sideshow. They have followed, like history, an interesting pattern. In 1924 the initial winter games were granted to France and Chamonix. In 1968, grown to full status with 35 events, the tenth winter Olympics were again granted to France and to Grenoble. The late General

Charles de Gaulle, and his prime minister, George Pompidou, later president of France, opened the games. Very much in evidence at Grenoble were two secret envoys of the United States—John A. Love, Governor of Colorado, and Mayor Tom Currigan of Denver. Their mission . . . . . lobbying for the 1976 winter games which were awarded to Denver.

According to the citizens of Grenoble, their city has "a mountain at the end of every street, a new delight on every mountain." Just as before the Romans, when it was the hamlet of Cularo, it sits in a valley of alpine majesty from the shores of the Isere River to the snowy slopes of mountains topped by Mont Blanc (15,781.5 feet), over twice the height of Mexico City and higher even than legendary Mount Olympus.

The installations of these Grenoble games, spread over 75 miles, which cost over $240,000,000 United States dollars, were begun January 28, 1964. They included a 60,000-seat stadium (practically the same size as the Munich Stadium for the 1972 summer games) built for the opening ceremony only, three villages, a 12,000-seat ice rink stadium, 67 miles of new trails, two new airports, a new hospital, nine miles of new ski roads, 90 meter and 70 meter launching pads for guided skiers, and a million dollars of abstract sculpture. The French know glory and glamor without being stuffy. Although preceded by rain, snow and fog, the opening day, February 6th, 1968, was perfect. The 1,355 athletes from 37 countries (38 entered originally were ready for the opening ceremony, as were 7,025 officials, 3,182 newspaper correspondents, 1,521 radio and TV personnel. The 3,500 members of the French Alpine Troops deployed in the vicinity breathed easy as a blinding snowstorm on February 3rd took care of everything. A smaller and less well-equipped Austrian Army had to supply the snow for the 1964 games. Unlike Innsbruck, where arrogant police were anxious to arrest Olympic athletes and spectators, the French were sophisticated and suave. The Grenoble gendarmes were firm but friendly, but were in great part replaced by 300 attractive young girl interpreters and hostesses, dressed up in red bunny uniforms with tight blue pants, strategically deployed and with pleasant manners. Needless to say, there were no incidents, only fraternization. Over 60,000 people filled the $600,000 temporary stadium as the sun appeared as if on cue. The usual ceremony was on a scale comparable with that of any summer Olympics but with a few added French innovations. Thirty-two thousand paper roses sprayed with French perfumes were dropped from the sky, and French Army parachutists were dropped

206

unerringly from above into the five Olympic rings painted on the field inside the stadium. French Army jets zoomed down and began skywriting the five colored Olympic rings in smoke.

At the proper dramatic moment Avery Brundage, president of the I.O.C., took the podium, and after asking for "a less materialistic and happier and more peaceful world" asked General de Gaulle, president of France, to open the games. This the latter did—solemnly—and then, without further comment, he sat down. The parade was impressive with multi-colored uniforms of every type. The largest team in the games was the 251-member contingent of ABC—which included Dick Button, twice a gold medalist—to televise the games for an estimated audience of over 100,000,000 people in 33 countries at a cost of $55,000,000; but this team did not march in the parade.

The press was requested to play down two subjects controversial in the field of sports. The most interesting was the matter of the sex tests—namely the I.O.C.'s saliva or chromosome test for all women competitors, approved by the International Sports Medical Federation (FIMS). These resulted from past cases involving women track and field competitors barred by their world body and involved medication to stop menstruation and injection of male hormones to increase physical stamina and muscular development or tone, sometimes also causing breaking of the voice, hair growth and other changes. This was reportedly a common practice in the all-out effort of some countries to win more events in the last three Olympics for propaganda purposes. The I.O.C. played ostrich although secrecy was impossible. The authorities either had to test all women athletes or none, and if a contestant refuses to take the test or is disqualified, her entry but failure to appear is immediately known. However, the press showed great consideration for the I.O.C. and the matter was swept under the rug. Suffice it to say, however, that a two-time winter gold medal woman winner in 1964 either refused to take the chromosome test or failed to pass it at Grenoble. At Mexico City this issue was again hushed up with the help of the press with respect to the major women's track and field teams.

The other subject was one brought up by Mr. Brundage, again, on professionalism. While "IBM," "OMEGA," "ABC" and other signs and promotion material were frequently in evidence at Grenoble and an advertiser had a credit on the Olympic tickets at Mexico for advertising purposes, it was because these manufacturers or companies contributed their services or equipment or money to the I.O.C. and to national Olympic or Olympic organizing committees. In the winter biathlon, modern pentathlon, and in all shooting competitions in the Olympics, the pistols, revolvers, rifles and shotguns can easily be recognized as can their manufacturers. Their use in pictures in connection with the Olympics in the news or in promotional material has never raised any complaint. In the equestrian events the name and the identity of the horses and their pictures raise no questions, even though the performances of the horses in the Olympics may greatly influence their sales value—to their owners. In Olympic yachting, designers and builders receive due credit. Yet the I.O.C. and Mr. Brundage suddenly made a big issue out of ski and skate manufacturers having their imprint or trademark or even their copyrights on their equipment. In most cases this equipment was given in large quantity as an important contribution to the individual Olympic contestant or the national team involved. Naturally a manufacturer has the legal right to have his imprint or trademark, and even more so his patent identification, on his products. Not even the I.O.C. on Mount Olympus can interfere with this. So unless the athlete issues an endorsement or testimonial, either for the equipment, or more specifically for money, or conspires to get his equipment photographed, he can not be criticized or put under surveillance by committees—who also accept help.

With the exception of I.O.C. problems, the 1968 winter games were free of incidents. Everyone had compliments for the French hosts except the Austrian skiers who believed French officials had favored Jean Claude Killy in the last of his three victories over one of their skiers, Karl Schranz, who was disqualified for skipping two gates. The competitions were never so hotly contested, nor were there ever so many competitors and spectators at so many events before. The United States, disappointed at its showing, with better luck and without its skiers suffering accidents, falls and sickness, might well have had at least three or four gold medals and two more silver or bronzes. Terry McDermott of Birmingham, Michigan, could easily have won the 500-meter skating if he had not drawn twenty-seventh position on a soft and melted rink. Tom Wood of Bloomfield Hills, Michigan, in the men's figure skating was second by only 5 points out of 2,000. As it was on an overall point basis without even considering population differences, Norway won, with Russia second, Austria third; then came Sweden, France, Netherlands, Finland, Italy, the United States, West Germany, East Germany, Czechoslovakia, Switzerland, Canada and Romania. It is clear from these results that the state subsidization of amateur athletes for propaganda purposes is failing for the same reason that collectivism in the twentieth century is not succeeding in industry and agriculture. It eliminates individual incentive, as presaged by this writer both before and after Tokyo. The state subsidization of athletes is only good for one generation—unless ex-athletes are taken care of for life. Otherwise, only the true amateur athlete will have the incentive and dedication to his sport to compete and then, for some future help in competitive endeavors because of the prominence he has attained in amateur sports. Three scintillating personalities dominated the Grenoble games with the greatest of dedication and incentive. Jean Claude Killy of France, a descendent of the Kellys of Erin, won three gold medals and the title of the "Superman of Skiing." He had won sixteen out of twenty competitions in 1967, and two previous world's championships. Old Eugenio "Red" Monti of Italy, age 40, speed king, won two gold medals in bobsledding on top of nine world's championships. He had won two silver and two bronze medals in past Olympics. Peggy Fleming, dark, shapely, glamorous figure skating gold medalist from Colorado State College who loves chocolate and whipped cream but only weighs 100 lbs., may now attain greater fame in the movies and show business than Sonja Henie.

One thing is certain—the winter games are growing in popularity and are increasing the interest in, and importance of, the Olympic games and Olympic ideals. They point to the fact that human beings all over the world in cold or tropical climates want peaceful, friendly competition in sports, sportsmanship and entertainment.

The 1972 and 1976 winter games are covered in chapters XX, XXI, and appendix.

1. SKIING

The Alpine skiing in 1968 was set in Chamrousse, a small resort near Grenoble but a mile above sea level. Poor visibility and strong gales that swept over the snow resulted in great difficulties. The Nordic skiing, namely the long distance ski races, were held at Autrans in what the French properly call the Norway of the Alps. Of course, the Norwegians were in their element but were surprised when Franz Keller of West Germany won the Nordic combined and they lost both ski jump events—from the 70-meter platform to Jiri Raska of Czechoslovakia and to Vladimir Beloussov of Russia from the 90-meter platform, who outjumped Raska in second place by half a meter. For the second time since this event was added at Innsbruck it attracted an audience of over 100,000 persons.

2. FIGURE SKATING

Skating is a natural means of transportation in icy countries, and ice skates were probably an offshoot of skis and snowshoes. When it was necessary to move faster over icy surfaces, man was forced to use smaller and thinner bone runners. Later, by experimental smoothing and working of the bones, he learned that a flat bottom on the runner would permit a swift, gliding motion, and in this way, ice skates were developed.

As far as the development of skating as a sport is concerned, it is known that Scotland showed an early interest in it. In fact, in 1642 there was a well-established Skating Club of Edinburgh. When the Scots migrated to Canada, skating flourished and regular tournaments were held before the turn of the nineteenth century. The first American to win in any of these tournaments was Benjamin West, the artist, who spent a lot of time in Europe sometime in the 1770's.

In the United States, although skates were in use in the northeastern states for transportation, the practical New Englanders did not use them, as far as is known, for sport's sake until prompted by Canadian enthusiasm, and it was not until a technical improvement was made in the skates themselves that figure skating became really popular. Around 1850 E. W. Bushnell of Philadelphia revolutionized the skating world when he came out with a pair of skates with steel blades. These could be bought for thirty dollars, which represented quite an amount at that time. Despite the price, he was overwhelmed with orders and was able to produce them at a lower price, and they were soon in use all over the world. Steel blades were especially important in fancy figure skating, for they enabled performers to do artistic twists and turns on blades which did not have to be constantly re-sharpened.

Later it was an American who popularized figure skating throughout the world. This American was Jackson Haines, a ballet master who, in the slump following the Civil War in America, was not getting the business he had before the war. Not wishing to give up his profession, he packed up and went to Vienna where dancing seemed more likely to furnish him a livelihood. When he got there he found that in addition to their love for dancing, the Austrians also liked to skate —so, why not combine the two and skate to music? He transferred first the waltz and later other dance steps to the ice, and his idea and routines were copied throughout Europe, Canada, and the United States. He made a name for himself, with this innovation and in Europe he was known as the "American Skating King." With his reputation made, he was able to establish schools, and his pupils improvised even further. One pupil in particular, Louis Rubinstein, a Canadian, came back to North America in 1878 and formed the Amateur Skating Association of Canada. Interest spread to America, and in 1887, the Skating Club of the United States was formed in Philadelphia. Beyond this small group, however, comparatively little interest was evinced until 1908, when figure skating was first included in the Olympic games.

The 1908 events in the first Olympic skating competitions held in England were the same as we have today, individual or singles for men and women and pairs, although there was an extra event in these Olympics probably comparable to our present free style part of the skating program. Generally, skating is judged 60 per cent on prescribed classical school figures or patterns and 40 per cent on free skating, where it is up to the individual to add all the dash and dazzle he can. The 1908 men's singles championship was won by Ulrich Salchow of Sweden, for whom a special figure that he performed is named. Mrs. E. Syers of Great Britain won the same title for the women, and the special figure winner was N. Panin of Russia. Despite the wonderful showing of Panin, Russia did not enter any skating events again until 1956. The honors in pairs went to Miss Hubler and Mr. Burger of Germany.

One of the participants in the 1908 skating events was Irving Brokaw of New York, who had gone to Europe to study. Although Brokaw didn't win any medals, his participation in the games and subsequent discovery of the enthusiastic following the sport was gaining prompted him, upon his return to the United States, to lecture on the sport and to organize American competitions.

In the war years that followed, the sport was eclipsed, but was resumed again in 1920. In the 1920 Olympics in Belgium, American representation was doubled; we had two members, and therefore, a figure skating team—Miss Theresa Weld and Nathaniel Niles. Ulrich Salchow, who had won

211

the last Olympic men's title and was eleven times world's champion, came in fourth, which should prove the quality of the competition. Grafstrom, another Swede, came in first and Niles placed sixth, surpassing both the English and Swiss national champions in performance. In the pair event, the Jakobssons of Finland, world's amateur champions for some time, won the gold medal, and Miss Weld and Mr. Niles came in fourth. Here also, it is to be noted that the Olympics had brought on annual world's championships between Olympiads. In the ladies singles, Theresa Weld did very well again, placing third to two Swedish skating stars.

Four years later, in 1924, the winter games, including figure and speed skating, were officially recognized as part of the Olympic program and the French arranged a complete series of winter sports at Chamonix which were a great success.

The contestants in figure skating included the best in the world—almost all the amateur champions of their countries. In men's figures, Grafstrom again placed first, although because of temporary illness he did not show the absolute perfection displayed at the Antwerp games in 1920. Nathaniel Niles of the United States came in sixth, just as he had in 1920, with Willi Böckl of Austria and Gautschi of Switzerland moving into second and third places formerly held by Scandinavians. Mrs. Herma von Szabo Plank, world's champion for two years, won the women's singles. Second to Mrs. Plank was America's Beatrix Loughran. Theresa (Weld) Blanchard, the former 1920 team member, was fourth. In the pair skating, two newcomers to the Olympics, Miss Engelman and Mr. Berger of Austria, came in first and Mrs. Blanchard and Mr. Niles placed sixth.

The interest aroused by the elaborate series of winter games staged at the Olympics at Chamonix enabled the United States to send a strong team to the second winter games in 1928. At these games, held in St. Moritz, was a gathering of the world's greatest amateur skaters, and Salchow, 1908 Swedish Olympic gold medal winner and now president of the International Skating Federation, observed that the amateurs present outperformed the professionals of the time. In the women's event, the unanimous choice for first place was a young Norwegian girl who was going to have a great influence on the growth of figure skating. This new Olympic winner was Sonja Henie, who in addition to her top skating performances added glamor to an already exciting sport. In the same event, Beatrix Loughran and Maribel

Vinson of the United States placed third and fourth respectively. Miss Loughran and Sherwin Badger placed fourth in the pair event. In the men's singles Grafstrom of Sweden won his third Olympic gold medal.

In 1932 the winter games were held at Lake Placid, New York, and Sonja Henie, the "girl in white," won top honors for women again and was seen by large crowds of Americans for the first time. Maribel Vinson moved up to third place in women's figures at Lake Placid. In the men's figures, Grafstrom of Sweden, three times Olympic champion, placed second to Karl Schafer of Austria. The American Roger Turner, who had placed tenth in the last Olympic games, placed sixth in this event. In pairs, Mr. and Mrs. Brunet of France won the gold medal for the second time and the American pair, Beatrix Loughran and Sherwin Badger, came in a close second.

The 1936 events were held at Garmisch-Partenkirchen, Germany. In the men's competition Karl Schafer of Austria won first place for the second consecutive time, with Ernst Baier of Germany winning second place. George Hill, a 17-year-old newcomer and American champion, placed twelfth out of twenty-five competitors.

Sonja Henie retained her Olympic championship and won for the third successive time first place in the competition for women. Cecilia Colledge of Great Britain gave a brilliant performance in the standard school figures but fell down in the free skating figures, placing second to Miss Henie. Maribel Vinson of New York, medal winner in 1932, took fifth place. A speedy pair from Germany, Maxie Herber and Ernst Baier, gave a fascinating gold medal perfomance in the pair event consisting mostly of "shadow skating"— that is, skating side by side and executing the same steps in perfect unison without touching one another. In the same event, Maribel Vinson and George Hill placed fifth.

It was not until after the 1936 Olympics, however, that skating became truly widespread in the United States. Sonja Henie had now abandoned the ranks of the amateurs and was brought to New York, where her ice show had a booming success. Immediately other ice revues imitated her show, and ice carnivals became gigantic spectacles which attracted enormous audiences throughout the country—which, in turn, popularized skating.

At St. Moritz in 1948, after a twelve-year interim, the winter games were resumed. The proof of the growing popularity of the sport in the United States, with the consequent increase in competition and experience and the improvement of performance was the fact that an American won a first-place gold medal in figure skating for the first time: 18-year-old Dick Button of Englewood, New Jersey, became the new men's champion. In addition to his winning top honors, two other Americans, John Lettengarver and James Grogan, placed fourth and sixth. The second and third places in men's figures were taken by Hans Gerschwiler of Switzerland and Edi Rada of Austria. Another new champion came into the limelight in the women's competition, and the tradition of glamor in the sport was maintained by the blonde and beautiful Barbara Ann Scott of Canada, who won the gold medal for women's figures. Yvonne Sherman of the United States came in sixth.

In the event for pairs, the Belgian duo of Micheline Lannay and Pierre Baugniel managed to outperform other very strong contenders. The American pair of Yvonne Sherman and Robert Swenning came in fourth, while the brother and sister team of Karol and Peter Kennedy placed sixth.

In 1952, the American team's hard work and the ever-increasing popularity of skating in the United States really paid off, and the Americans won more places than any previous figure skating team had. Dick Button won his second Olympic championship and everyone on the team finished in the top six. In the men's competition James Grogan placed third, with Hayes Jenkins fourth. Jeanette Altwegg of Great Britain, who was third in 1948, came in for top honors in 1952, with Tenley Albright a close second. In this same event, Sonya Klopfer and Virginia Baxter placed fourth and fifth respectively. In pairs, a German couple, Ria and Paul Falk, skated through for top honors, with the U.S. pair, Karol and Peter Kennedy, holding second place and Janet Gerhausen and John Nightingale taking fifth place.

After these games, Button turned professional and so stepped aside to let someone else have a try in the 1956 Olympics. Button, all-time great in the art of skating, won not only two Olympic titles but five straight world championships, seven consecutive U.S. titles, and three successive North American crowns, an all-time record.

In 1956, the Olympic figure skating championships were very closely contested among the Americans. Tenley Albright of Boston, silver medal winner in 1952, won first place in the women's event despite a deep cut in her right ankle suffered during pre-Olympic practice. Carol Heiss came in for second place, missing first place by only 1.5 points. Ingrid Wendl of Austria was third. In the men's competition, the judging was even closer. Hayes Jenkins won the gold medal, and Ronnie Robertson, in second place, was only one point behind. Hayes' younger brother, Dave Jenkins, won third place.

Probably the most popular event at Squaw Valley in the 1960 winter games was the figure skating, thirty-three countries originally entered the winter games with thirty attending. This winter Olympics and especially the figure skating were seen by a record audience of millions of TV viewers throughout North America, and, via video tape, the entire world. In the men's event the U.S.'s David Jenkins, 25-year-old medical student, 5' 6", 127 pounds, did everything but leap out and over the arena and won going away for his second Olympic crown. Don Jackson of Canada, aged 19, a pupil of the famous Pierre Brunet, twice gold medalist Olympic figure skater, came in third. Carol Heiss of the United States won the ladies' event, proving again the importance of coaching, as she was a long-time pupil of Pierre Brunet who is the dean of figure skating coaches. To indicate the tenseness of this great ballet competition on ice, seven of the 26 girls from 12 nations crashed on the ice and two collapsed in the thin air of high altitude. In the pairs the Canadian couple of Paul Brown and Barbara Wagner won.

The very first gold medal to be won at Innsbruck in 1964 went to a Russian husband and wife, Oleg Protopopov and Ludmilla Belousova, and brought back memories of the romantic team of Andree Joly and Pierre Brunet of France, who won in 1928, then got married to win again as Mr. and Mrs. Brunet in 1932. Fourteen-year-old Scott Allen of the United States won the only U.S. medal, taking third place in the men's figure skating, won by Manfred Schnelldorfer of West Germany, who skated by the favorite, Alain Colmat of France. However, the great star of the figure skating events was Sjoukje Dijkstra of Holland, who had come in a close second to Carol Heiss in 1960. Her performance and personality were reminiscent of Sonja Henie.

The 1968 Grenoble figure skating competition was held in the magnificient Stade de Glace in Grenoble specially built for the occasion. Oleg and Ludmilla had no trouble repeating their 1964 Olympic triumph and their 1963 and 1966 world championships. Wolfgang Schwartz of Austria won the men's figure skating event while Peggy Fleming broke up the show with her stellar performance in the ladies figure skating.

215

3. Speed Skating

Speed skating grew along with figure skating and also gained most of its impetus from the Olympic games. Even though speed skating came before the introduction of complicated figures, it did not have the wide appeal of the latter, and it wasn't until the 1924 Olympics that speed skating contests were held.

Traditionally the Europeans, especially the Scandinavians, have been great skaters. In speed skating, particularly in the longer races, the north Europeans have surpassed other countries because of their stamina and their conditioning in cold climates.

In the 1924 Olympics, this tradition was upheld and the Finns gained the three top places in the 1,500-, 5,000-, and 10,000-meter races. However, in the shorter 500-meter race, Charles Jewtraw of the United States won a gold medal.

Before the winter games of 1928, it looked as though the United States had a real winner in the 10,000-meter race in Irving Jaffee. Unfortunately, because of improper ice conditions, the event had to be officially canceled, although Jaffee won the informal contest which was run off. He also came in fourth in the 5,000-meter race. Other Americans who did well were O'Neil Farrell, who tied for third in the short race; Edward Murphy, fifth in the 1,500 and 5,000 meter. Clas Thunberg of Finland and Bernt Evensen of Norway tied for first place in the 500 meter. Thunberg also came in to win his second gold medal in the 1,500 meter but failed to repeat his 1924 victory in the 5,000-meter event, which was won by Ivar Ballangrud of Norway.

The Lake Placid games of 1932 were won by the United States. However, there was not as much competition as there might have been because of the traveling time and expense involved. Jack Shea won the 500-meter and 1,500-meter races, and Irving Jaffee came in first for the 5,000- and 10,000-meter gold medals. In the latter, Ballangrud, the 1928 Olympic champion, came in second. Americans also scoring points were Edward Murphy, O'Neil Farrell, Ray Murray, Herbert Taylor, Edwin Wedge and Valentine Bialas.

In the games of 1936, the Americans seemed to be resting on their 1932 laurels, for no United States skater placed in speed skating. The great Norwegian ace, Ivar Ballangrud, won three events—the 500-, 5,000-, and 10,000-meter races—and placed second in the 1,500 meter, which was won by a fellow countryman of his, Charles Mathisen.

During the years between 1936 and 1948, the Americans started to pick up again in speed skating. In the 1948 Olympic winter games the Scandinavians were all-powerful: The Norwegians won three races, and Seyffarth of Sweden won the 10,000 meter. Kenneth Bartholomew and Robert Fitzgerald of the United States tied for second place in the 500-meter race, with Kenneth Henry and Delbert Lamb taking fifth and sixth places. John Werket was sixth in the 1,500 meter.

At Oslo in 1952 a Norwegian truck driver, Hjalmar Andersen, gave a real show and won the first triple championship in speed skating since Ivar Ballangrud, also of Norway, had performed the same feat in 1936. For Andersen to accomplish this, he had to break a world record and two Olympic records. The only title he missed was the 500 meter, which Kenneth Henry of the United States won; Donald McDermott, also of the United States, was second.

In 1956 Russia returned to Olympic skating after an absence of forty-eight years and won three out of four gold medals: Evgeny Grishin won the 500 meter, E. Grishin and Y. Mikhailov tied for first in the 1,500 meter, and Boris Shilkov won the 5,000 meter. In accomplishing this feat, they also set two world records and three Olympic records. But the 10,000 meter race was won by Sigge Ericsson of Sweden, who also set an Olympic record. The only American to place was Carow, who came in sixth in the 500 meter.

Speed skating in 1960 was dominated by Russia. Added to the schedule were 500-, 1,000-, 1,500- and 3,000-meter speed skating for women, all won by Russia except the 500-meter to Frau Helga Haase of Germany. In the four men's events of 500, 1,500, 5,000 and 10,000 meters, Russia won two, Norway one, and the 1,500 meter was a tie between E. Grishin of Russia and R. Aas of Norway. To show coincidence on the ice, in 1956 Grishin also tied with one of his team mates in this event. As Grishin won the 1956 and 1960 500 meter event, he picked up four gold medals on the ice in two Olympics or perhaps one should say three-and-a-half gold medals.

At Innsbruck speed skating set new highs in many directions. Lydia Skoblikova of Russia won and set new records in the 500-, 1,000-, 1,500-, and 3,000-meter women's skating, the first person ever to win four gold medals in a single winter Olympics.

One of the greatest victories of the Austrian games was the upset win of the U.S. speed skater Terry McDermott, but there was no way to question his triumph, for he beat the

217

world's champion, 1960 and 1956 Olympic winner Eugeny Grishin and also broke the world and Olympic record. McDermott's gold medal was the only one won by the United States at the 1964 winter games. According to McDermott, there is a rising interest in speed skating for men in the United States, and with it he believes will come better and more winning Olympic performances, also encouragement for girl's speed skating. What is important is the United States to have speed skating rinks all over the country. Terry McDermott's upset victory and world's record was the first U.S. win in speed skating since 1932—a span of 32 years.

The Grenoble speed skating demonstrated the increased popularity of this sport and the fact that new world records would follow world famous skaters such as Erhard Keller of Germany, Kees Verkerk of Holland, Fred Maier of Norway and Johnny Hoeglin of Sweden. In the women's events Lydia Skoblikova of Russia, winner of six out of eight medals in 1960 and 1964 was entered but was eliminated.

The 500 meter with 48 skaters from 24 countries was won by Erhard Keller of Germany with Terry McDermott of the United States and Magne Thomassen of Norway tied for second. The 1,500 meter was won by Kees Verkerk of Holland over 52 other skaters from 17 countries. The 5,000 meter was won by Fred Maier of Norway with a new world record. There were 38 contestants from 17 countries. The 10,000 meter competition was held in heavy wind conditions between 28 contestants from 13 countries with Johnny Hoeglin of Sweden winning over Fred Maier of Norway by 3/10ths of a second.

Ludmila Titova of Russia won the women's 500 meter with Mary Meyers, Dianne Holum and Jennifer Fish all of the United States tied for second place. Carolina Geijssen of Holland won the 1,000 over Titova of Russia by 3/10ths of a second with the U.S.'s Dianne Holum in third place. The women's 1,500 was won by Kaija Mustonen of Finland with the Dutch pair, Geijssen and Christina Kaiser next. The 3,000 meter, the longest women's event, was won by Holland's Johanna Schut with Miss Mustonen of Finland second and Christina Kaiser of Holland third.

Just as in swimming many spectators believe the events are too similar and if rested the same contestants would win any number of medals.

4. Bobsledding

Man probably made his first attempt at sledding when he discovered that he could get down a steep, snow-covered hill faster by just sitting down than by trying to make it on foot. This must have proved chilly, however, so some bright soul stretched animal skins to sit on between two bone runners.

This invention may also have grown out of the necessity to transport large animals home for food. The Algonquin Indians of North America had something similar to this in their toboggan (Canadian French adaptation of the Indian word), which was made of wood.

The toboggan is really the forerunner of the modern bobsled, and the use of it in sports can be attributed to a group of Americans and Englishmen who vacationed in the Swiss Alps around the year 1890. This group of vacationers, bored by the peaceful activities offered them, were looking for something to do that would be a little more thrilling than padding over the Alps on snowshoes. They fashioned a long adaptation of the toboggan, proceeded to lay out a course on the mountain, and were soon rocketing down dangerous mountain slopes in suicidal fashion. Other thrill seekers joined them, and even though most people at the time looked upon the devotees of this sport as outright maniacs, the real fans eventually found tobogganing too safe and tame and began to search for something even more adventurous to do. They discovered that if the toboggan were mounted on wooden runners, a far greater speed could be attained, but also the danger was greater because the higher center of gravity made the vehicle trickier to control on turns.

About 1895, new recruits began to appear who developed a heavier sled with added ballast to help keep it on the course—a speedier sled but a safer one. These new sleds were called bobsleighs (bob, because riders would "bob" to increase speed on a straightaway; that is, at command from the brakeman they would bob into a forward position after leaning backward as far as possible; this action, which must be performed in perfect unison by the whole team, can make the sled actually jump forward and thus cut seconds from the time in racing). Enthusiasts of racing with these new sleds joined a toboggan club which had many members, but they eventually found the tobogganers' rules too tame for them and branched off on their own. They laid out their own course in the Swiss Alps, the famous and dangerous Cresta Run. In the original rules for bobsled racing, it was required that two

219

of the passengers be women—whether to add decoration or weight was never explained by the original rule makers—but women willing to rocket down the Alps at breakneck speeds were few and far between, so "two stout men" were substituted on the original five-man crew. The sport drew a larger number of fans each year while new features on the sleds were being developed to increase the speed even more; consequently, the Cresta Run became too dangerous, and an artificial run was built in St. Moritz in 1904. By the outbreak of World War I, there were some hundred bobsled courses in Europe.

National championships were soon held, and by 1924, when the winter games were first included officially as part of the Olympic program, the bobsledders made the most of the occasion and had their first international race, which was won by the four-man Swiss sled driven by E. Scherra.

Enthusiastic Americans vacationing in Switzerland entered into the thrilling sport wholeheartedly and obtained permission to represent their country in the 1928 Olympics. They carried off the Olympic competition that year, with Billy Fiske driving the 5-man team to victory and John Heaton piloting the other 5-man team for second-place honors. John Heaton also won first place in skeleton sled, with his brother Jennison winning second place. This victory was the beginning of many U.S. victories in this sport.

By the time of the 1932 Olympics, iron runners had been developed, and the Americans, with typical Yankee ingenuity, had inserted these runners in the bottoms of wooden shoes, and experimented with a V-shaped runner. This shape increased speed but cut up the track considerably, and after this competition only runners in the shape of arcs or true circles were allowed, with specific diameters. The Americans really clobbered their opponents in the bobsledding events at Lake Placid. They won first and second places in the four-man event, and in an unexpected upset, Hubert and Curtis Stevens came in first in the two-man, in which another American pair placed third. The National Amateur Athletic Union and the United States Olympic Committee were a little upset before the Lake Placid games because some bobsledders had protested that the teams had not been selected by competition, as demanded by the rules; but the results achieved silenced most of the complaints.

By 1936 the Americans had again added to the development of the sled by substituting steel planks for wooden ones, which made the sleds more flexible and cut down the friction between the runners and the ice. This was done by Bob and Bill Linney of New York, who also are credited with the first use of push handles to insure a fast start. On a running start, all four men could now push and then jump on as soon as they crossed the starting line. These refinements made for faster time.

At Garmisch, the Americans came through again to claim top two-man honors, with Ivan Brown and Bob Washbond winning the gold medal. This was quite an accomplishment, as several team members were injured in the trials because of the soft foundation of the course.

In 1948—with Fox of the 1936 team as coach and Curtis Stevens, the winning brakeman in 1932 and team member in 1936, as manager—things seemed to look promising. F. Fortune and S. Carron of the United States came in third to win a bronze medal in the two-man event. In the four-man event, the United States came through with flying colors and the team of F. Tyler, P. Martin, E. Rimkus, and W. D'Amico captured first place.

Before the games at Oslo in 1952 an amusing incident took place which illustrates the importance of the weight of the team members in bobsledding. The team was supposed to fly to London non-stop before going on to Oslo, but the airline transporting them had not taken into account the fact that many of the passengers represented Olympic bobsled beef, and a special stop had to be made at Gander because of the unexpected weight load.

In the actual game, it was time for another country to prove its strength, and the astute strategy of the Germans brought them a win. In the trial runs, the Germans observed that both the American and Swiss teams were making better time than they were, and decided to sacrifice one team by removing all the heavy men from their number-two team and transferring them to their number-one team. This tactic paid off, for the added weight gave them superior pickup power and they plummeted to victory in both the two- and four-man events. The United States placed second in both events—Stan Benham and Pat Martin in the two-man, and Benham piloting the four-man run.

The fact that the 1956 games were held at Cortina, Italy, seemed to give impetus to the host nation and for the first time an Italian team won first place in bobsledding. Lamberto Dalla Costa drove the gold-medal pair in the two-man event, and Eugenio Monti piloted for second place in both the two- and the four-man events. Switzerland won top

221

honors in the four-man, and the United States came in third, with Art Tyler driving. The following countries entered at least one bobsled crew in the Olympics; Russia, Germany, the United States, Switzerland, France, Belgium, Sweden, Austria, Italy, Norway, Finland, and Argentina. Needless to say, each team entered in this event usually brings its own team physician and nurse to apply treatment to contusions and abrasions.

The modern bobsled, with streamlined cowl and wheel-type steering, able to reach speeds of as high as 89 miles per hour, is a far cry from the animal-skin and bone combination used by primitive men. To ride in this ice rocket on treacherous mountain slopes, where a single slip can cause death, is to participate in a sport for only the most daring—a sport rightly called "the champagne of thrills."

Both bobsledding events were dropped at Squaw Valley because of lack of proper facilities, but at Innsbruck there were both two-man and four-man bobsledding events, with three tobogganing competitions: one-man individual, two-man, and women's individual.

The Canadian four-man team win in the four-man bobsled event was the "biggest upset in bobsledding history." The tobogganing races were exciting, although there is still some question as to whether the vehicles used in these competitions are luges (French), rodes (German) or toboggans (American-Canada and U.S.).

The two-man bobsled world's Olympic championships were held an hour's ride from Grenoble at Alpe d'Huez in 1968. Every possible problem and delay resulted in the later stages of the competition being held at 5 a.m. with 160 searchlights in use along a 1,641-yard track which sometimes proved unusable. The two teams of veteran Eugenio Monti, his brakeman Luciano de Paolis, and German hotel-owner Horst Floth, supported by his brakeman Pepi Bader each had four runs. Monti's earned a new world's record but the grand total of the four-runs were equal. Based on the rule book, Monti won because his first run was better than his rival's.

The four-man bobsled was also won by a Monti team. The bobsledding featured 41 bobs from 11 countries.

The tobogganing or luge contests started at Innsbruck were held at Villard de Lars over a run of 1,000 meters with five bends, six hairpin bends and one labyrinth. Austria, West Germany and East Germany dominated this sport—the one man event was won by Schmid of Austria with Köbler and Bonsack, both from East Germany, next. The two-man event was won by the East German pair of Köbler and Bonsack, with Schmid and Walch of Austria second, and Winkler and Nachman of West Germany, third. The ladies' event ended in a U.N. type of debate as the winning team from East Germany was accused of heating its runners before the race which makes the sleds move faster and is illegal. The result was the three first finishers from East Germany were disqualified with Erica Lechner of Italy getting the gold medal and Christa Schmuck and Angelika Duenhaupt—both of West Germany—the other two medalists.

5. Ice Hockey

Ice Hockey is an icy offshoot of field hockey, which was played by the Persians, Greeks, and Romans in ancient times and was played widely in France, England, and India in modern times. The sport spread throughout Europe, and the Irish and Scotch have always had the reputation of being great hockey players. There are stories of really wild and fierce slamming around between players in the "good old days." The legend of typical Irish temper can be substantiated by the story told about Lalrad Loingsech before he became King of Ireland some time before the Christian Era. The legend goes that he was born dumb, but one day, while he was playing hockey, an opponent gave him such a whack on the shins that he screamed for the first time in his life and thereafter regained his speech. Migrants from Europe brought the sport to Canada, where originally broom handles and even tree branches were used for hockey sticks.

When methods of making artificial ice were developed and indoor rinks came into use, enthusiasm for the sport spread to America, and the Canadians, who had been holding official hockey matches since the middle of the nineteenth century, really developed the sport and taught the Americans the art of playing it. Canadians have proved their prowess in ice hockey for many years. Even with international competition, Canada has upheld its high standard of performance and has won all Olympic ice hockey competitions since 1920, except in 1936, 1956 and 1960 when Great Britain, Russia and the United States won top honors.

Americans have usually done well in this event, and came in second to the Canadians in 1920 and 1924. In 1928, for the first time, the United States was not represented, but took second-place honors again in 1932. In 1936 the American team was dropped to third by the British, with Canada again the winner.

223

American ice hockey representation in the 1948 winter games in St. Mortiz caused quite a controversy. Two American teams were sent to the games, one chosen by the Amateur Hockey Association and the other the choice of the United States Olympic Committee. The Swiss favored the Association's team, but then the United States Olympic Committee threatened to withdraw American participation in all winter events. The International Olympic Committee settled the situation by barring both teams from competition. However, the Swiss went ahead and scheduled the Amateur Hockey Association team, and the International Olympic Committee, in turn, struck hockey from the program. Then the Swiss threatened to call off the winter games. The matter was finally settled by letting the team play but not giving it official rating.

Fortunately, things went more smoothly in 1952. The Americans tied with the Canadians in the final game, but Canada, with an unbeaten record, won first place.

At the Cortina games in 1956 Russia moved in to win the gold medal, with the United States second and Canada third. Sweden, Czechoslovakia, and Germany took fourth, fifth, and sixth places respectively.

At Squaw Valley, although considered an underdog and scheduled for fourth place behind Russia, Canada and Czechoslovakia, the U.S. hockey team won the world's Olympic championship. The key game was that won over Canada 2-1. Team coach Jack Riley of West Point called his outfit a team of destiny and inspired it to great effort. He was a former Dartmouth star and member of the 1948 U.S. Olympic hockey team. The United States was undefeated in the Olympic tournament, with 5 wins. Canada was second with 4 and one loss, Russia third with 2 wins, 2 losses, and 1 tie and Czechoslovakia fourth with 2 wins and 3 losses.

Russia's ice hockey team, the favorite at Innsbruck in 1964, won all seven games in the round-robin competition. With 5 wins and 2 losses each, Sweden, Czechoslovakia and Canada tied for second. The U.S. team, upset champions in 1960, won only two of their seven games, although Tom Yurkovich, and after he was injured, Pat Rupp, were outstanding goal tenders for the United States.

The 1968 ice hockey tournament was one of the most exciting ever. Coming up to the final matches in dramatic style three teams were even for the gold medal—Russia, Czechoslovakia and Canada. In the tourney's greatest game the Czechoslovakian team after seven years of waiting upset the Russians 5-4, but in a letdown Czechoslovakia was tied by Sweden, and the Soviet Union crushed Canada, so the final standings were: first, U.S.S.R.; second, Czechoslovakia; third, Canada; fourth, Sweden; fifth, Finland; sixth, the United States.

6. BIATHLON

The International Union of the modern pentathlon was responsible for the introduction into the winter games of an equivalent event to the modern or military pentathlon in the regular games. This event, called the biathlon, consists of cross-country skiing and rifle shooting in snow-covered terrain. In the first such Olympic competition Klas Lestander of Sweden won. This was a surprise as the 1959 world's champion, Vladimir Melanjin, and Alexander Privalov, who defeated him in Russia just before the games, were the favorites. Lawrence Damon, U.S. champion, was expected to finish near the top as he had defeated Lestander in the 1959 North American championship over the same McKinney Creek course near Squaw Valley. Finnish Antti Tyrainen was second, Privalov third, Melanjin fourth— Damon twenty-fourth with 13 misses in the shooting costing him a 26-minute addition (2 min. per miss) to his time, which was among the fastest.

At Innsbruck the combined skiing and rifle shooting event, the biathlon, involved 49 competitors representing 11 nations. The favorite, Vaikko Hakulinen of Finland, finished in fifteenth place as Vladimir Melanjin and Alexander Privalov, both of the Soviet Union, and O. Jordet of Norway, led the field in that order. The U.S. Army, which so far represents the United States in this sport, placed its men sixteenth, thirtieth, thirty-sixth and thirty-ninth.

In the future the United States Ski Association is reportedly going to take this sport over, together with the National Rifle Association. As in the case of the modern pentathlon, it seems that no army can control a sport without major help from civilians.

The biathlon, the winter equivalent of the modern pentathlon and governed by the same world body, was expanded at the Grenoble games in 1968. In addition to the individual championship and competition a team or relay contest was added, also featuring skiing and rifle shooting. Sixty contestants from sixteen countries competed in a 20-kilometer race and four shooting series of five shots each. Magnar Solberg of Norway with a perfect shooting score won the

225

individual gold medal. In the first Olympic team or relay contest the Russians won with Norway second and Sweden third. Fourteen national teams were entered.

CHAPTER XVIII

Wrestling

WRESTLING AS an athletic posture of man goes back, along with boxing, to prehistoric days. Prehistoric man had to wrestle wild beasts in close encounter, and, realizing he had to school himself in the struggle for survival, he may have practiced holds and grips in friendly demonstrations or contests with members of his family or with his neighbors.

Wrestling as a sport undoubtedly goes further back than any existing records. Wall paintings found in the tombs of Beni Hasan, a village in Middle Egypt, show that Egyptians 5,000 years ago knew nearly every wrestling hold we know today. There is definite historical evidence that wrestling was an important part of sports programs and festivities in ancient Greece and we find actual records of wrestling as the final event in the original or warrior's pentathlon after the eighteenth Olympic games, *circa* 708 B.C. Later wrestling became a separate event in the Olympics.

Any consideration of wrestling and the ancient Olympics cannot ignore one of the greatest names in both; Milo of Crotona, the greatest wrestler of antiquity. Although he was mainly a wrestler, he showed great abilities in boxing and in the pancratium. As a boy Milo won the boys' wrestling championship at the Olympic, Pythian, and other games. Later, he won many wrestling and pancratium championships, including six Olympic wrestling championships—which would make him the world's wrestling champion for twenty-four consecutive years.

Milo's strength was fabulous. When he was a small boy, he began carrying a young calf on his shoulder and continued to carry the calf every day thereafter until it had become a full-grown bull. Milo could, therefore, be called a star in the sport of weight lifting. He performed all manner of tricks to confuse his enemies, amuse his friends, and attract publicity. One of these was to grasp a pomegranate and challenge anyone to take it away from him. Not only was it impossible to do so, but his powerful grip was so controlled that the fruit was never crushed or damaged in any way. He could stand on a greased discus and make a fool of anyone who tried to push him off it. Another popular feat of Milo's consisted of having a cord tied tight around his head, then holding his breath and making the veins on his head swell until the cord broke, but Milo's tricks and own confidence in his strength proved his undoing in the end. No human being ever threw him in wrestling, but when he tried to replace a wedge in a tree trunk with his hand it became hopelessly entrapped in the aperture and poor Milo was eaten by wild animals. Milo of Crotona was not only never downed in twenty-four years—he never even fell to his knees. He was also known as a great eater. According to records that have come down to us, at one meal he ate seventeen pounds of meat and bread washed down by five quarts of wine. Wrestling in ancient Greece seems to have promoted good health, and wrestlers went on competing for twelve to twenty-four years.

In Japan, a most popular form of wrestling is Sumo, which started over two thousand years ago and is still popular. The champion Sumo wrestlers weigh 300 pounds or more and wear nothing but an ornamental loincloth. Their matches are held in a small, soft, sanded ring marked off with rice straw, and unfair play is scrupulously avoided. The object in Sumo is to push an opponent out of the ring or throw him to the floor. The slightest touch of knee or finger to the ground is a fall. Nearly all countries had similar ancient forms of wrestling, such as the Glima of the Icelanders, the Schwingen of the Swiss, the Cumberland of the Irish, and the Lancashire of the Scotch. In Greco-Roman wrestling, still popular in many countries and still on the Olympic program, the rules stipulate that legs cannot be used for attack or defense and that every hold must be above the belt. This is the type of wrestling that was practiced in ancient Greece and in the early Olympics. Wrestling is centuries old in the civilizations of India and China and has also been popular in Germany for centuries. Catch-as-catch-can wrestling is the product of America. All American wrestling was amateur at first, and friendly wrestling was held outdoors at picnics and fairs—witness the bouts of Abraham Lincoln. However, after a while, the best wrestlers went on tour, meeting all comers outdoors, and the sport began to achieve a wide popularity.

Wrestling in the early days was developed and improved by the Olympic games, where the greatest wrestlers from the known world vied for world's championships, not only in wrestling but in the pancratium. The competition was tough. In one contest an ancient Greek wrestler named

Archacian was awarded the Olympic championship when a toe hold he finally put on his opponent made the latter give up. However, during the contest, Archacian had been under the pressure of such terrific headlocks and strangle holds that when his opponent quit, Archacian rolled over, was proclaimed champion, and then died. In the pancratium we have really the beginning of the catch-as-catch-can, which would permit a toe hold or any other type of hold; in the Greco-Roman or normal wrestling as practiced by the Greeks, such holds would have been ruled illegal.

The ancient Greek wrestlers generally overcame the ancient Greek boxers in the pancratium. We find that the boxers were often being subdued by flying mares, leg holds, toe holds, strangle holds, headlocks, kicking, and above all else by the bending back of the fingers. This last trick not only made many a boxer quit, but ruined many a Greek fist for all time. The most famous exponent, if not the originator, of the technique of bending a man's fingers backward until he yelled "Uncle" or until his fingers and hands were broken is believed to be the great Greek wrestler Sostratos, who won the 104th, 105th, and 106th Olympic wrestling championships (364-356 B.C.), and also took on all boxers at one of these Olympics, winning both the wrestling and pancratium titles.

During the Middle Ages, when most competitive athletics disappeared, international tournaments in wrestling and wrestling matches at great parties given by kings were very popular—particularly in France and England. Francis I of France (1515-1547), the builder of Fontainebleau, became annoyed because French wrestlers were losing consistently to English wrestlers.

When the Spanish and the English, the Dutch and the French began colonizing North America, they found that wrestling was very popular among the Indians and that there was considerable wrestling in the early Americas. The early wrestlers in the United States, such as Ernest Roeber and William Muldoon, followed Greco-Roman rules, but the average neighborhood wrestler, not caring much about rules, adopted catch-as-catch-can methods. Hence the term "catch-as-catch-can wrestling."

Naturally, the first modern Olympics in 1896 included wrestling matches as an important part of the program. In the contest at Athens, five champions (listed as such)—two of them Greeks—took part. The only type of wrestling at the first Olympics was in the Greco-Roman style, and according to the records only one championship was contested, which was won by Schumann of Germany.

There is no record of any wrestling in the 1900 Olympic games, but in 1904, at St. Louis, there was competition for seven wrestling championships in seven classes; all the championships were won by Americans, and the entire competition was on a catch-as-catch-can basis.

After the 1904 Olympics, there was a split-up between the Greco-Roman wrestling, based upon the ancient Olympic style, and the "new" wrestling. In the Greco-Roman, holds were only allowed above the waist. Generally speaking, catch-as-catch-can is of American origin, but various types of catch-as-catch-can had appeared in the first part of the twentieth century in other countries. The Swiss had developed a sort of national sport of "catch" wrestling; the Japanese, with jujitsu, had departed from Greco-Roman. Sumo wrestling was a combination of Greco-Roman and catch-as-catch-can. The Turks had also developed a very tough—and cruel—version of catch-as-catch-can. England had developed its catch-as-catch-can from the Cumberland and Westmoreland styles, which had originally approximated the Greco-Roman. France stuck pretty closely to Greco-Roman until about 1913, when catch-as-catch-can began to appear there for the first time.

In the 1906 Olympics at Athens there were wrestling competitions, with Germany winning the unofficial team title, although the Germans did not win a single individual championship. At the Athens games—unlike the St. Louis games —only Greco-Roman rules were used, and the two Americans who were contestants were at a great disadvantage. J. Jensen of Denmark won the heavyweight championship; W. Weckman of Finland won in the middleweight class and Watzl of Austria in the lightweight class.

The fourth Olympiad at London in 1908 was the first to recognize the two schools or classifications and there were separate competitions in catch-as-catch-can and Greco-Roman wrestling. The Americans showed to advantage in the catch-as-catch-can wrestling, although the British won three titles to the United States' two. In Greco-Roman, the Swedes, the Finns, the Italians, and the Hungarians won titles.

The fifth Olympic games in Stockholm in 1912 demonstrated the fact that wrestling as a universal and ancient sport was going to be handicapped—for a while, at least— by the fact that there was great variance between the styles and rules of the several countries. The Swedes did not even recognize catch-as-catch-can wrestling, so Olympic competition was limited to Greco-Roman rules; as a result, Finland and Sweden dominated the Olympic wrestling competition, with three championships being won by Finland and two by Sweden. In the light heavyweight class, A. O. Ahlgren of Sweden and J. Boling of Finland drew, after over nine hours of continuous wrestling.

During World War I wrestling, like boxing and fencing, progressed greatly, particularly catch-as-catch-can. The 1920 Olympics at Antwerp presented really outstanding contestants from a great many countries in both catch-as-catch-can and Greco-Roman. At the 1920 or seventh Olympiad, in the catch-as-catch-can class the United States found very worthy competition from English, South African, and Indian teams as well as from the Finns. However, the surprise at the meet was the ability of the Swiss, who up to that time had had no reputation for either ability or knowledge of the game. However, the Swiss had wrestled catch-as-catch-can for many decades. They won one championship and would probably have taken another but for the injury of one of their athletes, who was forced to forfeit his final bout. The rules covering the meet were very unsatisfactory to the American team in that leg scissors were barred. The American form of catch-as-catch-can had used leg and scissor holds on the head and various parts of the body to great advantage.

The final score was the United States 9½, Finland 8, Sweden 5 1/3, Switzerland 5, and England 2. C. E. Ackerly of Cornell University was the only American to win an individual championship. In the middleweight division, Charles F. Johnson of Quincy, Massachusetts, won third place, and in the light heavyweight class, Walter Maurer of the Chicago Hebrew Institute won third place. Nat Pendleton of Columbia University and the New York Athletic Club won second place in the heavyweight division, and Fred Meyer was tied for third place in the same class. The decision which took the final match from Pendleton, a great amateur wrestling star who later became a tough guy in Hollywood pictures, was probably one of the most unpopular of many unsatisfactory and unfair decisions. It is interesting to note that one of the toughest members of the U.S. wrestling team at the 1920 Olympics was Paul Berlenbach, who later turned to boxing and became the professional light heavyweight world's champion.

In the Greco-Roman wrestling, the belief of the Americans that American versatility and aggressiveness would give some men with practically no training a chance was proved incorrect—no points were won by American entries. Greco-Roman team honors were won by Finland.

These Olympics showed that, while the popularity of wrestling extended throughout the world, there was no standardization of rules and methods, and that a standardization of the rules in both types of wrestling would be necessary before free and effective competition could be achieved.

The eighth Olympiad at Paris in 1924 presented the best wrestling competition there had been in any modern Olympics. In the Greco-Roman there were 250 competitors, representing twenty-four countries. As in 1912 and 1920, the Finns and the Swedes dominated the competition, Finland winning the unofficial team championship, with Sweden second, Estonia third, and France fourth—Hungary being a close fifth. The American wrestlers decided that until they learned how to wrestle the Greco-Roman style they would not try to compete.

In the catch-as-catch-can, however, the United States won its first overwhelming victory in wrestling, scoring 49 points to win the unofficial team championship, Finland and Switzerland tying for second with 33. There were 187 contestants entered, representing sixteen nations. The United States won four individual world's championships. Robin Reed of Oregon Agricultural College won in the featherweight class and was considered by many to be the best wrestler of this Olympiad. In fact, many experts consider him, pound for pound, one of the greatest amateur and Olympic wrestlers of modern times. Russell Vis of the Los Angeles Athletic Club won in the lightweight class, John P. Spellman of Brown University in the light heavyweight class, and Harry Steele of Ohio State University in the heavyweight class. In addition, second place in the featherweight class was won by Chester Newton of the United States, and third place in the bantamweight was won by Bryant Hines. The wrestling started on July 11th and ran morning, afternoon, and night through July 15th. Due to the fact that many of the officials were inexperienced, and the fact that the rules had still not been properly standardized, there were some very bad decisions. However, after a meeting of the International Wrestling Federation there was hope that the various countries would standardize their rules and afford wrestling the same opportunity for progress as other sports. W. E. Cann was the U.S. wrestling coach. The wrestling took place in the Velodrome d'Hiver, the

Madison Square Garden of Paris, and was very well attended.

International competitions in the years between Olympics, in both catch-as-catch-can and Greco-Roman wrestling, contributed greatly to the advance of the sport between 1924 and 1928. However, there still was great variation in interpretation of the rules. The development of catch-as-catch-can was undeniably American, but—with the exception of the Swiss—European countries preferred the Greco-Roman style. Other countries differed with the United States, even in the catch-as-catch-can style, with respect to holds, especially leg holds and particularly the body and head scissors. These holds, perfectly legitimate from the U.S. standpoint, were barred in the Olympic games. Also from the beginning of the modern form of wrestling one element of the sport had been perennially debated—the rolling fall. In Greco-Roman wrestling, where only the arms are employed, athletes may remain in position, and fast falls are allowed since the lower body and limbs are always free. As a result of the freedom of the limbs, wrestlers can usually prevent a roll, and, if they can't, can very easily bridge. When the legs are tied up in catch-as-catch-can, as they are much of the time on the offensive, the high bridge is impossible and rolling falls must work a great unfairness. The Greco-Roman influence has also made ruling on the flying fall difficult. While the contestants are on their feet, one can pick his opponent up bodily, throw him squarely on his shoulders, and—even though the touch may be only momentary—score a fall. However, when the men are on the mat in catch-as-catch-can, with one man on the offensive or behind his man, as it is called, then the pin fall should be required, with the shoulders held to the mat for a perceptible length of time (two seconds). In 1938 the complaint was that U.S. wrestlers were eliminated on the basis that any roll, however fast, meant a fall.

George Pinneo was the U.S. coach in 1928. The Greco-Roman wrestling unofficial team title was won by Germany, while Finland won the catch-as-catch-can unofficial team title. Allie Morrison won the featherweight world's title for the United States. Lloyd Appleton of the United States, now wrestling coach at West Point, was second in the welterweight class. Among the heavyweights who were also-rans in these Olympics were Earl MacCready of Canada and Ed Don George of the United States. Both of these men, although they were unsuccessful in the Olympics, went on to great prominence in professional wrestling. MacCready, a Canadian, learned his wrestling in the United States, at Oklahoma A. and M. He was national intercollegiate heavyweight champion of the United States in 1928, 1929, and 1930, and national AAU title holder in 1930. He later became one of the best wrestlers in the world. G. W. Streit, Jr., of Birmingham, Alabama, manager of the 1924, 1928, and 1932 U.S. wrestling teams, deserves great credit for his firm but sportsmanlike complaints and arguments on the differences in rules.

The 1932 Olympic games again presented fine competition in wrestling. The American team was considered the best-balanced wrestling team ever to represent the United States. Its coach was Hugo Otapalik. The U.S. team won three first places and two seconds in the catch-as-catch-can division. R. E. Pearce of the United States won the bantamweight championship; Edgar Nemir of the United States was second in the featherweight class; Jack Van Bebber, another U.S. all-time great, won the welterweight title. Peter J. Mehringer of the United States won the light heavyweight title, and John Riley was second in the heavyweight class to Johan Richtoff of Sweden, who won the heavyweight Olympic title in 1928, besting both George and MacCready. In the Greco-Roman wrestling the United States had no entries, but many countries were represented from Scandinavia, continental Europe, and Asia, with Sweden winning the unofficial team title.

Just as in other sports, the interest engendered by the Olympic games and by international amateur wrestling competition and intercollegiate and amateur competition within various countries—particularly the United States—developed great coaching, which in turn improved performance. Prominent among the coaches was the one who created the greatest college wrestling teams in the United States—those of Oklahoma A. and M. College. For decades a mild little man named Ed Gallagher held forth there as coach and annually developed smart, clean, aggressive, splendidly conditioned teams that won many intercollegiate championships. He also trained many Olympic wrestlers.

As a result of the standardization of wrestling all over the world and of greater interest in this sport inspired by the Olympics, a larger number of entrants and better competition and performance marked the eleventh Olympiad at Berlin in 1936. The American Olympic team was managed again by G. W. Streit, Jr. The coach of the U.S. team was William H. Thom of Indiana, ably assisted by honorary coach

233

and advisor Ed Gallagher of Oklahoma A. and M. The unofficial catch-as-catch-can wrestling team championship went to the United States, which won one first place and three seconds. The wrestling competition attracted twenty-eight countries. Ross Flood of Blackwell, Oklahoma; Francis E. Millard of North Adams, Massachusetts; and Richard L. Voliva of Bloomington, Indiana, finished second in the bantamweight, featherweight, and middleweight classes respectively. Sweden was second in the unofficial team championship, with one first, one second, and two third places. The Greco-Roman team championship went to Sweden.

For the first time in Olympic competition the same man won both the catch-as-catch-can and the Greco-Roman titles. Kristjan Palusalu of Estonia won the heavyweight championship in free style wrestling and the heavyweight championship in Greco-Roman style. The wrestling at these Olympics was held at Deutschland Hall, and a capacity crowd attended every session. There was some trouble with officiating, but sportsmanship, as usual, won out. The officiating in wrestling has now improved, as the rules have become more and more standardized over the years.

The fourteenth Olympiad in London in 1948 brought out tremendous competitions in both catch-as-catch-can and Greco-Roman wrestling. The unofficial team championship in catch-as-catch-can was won by Turkey and in Greco-Roman by Sweden. The U.S. team was managed by Clifford Keen of Michigan and coached by Art Griffith of Oklahoma A. and M. The team was helped by a number of ex-coaches and Olympic wrestlers, among whom was Ed Don George. The U.S. team won two championships, one second place, one third, one fifth, and one sixth. Behind Turkey in unofficial first place in the team scoring was Sweden, with the United States third. It is interesting to note that the Turkish team that won and the four Turkish champions who took individual titles were all men in their thirties. From the days of the ancient Olympics to the present, good wrestlers have had far longer competitive lives than top competitors in any other sport, except fencing. In Europe and the United States many men wrestle competitively for as long as twenty years. G. Leeman took second in the bantamweight class, R. Hutton of the United States sixth in the heavyweight. W. Koll was fifth in the lightweight, L. Merrill third in the welterweight. G. Brand of the United States was first in the middleweight class, and H. Wittenberg of the United States was first in the light heavyweight class.

Wittenberg, incidentally, was considered by many the most outstanding wrestler in the 1948 Olympic games and is considered by most experts to be one of the best amateur wrestlers ever developed in the United States. He won the national light heavyweight championship in the United States in 1943 and 1944, and again in 1947 and 1948, representing the New York Police Sports Association. Wittenberg won almost 500 matches in succession between 1938 and 1952 before he was beaten by Dale Thomas of East Lansing, Michigan, in the light heavyweight class final for the 1952 Olympic games. He had then been wrestling for almost twenty years. Later he defeated Thomas several times, and again wrestled for the United States in 1952.

In 1948 the catch-as-catch-can wrestling was dominated by the Turks. The Greco-Roman wrestling unofficial team championship was won by Sweden. As usual, the United States did not participate, although interest in Greco-Roman wrestling was beginning in the United States.

In 1948 one thing was certain—that interest in both styles of wrestling was increasing all over the world, with the result that the United States appeared to be falling behind even in the catch-as-catch-can style which it had developed.

The 1952 Olympiad at Helsinki marked the return of Russia into Olympic competition, and it dominated both catch-as-catch-can and Greco-Roman styles. Competitors from thirty-five nations entered the free style or catch-as-catch-can at this Olympiad. Some rather unusual occurrences on the U.S. Olympic team prior to the final Olympic meet are worthy of notice. One was that light heavyweight Dale Thomas of Michigan State College defeated heavyweight Kerslake twice, but was not allowed by the Olympic officials to wrestle in that class, because he had previously been entered as a light heavyweight. So Kerslake represented the United States in the heavyweight class. Wittenberg had won over Thomas in the light heavyweight class, although Thomas had broken Wittenberg's extraordinary string of victories in the tryout. Raymond Schwartz was the U.S. coach and B. R. Patterson the manager. Advance reports were that Iran, Turkey, Sweden and Russia had terrific teams. The Russians did, and won practically everything. Russia was the unofficial team champion of Greco-Roman and catch-as-catch-can. In Greco-Roman, Hungary was second. In catch-as-catch-can, Sweden was a very close second and Turkey a close third.

In catch-as-catch-can, J. Henson of the United States was

235

third in the featherweight class and T. Evans of the United States was second in the lightweight class. W. Smith of the United States won the title in the welterweight class in an interesting manner. He lost a split decision to Berlin of Sweden, then defeated Modjtabavi of Iran by a fall. Then the Iranian soundly beat the Swede, thus giving Smith the world's title. In the light heavyweight class, Henry Wittenberg, one of the greatest American wrestlers of all time but certainly not at his best after twenty years of competition, lost a hairline decision to Palm of Sweden for the Olympic crown—which Wittenberg had won in 1948. Wittenberg was a great sportsman, and therefore was proud to take second place. W. Kerslake was fifth in the heavyweight class and increased his experience, which enabled him to win, in 1953, not only the heavyweight national championship in the United States in the catch-as-catch-can but also the heavyweight championship in the first Greco-Roman tournament ever held in the United States. In wrestling, the popularity of a European specialty inspired through the Olympics sufficient interest to lead to national tournaments and championships in the United States.

The future of wrestling is bright. It has been developed and improved, and standardized throughout the world, by the Olympic games. Many people believe that wrestling in the future will be dominated someday by Japan, which would mean that the modern sport of wrestling in both the catch-as-catch-can and Greco-Roman styles had circled the globe. Certainly the 1952 victory of Russia as a newcomer to Olympic wrestling shows that supremacy in sports moves around.

The United States, for the first time in the history of the modern Olympics, sent two complete wrestling teams to Melbourne, one catch-as-catch-can and one Greco-Roman. Several years ago the United States AAU, in order to help standardize international wrestling, adopted the international rules, even in catch-as-catch-can, although they deviated from former AAU regulations and handicapped U.S. wrestlers for a short time. In 1956, for the first time, wrestlers from all over the world were able to compete, in both schools of wrestling, under rules that will be familiar to all competitors, from Argentina to Zanzibar and from Australia to Yugoslavia.

Thirty nations sent wrestling representatives to Melbourne. There were 195 competitors—110 for catch-as-catch-can or free style, and 85 for the Greco-Roman—and 312 bouts. In the catch-as-catch-can wrestling, the unofficial team champion was Turkey. In the Greco-Roman, the championship was won by Russia with five gold medals, one silver and one bronze. The standard of the competition in both styles was very high. The most unusual event of the competition was the final heavyweight Greco-Roman match between W. Dietrich of Germany and A. Parfenov of Russia. The German won after having won four other bouts. However, after a Russian protest, the decision was reversed and A. Parfenov of Russia was awarded the title. The outstanding wrestlers in the tournament were Japan's S. Sasahara, winner of the featherweight free style, and Turkey's H. Kaplan, heavyweight free style champion. There were only two U.S. medal winners: B. Hodge, who placed second in the middleweight free style, and P. Blair, who placed third in the light heavyweight free style.

In the renovated Basilica of Massenzio in the center of old Rome, amid the ruins of the eternal city, in two and sometimes three rings, both the free style and Greco-Roman 1960 Olympic wrestling tournaments were run off. Three-hundred and thirty-six wrestlers from 54 countries competed in the open vaults of a building built in 300 A.D. In this imposing setting, Turkey won four gold medals and two silver in free style and three gold medals in Greco-Roman. The Turks, always a powerful mat entry, the United States, Russia and husky German heavyweight, Wilfred Dietrich, were the stars.

The United States made its best showing in this sport in 28 years by collaring three free style gold medals. The United States also won a fourth and two fifths. The United States start in Greco-Roman wrestling was not impressive but hopeful and a great improvement. Dietrich, second in Greco-Roman in 1956, was again second in this competition but doubled up and won the free style heavyweight title. All U.S. free style Olympic champions were from the center of wrestling in the United States—Oklahoma. An unfortunate incident marred the meet—namely a Bulgarian Greco-Roman heavyweight wrestler, himself out of first place contention, was believed to have thrown his bout to Kardidze of Russia and consequently handed the Russian the Olympic championship. The International Wrestling Federation reportedly made a strange ruling. The Russian was confirmed as champion but the Bulgarian was disqualified and barred from further competition.

The overall honors for catch-as-catch-can or free-style wrestling at Tokyo went to the Japanese—three gold medals (36 points) with Bulgaria, Russia and Turkey next (37-35 1/3-34). The United States won a bronze medal when middleweight Daniel Brand got to the semifinals, and also two fourth places. Russia showed up best in the Greco-Roman, although Japan earned two more gold medals. The competitions were unusually well staged in the impressive Komazawa Gymnasium and featured 312 competitors from 44 nations.

The free-style and Greco-Roman wrestling tournaments were held in the Pista de Hielo (Ice Skating Rink) in Mexico City. There were 164 free style competitors from 38 countries and 179 from 37 countries in the Greco-Roman. In each round wrestlers with 6 bad points or more were eliminated. Bad points were compiled as follows: victory by fall, 0 bad point; decision on points, 1 bad point; draw, 2 bad points; defeat on points, 3 bad points; and fall, 4 bad points. Russia won both on all-around scoring. The biggest surprise at Mexico was the wrestlers from Mongolia who captured four medals in the free style and who undoubtedly will be heard about in the future. The Turks, on the other hand, continued their decline that started at Tokyo. The United States won two silver medals: Richard Sanders in the flyweight class and Donald Behm in the bantamweight class won the medals.

JUDO

Judo (Jujitsu or Jujuitsu) as a sport, namely a form of wrestling or personal combat, was added to the Olympic program for the 1964 games at Tokyo. Basically the defense and even offense depends largely upon the skill of using the opponent's strength, weight and momentum to halt, injure or defeat him, and upon the skill of applying pressures to throw the opponent off balance. A bout, which has certain ceremonies, starts with the adversaries holding the collar of each other's kimona or jacket. It is believed this art, science and sport was brought to Japan from China thousands of years ago but became very popular and is now almost the national sport of Japan. By 1900 judo had spread throughout Asia and Europe. It became well known in America during World War I and World War II.

The first Olympic judo competition was held in 1964 in the colorful pagoda-like Nippon Budokan Hall. It was conducted with all the proper ceremony and the contests proved so popular that there is little doubt that it will become a regular feature.

An American, Jim Bregman of Arlington, Virginia, a student studying economics and judo in Japan, earned honors in judo when he won an Olympic bronze medal in the middleweight division. The Japanese, as expected, won three out of

238

the four classifications, although surprisingly enough the winner of the unlimited division was a 6-foot 5-inch, 250-pound "physical ed" instructor from Netherlands. Anton Gessink defeated Japan's champion Akio Kaminaga for the second time in the finals. Gessink has been world's champion since 1961. He was congratulated by Prince Bernhard, who was an enthusiastic spectator at Budokan Hall. Twenty-nine countries were represented.

There was no judo in the 1968 games in Mexico, but judo returned to the Olympic program at Munich.

CHAPTER XIX

Yachting

THE OLYMPIC sport of yachting covers sailing races of smaller craft generally referred to throughout the world as yachts. Yacht racing dates from the beginning of the nineteenth century. Long before that, however, Queen Elizabeth had a pleasure ship called a yacht—in 1588. Charles II of England was given a yacht by the Dutch in 1660. He later designed his own 25-ton yacht, called *Jamie*. This yacht was built at Lambeth in 1662. Shortly thereafter *Jamie* raced a small Dutch yacht with the Duke of York at the helm, from Greenwich to Gravesend and back, and won. The King was steering *Jamie*. The winner collected a 100-pound wager. This is considered the first yachting race between two amateurs. The first sailing club was founded in 1720. It was called the Royal Cork Yacht Club, and it was established in Ireland.

The oldest surviving (though it was not the first established) yacht club in the United States is the New York Yacht Club, founded in 1844. However, records indicate that even in colonial times there were privately owned yachts used principally for pleasure and that some of them actually raced. International yacht racing began in 1851, when a syndicate of New York Yacht Club members built a 101-foot schooner, the *America*, and sailed her to England, where she proved much faster than the British yachts. Thus were started the famous international sailing matches, continued through 1937, in which numerous British, Canadian, and American yachtsmen attempted to take the so-called championship cup from the New York Yacht Club. Ocean-racing yachts range in size from approximately 53 feet down to 35 feet in length, and the races are won or lost on corrected time, each yacht receiving an allowance from the largest, or scratch boat, in proportion to its size and potential speed.

Many changes in the designs of yachts and in the rules and regulations of yacht racing have taken place through the years, but one of the most significant contributions to the sport was made by J. Scott Russell, who, in 1848, argued against the wisdom of building sailing vessels on a cod-head and mackerel-tail plan and enunciated the wave-line theory.

The first international rules were laid down in 1904, with the Germans, French, and British agreeing to them; the United States did not send an official representative to the conference. The second series of international rules was agreed to during 1919 and 1920.

The class, or closed-course, racing in the Olympics of today is based on the one-design racing sloop. This type of racing was intended as the poor man's racing, for the boats involved cost as little as $250—that is, they did back in 1911, when this branch of the sport was organized. The poor man's racing boat at this time was the Star Class, a 23-foot, thin-keeled sloop. The main sponsor for this type of boat was an American, George A. Corry. As a proof of his vision this class today numbers over 5,000 boats belonging to over 200 fleets scattered around the world in every continent. Racing associations have grown up everywhere there is water, and in addition to the Olympics there are world, continental, and national championships annually. Yachting as a sport gains most of its publicity from racing, but racing is a very small part of the sport of sailing.

In the wake of the Stars, hundreds of other one-design classes became popular—most of them under 40 feet in length, many under 20—many of them holding annual or biennial world's championships. Some of the best known of these are Snipes, Comets, Lightnings and Thistles. Yachting has become a completely amateur sport, and there are no longer any professional racing-yacht skippers. In yacht racing there are hundreds of championships, but there is no one overall champion. All classes have their own champions, but they rarely meet each other and there is no final way of deciding that one skipper or one group of sailors or one type of boat is at the top of the entire sport.

In 1896, at the first Olympiad in Athens, plans had originally been made to have an exhibition regatta, including some sailing ships, but a storm came up on the day it was to be held and it was canceled. In 1900, at the second Olympic games in Paris, sailing competitions were held, with France winning the all-around championship in yachting. Switzerland was second, which reminded everyone that there really was a

Swiss Navy, even though it might sail or steam on lakes. The competition was restricted to a 6-meter class, 8-meter class, two-ton boat, and ten-ton boat. There was no yachting in 1904, obviously because there were no lakes or oceans suitable for sailing near St. Louis, Missouri. There is also no record of any official sailing or yachting in the 1906 Olympics, but naturally there were official yachting competitions in the 1908 Olympics at London, which Great Britain won on an overall basis. The competitions were in 6-meter, 7-meter, 8-meter, and 12-meter, and for the first and only time in the Olympics the British introduced motorboat racing with three classes.

In the 1912 Olympic games in Sweden there was great interest in the sailing competitions, which were won by Sweden. There were a 6-meter class, an 8-meter class, a 10-meter class, and a 12-meter class. In the 1912 Olympics, Russia was one of the participants, placing third in the 10-meter class.

At the seventh Olympiad, the yachting competitions were held at Ostend, with Norway winning the all-around competition; Sweden was second, Holland third, Great Britain fourth, Belgium fifth and France sixth. There were tremendous winds and a very rough sea, and the competition tested the courage of the contestants as well as the seaworthiness of their craft. After the games a very big step was made for the future of yachting competitions in the Olympics, for the Olympic Congress decided that standardization was essential, and therefore yachting programs for Olympic games were put under the control of the International Yachting Federation. This organization was charged with the preparation of the program for future Olympics and with notifying the various countries of the program a considerable time ahead of each Olympiad. It was ruled that the events would consist of yachts of 6 meters and 9 meters and probably one of 5 meters or less, that the yachts could be built anywhere but that they had to be manned by citizens of the competing countries and that yachts of 5 meters should have but one man on board, of 6 meters three, of 8 meters five, and, of course, that all crews had to be amateurs. The unfortunate part about this excellent arrangement was that the International Yachting Federation did not include the membership of the United States. However, the Olympic Congress stated that they would press the United States to join the organization.

The eighth Olympiad in 1924 in Paris brought together entries from 19 nations in yachting. These nations finished on an all-around basis in yachting in the following order: first, Norway; second, Belgium; third, Holland; fourth, France; fifth, Denmark and Great Britain, tied; seventh, Finland and Sweden, tied; ninth, Spain and Argentina, tied; eleventh, Cuba; twelfth, Italy; thirteenth, Switzerland; fourteenth, Czechoslovakia, fifteenth, Poland; sixteenth, Monaco; seventeenth, South Africa; eighteenth, Canada; and nineteenth, Portugal. The events were the monotype or dinghy class, the 6-meter, and the 8-meter. The races were staged at Meulan-les-Mureaux and also in the harbor at Le Havre. There was more than passing interest in the yachting events, for there were actually over 9,000 spectators on hand.

International competitions involving Americans between the 1924 and 1928 Olympic games finally got the United States into Olympic yachting. The United States also joined the International Yacht Racing Union and submitted entries in the monotype class, the 6-meter, and the 8-meter for the next Olympics.

In the ninth Olympiad yachting championships in 1928 the final standing in the 8-meter class was as follows: first, France; second, Holland; third, Sweden; fourth, Italy; and fifth, Norway. Argentina, Great Britain, and the United States were eliminated or withdrew. In the 6-meter class: first, Norway; second, Denmark; third, Estonia; fourth, Holland; fifth, Belgium; sixth, the United States and seventh, Sweden. Germany, Hungary, France, Italy, Spain and Portugal were eliminated. In the monotype, or 12-foot class: first, Sweden; second, Finland; third, Italy; fourth, Norway; fifth, Holland; sixth, Germany; seventh, Lithuania; eighth, Great Britain; ninth, Denmark; and tenth, the United States, with Sweden winning the unofficial all-around championship.

The tenth Olympiad at Los Angeles featured great competition in the yachting events. There were four classes—6-meter, 8-meter, the famous Star class, and the monotype. According to the rules, the monotype was to be manned by one man, the Star by two, the 6-meter by five, and the 8-meter by a crew of seven. The United States, for the first time, won the all-around yachting championship. The events were run in Los Angeles harbor with the assistance of the U.S. Navy and Coast Guard. There was tremendous competition in the preliminaries, semifinals, and final tryouts to represent the U.S. Owen Churchill was manager of the U.S. Olympic champions in yachting, and was again manager in 1936.

At the 1936 Olympics in Berlin the yachting competitions

were held at Kiel and run by the German Navy. Owen Churchill's *Angelita* was the U.S. entry in the 8-meter class, William A. Bartholomae, Jr.'s *Mystery* was the U.S. entry in the 6-meter class, and Frank B. Jewett, Jr. was the U.S. entry in the monotype class. *Three Star Too,* with W. Glen Waterhouse, as captain, and Woodbridge Metcalf, was the American entry in the Star class. The all-around yachting was won by Germany, with Great Britain second, Italy third, Sweden fourth, and Norway next. The United States did not fare so well, coming in tenth in the 8-meter class, ninth in the 6-meter class, fifth in the Star class, and ninth in the monotype. There were 26 nations competing, with Chile, Uruguay, Turkey, and Brazil as newcomers. The monotype boat of each team was supplied by the Olympic Organizing Committee of the host country.

The fourteenth Olympiad at London brought together entries from 21 countries in the yachting competitions, which consisted of five events—6-meter class, Dragon class, Star class, Swallow class, and Firefly class. They were held at Torquay, Devon, England, with an impressive ceremony at historic Torre Abbey. The competition, held in Tor Bay, was run with the assistance of the British Navy, and anchored at the scene of the competition were the British battleships *Anson* and *King George V,* the aircraft carrier *Victorious,* and a score of American, French, British, and Belgian ships, two Swedish training ships, and the Norwegian royal yacht, with the Crown Prince of Norway aboard. The countries scored in the following order on an all-around basis: United States, Norway, Denmark and Sweden. The manager of this U.S. Olympic championship team was Lee Loomis.

The fifteenth Olympiad in Helsinki in 1952 brought out more competitors and greater performances than ever before in the yachting events. The events, held in the bautiful harbor of Helsinki, were run in impeccable style by the Finnish Olympic Sailing Committee, assisted by a distinguished jury headed by Crown Prince Olaf of Norway and Sir Jeffrey Lowles of the United Kingdom. The members of the visiting yachting teams were housed in the private residences of the yachtsmen of Helsinki.

The captain of the U.S. team was again Owen P. Churchill, and for the first time there was a woman manager, Mrs. Millie Horton, whose husband, William Horton, was the skipper of the U.S. boat in the Dragon class—his crew were William, Jr., and Joyce Horton. Twenty-eight nations participated. There were five events—the 6-meter

243

class, the 5.5-meter class, the Dragon, Star and Finn class (the Finn class being the equivalent of the old monotype). An interesting feature of this competition was the entry and excellent showing of Russia, a nation returning to the yachting competition after a long absence. The entry of Russia suggested to some that yachting, like riding or fencing, is not restricted to any one class.

The unofficial 1952 all-around yachting championship wound up with the United States first, Norway second, Italy third, Denmark fourth, Sweden fifth, and Portugal sixth. The Finn class, which to many is the greatest test in the yachting competition and was the one in which there were representatives from every country, wound up with the countries finishing in the following order: Denmark, Great Britain, Sweden, the Netherlands, Austria, Norway, Italy, Canada, Brazil, Spain, France, Russia, Switzerland, the Bahamas, Germany, South Africa, Portugal, Belgium, Finland, Uruguay, Ireland, Australia, Yugoslavia, Cuba, Argentina, Greece, Japan and the United States.

The yachting regatta of the sixteenth Olympic games was held in Port Philip Bay, only a few miles from the Olympic stadium. Port Philip Bay is 45 miles wide and has 1,400 square miles of open water. This was, therefore, a sailing area of unusual size to most of the visiting yachtsmen. The wind, usually southwesterly, was cold and strong and at times whipped the bay into a raging surf. One hundred and seventy-eight yachtsmen representing 28 nations, with 51 racing yachts of the greatest craftsmanship in this field, were present. Twenty boats for the individual dinghy series were provided by Australia. These were drawn by lot.

Sweden won the unofficial all-around team championship taking two firsts and one fifth. The unusual feature in the regatta was the disqualification of New Zealand's "Red Dragon" (in the Dragon Class) twice due to two protests— one by Britain's "Bluebottle" and the other by Argentina's "Pampero." The skipper of the New Zealand boat tacked improperly, with near collisions, in both cases. Another feature of the regatta was the tie between Sweden and Denmark in the Dragon Class. The two yachts representing these two countries were so evenly matched that at the end of one week's sailing they tied with the same score. But Sweden was awarded the gold medal on a countback on placings. The determination of this tie was very important, for had Denmark won the tie, her "Tip" would not only have won the

Dragon Class but Denmark and not Sweden would have won the unofficial all-around championship in yachting.

Denmark came back, however, in 1960 on the Bay of Naples to win the unofficial yachting title it almost won in 1956. The growing popularity of this sport, once reserved only for the very rich, was proven by the fact that 287 competitors from 46 nations sailed 138 yachts in the five classes. Fifteen medals were divided among eleven nations, with Denmark taking home one gold and two silver medals. Russia broke through to win a gold and a silver with the United States winning a gold and a bronze. Strange as it may seem, the proletariat Russians in 1960 won the dressage in equitation, the overall fencing and a yachting crown. The outstanding personality of the regatta was Paul B. Elvstrom, Denmark's master of small boats, who collected a gold medal in the Finn class for the third straight time and his fourth Olympic championship as he won in the firefly class in 1948. The United States won the big 5.5 class with the U.S.-designed and built-Minotaur which Skipper O'Day purchased after his winning boat in the U.S. Olympic tryout was damaged.

The United States won the all-around yachting crown on Sagani Bay near Tokyo in 1964 with two close seconds (in the Star class, Richard Stearns and Lynn Williams, and in the Finn Class, Peter Barrett) and three thirds. Germany was second with one first, one second, one fifth and one sixth, and Denmark a whisper behind with one first, one third and one fourth. The gold medals in the five events were won by Australia, Denmark, Bahamas, New Zealand and Germany. Forty-two countries were represented. For the first time in Olympic history the United States won a medal in each of the five events.

The United States again won the all-around yachting honors at the 1968 Olympics in Mexico. The yachting events were held at Acapulco, famous resort of millionaires. There were new problems there, high humidity, burning heat and very special meteorological and oceanic conditions. The 5.5 meter class was won by the three Sundelin brothers from Sweden, the Dragon class by the U.S.'s Buddy Frederichs, the Flying Dutchman class was won by Britain's Rodney Patterson and Ian Macdonald Smith, the Star class was won by the U.S.'s Lowell North and Peter Barrett. The Finn class was won in a surprise victory by Russia's Valentin Mankin.

245

CHAPTER XX

The 1972 Games

THE XX OLYMPIAD in 1972 at Munich, West Germany, proved to be the worst and most disastrous in the long history of the modern games. While very little is known about the final ancient games, in 394 A.D., their reportedly unfair and unsportsmanlike nature, with fighting and murder rampant, must have had some similarity to the Munich games, which could presage another abandonment of the Olympics.

From the very beginning, the Munich games seemed fated for trouble. Max Schmeling—who had spent his earlier years in the Nazi German army—was sent to visit the United States, with German Olympic officials by the Munich Organizing Committee, to try to sell what U.S. sportswriters immediately started referring to as the Munich "Mini" Olympics. A warning sign went up. Instead of talking of a 100,000-capacity stadium, the Munich Organizing Committee began speaking of merely enlarging their stadium of some 40,000 capacity. They suggested that the games were getting too big and therefore there should be more emphasis on TV coverage. The committee wanted to limit the number of spectators at the games by keeping the stadium relatively small and intimate, which would make the Munich games easier for the spectators to view. This was their beginning plan, but in the end they compromised.

The committee also commandeered all hotel accommodations within seventy-five miles of the center of Munich, and even regular clients of Munich hotels were told they could not get any reservations or accommodations during the games anywhere within that radius. This immediately was a further danger signal to all those persons who were planning a normal trip to the Olympic games. Actually it was reported much later that during the Olympics there were many vacant accommodations in Munich, yet no proper reservations could be obtained sufficiently ahead of time to make for safe planning. Even members of the Jury d'Appel with certificates from world sports bodies and those with authentic press credentials could not get reservations.

From the beginning, no proper plans for special security were made, although, as has since been ascertained, warnings were duly given. The Germans apparently believed that Munich could have no security or police problems because the German police and security were adequate. No corrective or protective police measures were taken in time to prevent the murders and chaos that were the tragic climax of the games. The liquidation of all the Israeli hostages and most of the terrorists might well have been avoided if there had been sufficient security and if the police had not overreacted.

And the Munich fiasco did not stop with the Germans. The U.S. Olympic teams suffered every possible bad break, many of them chargeable to the U.S.O.C. management. However, it seems that a conspiracy—or at the least a combined intent caused by human jealousy—was present on the part of the Communist countries on one hand, and those of the Third World on the other, to "get the U.S."

Jesse Abramson has covered every one of the Olympic summer games from the 1928 Amsterdam games to the Munich games and remembers that earlier he decoded Grant-land Rice's dispatches from the 1924 Paris games. Abramson states without hesitation that the 1972 games were dominated by one thought—"Get America!" Either that, he says, or Murphy's Law was in operation for the United States, especially for the track team: "Everything that could go wrong did go wrong."

One significant example was the unexpected and arbitrary disqualification of a vaulting pole that had not just once, but twice, been previously approved. This pole had been used by the world's outstanding pole-vaulters for more than a year before the games, including three vaulters from the United States. Indicating the unfairness of this unusual act of officialdom is the fact that the world's record pole vault by one of the U.S. entries was 18′ 5¾″, yet the winning height at Munich, negotiated by a German, was only 18′ ½″, almost half a foot short. Thus a U.S. gold medal was lost.

The officiating and decisions in many sports were almost unbelievably bad. The hosts even admitted this, but nothing positive or constructive was done about it beyond firing a lot of officials. After the fact, there were profuse regrets and apologies.

When Reynaud Robinson and Eddie Hart, top U.S. sprinters, were told the wrong starting time for their quarter final heat by Coach Stan Wright (with no followup by the U.S. Olympic team officials or the officials running the events) and were eliminated, it cost the United States one or perhaps two more Olympic gold medals. The Russian Borsov made no world championship time or any time comparable to that of the eliminated runners, and his performance in the relay was not up to the best of U.S. runners.

Uninfluenced except by bad luck, Rich Wohluter of Notre

Dame fell during the 800-meter heat and another probable medal was lost to the United States. Finally, as a capper on the fiasco of the games themselves, Vince Matthews and Wayne Collett, who ran first and second in the 400-meter final, in a planned or perhaps spontaneous display of bad manners or lack of patriotism, refused to show normal respect either to their country's flag and anthem or to the Olympic ceremony on the victory stand, notwithstanding the thousands of years of Olympic grandeur. Julius Song from Kenya, who finished third, stood at rigid attention on the stand, in contrast to the two Americans. Their treatment by the I.O.C. —lifetime expulsion from the Olympics—if harsh, was certainly well deserved. Matthews, in an excuse quoted in *The New York Times,* proved he should have remained silent. "I am an athlete, not a politician. . . . I never stand at attention. . . . True I was clowning around with my medal, but it was mine."

Because of the lifetime Olympic ban against Matthews and Collett and the injury to another U.S. sprinter, only three able-bodied men were left, out of the six entered for the four-time 400-meter relay. Although the I.O.C.'s own ban of Collett and Matthews should not have applied against the U.S. team, the no-substitution rule was not changed and the United States was eliminated. So another surefire gold medal, in the 1,600 relay, was lost, probably influenced by political discrimination. (The I.A.A.F., realizing the absolute unreasonableness of the ruling, changed the rule—but effective as of the 1976 Olympics.)

Billy Fordjour of Ghana, a senior at Harvard Payne College in Texas, and Jim Ryun tangled feet as the two trailed in the last 500 meters of a 1,500-meter heat. Eighty meters behind, Ryun tried but finished out of the running. Although he had broken the world's record for the 1,500-meter in 3:33.1 in 1967, he never could come back and was followed by hard luck thereafter—the Munich Olympics were no exception. In the mix-up on the ground Ryun was spiked in both ankles, yet he was, in his own words, playing it smart by lying back to merely qualify in the heat. A protest filed by Ryun was turned down by the Jury d'Appel. A strange slant on this incident must be mentioned here. The reporter for the Agence Presse, who reportedly was the nearest person to the fall, stated: "Ryun was given a sudden and violent dig in the ribs by a runner alongside of him . . . the blow Ryun received in the side looked like something from a karate exhibition." Could Ryun have been purposely knocked into the Ghana runner by one of the many Munich "get the U.S." conspirators? The winning time of the 1,500 at Munich was 3:36.3 . . . slower than Jim Ryun's best.

The U.S.O.C. and the management of the U.S. Olympic teams were severely criticized. There can be no question that many errors can be blamed on them, but there is no evidence that the U.S. government and the U.S. Congress could do better. The present management and concept has not done badly in eighty years. A currently U.S. government-run sport and Olympic team in the modern pentathlon is probably the worst-run of any of this country's teams, with the poorest results.

A new sport (which is hardly athletic) has been introduced—the slalom. Replicas of the Olympic slalom course were used for practice—but only in East and West Germany —for many months before the games. The two Germanys had an almost clean sweep and East Germany won all four gold medals. The performance of East Germany in women's track and field is worthy of special note. The new world records set were standouts, worthy of special commendation.

Certainly Olympic sports and Olympic events should not be increased lightly. With proper pruning, the great Olympic tree can possibly be saved. But if too many suckers are encouraged and cross branches allowed to weaken proper growth, the tree will die. Let us examine the recent proliferation of events and sports.

The four-event slalom is an excellent example. Adding these four events to the games was hardly justified, since the results were almost preordained. Within twelve Olympiads (1928–1976), swimming expanded from fifteen events to thirty-three, while track and field went from twenty-seven events to thirty-eight! It is important to remember that every time the number of sports and events increase, so do the points, the number of athletes, spectators and officials, the heats and time, installations and equipment needed, number of days of competition, etc., etc. The result may well become a Frankenstein's monster.

Altogether the Munich games involved poor officiating, protests and bad sportsmanship, political interference, bias, disqualifications, and murder. Certainly the Germans must have wished that they had not bid for, obtained, or conducted the games as they did.

Notwithstanding the original German "Mini" Olympic plans, the Munich games were the biggest—although the worst—of the modern games, if this is any consolation. A well-known sportsman commented that Baron de Coubertin, the French founder of the modern games, in 1896, must have turned over in his grave at so many unhappy and tragic incidents at Munich. No one was sorry when the games were over. All who stayed away were delighted they did.

A news release of the U.S.O.C. named Valery Borzov of the Soviet Union as one of the great stars of the Munich games; yet his record of 0:10.14 in the 100 and 0:20.0 in the 200 did not match the existing world and Olympic records of 0:9.9 and 0:19.8 at the time. The real stars of the 1972 Olympic track competition were Finland and her two runners who won the 1,500-, 5,000-, and 10,000-meter runs. Pakka Vasala, running the 1,500-meter in 3:36.3, sprinting away from Kipchoge Keino at the finish, was impressive. Lasse Viren, a 24-year-old policeman with an Amish-style beard, who broke the Olympic 5,000-meter record with 13:26.4, was outstanding. This performance was in addition to his win in the 10,000-meter run in 27:38.4, even though he collided and fell on the 20th lap with the great Gammoudi running in his third Olympic game. Both men got up running, but Gammoudi gave up after one more lap. Viren caught up with the leaders in two laps and sprinted for the finish, winning by almost ten yards in a world and Olympic record time.

The marathon, as usual, stirred up lots of interest, especially because the United States (Frank Shorter) won for the first time since the disputed gold medal in this event was given to John Hayes in 1908, sixty-four years earlier.

United States swimmer Mark Spitz received the most personal publicity, but his seven gold medals (three as a member of relay teams) were for very similar performances. Experts chose Lasse Viren, the new flying Finn, as the standout, together with Ard Schenk, the Dutch speed skater, who won gold medals in the 1,500-, 5,000-, and 10,000-meter events. Since there are no skating relays in the Olympics, Schenk perhaps deserves equal honors with Spitz. The great success of East Germany was the result of particularly careful preparations and concentration in sports and events in which the United States was neither strong nor interested.

A great advantage to the Olympic movement was the final retirement of the late Avery Brundage who, at the age of eighty-seven, rather unwillingly gave up his unchallenged, despotic twenty-year reign as the I.O.C. president. As the great apostle of absolute purity in amateur sports, he was often referred to as pompous, acrimonious, assinine, archaic, unbending, autocratic and tyrannical, and his reactions to the Munich Olympic murders of eleven Israeli athletes represented, according to many, an example of insensitivity. Whatever may be said about Brundage, however, he was clearly a dedicated Olympian who contributed most of his time and efforts and much of his great fortune to the Olympic movement.

The new head of the I.O.C. is fifty-eight-year-old Lord Killanin of Ireland, who has been quoted as saying: "I can't see any objection for a stable boy or someone who rides horses for a living being an Olympic boxer." If this is acceptable, where would Lord Killanin draw the line? Could the boy who rides horses for a living perform on the long horse in gymnastics? Or be a modern pentathlon man, where one event is riding over a jumping course on a strange horse? Could a world's heavyweight champion collecting five million dollars per fight compete in freestyle wrestling as an amateur? Or does Lord Killanin prescribe to a world where there will be no professionals, only amateurs subsidized by the state, who might well run sports for propaganda purposes? If all governments take over amateur sports and the Olympics become a sort of battleground between countries, Lord Killanin may be faced with the same problems that terminated the games in 394 A.D. Let us hope this will not be the case, and let us review some of the results in the various sports at the Munich games.

ARCHERY

Archery returned to the Olympic games in Munich for the first time since 1920. This is the only sport that had a woman president of the world body, the Federation de Tir a l'Arc—Inger K. Firth of Great Britain. The Olympic archery competition was held separately but concurrently for men and women; the site was less than three miles from the Olympic Village. The men shot 288 arrows, 72 each from 90, 70, 50 and 30 meters away. John Williams, an eighteen-year-old private in the U.S. Army, from Pennsylvania, current world's champion, won with 2,528 points out of a possible 2,880 points. Gunnar Jarvil of Sweden was second with 2,481, and Edwin Eliason of the United States was fifth. Also from the United States, Doreen Wilber, with thirty years of competitive archery experience, won the women's competition with a score of 2,424, and Linda Myers was fifth.

251

The most important elements in all recent Olympic boxing competition, Munich included, have been: (1) poor decisions, many affected by political, ideological and national influences; (2) the finals often being anticlimactic after the semifinals; (3) the discovery of potential world professional titleholders, especially heavyweights: Frank Genaro, Fidel LaBarba, Pascual Perez, Jack Fields, Pete Sarron, G. Benvenuti, Floyd Patterson, Cassius Clay, Joe Frazier, George Foreman and now, according to many predictions, Teofilo Stevenson, the 1972 heavyweight Olympic winner.

A new trend is the appearance of boxers from the emerging nations of Africa. In 1972, five African nations captured seven medals.

Communist countries, however, got nine out of eleven gold medals, proving that amateurs in boxing are best in countries where they are subsidized and where there are no professional boxers, a natural development.

Lots of poor decisions in lots of sports were made at the Munich Olympics, many influenced by political and ideological thinking. Probably the greatest steals were in boxing, where the Olympic brass, ashamed of their decisions, developed the concept that the more judges, the fairer the decisions. At Munich there was a nonvoting referee who should have known what was going on in the ring better than anyone else, plus five—yes, one, two, three, four, five—judges to each bout who were kept circulating at ringside as if they were in a game of musical chairs! As Red Smith described it, this was so that their incompetence would not stagnate. One of the most questionable decisions favored Valery Tregubov, two-time European southpaw champion in the light middleweight class (156 pounds), over Reggie Jones, a U.S. boxer from Newark, New Jersey. The judge from Liberia gave all three rounds to Jones for a score of 60-57; the judge from Malaysia scored it 59-57 in favor of Jones; a judge from Yugoslavia voted for the Russian 59-58; and the judges from Nigeria and Netherlands scored 58 points for each fighter but checked the Russian as the winner. Although the total U.S. score was in favor of Jones by 294 to 290, he lost! Most experts gave Jones both the first round and the third, by a very wide margin. In fact, many experienced ringside observers thought the Russian was in very bad shape at the finish. The crowd threw paper and garbage into the ring after the bout in a super boxing booing demonstration that lasted all through the next three-round bout and into the following. Jones, twenty-one years old, was a lance corporal in the U.S. Marines. Tregubov, thirty years old, was an officer in the Red Army.

Olympic boxing has survived bad decisions for many years. In 1972 they were just as bad as before, or perhaps worse. There is apparently no solution to this, short of importing judges from outer space.

Cuba won the all-around honors in fisticuffs. Munich, notwithstanding mediocre boxing and very bad decisions, with the suspension of many officials, did produce one outstanding performer who needed no help from any officials— a young Cuban heavyweight named Teofilo Stevenson. Stevenson is reputed to be far more advanced in the gentle art than was Floyd Patterson, Cassius Clay, Joe Frazier or George Foreman at the time each won his respective Olympic title. However, Stevenson allegedly believes in Communism and is against professionalism. He is over twenty-one and, according to Castro's controlled releases, will be the first heavyweight (but not the first boxer) to be Olympic champion three times in succession. According to this statement, he will be at Montreal, reportedly with his Russian coach Chervonenko, who learned boxing from American movies of American world champions. The plans for Stevenson are similar to those that were followed by Laszlo Papp, who won three Olympic titles for Communist Hungary in 1948, 1952 and 1956. After more than eighteen years of amateur boxing for a mere living, he finally turned pro after he had gone over the hill. Cassius Clay's reputed single purse of five million dollars for a title fight should test Castro's might in keeping "Stevenson's right boxing for Castro's left," quoting Hartmut Scherzer in the U.S.O.C. 1972 book.

Canoeing and Kayaking

These water sports were, as usual, completely dominated by Communist countries. The Communist governments' subsidy of allegedly amateur athletics and their elimination of any professional sports has resulted in their capturing sixteen out of twenty-one medals in this category. The slalom (although performed in canoes or kayaks it can be considered a separate sport), added to the Olympic program by the East and West Germans, showed nine medals for the two Germanys out of twelve, with four gold medals for East Germany. Quite a number of experts question the wisdom of categorizing the slalom as a sport based on athletic ability.

253

CYCLING

Amateur cycling, after making a great comeback in Mexico City in 1968, further advanced itself at Munich when a new group of cyclists from East and West Germany and the Soviet Union joined battle with the cyclists from the old cycle strongholds of France, Australia, Denmark and Italy. Norway, in the person of Knut Knudsen, won its first gold medal in cycling ever when the twenty-two-year-old Knudsen traveled at fifty kilometers an hour to beat the former world's champion, Swiss Xaver Kurmann. Denmark's only gold medal for the entire Munich Olympics was won by Niels Fredborg, a twenty-five-year-old insurance clerk, in the 1,000-meter time trial. Daniel Morelon of France became the first man in seventy-six years to win back-to-back titles in the scratch sprint. However, he yielded his tandem crown, again with Pierre Trentin, to the Soviet Union. The winning Netherlands foursome in the team road race were disqualified as a result of urine analyses, but Netherlands came back when Hennie Kuiper won the individual road race. The Soviet Union won all-around honors in cycling.

EQUESTRIAN EVENTS

Probably the closest and most exciting competition at the Munich Olympics, and one projecting proper and outstanding Olympic sportsmanship, was the famous Prix de Nations Team Equestrian Jumping event. The morning round of team jumping in a light rain wound up as close as one-fourth of a point, or 0.25. The United States received a penalty because Shapiro exceeded the time limit over the course of fourteen jumps. The weather cleared in the afternoon in time for the closing ceremony following the finals of the Prix de Nations. The stadium was packed with more than 80,000 spectators. The final results were close indeed. In the second round of jumping, West Germany and the United States were each charged with sixteen penalties, while Italy overtook Great Britain to win the bronze medal. West Germany's margin of victory was one-fourth of a point, or 0.25, over the United States. This was some consolation to the host nation for all of its problems.

A very unusual group of competitors was involved in the equestrian dressage individual finals: Gold medalist Liselott Linsenhoff, a German millionaire factory owner who rode Piaff, a fourteen-year-old stallion; silver medalist Elena Petushkova (Russian wife of Valery Brumel, the Olympic high-jump champion at the Tokyo Olympics), with an Olympic veteran horse named Pepel; bronze medalist Josef Neckermann, a West German sixty-one-year-old department store magnate who recovered from an April spinal accident to ride Venetia, an eleven-year-old brown mare (this was his fourth win in four Olympic Games). West Germany was the equestrian all-around winner.

FENCING

An Olympic book, published by a Stuttgart, Germany, publisher, with U.S.O.C. members listed as editors, insists on ducking an issue. The book states that the Eastern European Socialist nations dominate the sport of fencing simply because they treat the discipline in dead earnest whereas the other former great fencing countries regard it as a weekend fancy. The fact is that the Communist countries now excel in fencing because their fencers are subsidized. Fencers in France, Italy, Belgium and other Western European countries —where the sport was initiated, coached, trained and developed—are now second-best. However, subsidy may lose its attractiveness eventually. In 1972, Italy won the men's sabre team world's championship and the women's individual foil championship; Switzerland came in second in the world's epee team; and France placed third in the men's individual foil and second in the men's individual epee . . . not bad for weekend dilettantes! Hungary won all-around honors in fencing.

GYMNASTICS

Japan firmly established its superiority in men's gymnastics in 1968 and again dominated this sport in Munich. Theirs was practically a clean sweep, with Sawao Kato, Erzo Kenmotsu and Akinori Nakayama. The women's gymnastic competition in Munich was among the most popular events. In fact, not a single ticket on any day was available for this competition. A seventeen-year-old Russian gymnast named Olga Korbut, 5′ 1″, 84 pounds when wet, almost became queen of the Munich Olympic Games, as Vera Caslavska had been queen of the Mexican games. However, poor little Olga missed out on the finals of the all-around competition and finished seventh, although she won the floor exercise and balance beam, came in second in uneven parallel bar, and finished fifth in long horse.

Olympic experts advise that a gymnastic installation in the future should be provided for 100,000 spectators, to accommodate those who want to enjoy the women's gymnastic competition.

Modern Pentathlon

The modern pentathlon, the super all-around event created originally to spread friendship among the military and at one time restricted to army and navy personnel, had fifty-nine competitors. Some twenty nations have extensive interest in this event. The Soviet Union won the team event. Andras Balczo of Hungary, five times world champion and a silver Olympic medalist, as well as five times a member of the world's championship Hungarian team, won the individual title. Balczo was seventeenth in riding, forty points behind the five top-point scorers, but second in fencing with forty-four victories out of fifty-eight bouts, which pushed him into second place. In shooting, his score of 192 out of 200 gave him twelfth place in that event. His 300-meter freestyle swimming time of 3:46.6 placed him twenty-fifth in this event, but he was third in the all-around standing at this point. So Balczo knew exactly what he had to do in the cross-country run, and he did it.

A bombshell disturbed the competition when tests showed as many as sixteen of the competitors had used tranquilizers for the shooting competition. This is specifically forbidden, and there had been major disqualifications because of the use of tranquilizers at the 1968 Olympic games at Mexico City. In 1972, however, after many secret meetings, the matter was swept under the rug. There were no disqualifications, although the rule against tranquilizers in shooting was well established and previously observed.

The 1974 U.S. modern pentathlon team, managed from Washington, and well illustrating the efficacy of U.S. government control, came in eleventh in the 1974 world's championship.

Rowing and Sculling

The Munich Olympic Organizing Committee spared no expense in the construction of the rowing course at nearby Feldmoching. Many rowing officials complained, however, when brisk head winds delayed the start of a semifinal for almost two hours. Although allegedly of no importance, on the day of the semifinals two of the lanes were renamed "loserstrasse." East Germany qualified in all seven events and the Soviet Union squeezed six into the finals. The U.S. eight

Jean Claude Killy, "The all-time Superman of skiing," was the winner of sixteen out of twenty competitions in 1967, two previous world championships, and three gold Olympic medals at Chamrousse, France, in 1968.
French Government Tourist Office

West German Walter Esser and "Angel" splashed past a watery spot in the riding event of the five-sport Modern Pentathlon.   *Wide World*

Women, who compete with men in several Olympic events, were represented in Munich by Mexican skeet shooting champion Nuria Ortiz.   *Wide World*

John Writer, 27, of Chicago, Illinois, 1972 Olympic champion with the small bore rifle, showed all the extra gadgets, rests, pads, grips, sights, and meters needed for the breathing and squeezing.
Wide World

Dorothy Hamill displays her gold medal after capturing the women's figure skating title in the 1976 Games. *Wide World*

Piet Kleine of the Netherlands winning the men's 10,000 meter speed skating in Innsbruck. Despite the snow, Kleine came within 28 hundredths of a second of the world record. *Wide World*

United States equestrian rider Edmund Coffin takes his horse "Bally-Cor" over one of the jumps during competition in the three day jumping event where he won the Gold Medal. *UPI*

Cuba's indomitable Teofilo Stevenson, right, comes in with a hard right stunning U.S.A.'s John Tate. Stevenson won his 2nd Olympic gold medal in Montreal and is an early favorite to capture a third in Moscow. *Wide World*

Leon Spinks, right, lands a right to Cuba's Sixto Soria. Spinks won the fight and the Olympic gold medal for the light heavyweight class. He then went on to defeat Muhammad Ali for the professional heavyweight championship, only to lose to Ali in return bout. *UPI*

Wide-angle photo shows more than 70,000 spectators jammed into Olympic Stadium to watch closing ceremonies of the 1976 Olympic Games. On the floor, dancers form Olympic rings around Indian tepees. *UPI*

lost to New Zealand, with East Germany and West Germany third and fourth, although both were local favorites. The coxless four was the tightest of all the races; East Germany beat Australia by less than one-third of a boat length. The major upset was the defeat in the single sculls of Alberto Demiddi of Argentina, European champion, by Yuri Malishev of the Soviet Union, age twenty-five. His fellow Soviet scullers, Tyukalov (1952) and Ivanov (1956–60–64), had won previous Olympic honors. East Germany won the all-around honors in rowing.

SHOOTING

Just imagine the progress in Olympic shooting—twenty nations shared in the points and in the first six places in eight events. A U.S. Olympic publication states that the greater number of shooters among the first six in all events were from socialist countries, with a comment that this was inconclusive evidence of where the interest center of the sport might be, implying that the United States was an also-ran. Yet an analysis of Olympic points as set up originally by the press and approved by Olympic management of all countries at a 1924 meeting, and the fairest possible method, shows that the winner of the Munich Olympic shooting events was— even without considering population—the United States, with 31 points to the U.S.S.R.'s 29 points and with two gold medals and two silver medals to their one gold medal, two silver medals, and one bronze medal. If Olympic points per million population were used as the criterion, the U.S. margin over the Soviets in shooting would be even wider.

SWIMMING AND DIVING

No sport in the Olympic parade of sports can match swimming for the almost unbelievable improvement in the record books. The Munich Olympic games saw the following sensational results. Out of twenty-nine events for men and women in swimming, there were twenty-two new world records surpassed, one world record equalled, and six new Olympic records broken. Mark Spitz capped fourteen years in competition swimming by winning four individual events and participating on three winning relay teams. The United States again won all-around swim honors, with only five members from the 1968 world championship team.

Probably one of the most irrational and unfair decisions at the Munich Olympic games, and certainly one that can be blamed on officials and not on the athletes, was the disqualification of sixteen-year-old Rick DeMont of the United States, which deprived him of a possible gold medal in the 400-meter freestyle swim. It also deprived the United States of another possible gold medal in the 1,500-meter, where DeMont was the world record holder. The disqualification was based on a urine analysis which showed faint traces of Ephedrine, a drug DeMont had been taking for his asthma all his life. "This was a gross injustice," said Peter Daland, coach of the U.S. male swimmers. "He was robbed because of the mistakes of adults." Deland blamed the U.S.O.C. physicians with the team, and the I.O.C. also gave the American doctors a reprimand: "The U.S. teams' medical authorities are responsible for this situation."

Out of this incident grew another strange decision. Brad Cooper of Australia, who ran second (1/100th of a second slower than DeMont), was awarded the gold medal, and Steven Genter of the United States, who came in third, was given the silver medal for second place. But no third or bronze medal was given to Tom McBreen of the United States, who came in fourth according to the Munich officials. The reason the officials gave was that McBreen had not been picked to take the dope test after the race. This fortunately was later reversed, but it is a further indication of the attitude of the officials toward the rules, or perhaps only toward the United States. Many persons believe that DeMont should be credited with overcoming his asthma to win a gold medal in the Olympics. There is no doubt that the U.S. Olympic medical staff knew of the medicine regularly taken by their athlete for a proven ailment, and they should certainly have done something about it. They should receive a gold medal for gross and total inefficiency! Incidentally, they refused to be interviewed by the press after this incident. The I.O.C. executive board turned down the U.S. appeal on DeMont, reportedly not even permitting him to swim in the 1,500-meter without his asthma medication.

Although Spitz broke all records with seven gold medals, it must be admitted that an analysis of his performance indicates an unusual similarity of events, namely, the 100-meter freestyle; the 200-meter freestyle; the 100-meter butterfly; the 200-meter butterfly; and three relays in which Spitz again swam 100 meters twice and 200 meters once. It could be compared to a champion sprinter running 60-, 100- and 200-meter dashes and four relays of the same distances. Spitz, however, should be given due credit, and he, of course, had nothing to do with the unusual opportunity given him.

The women's swimming was dominated by the United States as a team and by a fifteen-year-old Australian girl, Shane Gould, who is 5'7" tall and weighed 132 pounds. She swam twelve times to win three gold medals, one silver and one bronze. She drew a blank in a relay only because she was out of the running when she started on the last leg.

Diving events were dominated by team captain Micki King's great victory in the springboard event. She had failed to win in Mexico in 1968 when she accidentally hit the springboard on her next-to-last dive. She broke her arm but insisted on staying in the competition, finishing fourth. Her margin of victory over Ulrika Knape of Sweden, winner of the Munich platform event, was quite convincing—450.03 to 434.19.

WATER POLO

The water polo competition was, according to experts, the best ever, with the top teams extremely close. The final game, between Hungary and the Soviet Union, was reminiscent of this game at Melbourne in 1956, without the bad blood of that engagement due to the Hungarian revolution against Soviet control at that time. The final placement was: Soviet Union, Hungary, United States, West Germany, Yugoslavia and Italy.

TEAM GAMES

BASKETBALL

The final basketball game between the United States and the Soviet Union was perhaps the highwater mark of the "get the U.S." project of a number of countries and, more important, the officials of many countries. Although officially awarded the silver medal for second place, the U.S. team refused the medal, perhaps the first Olympic medal ever to be refused. The United States participants still believe they won, 50–49, in a regular 40-minute game.

Some strange decisions caused the United States the loss of thirty-six years of domination in basketball, a game invented by an American. According to various sources, the loss ended a winning streak of 62, 63 or 64 games.

The whole game was irregular. It began at the ridiculous hour of 11:45 P.M. and ended in chaos some time after 1 A.M., although players were around at courtside awaiting word of the protest as late as 5 A.M. The winning Soviet basketball decision clearly violated international rules on several counts. The contest lasted at least 40:03 minutes.

The Soviet team led until U.S. Doug Collins scored two foul shots with three seconds left, for a score of U.S. 50, U.S.S.R. 49. The rest of the action allegedly consumed less than three seconds, ending in a score of 51–50 in favor of the Soviet Union whose team had three scoring chances. An inbounds pass was deflected at mid-court, and the three seconds appeared over. The crowd rushed on to the court thinking the United States had won, but the clock definitely showed, as thousands noted, that there was one second to go. The officials ordered the crowd cleared and play resumed. The Soviets took the ball out of bounds with Thomas Miller, a 6′ 11″ forward, waving his arms to prevent the pass. An inbounds pass was short when the horn sounded. The U.S. players and the crowd rushed out on to the court again. The clock had not been reset and Robert Jones, Secretary General of the International Amateur Basketball Federation (F.I.B.A.), ordered three seconds, not one second, again posted on the clock. The Soviet goal was then accomplished. Two violations evident in the films of the game were not called. The referees were a Bulgarian and a Brazilian. All the pictures taken indicate the violations, yet a five-man jury of appeal decided against the U.S. appeal. The five-man jury consisted of representatives from Cuba, Poland, Puerto Rico, Spain and Italy. No further comment is necessary. Thus two or three bizarre seconds ended a thirty-six-year U.S. reign! The official finalists were: the Soviet Union, Cuba, Italy, Yugoslavia, Puerto Rico and Brazil.

FIELD HOCKEY

Munich witnessed the end of the postwar domination of hockey by Pakistan and India when West Germany's Michael Krause made the winning goal from ten yards out for a win over Pakistan. The victory ceremony was the scene of a near riot and an exhibition of the poorest type of unsportsmanship by the defeated team resulting in the banning of the Pakistani team's field hockey players from Olympic competition for life. The International Field Hockey Federation also banned Pakistan, the present world's champion, from all international competition for four years. The finalists were: West Germany, Pakistan, India, Netherlands, Australia and Great Britain, in that order.

HANDBALL

This sport, team handball, has reportedly been played in Europe for more than a century. It was on the Olympic program in 1936 at Berlin. It can be played outdoors or indoors; at Munich it was played indoors and involved sixteen teams. The finalists in order of finish were: Yugoslavia, Czechoslovakia, Romania, East Germany, the Soviet Union, and West Germany.

SOCCER

For the first time since the world qualifying rounds were inaugurated, twelve years before Munich, the United States won its way to the Olympic games tournament. The final result, in closely contested games projecting excellent sportsmanship, was: First place, Poland; second place, Hungary; and East Germany and the U.S.S.R. in a tie for third place. Over 80,000 spectators watched the West Germany–East Germany and Soviet Union–East Germany matches, while less than 30,000 watched the Poland–Hungary match for first place.

VOLLEYBALL

The competitions in volleyball in Munich could not match the violent enthusiasm exhibited in Mexico City, but probably what was missing in enthusiasm was made up by better team play and technique. The finalists in the men's competition were: Japan, East Germany, the Soviet Union, Bulgaria, Romania and Czechoslovakia. The United States lost three games out of three in the preliminary rounds. The finalists of the women's competition were: the Soviet Union, Japan, North Korea, South Korea, Hungary and Cuba.

TRACK AND FIELD

Some of the highlights of track and field events at Munich have already been covered at the beginning of this chapter. But there were other exciting happenings.

David Wottle, dirty golf cap and all, was the first American to win the 800-meter since Tom Courtney in 1956.

The steeplechase, won in 1968 by Amos Biwott of Kenya, has become a Kenya specialty because of the training methods there. Biwott led through most of the race at Munich but finished sixth, while two other Kenyans—Kipchoge Keino and Benjamin Jipcho—came in first and second. Keino's time was 8:23.6, a new Olympic and world record.

The winner in the 16-lb. hammer throw, A. Bondarchuk of the Soviet Union, broke the world and Olympic records by eight feet—not eight inches—at 248′ 8″.

In the women's track and field—especially in the field events—many world records were broken. There were such

261

almost unbelievable improvements as these: N. Chizhova of the Soviet Union put the shot 69′ 0″; the previous world record was 64′ 4″. F. Melnik threw the discus 218′ 7″; the world record up to then had been 191′ 2½″. Ruth Fuchs Egerman threw the javelin 209′ 7″, throwing out the world record of 198′ ½″.

The matter of hormone tests for all women athletes in the Olympic games has been a very controversial subject for many years; the question is again raised by the phenomenal performances of women athletes at Munich.

WEIGHT LIFTING

This event, categorized as a sport of Eastern European socialist nations, is a specialty which, if the United States and Americans wanted to develop for Olympic nationalist propaganda purposes, could easily be mastered. However, since athletes and the Olympics are considered in the United States as sports without national or political objectives, only those few U.S. athletes who are interested in weight lifting participate. Therefore the United States has not produced winning teams.

In 1968 Bulgaria did not place a single entry among the top six competitors in seven weight classes. However, with an expansion of the seven classes to nine in 1972, Bulgaria in four years of all-out interest attained the position of world leader in this sport, capturing three gold medals, three silver, and a fifth place. As a contrast, the Soviet Union, who won three gold medals, three silver and a fourth place in seven events in Mexico, only won three gold medals, one silver and one bronze out of nine events at Munich. United States weight lifters are not yet world contenders, but they are improving. Ken Patera, in the super heavyweight class, almost won a silver medal for the United States, but he unwisely selected a weight he could not lift and was eliminated.

WRESTLING

Wrestling in both styles, free and Greco-Roman, increased weight classifications by two—paperweight (106 lbs.) and super heavyweight (over 220 lbs.). In the freestyle, the United States made an unexpected and splendid improvement with three gold medals, two silver and one bronze out of ten classifications. Dan Gable, the world champion in the 149.5-lb. class, and Wayne Wells, former world champion at 163 lbs., won their classes decisively. Ben Peterson, notwithstanding one draw, won the 198-lb. class while his brother, John, came in second in the 180-lb. class. Comstock, Wisconsin, their home town, was very proud of its sons. Chris Taylor, the U.S. 425-lb. super heavyweight, entered in both the freestyle and Greco-Roman categories was, according to many, the victim of a poor decision in a bout against the Soviet's Alexander Medved, who won the super heavyweight gold medal. The loss may have also been the reason why Taylor received only the bronze medal. Taylor was also entered in the Greco-Roman, but an unfortunate draw pitted him in the first round against the cunning and experienced veteran of three previous games, William Dietrich, who won in short order. Double medals, a rare accomplishment, were won in both free and Greco-Roman style by Jan Karlsson of Sweden in the 163-lb. class, silver in freestyle and bronze in Greco-Roman. The only repeat gold medalist was Peter Kirov of Bulgaria, who had won in the 115-lb. class in Greco-Roman in 1968.

JUDO

At Tokyo, when judo first became an Olympic event, Japan won three out of four titles, although the Dutch giant schoolteacher, Antonius Geesink, won the open class. The star of the Munich judo competition was Wim Ruska of the Netherlands, who won both the heavyweight and the open class championships. When it was all over, Ruska announced his retirement. The judo competition was reorganized at Munich into six categories—light, welter, middle, light heavy, heavy, and open categories.

YACHTING

Kiel was the site of the 1936 Olympic yachting competitions and of the 1972 Olympic yachting competitions. Although it is considered the finest European yachting course, the weather conditions were bad, as if jinxed by the sad luck of the Munich games. On one day, all races had to be canceled. Two of the classes completed only six races instead of seven because of the weather. In a rearrangement of Olympic classes, the 5.5-meter class was dropped after 1968, and the International Yacht Racing Union added the soling class, with a three-man crew, and the tempest class, with a two-man crew. Eighteen medals in six events were almost equally distributed among nine countries. The United States won three medals; Australia was the winner on points.

WINTER OLYMPICS

The 1972 Sappora winter games featured many dramatic and unusual incidents. And there was plenty of snow, which had not been the case at Grenoble and Innsbruck. Unfortunately, there were very few heroes or heroines at the Sappora games. But there was one villain, according to many ski followers—the late Avery Brundage, I.O.C. president. He waged a personal war against the skiers with such effect that he, and he alone, brought about the expulsion of the great skier Karl Schranz of Austria from the games. Schranz was not only the first but the only winter Olympian disqualified after having already arrived in the Olympic Village. The strange part about it is that Brundage, on arriving in Sappora, stated to the press that he had a list of forty skiers who reportedly had broken the Olympic code because of alleged professionalism. What became of the other thirty-nine is not known. In fact, the fight of Brundage against professionalism began to seem more important than all of the athletic contests. Schranz was adjudged to be more guilty than, for example, Ard Schenk, the Dutch speed skater, or Galina Koulakova, the Russian cross-country skier, each a triple gold medalist, or Marie Therese Nadig, Switzerland's surprise winner of the downhill and giant slalom. Yet Schenk attracted as much, or more, attention than Schranz; Koulakova was, in many ways, as subsidized as Schranz; and Marie Nadig received as many free pairs of skis as Schranz ever did.

Schranz' guilt was not that he was employed by a ski manufacturer but that he represented what Brundage most disliked—an athlete making a living indirectly out of his success in sports. Schranz' absence definitely affected the performance of his teammates, especially Marie Proell, favorite in her ski disciplines as Schranz had been in his. Having to carry the weight of her country's hopes proved too much of a burden, and as a result she finished second, not once but twice, to the eighteen-year old Swiss Marie Nadig.

Switzerland went to great efforts to train and prepare their ski team for success, and they won three gold medals and two silver medals in the skiing events.

The greatest surprise of the ten days' competition in skiing was in the final event, when a complete unknown, Francisco Fernandez Ochoa from Navacherrada, in sunny Spain, won the first winter Olympics medal in the history of his country, in the men's slalom.

If Brundage believed that he was supported by the win of

the little-known Spaniard over the heavily subsidized national teams of the Soviet Union, East Germany, France, Italy, Austria and Switzerland, he may well have been disappointed when he learned that the Spanish team spent most of its summer training in Chile! The French skiing team went home very disappointed, with no gold medals. Barbara Cochran from Richmond, Vermont, was an unexpected U.S. gold medal winner in the slalom.

Scandinavian and Alpine countries have usually dominated the winter Olympics, and both the United States and the Soviet Union are ordinarily strong contenders. The Japanese and the East Germans upset this at Sapporo. East Germany's imposing list of medals at the winter Olympics was the achievement of a comparatively new country where sports is looked upon as a means of raising the national prestige. Training, competition and techniques are far more scientific there than elsewhere. The East German Olympic team was heavily supported by the East German government. Their successes in track and field, especially in the women's competitions and in the winter games, could make them a major rival or even a successor to the Soviet Union on total medals and points. The Japanese made great progress in winter sports. They spent over 40 million dollars on Sapporo; and the permanent installations, underground railroads and new roads will establish Sapporo as the winter sports center of Asia.

The biathlon encountered rough weather and a blizzard, and the competition had to be postponed after its start. Although the skiers could operate in the blizzard, the shooting was impossible as the targets were no longer visible. Magnar Solberg of Norway repeated his 1968 individual biathlon win; the Soviet Union won the team event. Finland and East Germany were a surprise second and third. This 20-meter cross-country race, with four shooting exercises, is attracting more and more interest. There were fifty-four participants from thirteen countries. The United States improved sufficiently to come in sixth, after Norway and Sweden.

An unusual incident was the victory of Irina Rodnina and Alexei Ulanov in the figure skating couple event, despite the fact that the partners were hardly speaking to each other and Ulanov married another girl right after the competition.

Probably the high-water mark of the winter games from the standpoint of the host country was the 70-meter platform jump. A Japanese, Yukio Kasaya, won, and Japan grabbed off the first three places. Jiri Rasha, the Czech Olympic champion at Grenoble, came in fifteenth. Japan also expected to win the 90-meter platform event, again with Kasaya, but he petered out and the Polish entry, W. Fortuna, won this ski jump event for his country.

The United States won the women's 500-meter speed skating event with Anne Henning, and the 1,500-meter event with Diane Holum, both winners making extraordinarily fast time.

Ice hockey, as usual, attracted some of the largest crowds at the winter games, but the tournament was disappointing. The longer the tournament lasted, the more the Canadian team was missed. The Canadians, five-time Olympic champions, came in only third at Grenoble and stayed away from Sappora, for no publicly announced reason. The United States finished an unexpected second to the Soviet Union, with East Germany, Czechoslovakia, Sweden, Finland and Poland winding up in that order.

CHAPTER XXI

The 1976 Games

THE 1976 OLYMPIC GAMES in Montreal, Canada, were marred by the boycott of twenty-seven countries and, some felt, poor management and poor planning. International Olympic Committee Director, Monique Berlioux, lamented, "The soul has gone out of the Olympics. The Games ended . . . as they started . . . clouded, however, by controversy and international political wrangling." Many journalists and sports writers pondered whether these games were the end of the Olympics and whether the world had outgrown the vision of Baron de Coubertin who had sought to bring brotherhood through sports when he founded the modern Games in 1892.

Despite their problems the XXI Games were not a failure in any sense. Athletes in Montreal set thirty-two world records, fifteen of them by Americans.

The Games started on a stormy note when twenty-seven countries pulled out of the Games to protest Canada's refusal to bar New Zealand on the grounds that its Rugby team had played in apartheid South Africa. The boycott affected five-hundred athletes, many of whom were already in Montreal, having trained and pointed towards the Games for years. The affect of the boycott on the athletes themselves was evident when James Gilkes from Guyana, a student at the University of Southern California, asked to be allowed to run independently since his country had boycotted the Games. However, the I.O.C. and the Canadian authorities refused to accept his entry. The boycott reduced the total number of competing nations by twenty-five percent and athletes by just under ten percent. Canada also refused to accept a Taiwanese team under its normal I.O.C. name of the Republic of China which it had previously agreed to accept.

Though the spectre of violence at the Munich Games hung over Montreal, there were few scares or rumors of terrorism. When Valery Borzov, double winner of the sprint in 1972, did not show for the 200-meter dash in which he was entered, there were reports that he had been threatened or kidnapped. Borzov eventually showed up, but the Russians soon had another incident on their hands when a 17-year-old diver disappeared and turned up the next day requesting political asylum in Canada. Officials angrily demanded that the boy be returned to Russian control and accused Canadian authorities of kidnapping him. Later the incident calmed down when it became apparent that a girl, not ideology, was the young diver's motivation.

Meanwhile, on the gymnastics mat, spectators watched to see if Olga Korbut, the extraordinary young gymnast who had captured the crowds and Olympic gold in Munich in 1972, would be able to extend her title in Montreal. While the Russian team of Korbut, the brilliant Nellie Kim, and the 66-pound Maria Filatova won the team gold medal, the spotlight for these Games belonged to a sprightly upstart from Romania named Nadia Comaneci who took three individual gold medals and startled observers with extraordinary performances that won her a perfect score.

While he fell just slightly short of Mark Spitz's six gold medals, the 6'6" John Naber was certainly the outstanding leader of the American men's swimming sweep, turning to the water for two backstroke golds, two more in the relays, and a silver behind teammate Bruce Furniss in the 200-meter freestyle. It was Naber who made a lasting impression after his triumphs, hurling himself back into the pool for victory laps, enveloping surprised rivals in vice-like bear hugs and launching into enthusiastic speeches about life and religion at the slightest provocation. Some teammates were mystified, even put off by Naber, especially when he pontificated about his religion. "I'm not a Jesus-freak," he said, "I'm just crazy about Jesus."

A latecomer to swimming, Naber had not started until the advanced age of 13 at which point he had to work hard to catch up, taking full advantage of his long arms and kicking with his oversized feet. "My foot size, 12 EEE, doesn't help me

267

much. Certainly no more than fins," he joked after capturing his medals.

In the track and field, the XXI Olympic Games' outstanding performances were registered by Finland's Lasse Viren, Cuba's Alberto Juantorena and American Bruce Jenner. Viren, the 28-year-old policeman, took an unprecented 5,000- and 10,000-meter double and nearly completed what would have been a mind-boggling triple when he finished fifth behind East Germany's Waldemar Cierpinski and silver medalist, American Frank Shorter, in the marathon. As he entered the track and field stadium at the finish of the marathon he was greeted with cheers of appreciation for his outstanding performances, but Viren ran amid controversy that had never pursued other long distance greats. It was first stirred by a barefooted victory lap with his shoes held aloft in his hands, a gesture officials felt was a commercial for the shoe brand distributed by his coach. Viren also became the center of the "blood doping" controversy of the Games. A shadowy, largely unexplored technique, "blood doping" is supposed to begin with the withdrawal of several pints of blood about three weeks before an event. Through a high protein diet, the athlete then replaces the lost blood cells. Then, when the stored-up blood is transferred back into the body, the athlete supposedly enjoys a far higher blood count and a greater oxygen supply. Doctors warn that the method may be dangerous and athletes who have experimented with this say it doesn't always work. Viren's pre-Olympic record was nowhere near his extraordinary performance in Montreal, and some critics credited his improvement to a tank full of high-Octane blood. But evidence to back up the charge was scarce, though Finnish doctors boasted on occasion of their advances on the field. Viren was also rumored to indulge in reindeer milk, but there was very little question that Viren's double was the most brilliant single achievement, especially after his performance in the marathon, at the 1976 Games.

Alberto Juantorena, standing head and shoulders above his competition, tore around the Olympic track, winning the 400- and 800-meter events and breaking the world record in the 800. Bruce Jenner was also to best the world record when he totalled up 8,618 points in the decathlon. Other record breaking performances including Hungarian Miklos Nemeth's javelin throw to beat the old world record by an amazing 14 feet, Sweden's Andrus Gärderud's 3,000-meter-steeplechase victory which lowered the standard in that event by four seconds and an American, Edwin Moser's 400-meter hurdles race for gold.

The Russian team took the unofficial team title with forty-nine gold medals and a total of one hundred twenty-five medals, but perhaps the biggest surprise in the team competition was the arrival of East German competitors who swept to forty gold medals, six more than the third place United States team, and added another seven more in the winter Games. The efforts of the East German sports system, completely government supported, were most evident in the women's track and field and swimming events. In track and field the women took gold medals in nine out of thirteen events, and in swimming they stroked to eleven out of thirteen wins, each of them a world's record. The East German effort stirred a great deal of controversy both in the sports and political worlds. In the United States, the President's Commission on Olympic Sports 1975-1977 proposed that the United States Government, from taxes paid by American citizens, supply a new organization with an initial appropriation of $215 million, to use for the complete reorganization of Olympic and amateur sports, and an added annual support by the taxpayers of $83 million per year for the further carrying out of this plan—a grand total of $464 million for the first four-year Olympiad. The plan included the creation of thirty-seven "National Sports Bodies" controlling various sports.

The appropriations originally cited in the report were eventually abandoned as too heavy an additional tax burden for the American tax payers. However, the Amateur Sports Act of 1978-79 (Bill S.2727) was later proposed, granting $30 million for the fiscal year 1979, $12 million for the creation of permanent training centers, and $18 million to be made available and used as best decided by the U.S. Olympic Committee.

The debate over the definition of amateur versus professional athlete continues on an international basis, and, despite fine showings by Americans in international contests and meets, it appears that the American government feels the need to socialize amateur sports in this country.

In the sports world itself, much of the controversy over the East Germans centered around the usage of anabolic steroids, hormonal drugs that increase the muscle mass dramatically and therefore greatly enhance the body's capacity for athletic performance and endurance. Previously these steroids have been the domain of weight lifters, and it is generally acknowledged that all weight lifters take them. But the broad-shouldered, deep-voiced, thick-waisted East German women that seemed so awesome may also have been benefitting from steroid programs.

Dr. Gibson Ariel of Amherst, Massachusetts, suggested that ninety percent of the shot putters and discus throwers use them and that usage is as widespread in the West as it is in the Communist countries. "I would be willing to predict that for the first ten places in every event, all the winners were on steroids."

Along with the winners, some losers were also on steroids and were disqualified when traces showed up in their urine tests, amongst them Mark Cameron, a United States weight lifter, and Peter Pavlasek of Czechoslavakia. Also disqualified and stripped of their gold medals were Zbigniew Kaezmarek of Poland in the lightweight class, and Valentin Khristov of Bulgaria in the heavyweight class.

It took a trio of strikingly different champions to maintain order on at least a few Olympic fronts. Just when the flashy platform diver Greg Louganis of the United States seemed likely to succeed Comaneci as television's airborn idol, the stylish Italian veteran Klaus Dibiasi, 28, asserted himself and became the first three-time winner in a men's aquatic event.

Wrestling's 350-lb. super-heavyweight lifter, Vasily Alexeev, defended his weight-lifting title with another of his world records that he has made almost routine. And, at the archery field, scrawny Darrell Pace, 19, proved that he is indeed the best target shooter in the history of the sport, breaking his own world's record which he had set two years before.

An unusual departure at Montreal was that all of the athletes, or even a great many of them, did not parade at the close of the Games. Only six competitors from each country were allowed to march, making representation of some of the stars of the Games inequitable. For example, the Americans did not include amongst their group any of the boxers who had fought to five gold medals.

Security conscious and drug conscious the Montreal Olympic Games were, but many felt they were the most poorly organized in years, rife with political opportunism and the example of government-developed sports programs.

But there was still a place for the original purpose of the Olympics and the strivings of amateur athletes, perhaps best exemplified by American Arnie Robinson, who won the long jump with a leap of 27 feet 4¾ inches after three solid years of grueling preparation while his wife held down two jobs to help pay the bills.

As the world prepares to come to Moscow for the 1980

Olympics the spectres of political ultra-nationalism and definition of "amateur athletes" hang over the Games and their future.

ARCHERY

The first event on the Montreal Olympic program was archery, a comparatively new event in the Olympics, but one which was won in both the men's and women's divisions by Americans Darrell Pace and Luann Ryon, Pace winning by the large margin of 69 points and Mrs. Ryon by 39.

BASKETBALL

Basketball competition in the Men's division at the Montreal Olympics was won easily by the United States, regaining the gold medal they had lost for the first time to Russia in 1972. The only surprise was that Yugoslavia outscored Russia for second place, with Canada fourth, Italy fifth, and Czechoslovakia sixth. In women's basketball, Russia won, with the United States second, Bulgaria third, Czechoslovakia fourth, Japan fifth, and Canada sixth.

BOXING

Boxing events were particularly excellent, and were complemented by better than usual officiating in Montreal. The influence of Muhammed Ali, who had won the 1960 Olympic heavyweight championship when he was known as Cassius Clay, and his style, a fast left hand and even faster feet, was evident throughout the events. Teofilo Stevenson, Cuba's heavyweight, took his second Olympic gold and started warming up for what seems to some an inevitable third in Moscow in 1980. The United States with five golds won the team title for the fifth time (1904, 1924, 1932, 1952, 1976).

EQUESTRIAN EVENTS

The equestrian events were outstanding and clearly won by West Germany for their third straight gold in team competition, with the United States in second place, taking gold medals in both the individual three-day event and the team three-day event. Switzerland and France each won a single gold medal.

FENCING

As usual, neither the United States nor Canada could place in any event. The Russians regained their unofficial team championship which they had lost to Hungary in 1972, but only captured the gold in the saber team and individual competitions. Sweden won the epee team title for the first time, and West Germany captured the honors in the foil team, again for the first time.

GYMNASTICS

For the fifth straight Olympic Games, the somewhat overlooked Japanese team captured the all-around team title and the overall men's gymnastics events. Russia took the women's team title, but gymnastics were dominated by Romania's Nadia Comaneci and her three gold medals in the balance beam, parallel bars, and all-around individual competitions. Peter Kormann won the first individual men's gold medal in 44 years for the United States in the floor exercise competition.

MODERN PENTATHLON

Here again, brand new winners impressed Olympic followers. In the past fourteen Olympiads in which the Modern Pentathlon had been contested, Sweden had taken home nine gold medals and Hungary three. In Montreal it was Poland's J. Pyciak-Peciak who took the individual gold medal, while the unheralded and unexpected team from Great Britain took the team title. The American team managed fifth place, after Russia was disqualified, with the best individual performance by John Fitzgerald who finished sixth.

ROWING

The Communist countries dominated the rowing events in this Olympiad with the East German's taking five gold medals, one silver, and two bronze; Russia, one gold, two silver, and a bronze in men's rowing. East Germany's four gold and two silver, Bulgaria's two gold and one silver, and Russia's two silver and three bronze controlled the women's division.

SHOOTING

Six Olympic records and three world records were bettered in the shooting competition, with both the East Germans and the Americans taking two gold medals each.

SOCCER

The East Germans controlled the soccer pitch, edging out Poland, Russia, and Brazil in that order for the gold medal.

SWIMMING

Just as the East Germans dominated the women's events, the American men dominated their side of the swimming. The United States won twelve of thirteen events and took home ten silver medals as well. The American women fared far less well, winning only two golds after having swept eight in Munich.

WEIGHT LIFTING

According to many, this sport should have been labeled "The Clash of the Montreal Olympics." The two strongest men in the world were to meet, Alexeev, the defending Olympic champion from Russia, against Platchkov, the Bulgarian world-record holder. Not even standing-room tickets existed for the competition, but, at the last minute, Platchkov was withdrawn because of illness. Although the competition ended on July 27th, the final decisions on gold-medal winners in the lightweight and heavyweight divisions were not made for several months. A total of ten lifters, including the gold medalists in these two divisions, were disqualified as a result of a test for anabolic steroids. The tests for drugs were compulsive for the first time at Montreal. There was also a change in the number of lifts to arrive at credited weight, thereby creating new standards for Olympic and world records.

WRESTLING

In catch-as-catch-can the United States sent six of its ten entries to the finals, winning only one gold but capturing three silvers and a bronze. John Peterson won the gold in the middleweight class. The Greco-Roman competition was dominated by the Eastern Europeans despite notable improvement by the Americans.

YACHTING

New classes changed the face of the yachting competition dramatically with the 470 class and the Tornado class replacing the former Star and Dragon classes. The United States won the silver in the Soling class with "Good News," as the West Germans took the unofficial team championship.

WINTER GAMES

The 1976 Winter Games in Innsbruck, Austria, hosted a total of thirty-six nations, though only nineteen nations managed to have athletes placed in the top six of any event. The return to Innsbruck, the site of the 1964 Games, was a delight for many, and more than 60,000 attended the Parade of Nations which preceded the Games and the formal opening conducted by Dr. Rudolf Kirschenschlagerr, president of Austria. In figure skating, the artistry of John Curry of Britain and Dorothy Hamill of the United States was unbeatable, as both captured gold medals. Irina Rodnina of Russia repeated her gold-medal performance in the pair skating, but with a different partner than in 1972, Aleksandr Zaitsev.

Jan E. Storhalt of Norway celebrated his 27th birthday by winning the 1500-meter speed-skating event in record time. Peter Mueller, United States speed skater, who was engaged to marry Leah Poulos, another United States skating medal winner, won the 1,000 meters. Mueller's win ended the twelve-year gold-medal drought in speed skating for the United States at the Winter Games. The last previous gold medalist was Terry McDermott in the 500 meters in 1964. Poulos was fourth in the 500 meters, second in the 1,000 and sixth in the 1,500, in the women's competition. Tatiana Averina, speed-skating ace of the Soviet Union, won four medals including two gold. Sheila Young of the United States took the 500 meters in record Olympic time. For the first time an American showed up very well in Nordic skiing, as Bill Koch placed second in the 30-kilometer cross-country. East Germany made a clean sweep in luge and bob sled. Russia won the ice hockey gold medal, while Czechoslovakia was a surprising second.

In alpine skiing, Austria's Franz Klammer took the dramatic downhill and Rosie Mittermaier came within tenths of a second of capturing all three women's races. As it was, she took home two gold medals in the downhill and the slalom.

CHAPTER XXII
The Future and its Problems

THE OLYMPIC IDEA and the modern Olympic games have now progressed so tremendously that they have created stupendous problems. The creators of the modern version of the ancient games would be aghast at the immensity of the Olympiads of today. The games now involve some 9,000 athletes from millions of candidates, hundreds of millions of dollars in costs to stage, over $10 million in gate receipts, ever-rising millions of dollars in ancillary rights based on such inventions of man as the motion picture, radio, television, video tape, etc. In a fraction of a second Olympic events are now seen or heard all over the world. Soon 500,000,000 radio and TV sets can be tuned in on the Olympic games at one and the same time.

With this tremendous spectacle come such problems as the maneuvers and intrigues of selecting or assigning the games to certain cities and countries, and the transportation of teams thousands of miles. In addition, a city must not only be confirmed by the Olympic Committee and the government of its country, but its national government must certify that the athletes of all countries eligible for participation in the Olympic games in question will receive visas, no matter what the international situation may be six to eight years in the future. This means that the Olympics and the International Olympic Committee believe that athletics, sports and sportsmanship are above the U.N., nations, national loyalties or politics. Perhaps they should be, but unfortunately, in our modern world, they can't always surmount international or political situations.

It has also been discovered, as asserted by *Scientific American* and the U.S. Space Agency, that no two cities offer equal conditions for the athlete in any sport because of variation in gravity pull, depending on the distance of the cities from the equator. This difference can well mean variations in athletic performance comparable to those based on high altitude. For instance, based on gravity pull alone there is slightly over six inches difference in the throwing of a javelin, all other things being equal, between Helsinki and Melbourne, and slightly over an inch and a quarter in the hop, step and jump between Los Angeles and Moscow. The International Olympic Committee and various world sports bodies will soon have to get their slide rules out and allow for this in their world and Olympic record marks. This, of course, is a less difficult and more tangible complication than the many involving the growth and expansion of the games and their national and political problems.

In the old days when life was simple and the Olympic games consisted of one event, it was held in a neutral site and even wars did not stop it. Today wars involve the whole world, and there is no Olympia or Mount Olympus. However, nothing can be done about the increase of events and sports and the increase of competitors and spectators. Before this book has vanished completely, the Olympics will involve over 20,000 athletes from over 200 countries instead of 8,500 from 121 countries (1972 statistics) and over 300 events instead of 235. The summer games alone will last at least five weeks. Eventually the problem of numbers of contestants and events will have to be solved by one of two methods or both. Currently, in soccer and several other team sports, there are area eliminations to limit the number in the finals at the actual Olympiad. This principle could be applied more and more. Next, track and field entries are limited or partially limited to contestants whose officially recorded performances during some reasonable period before the games entitles them to hope for a winning performance. Unless these qualifying performances in time, distance, height, weight, etc., can be satisfied, the contestant is eliminated or not qualified to perform in the games. This principle can also be fairly and practically applied in many events.

With respect to added sports and events this also can be reasonably resolved. Naturally the Olympics must include more events and sports as well as more contestants and nations. No one can stop progress or the natural development of sports. The Tokyo Olympics prove this and definitely indicate that the International Olympic Committee has no intention of limiting additions. If volleyball, both for men and women, involving large teams but of no great proven popularity in the world, has been admitted, there is no reason for the future exclusion of baseball or for not readmitting polo. Tennis and rugby football should be returned to the games as archery has been. If judo, which has a limited following in the entire world, can be added to the Olympic cavalcade together with both freestyle and Greco-Roman wrestling, there is no reason why bowling—one of the most popular sports in the world—should not be added at some later date.

The financial side of the games poses a far greater problem: how to raise the money for the costs of the installation and equipment and the staging of the games—held at a different spot every four years. Still another problem for each nation (some are poorer than others) is how to raise the money to develop, train and send a team to some point, sometimes at the other end of the world. This has made many practical persons agree that the games should from now on rotate only between about a dozen very large cities with permanent installations and equipment to eliminate the major initial costs. The amount saved can then be applied through that city's contribution to helping pay for the transportation of visiting teams. By selecting very large centers of population without regard to the millions of dollars from tourists, the gate receipts can, with proper management, increase from $10 to $20 million, and the various ancillary rights can be more easily and cheaply harnessed for more revenues than at some remote site. In the future, a city with every installation already available could bid millions of dollars to get the Olympic games, and this money could be used to train, equip and bring teams from all over the world. Cities like Rome, Tokyo, Mexico City, Los Angeles, Moscow, Rio de Janeiro, with a 200,000 capacity stadium, all after spending millions of dollars for installations or with existing installations, could bid for the games. A bid of $100 million or less could take care of the training, expenses and transportation of many teams—yet save useless expenditures.

All these and many more modern developments, improvements or changes could perhaps be studied by younger and less tradition-steeped management. This implies a problem which is often debated—whether or not the International Olympic Committee is, in fact, an aged, self-perpetuating organization, one that may forget it is not above diplomatic protocols, laws, and the dignity and rights of individuals. Prince Axel of Denmark tried to convince his Olympic colleagues they should quit at 70 and proved his adherence to his own beliefs by resigning in 1948 at that age. Government and private enterprise usually retire executives at 65. But Mr. Avery Brundage was holding on for dear life in 1972 at age 87. Armand Massard, the senior vice president from France, resigned before the 1968 games at 79. The Marquess of Exeter, who has been many times an unsuccessful candidate, won the 1928 Olympic high hurdles event as Lord Burghley. He would have liked to succeed Brundage. However, kings and lords are no longer expected trimmings to the games. Many believe the members of the I.O.C. are out of tune with present-day changes, while still others consider the maturity, age and experience of the I.O.C. members invaluable.

For those who build all kinds of stories about Olympic properties, ideas, scoring systems, etc., there usually are some shocks. For instance, not long ago, a highly competent member of the staff at Olympic House came up with the startling statement that the late Arthur Lentz had, a few years before, developed a method of scoring points for comparisons of national performances in the various sports and on an over-all basis, namely, the scoring in each event of 7-5-4-3-2-1 points for first, second, third, fourth, fifth and sixth places. However, if Lentz were alive today, he would certainly deny being the creator of a system used in intercollegiate track meets as far back as the 1920s in the United States, and perhaps long before that. Also the gold medal scoring or ranking of nations by the number of gold medals, mentioned as a sort of creation of our present day, is as old as the ancient games. There are tables showing Olympic championships by city-states going back to the ancient games. Although oak wreaths were awarded to the winners in ancient times instead of gold medals, yet city-states vied with each other for the most winners. Scoring by the number of championship victory wreaths can also be associated with the first modern games, in 1896. As to point scoring, in 1924 the author, as the U.S. Olympic Committee's interpreter, remembers a Paris conference and luncheon conducted in French and presided over by no less than the Baron de Coubertin, father of the modern games, and with Colonel Thompson, then head of the U.S.O.C., present, as well as many other Olympic leaders. The conference included a discussion about scoring.

Although everyone believed that any scoring system should be discouraged for any determination of an alleged national winner (which would not be consistent with the Olympic concept), all agreed that no matter what efforts were made by Olympic organizations, the press would come up with all sorts of conclusions on the ultimate victor. Everyone also agreed that as the Olympics developed and the number of athletes and the number of nations participating increased, the scoring should be on the basis of 10-5-4-3-2-1 points for first, second, third, fourth, fifth and sixth places. It was pointed out at this luncheon that the 7-5-4-3-2-1 scoring system, suggested by U.S. college track and field officials and reportedly used in intercollegiate track meets in the United States, would not be right for the Olympics. It was agreed that in world competition, that is, in the Olympic scoring, the first place, which meant the whole world's championship and an almost immortal honor, had to rate higher than also-rans, even if they were finalists. It was brought out that if a 7-5-4-3-2-1 scoring was used, a second and third in the Olympics would be 9 points, or 2 points better than an all-world title, and even a third and fourth, totaling 7, would equal the points of the world winner. In fact, a third, fifth and sixth, totaling 7 points, would also equal the winner. On the other hand, the 10-5-4-3-2-1 scoring placed the proper premium and emphasis on the world's championship in a competition involving hundreds of thousands of athletes.

In fact, in discussions among Olympic representatives and leaders in Paris in 1924, a new method of scoring or a further development was discussed which, according to many, had been recommended if not first suggested by Gen. Douglas MacArthur at the 1920 Olympics, when he was president of the U.S.O.C. It went one step further than the 10-5-4-3-2-1 scoring system, generally accepted as the best and fairest system by Olympic officials and the press. From De Coubertin to Grantland Rice, both present in Paris in 1924, this new idea was considered as the best criteria of national Olympic performance.

According to General MacArthur, the only true evaluation of the comparative Olympic or athletic accomplishment of countries had to take into account the population of the competing countries. In other words, the total Olympic point score of each country should be divided by that country's population to arrive at the number of Olympic points per million population. Any other comparison could not possibly mean anything, especially if the Olympic games grew, as they did, to include many countries of every size. Otherwise, how could a country with a 100-million population be compared with a country with a 5-million population—certainly not on point scoring alone.

For some reason, this very sound idea was forgotten until 1936 and later in 1956 when several countries, notably Germany and then the Soviet Union, went all out, by every possible national and government means, to swamp other countries at the Olympics for national, political and ideological propaganda. Even so, their all-out efforts and large populations did not spell true superiority when compared with smaller but more truly athletic and sports-minded countries. For instance, Germany, the leader in total points in 1936, was not even near the top in points per million population and in 1956, neither the Soviets nor the Americans won at Melbourne on the basis of Olympic points per million population. Australia, Finland and Sweden were the actual leaders—all three scored over 20 points per million population against only 3.53 and 3.44 for the United States and the Soviet Union respectively. So if anyone insists on rating the athletic prowess of a country by Olympic scoring, the only possible comparison is by Olympic points per million population.

Another myth is that which surrounds the famous Olympic

279

symbol, the five interlocking circles representing the five continents. According to many, this is a property of the I.O.C., and its various applications on national emblems were developed by the various committees; for example, the super-imposing of the five interlocking circles on the U.S. shield is reportedly a recent creation of the U.S.O.C. The symbol was allegedly first used at the 1924 games. But it is actually far from modern. The official guide and report of the 1896 games, endorsed by his royal highness, Crown Prince Constantine of Greece, with a prologue by Timoleon Philemon, secretary general of the games has, on page 63, the U.S. Olympic shield, down to the thirteen stripes and the five interlocking rings. And to go back even further, any number of Olympic four and five interlocking circles on marble plaques or floors have been found at Olympia dating back to 500 B.C. Four interlocking circles found on the altar at Delphi and definitely connected with the ancient games, are considered by experts to be 3,000 years old.

To return to the scoring, since I was present and participated in the first discussion and informal approval of the most reasonable scoring system, points per million population, I decided to set it up in tables in the appendix of earlier editions of this book for the information of all concerned. I have received hundreds of letters from all over the world commenting favorably and agreeing that it is the only true way of evaluating the comparative athletic accomplishments of various nations at the Olympics. With the number of a nation's contestants further limited in track and field to performance rather than to the size of the country or the wealth of its Olympic committee, the new method is the only proper basis for comparing national amateur athletic prowess. In the appendix are tables showing the standing of countries in the last few games based on this system. While all three methods described above are often referred to, the last is the most logical and certainly the most accurate in comparing the Olympic accomplishments of countries of very different populations. For instance, if Finland with 5 million or less persons makes 98.5 points it is superior in athletic prowess to Great Britain with over 51 million population with 180.5 points for that Olympiad.

Constant progress is proven by a recent innovation. The Tokyo Olympic Organizing Committee on October 11 to 16, 1963, one year before the games, held a preview or rehearsal of the forthcoming 1964 games. This international sports week was held in Tokyo and involved over 600 athletes from

30 nations in 18 events. It gave the teams and coaches a chance to study climatic and terrain conditions and the facilities a year ahead. It also gave the organizing committee an opportunity to perfect their preparations and check their plans. This preview cost over $1 million. The Mexican Olympic Committee, not to be outdone by its predecessor and to enable visiting athletes to get used to competing at Mexico City's high elevation, held similar pre-Olympic games, October 12 to 27, 1967. Munich preview did not follow suit. These preview pre-Olympics or rehearsals should indicate that Olympic problems of the future will be solved and that the games are certainly here to stay. This is important, for there is no question that they constitute man's oldest and greatest show and one of man's greatest hopes for future peace and goodwill among nations and their peoples.

To further the Olympic ideals and their results and objectives, a perfectly obvious but heretofore unthought of development may well do much to enhance the beneficial impact of the games. When Sir George Robertson died in London early in 1967, the last surviving athlete in the first modern Olympic games at Athens in 1896 passed away. However, some 72,000 athletes have been competitors in the modern Olympic games. To bring together top athletes with the experience of the sportsmanship and international understanding created or developed by the games, an Olympian organization, namely a club of all former Olympians, seemed a great idea to a U.S. engineer, Samuel Norton Gerson. Gerson was a silver medalist in wrestling at the 1920 Antwerp games. He became interested, as a hobby, in becoming a historian of the games and of corresponding with former Olympic athletes all over the world. This led ultimately to the organization of the Olympians on both a U.S. and international scale. The result has been the organization and frequent meetings of "Olympians" in various countries and the "Olympians International." At the second meeting of the international body at Tokyo in 1964 Edgar S. Tanner of Australia was re-elected president with Samuel Gerson as secretary-treasurer-historian. Thirty-two countries have organized Olympians. According to the Olympians there are approximately 40,000 former Olympic athletes living in the world today and of these some 5,500 are in the United States. A recent president of the U.S. Olympians is Pierre Brunet, gold medalist in figure skating in 1928 and 1932 for France. The purpose of the organization of the alumni of the Olympic games is:

"To support the world movement to achieve and maintain

281

international peace and goodwill through, among other media, sports competitions among the nations on the basis of ancient Greek Olympic ideals of sportsmanship.

"To stimulate interest in the Olympic games.

"To maintain fellowship among former Olympic competitors, officials, managers, coaches and trainers all over the world."

COMPLETE APPENDIX

MODERN OLYMPIC GAMES

Number	Year	Site	Nations Entered	Number Contestants	Winner (Unofficial)
I	1896	Athens	13	484	Greece
II	1900	Paris	16	1505	France
III	1904	St. Louis	7	1609	United States
#	1906	Athens	21	901	France
IV	1908	London	22	2666	Great Britain
V	1912	Stockholm	27	4742	Sweden
VI	1916	Berlin	—	—	Canceled (World War I)
VII	1920	Antwerp	26	2741	United States
VIII	1924	Paris	45	3385	United States
IX	1928	Amsterdam	46	3905	United States
X	1932	Los Angeles	39	2403	United States
XI	1936	Berlin	51	4069	Germany
XII	1940	(Tokyo) Helsinki	—	—	Canceled (World War II)
XIII	1944	Unawarded	—	—	Canceled (World War II)
XIV	1948	London	59	6005	United States
XV	1952	Helsinki	69	5867	United States
XVI	1956	Melbourne	67	3539	U.S.S.R.
XVII	1960	Rome	84	5396	U.S.S.R.
XVIII	1964	Tokyo	94	5541	U.S.S.R.
XIX	1968	Mexico City	109	6082	United States
XX	1972	Munich	121	8512	U.S.S.R.
XXI	1976	Montreal	87	7840	U.S.S.R.
XXII	1980	Moscow			
XXIII	1984	Los Angeles			

Unofficial or extra Olympics.

OLYMPIC WINTER SPORTS

Number	Year	Site	Nations Entered	Number Contestants	Winner (Unofficial)
I	1924	Chamonix	16	306	Norway
II	1928	St. Moritz	25	518	Norway
III	1932	Lake Placid	17	307	United States
IV	1936	Garmisch-Partenkirchen	28	756	Norway
V	1948	St. Moritz	29	932	Sweden
VI	1952	Oslo	30	1178	Norway
VII	1956	Cortina D'Ampezzo	32	1117	U.S.S.R.
VIII	1960	Squaw Valley	30	782	U.S.S.R.
IX	1964	Innsbruck	37	1192	U.S.S.R.
X	1968	Grenoble	37	1355	Norway
XI	1972	Sappora	31	920	U.S.S.R.
XII	1976	Innsbruck	38	1450	U.S.S.R.
XIII	1980	Lake Placid			
XIV	1984				

Recapitulation

Number of Modern Olympics held:--- 19

UNOFFICIAL WINNERS
(Based on 10-5-4-3-2-1 Scoring)

United States	8	Great Britain	1
U.S.S.R.	5	Germany	1
France	2	Sweden	1
		Greece	1

283

CHAMPIONSHIPS (WON) BY NATION

I. MODERN OLYMPICS 1896

Athens

NATION	CYCLING	FENCING	GYMNASTICS	SHOOTING	SWIMMING	TENNIS	TRACK & FIELD	WRESTLING	TOTAL
United States	—	—	—	2	—	—	9	—	11
Greece	1	1	2	3	—	—	1	1	8
Germany	—	—	5	—	—	½	—	1	6½
France	4	1	—	—	—	—	—	—	5
Great Britain	—	—	—	—	—	1½	1	—	2½
Australia	—	—	—	—	—	—	2	—	2
Austria	1	—	—	—	1	—	—	—	2
Hungary	—	—	—	—	2	—	—	—	2
Denmark	—	—	—	—	—	—	1	—	1
Switzerland	—	—	1	—	—	—	—	—	1

284

CHAMPIONSHIPS (WON) BY NATION

II. MODERN OLYMPICS 1900

Paris

NATION	ARCHERY	BOWLING	CROQUET	CYCLING	FENCING	GOLF	GYMNASTICS	POLO	ROWING	SHOOTING	SWIMMING	TENNIS	TRACK & FIELD	WATER POLO	YACHTING	TOTAL
France	2	2	3	1	2	—	1	—	1	8	1	—	1	—	6	28
United States	—	—	—	—	—	2	—	—	1	1	—	—	18	—	—	22
Great Britain	—	—	—	—	—	—	—	1	—	—	2	4	4	1	2	14
Switzerland	—	—	—	—	—	—	—	—	—	6	—	—	—	—	1	7
Germany	—	—	—	—	—	—	—	—	1	—	2	—	—	—	2	5
Belgium	—	—	—	—	—	—	—	—	—	3	—	—	—	—	—	3
Australia	—	—	—	—	—	—	—	—	—	1	2	—	—	—	—	3
Netherlands	—	—	—	—	—	—	—	—	1	1	—	—	—	—	—	2
Denmark	—	—	—	—	—	—	—	—	—	2	—	—	—	—	—	2
Canada	—	—	—	—	—	—	—	—	—	1	—	—	—	—	—	1
Cuba	—	—	—	—	1	—	—	—	—	—	—	—	—	—	—	1
Hungary	—	—	—	—	—	—	—	—	—	—	—	—	1	—	—	1

CHAMPIONSHIPS (WON) BY NATION

III. MODERN OLYMPICS 1904

St. Louis

NATION	ALL AROUND	ARCHERY	BOXING	CURLING	CYCLING	FENCING	GOLF	GYMNASTICS	LACROSSE	ROQUE	ROWING	SOCCER	SWIMMING	TENNIS	TRACK & FIELD	WATER POLO	WRESTLING	TOTAL
United States	—	6	7	3	7	1	1	8	—	1	5	—	5	2	24	1	7	78
Cuba	—	—	—	—	—	5	—	—	—	—	—	—	—	—	—	—	—	5
Germany	—	—	—	1	—	—	—	—	—	—	—	—	4	—	—	—	—	5
Canada	—	—	—	—	—	—	1	—	1	—	—	1	—	—	1	—	—	4
Hungary	—	—	—	—	—	—	—	—	—	—	—	—	2	—	—	—	—	2
Greece	—	—	—	—	—	—	—	—	—	—	—	—	—	—	1	—	—	1
Ireland	1	—	—	—	—	—	—	—	—	—	—	—	—	—	—	—	—	1

CHAMPIONSHIPS (WON) BY NATION
UNOFFICIAL OLYMPIC GAMES 1906

Athens*

NATION	CYCLING	FENCING	GYMNASTICS	ROWING	SHOOTING	SOCCER	SWIMMING	TENNIS	TRACK & FIELD	WRESTLING	TOTAL
France	1	3	1	1	4			3	1		14
United States		1							11		12
Greece				1	2		1	1	3		8
Great Britain	2				2		1		3		8
Italy	3			4							7
Germany		2	1				1		1	1	6
Switzerland					5						5
Norway					3				1		4
Austria			1				1			1	3
Denmark						1				1	2
Finland									1	1	2
Sweden									2		2
Canada									1		1
Hungary							1				1

*(Vitally important in development of games as marks end of efforts to have Greece as permanent site.)

287

CHAMPIONSHIPS (WON) BY NATION
IV. MODERN OLYMPICS 1908
London

NATION	ARCHERY	BOXING	CYCLING	FENCING	FIELD HOCKEY	GYMNASTICS	LACROSSE	MOTOR BOATING	POLO	RACQUETS	ROWING	RUGBY	SHOOTING	SKATING	SOCCER	SWIMMING	TENNIS	TRACK & FIELD	WATER POLO	WRESTLING catch-as-catch-can	WRESTLING Greco-Roman	YACHTING	TOTAL
Great Britain	2	5	5		1			2	1	2	4		6	1	1	4	6	8	1	3		4	56
United States													3			1	1	15		2			22
Sweden						1							2	1		1		2			1		8
France	1		1	2				1															5
Canada							1						1					1					3
Germany														1		2							3
Hungary				2																	1		3
Italy						1															1		2
Norway													1										1
Australia												1											1
Belgium													1										1
Finland																					1		1
Russia														1									1
South Africa																		1					1

288

CHAMPIONSHIPS (WON) BY NATION

V. MODERN OLYMPICS 1912

Stockholm

NATION	CYCLING	EQUESTRIAN	FENCING	GYMNASTICS	MODERN PENTATHLON	ROWING	SHOOTING	SOCCER	SWIMMING (men)	SWIMMING (women)	TENNIS	TRACK & FIELD	WATER POLO	WRESTLING	YACHTING	TOTAL
Sweden	1	4	—	1	1	—	7	—	2	1	—	5	—	1½	1	24½
United States	—	—	—	—	—	—	7	—	2	—	—	14	—	—	—	23
Great Britain	—	—	—	—	—	2	1	1	—	1	2	2	1	—	—	10
Finland	—	—	—	—	—	—	—	—	—	—	—	6	—	3½	—	9½
France	—	1	—	—	—	—	2	—	—	—	3	—	—	—	1	7
Germany	—	—	—	—	—	1	—	—	3	—	1	—	—	—	—	5
Norway	—	—	—	1	—	—	—	—	—	—	—	1	—	—	2	4
South Africa	1	—	—	—	—	—	—	—	—	—	2	1	—	—	—	4
Canada	—	—	—	—	—	—	—	—	2	—	—	1	—	—	—	3
Hungary	—	—	2	—	—	—	1	—	—	—	—	—	—	—	—	3
Italy	—	—	1	2	—	—	—	—	—	—	—	—	—	—	—	3
Australia	—	—	—	—	—	—	—	—	1	1	—	—	—	—	—	2
Belgium	—	—	2	—	—	—	—	—	—	—	—	—	—	—	—	2
Denmark	—	—	—	—	—	1	—	—	—	—	—	—	—	—	—	1
Greece	—	—	—	—	—	—	—	—	—	—	—	1	—	—	—	1

CHAMPIONSHIPS (WON) BY NATION
VII. MODERN OLYMPICS 1920
Antwerp

NATION	ARCHERY	BOXING	CYCLING	EQUESTRIAN	FENCING	FIELD HOCKEY	GYMNASTICS	ICE HOCKEY	MODERN PENTATHLON	POLO	ROWING	RUGBY	SHOOTING	SKATING	SOCCER	SWIMMING (men)	SWIMMING (women)	TENNIS	TRACK & FIELD	WATER POLO	WEIGHT LIFTING	WRESTLING catch-as-catch-can	WRESTLING Greco-Roman	YACHTING	TOTAL
United States		3									3	1	13			7	4		9			1			41
Sweden			1	4			1		1				1	2		3			1			1	2	2	19
Finland														1					9			2	3		15
Great Britain		2	1			1				1								2	5	1				1	14
Norway											1		5						1					7	14
Italy			1	1	5		2				1								2		1				13
Belgium	4		1												1						1			1	10
France		1	1		1													2	1		2				8
Canada		1						1											1						3
Denmark													1				1								3
Netherlands			1																					2	3
South Africa		1																1	1						3
Switzerland											1											1			2
Brazil													1												1
Estonia																					1				1

290

CHAMPIONSHIPS (WON) BY NATION
VIII. MODERN OLYMPICS 1924
Paris

The winter-games columns (SKIING, SPEED SKATING, FIGURE SKATING, ICE HOCKEY, BOBSLEDDING) are grouped under the heading **I. WINTER GAMES**.

NATION	TOTAL	YACHTING	WRESTLING Greco-Roman	WRESTLING catch-as-catch-can	WEIGHT LIFTING	TENNIS	WATER POLO	SWIMMING (women)	SWIMMING (men)	SOCCER	RUGBY	ROWING	POLO	MARKSMANSHIP (target)	MARKSMANSHIP (hunting)	GYMNASTICS	FENCING	EQUESTRIAN	CYCLING	BOXING	TRACK & FIELD	MODERN PETATHLON	SKIING	SPEED SKATING	FIGURE SKATING	ICE HOCKEY	BOBSLEDDING
United States	46			4		5		6	7		1	2		3	2	1				2	12			1			
Finland	17		3	1																	10			3			
France	13		1		2		1							1	1		3		4								
Great Britain	10							1				2			2					2	3						
Norway	9	2													2					1			4				
Italy	8				3											2	1		1		1						
Switzerland	5			2												2											1
Sweden	4																	2				1			1		
Belgium	4	1															1			2							
Netherlands	3											1						2									
Australia	2								1												1						
Austria	2																								2		
Denmark	2																1		1								
Hungary	2													1			1										
Yugoslavia	1															1											
Argentina	1												1														
Canada	1																									1	
Czechoslovakia	1															1											
Estonia	1		1																								
South Africa	1																		1								
Uruguay	1									1																	

291

CHAMPIONSHIPS (WON) BY NATION
IX. MODERN OLYMPICS 1928
Amsterdam

NATION	Bobsledding	Ice Hockey	Figure Skating	Speed Skating	Skiing	Modern Pentathlon	Track & Field (men)	Track & Field (women)	Boxing (men)	Cycling	Equestrian	Fencing	Field Hockey	Gymnastics	Rowing	Soccer	Swimming (men)	Swimming (women)	Water Polo	Weight Lifting	Wrestling catch-as-catch-can	Wrestling Greco-Roman	Yachting	TOTAL
	II. WINTER GAMES																							
United States	2						8	1							2		5	5			1			24
Finland				1½			5														2	1		9½
Germany								1			2	1			1			1	1	1½		1		9½
Sweden			1			1											1				2	2	1	9
France			1							1		2								1			1	7
Italy									3	1		2			1									7
Switzerland														5	1						1			7
Norway			1	1½	3																		1	6½
Netherlands									1	1	2							1						5
Canada		1					2	1																4
Hungary									1			2												3
Argentina									2								1							3
Denmark										3														3
Great Britain							1								1									2
Czechoslovakia											1			1										2
Egypt																				1		1		2
Estonia																					1	1		2
Japan																	1							1½
Austria																				1				1
Australia															1									1
India													1											1
Ireland							1																	1
New Zealand									1															1
Poland								1																1
South Africa							1																	1
Spain											1													1
Uruguay																1								1
Yugoslavia														1										1

292

CHAMPIONSHIPS (WON) BY NATION
X. MODERN OLYMPICS 1932
Los Angeles

NATION	III. WINTER GAMES — ICE HOCKEY	FIGURE SKATING	SPEED SKATING	SKIING	SLEDDING	MODERN PENTATHLON	TRACK & FIELD (men)	TRACK & FIELD (women)	BOXING	CYCLING	EQUESTRIAN	FENCING	FIELD HOCKEY	GYMNASTICS	ROWING	SHOOTING	SWIMMING (men)	SWIMMING (women)	WATER POLO	WEIGHT LIFTING	WRESTLING catch-as-catch-can	WRESTLING Greco-Roman	YACHTING	TOTAL
United States			4		2		11	5	2		1			5	3		3	6			3		2	47
Italy							1			3		2		4		1						1		12
France		1								1	2	2								3	1		1	11
Sweden				1		1										1					2	4	1	10
Japan							1				1						5							7
Finland				1			3														1	1		6
Hungary									1			2		2					1					6
Great Britain							2								2									4
Argentina							1		2															3
Australia										1					1			1						3
Canada	1						1		1															3
Germany															1					1		1		3
Norway				2																				2
Austria		1										1												2
Netherlands										1	1													2
Ireland							2																	2
Poland							1	1																2
South Africa									2															2
Czechoslovakia																				1				1
India													1											1

293

CHAMPIONSHIPS (WON) BY NATION
XI. MODERN OLYMPICS 1936
Berlin

NATION	TOTAL	YACHTING	WRESTLING Greco-Roman	WRESTLING catch-as-catch-can	WEIGHT LIFTING	WATER POLO	SWIMMING (women)	SWIMMING (men)	SOCCER	SHOOTING	ROWING	POLO	GYMNASTICS	FIELD HOCKEY	FIELD HANDBALL	FENCING	EQUESTRIAN	CYCLING	CANOEING	BOXING	BASKETBALL	TRACK & FIELD (women)	TRACK & FIELD (men)	MODERN PENTATHLON	SLEDDING	SKIING	SPEED SKATING	FIGURE SKATING	ICE HOCKEY
																									IV. WINTER GAMES				
Germany	36	1		1	1					1	5		6		1		6		3	2		2	3	1		2		1	
United States	25			1	1		2	4			1										1	2	12		1				
Hungary	10		1	2		1		1								3				1		1							
Finland	8		1	2																1			3			1			
Italy	8	1							1							4				1		1							
Norway	8									1																2	4	1	
Sweden	6		3							1																2			
France	6				1													3		2									
Netherlands	6	1					4											1											
Japan	5							3															2						
Great Britain	4	1									1												1						1
Austria	4																		3									1	
Czechoslovakia	2																		2										
Argentina	2																			1									
Egypt	2				2																								
Estonia	2		1	1																									
Switzerland	1																								1				
India	1													1															
New Zealand	1																						1						
Turkey	1		1																										

294

CHAMPIONSHIPS (WON) BY NATION
XIV. MODERN OLYMPICS 1948 — London
V. WINTER GAMES

NATION	TOTAL	YACHTING	WRESTLING Greco-Roman	WRESTLING catch-as-catch-can	WEIGHT LIFTING	WATER POLO	SWIMMING (women)	SWIMMING (men)	SOCCER	SHOOTING	ROWING	GYMNASTICS	FIELD HOCKEY	FENCING	EQUESTRIAN	CYCLING	CANOEING	BOXING	BASKETBALL	TRACK & FIELD (women)	TRACK & FIELD (men)	MODERN PENTATHLON	SLEDDING	SKIING	SPEED SKATING	FIGURE SKATING	ICE HOCKEY
United States	41	2		2	4		4	8		1	2				1		1		1	1	11		1	1	1	1	
Sweden	21		5						1			1		3	1	3	4			2	5	1		3			
France	11		1	1						1				3	1	2		2		1	1			2			
Hungary	10					1				1	1	3		1				1			1						
Italy	9			1						1		4					3	1			1		1	2			
Switzerland	8											1		1			1	1			1		1	1		1	
Finland	7			1																							
Czechoslovakia	6			4													3										
Turkey	6		2																								
Denmark	5	1																									
Netherlands	5						2													4							
Norway	5	1					1											2					1	2	3		
Argentina	3										2										1						
Belgium	3																				1						
Great Britain	3	1														1					1					1	
Australia	2																1										
Austria	2																										1
Canada	2												1														
Egypt	2				2																						
Mexico	2														2												
South Africa	2																				1					1	
India	1												1														
Jamaica	1																				1						
Peru	1	1								1																	

CHAMPIONSHIPS (WON) BY NATION
XV. MODERN OLYMPICS 1952 — Helsinki

Winter-games columns (Bobsledding, Figure Skating, Ice Hockey, Skiing, Speed Skating) are from **VI. WINTER GAMES**.

NATION	Bobsledding	Figure Skating	Ice Hockey	Skiing	Speed Skating	Modern Pentathlon	Track & Field (men)	Track & Field (women)	Basketball	Boxing	Canoeing	Cycling	Equestrian	Fencing	Gymnastics	Rowing	Shooting	Soccer	Swimming (men)	Swimming (women)	Water Polo	Weight Lifting	Wrestling catch-as-catch-can	Wrestling Greco-Roman	Yachting	Field Hockey	TOTAL
United States		1		2	1		14	1	1	5	1					2	1		6	2		4	1		2		44
U.S.S.R.								2							9	1	1					3	2	4			22
Hungary						1	1			1				2	2		1	1		4	1			2			16
Sweden						1	1				1		4		2								2	1			12
Norway				4	3												2								1		10
Finland				3						1	4													1			9
Italy				1			1			1		2		3											1		9
Czechoslovakia							3	1		1	1					1											7
Australia								3				2							1								6
France											1		1	2		1			1								6
Germany	2	1																									3
Austria				2																							2
Belgium												2															2
Denmark											1														1		2
Canada			1														1										2
Great Britain		1											1														2
Jamaica							2																				2
South Africa								1												1							2
Switzerland															2												2
Turkey																							2				2
Argentina																1											1
Brazil							1																				1
Japan																							1				1
Luxembourg							1																				1
New Zealand								1																			1
Poland										1																	1
Romania																	1										1
Yugoslavia																1											1
India																										1	1

CHAMPIONSHIPS (WON) BY NATION
XVI. MODERN OLYMPICS 1956
Melbourne
VII. WINTER GAMES

NATION	TOTAL	Field Hockey	Yachting	Greco-Roman Wrestling	catch-as-catch-can Wrestling	Weight Lifting	Water Polo	Swimming (women)	Swimming (men)	Soccer	Shooting	Rowing	Gymnastics	Fencing	Equestrian	Cycling	Canoeing	Boxing	Basketball	Track & Field (women)	Track & Field (men)	Modern Pentathlon	Speed Skating	Skiing	Ice Hockey	Figure Skating	Bobsledding
U.S.S.R.	43*			5	1	3				1	3	2	11				2	3	1	2	3	1	3	2	1		
United States	34		1			4		3	2		1	3						1	1	4	15	1				2	
Australia	13							3	5							1				1	2						
Sweden	10*		2	1											1		2					1	1	1			
Hungary	9*						1	1	1				1	3			1	1									
Italy	9*			2										2		2											1
Germany	7*							1							3			1									
Finland	6			1							1		1				1							1			
Great Britain	6		1					1						1	2			1									
Romania	5										1						3	1									
Austria	4				1																			3		1	
France	4		1					1				1		1		3											
Japan	4				1				1				2														
Norway	3		1																					2			
Switzerland	3																							2			1
Turkey	3				3																						
Canada	2										1	1															
Iran	2				2																						
New Zealand	2		1																		1						
Brazil	1																				1						
Bulgaria	1				1																						
Czechoslovakia	1																			1							
Denmark	1		1																								
India	1	1																									
Ireland	1																				1						
Mexico	1								1																		
Poland	1																			1							

*These include full credit for ties for Olympic first place.

297

CHAMPIONSHIPS (WON) BY NATION

XVII. MODERN OLYMPICS 1960 — Rome
VIII. WINTER GAMES

NATION	Biathlon	Figure Skating	Ice Hockey	Skiing	Speed Skating	Modern Pentathlon	Track & Field (men)	Track & Field (women)	Basketball	Boxing	Canoeing	Cycling	Equestrian	Fencing	Gymnastics	Rowing	Shooting	Soccer	Swimming (men)	Swimming (women)	Water Polo	Weight Lifting	Wrestling catch-as-catch-can	Wrestling Greco-Roman	Yachting	Field Hockey	TOTAL
U.S.S.R.				1	5		5	6		1	3	1	1	3	10	2	2					5		3	1		49
United States		2	1				9	3	1	3						1	1		6	5		1	3		1		37
Germany				3	1		2				1		1	1		3	1			2			1				15
Italy							1			3		5	1	2							1						13
Australia							1						2						4	1							8
Turkey																							4	3			7
Hungary						2				1	1			2													6
Poland							2			1												1					4
Sweden	1			2							1																4
Norway				1	2																				1		4
Japan															4												4
Finland				2											1												3
Romania								1									1							1			3
Czechoslovakia										1					1	1											3
Great Britain							1													1							2
France				1																							2
Austria				1													1										2
Switzerland				2																							2
Canada		1		1																							2
New Zealand							2																				2
Denmark											1														1		2
Greece																									1		1
Ethiopia							1																				1
Pakistan																										1	1
Yugoslavia																		1									1
Bulgaria																								1			1

IX. WINTER GAMES — Innsbruck
CHAMPIONSHIPS (WON) BY NATION — XVIII. MODERN OLYMPICS 1964 — Tokyo

NATION	Biathlon	Tobogganing	Bobsledding	Figure Skating	Ice Hockey	Skiing	Speed Skating	Modern Pentathlon	Track & Field (men)	Track & Field (women)	Basketball (women)	Boxing	Canoeing	Cycling	Equestrian	Fencing	Gymnastics	Rowing	Shooting	Soccer	Swimming (men)	Swimming (women)	Water Polo	Weight Lifting	Wrestling catch-as-catch-can	Wrestling Greco-Roman	Yachting	Judo	Field Hockey	Volleyball	TOTAL
U.S.S.R.	1			1	1	3	5	1	2	2		3	2			3	4	2	1			1		4	2	2				1	41
United States									12	2	1	1						1			9	7		1	3						37
Japan												1					5							1	3	2		3		1	16
Germany		2		1									2	1	2	1		2	1								1				13
Hungary								1				2	1			4				1			1								10
Italy												3		3	1	1			1		1										10
Poland									1	1		3				1								1							7
Australia										1											3	1					1				6
Finland						3																			1	2					6
Sweden						2							1						1							1					5
Great Britain			1						2	2																					5
Czechoslovakia													1				3		1												5
France						3								1																	4
Austria		1				3																									4
Bulgaria																									2	1					3
New Zealand									2																		1				3
Norway						2	1																								3
Netherlands				1																		1						1			3
Belgium									1					1																	2
Yugoslavia												1														1					2
Denmark														1													1				2
Turkey																									1	1					2
Canada			1												1																2
Romania													2																		2
Ethiopia									1																						1
Bahamas																											1				1
Switzerland															1																1
India																													1		1

WINTER: 7 SPORTS—30 EVENTS   SUMMER: 21 SPORTS—167 EVENTS   TOTAL: 28 SPORTS—197 EVENTS

CHAMPIONSHIPS (WON) BY NATION

XIX. MODERN OLYMPICS 1968 — Mexico City
X. WINTER GAMES — Grenoble

NATION	Biathlon	Toboggan	Bobsled	Figure Skating	Skiing (men)	Skiing (women)	Speed Skating	Speed Skating (women)	Ice Hockey	WINTER GAMES	Modern Pentathlon	Athletics (men)	Athletics (women)	Basketball	Boxing	Canoeing	Cycling	Equestrian	Fencing	Gymnastics	Rowing	Shooting	Soccer	Swimming (men)	Swimming (women)	Water Polo	Weight Lifting	Wrestling catch-as-catch-can	Wrestling Greco-Roman	Yachting	Field Hockey	Volleyball	SUMMER GAMES	GRAND TOTAL
United States	—	—	—	1	—	—	—	—	—	1	—	12	3	1	2	—	—	—	—	—	—	1	—	11	12	—	—	2	—	2	—	—	45	46
U.S.S.R.	1	—	—	1	1	—	—	1	1	5	—	3	1	—	3	2	—	1	3	4	1	2	—	—	—	—	3	2	1	1	—	2	28	33
France	—	—	—	—	3	1	—	—	—	4	—	1	—	—	—	—	4	1	1	—	1	2	—	—	—	—	—	—	2	1	—	—	7	11
Japan	—	—	—	—	—	—	—	—	—	0	—	1	—	—	1	—	—	—	—	5	—	—	—	—	—	—	1	3	—	—	—	—	10	10
Hungary	—	1	—	—	1	—	—	—	—	0	1	1	1	—	1	2	—	1	2	—	2	1	1	2	1	1	—	—	—	—	—	—	10	10
East Germany	—	1	—	—	—	—	1	1	—	1	—	1	1	—	—	2	1	—	—	—	2	1	—	2	—	—	—	3	2	—	—	—	9	10
Czechoslovakia	—	—	—	—	1	—	1	—	—	1	—	1	1	—	1	—	1	1	—	4	—	1	1	—	—	—	1	—	2	—	—	—	9	10
West Germany	—	—	—	—	1	1	—	—	—	2	1	—	1	—	1	1	1	1	1	—	1	—	—	—	—	—	—	—	—	—	—	—	6	8
Norway	1	—	—	—	3	1	1	—	—	6	—	—	—	—	—	—	—	—	—	—	—	1	—	1	—	—	—	—	—	—	—	—	1	7
Italy	—	1	2	—	1	—	—	—	—	4	—	1	—	—	1	1	1	1	1	—	—	—	—	1	—	—	—	—	—	1	—	—	3	7
Netherlands	—	—	—	—	—	—	1	2	—	3	1	1	1	—	—	1	1	—	—	—	—	—	—	—	1	—	—	—	—	—	—	—	4	7
Poland	—	—	—	—	—	—	—	—	—	0	1	1	1	—	1	—	1	1	—	—	1	—	—	—	—	—	—	—	—	—	—	—	6	6
Australia	—	—	—	—	—	—	—	—	—	0	—	1	1	—	—	—	—	—	—	—	—	—	—	2	1	—	—	—	—	—	—	—	5	5
Great Britain	—	—	—	—	—	—	2	1	—	0	—	1	1	—	—	—	—	1	—	—	—	1	—	—	1	—	—	—	—	—	—	—	5	5
Sweden	—	—	—	1	2	2	—	—	—	3	1	1	—	—	—	1	1	—	—	—	—	1	—	2	1	—	—	—	—	1	—	—	2	5
Romania	1	—	—	—	—	—	—	—	—	0	—	—	2	—	—	1	—	—	1	—	—	—	—	—	—	—	—	—	—	—	—	—	5	5
Austria	—	1	—	1	1	1	—	—	—	3	—	—	—	—	—	—	—	—	—	—	—	—	—	—	—	—	—	—	—	—	—	—	0	3

Table of Olympic medals by nation and sport.

NATION	Biathlon	Toboggan	Bobsled	Figure Skating	Skiing (men)	Skiing (women)	Speed Skating	Speed Skating (women)	Ice Hockey	WINTER GAMES	Modern Pentathlon	Athletics (men)	Athletics (women)	Basketball	Boxing	Canoeing	Cycling	Equestrian	Fencing	Gymnastics	Rowing	Shooting	Soccer	Swimming (men)	Swimming (women)	Water Polo	Weight Lifting	Catch-as-catch-can Wrestling	Greco-Roman Wrestling	Yachting	Field Hockey	Volleyball	SUMMER GAMES	GRAND TOTAL
Mexico										0					2									1									3	3
Kenya										0		3																					3	3
Yugoslavia										0										1					1	1							3	3
Iran										0																	1	1					2	2
Turkey										0																		2					2	2
Canada						1				1								1															1	2
Finland								1		1											1												1	2
Bulgaria										0																			2				2	2
New Zealand										0								1															1	1
Ethiopia										0		1																					1	1
Tunisia										0		1																					1	1
Denmark										0							1																1	1
Pakistan										0																					1		1	1
Venezuela										0					1																		1	1
TOTALS	2	3	2	3	10	6	4	4	1	35	2	24	12		11	7	7	6	8	14	7	7	7	17	16	1	7	8	8	5	1	2	172	207

CHAMPIONSHIPS (WON) BY NATION

XI WINTER GAMES — Sapporo | **XX MODERN OLYMPIC GAMES 1972 — Munich**

NATION	Biathlon	Toboggan	Bobsled	Figure Skating	Skiing (men)	Skiing (women)	Speed Skating (men)	Speed Skating (women)	Ice Hockey	Ski Jumps	WINTER GAMES	Track & Field (men)	Track & Field (women)	Modern Pentathlon	Basketball	Boxing	Canoeing	Slalom	Cycling	Equestrian	Fencing (men)	Fencing (women)	Gymnastics (men)	Gymnastics (women)	Rowing	Shooting	Soccer	Swimming (men)	Swimming (women)	Water Polo	Weightlifting	Wrestling Freestyle	Wrestling Greco-Roman	Judo	Yachting	Field Hockey	Volleyball	Archery	Handball	SUMMER GAMES	GRAND TOTAL
U.S.S.R.	1	—	—	1	2	3	—	—	1	—	8	6	3	1	1	2	6	—	2	2	1	1	2	4	2	1	—	—	—	1	3	5	4	1	1	—	1	—	—	50	58
United States	—	—	—	—	—	1	—	2	—	—	3	6	1	—	—	1	—	—	—	—	—	—	—	—	—	2	—	9	8	—	—	3	—	—	1	—	—	2	—	33	36
East Germany	—	2	—	—	1	—	—	—	—	—	3	1	6	—	—	1	—	4	—	—	—	—	1	2	3	—	—	2	—	—	—	—	—	—	—	—	—	—	—	20	23
West Germany	—	—	1	—	—	—	1	1	—	—	3	2	4	—	—	—	1	—	—	3	—	—	—	—	2	—	—	—	—	—	—	—	—	—	—	1	—	—	—	13	16
Japan	—	—	—	—	—	—	—	—	—	1	1	—	—	—	—	—	—	—	—	—	—	—	5	—	—	—	—	1	1	—	—	2	—	3	—	—	1	—	—	13	14
Australia	—	—	—	—	—	—	—	—	—	—	0	—	—	—	—	—	—	—	—	—	—	—	—	—	—	—	—	1	5	—	—	—	—	—	2	—	—	—	—	8	8
Poland	—	—	—	—	—	—	—	—	—	1	1	1	—	—	—	1	1	—	—	—	2	—	—	—	—	—	1	—	—	—	1	—	—	—	—	—	—	—	—	7	8
Netherlands	—	—	—	—	—	—	3	1	—	—	4	—	—	—	—	—	—	—	1	—	—	—	—	—	—	—	—	—	—	—	—	—	—	2	—	—	—	—	—	3	7
Italy	—	1	—	—	1	—	—	—	—	—	2	—	—	—	—	—	—	—	1	1	1	1	—	—	—	—	—	1	—	—	—	—	—	—	—	—	—	—	—	5	7
Hungary	—	—	—	—	—	—	—	—	—	—	0	—	—	1	—	1	1	—	—	—	2	—	—	—	—	—	—	—	—	—	1	—	—	—	—	—	—	—	—	6	6
Bulgaria	—	—	—	—	—	—	—	—	—	—	0	—	—	—	—	—	—	—	—	—	—	—	—	—	—	—	—	—	—	—	3	1	2	—	—	—	—	—	—	6	6
Sweden	—	—	—	—	1	—	—	—	—	—	1	—	—	—	—	—	—	—	1	—	—	—	—	—	—	1	—	2	—	—	—	—	—	—	—	—	—	—	—	4	5
Norway	1	—	—	—	1	—	—	—	—	—	2	—	—	—	—	—	—	—	1	—	—	—	—	—	—	—	—	—	—	—	1	—	—	—	—	—	—	—	—	2	4

NATION	Biathlon	Toboggan	Bobsled	Figure Skating	Skiing (men)	Skiing (women)	Speed Skating (men)	Speed Skating (women)	Ice Hockey	Ski Jumps	WINTER GAMES	Track & Field (men)	Track & Field (women)	Modern Pentathlon	Basketball	Boxing	Canoeing	Slalom	Cycling	Equestrian	Fencing (men)	Fencing (women)	Gymnastics (men)	Gymnastics (women)	Rowing	Shooting	Soccer	Swimming (men)	Swimming (women)	Water Polo	Weightlifting	Wrestling Freestyle	Wrestling Greco-Roman	Judo	Yachting	Field Hockey	Volleyball	Archery	Handball	SUMMER GAMES	GRAND TOTAL
Great Britain	—	—	—	—	—	—	—	—	—	—	0	—	1	—	—	—	—	—	—	2	—	—	—	—	—	—	—	—	—	—	—	—	—	—	1	—	—	—	—	4	4
Switzerland	—	—	1	—	1	2	—	—	—	—	4	—	—	—	—	—	—	—	—	—	—	—	—	—	—	—	—	—	—	—	—	—	—	—	—	—	—	—	—	0	4
Czechoslovakia	—	—	—	1	—	—	—	—	—	—	1	1	—	—	—	—	—	—	—	—	—	—	—	—	—	—	—	—	—	—	—	—	1	—	—	—	—	—	—	2	3
Romania	—	—	—	—	—	—	—	—	—	—	0	—	—	—	—	—	1	—	—	—	—	—	—	—	—	—	—	—	—	—	—	—	2	—	—	—	—	—	—	3	3
Finland	—	—	—	—	—	—	—	—	—	—	0	3	—	—	—	—	—	—	—	—	—	—	—	—	—	—	—	—	—	—	—	—	—	—	—	—	—	—	—	3	3
Cuba	—	—	—	—	—	—	—	—	—	—	0	—	—	—	—	3	—	—	—	—	—	—	—	—	—	—	—	—	—	—	—	—	—	—	—	—	—	—	—	3	3
France	—	—	—	—	—	—	—	—	—	—	0	—	—	—	—	—	—	—	1	—	—	—	—	—	—	—	—	—	—	—	—	—	—	—	1	—	—	—	—	2	2
Kenya	—	—	—	—	—	—	—	—	—	—	0	2	—	—	—	—	—	—	—	—	—	—	—	—	—	—	—	—	—	—	—	—	—	—	—	—	—	—	—	2	2
Yugoslavia	—	—	—	—	—	—	—	—	—	—	0	—	—	—	—	1	—	—	—	—	—	—	—	—	—	—	—	—	—	—	—	—	—	—	—	—	—	—	1	2	2
Austria	—	—	—	1	—	—	—	—	—	—	1	—	—	—	—	—	—	—	—	—	—	—	—	—	—	—	—	—	—	—	—	—	—	—	—	—	—	—	—	0	1
New Zealand	—	—	—	—	—	—	—	—	—	—	0	—	—	—	—	—	—	—	—	—	—	—	—	—	1	—	—	—	—	—	—	—	—	—	—	—	—	—	—	1	1
Denmark	—	—	—	—	—	—	—	—	—	—	0	—	—	—	—	—	—	—	1	—	—	—	—	—	—	—	—	—	—	—	—	—	—	—	—	—	—	—	—	1	1
Uganda	—	—	—	—	—	—	—	—	—	—	0	1	—	—	—	—	—	—	—	—	—	—	—	—	—	—	—	—	—	—	—	—	—	—	—	—	—	—	—	1	1
Spain	—	—	—	—	1	—	—	—	—	—	1	—	—	—	—	—	—	—	—	—	—	—	—	—	—	—	—	—	—	—	—	—	—	—	—	—	—	—	—	0	1
North Korea	—	—	—	—	—	—	—	—	—	—	0	—	—	—	—	—	—	—	—	—	—	—	—	—	—	1	—	—	—	—	—	—	—	—	—	—	—	—	—	1	1
TOTALS	2	3	2	3	8	6	4	4	1	2	35	24	14	2	1	11	7	4	7	6	6	2	8	6	7	8	1	17	16	1	9	10	10	6	6	1	2	2	1	195	230

CHAMPIONSHIPS (WON) BY NATION

NATION	\[XIII WINTER GAMES – Innsbruck\]										\[XXI MODERN OLYMPIC 1976 – Montreal\]																										
	Biathlon	Luge	Bobsled	Figure Skating	Skiing (Men)	Skiing (Women)	Speed Skiing (Men)	Speed Skiing (Women)	Ice Hockey	WINTER GAMES	Modern Pentathlon	Athletics (Men)	Athletics (Women)	Basketball	Boxing	Canoeing	Cycling	Equestrian	Fencing	Gymnastics	Rowing	Shooting	Soccer	Swimming (Men)	Swimming (Women)	Water Polo	Weightlifting	Wrestling (Freestyle)	Wrestling (Roman-Greco)	Yachting	Field Hockey	Volleyball	Archery	Handball (Team)	Judo	SUMMER GAMES	GRAND TOTAL
U.S.S.R.	2	—	—	2	2	2	2	2	1	13	—	2	2	2	1	6	1	1	3	7	1	1	—	—	2	—	7	5	7	—	—	—	—	2	2	49	62
East (GDR) Germany	—	3	2	—	1	—	1	1	—	7	—	2	9	—	1	3	1	1	—	—	9	2	1	1	11	—	—	1	1	1	—	—	—	—	2	40	47
U.S.A.	—	—	—	2	—	1	1	—	—	3	—	6	—	1	5	—	—	2	2	—	—	2	—	13	2	1	—	1	—	2	—	—	2	—	—	34	37
West (Ger) Germany	—	2	—	—	—	—	—	—	—	2	—	—	—	—	1	1	—	2	2	—	3	1	—	—	—	—	—	—	2	—	—	1	1	—	—	10	12
Japan	—	—	—	—	—	—	—	—	—	—	1	—	—	—	—	—	—	—	—	3	—	—	—	—	—	—	—	—	—	—	—	—	—	—	3	9	9
Poland	—	—	—	—	1	1	—	—	—	2	—	2	1	—	1	—	1	—	—	—	—	—	—	—	—	—	—	—	1	—	—	1	1	—	—	7	7
Finland	—	—	—	—	1	1	—	—	—	2	—	2	—	—	—	—	—	—	—	—	1	—	—	—	—	—	—	—	1	—	—	—	—	—	1	4	6
Cuba	—	—	—	—	—	—	—	—	—	—	—	2	—	1	3	—	—	—	—	—	—	—	—	—	—	—	—	—	—	—	—	—	—	—	—	6	6
Bulgaria	—	—	—	—	—	—	—	—	—	—	—	—	1	—	—	—	—	—	—	1	2	—	—	—	—	—	2	2	1	—	—	—	—	—	1	6	6
Hungary	—	—	—	—	—	—	—	—	—	—	—	1	—	—	—	1	1	—	1	1	—	—	—	—	—	1	—	—	—	—	—	—	—	—	—	4	4
Romania	—	—	—	—	—	—	—	—	—	—	—	—	—	—	—	1	—	—	1	3	—	—	—	—	—	—	—	—	—	—	—	—	—	—	—	4	4
Norway	—	—	—	—	1	—	2	—	—	3	—	—	—	—	—	—	—	—	1	—	1	—	—	—	—	—	—	—	—	1	—	—	—	—	—	1	4
Sweden	—	—	—	—	—	—	—	—	—	—	—	1	—	—	—	—	—	1	1	—	—	1	—	—	—	—	—	—	—	1	—	—	—	—	—	4	4

NATION	Biathlon	Luge	Bobsled	Figure Skating	Skiing (Men)	Skiing (Women)	Speed Skating (Men)	Speed Skating (Women)	Ice Hockey	WINTER GAMES	Modern Pentathlon	Athletics (Men)	Athletics (Women)	Basketball	Boxing	Canoeing	Cycling	Equestrian	Fencing	Gymnastics	Rowing	Shooting	Soccer	Swimming (Men)	Swimming (Women)	Water Polo	Weightlifting	Wrestling (Freestyle)	Wrestling (Roman-Greco)	Yachting	Field Hockey	Volleyball	Archery	Handball (Team)	Judo	SUMMER GAMES	GRAND TOTAL
Great Britain				1						1	1													1						1						3	4
Italy					1					1									1					1												2	3
Austria					2					2																											2
France												1						1																		2	2
New Zealand												1																			1					2	2
Czechoslovakia																	1					1														2	2
Switzerland					1					1								1																		1	2
Yugoslavia																1													1							2	2
Denmark																														1						1	1
Mexico												1																								1	1
Holland							1			1																											1
Canada						1				1																											1
Trinidad												1																								1	1
Jamaica												1																								1	1
No. Korea																						1														1	1
So. Korea																												1								1	1
TOTALS	2	3	2	4	10	5	6	4	1	37	2	23	14	2	11	11	6	6	8	14	14	7	1	15	15	1	9	10	10	6	1	2	2	2	6	198	235

305

1956

UNOFFICIAL OLYMPIC RANKINGS

on basis of

Points Scored Per Million Population

1956 Ranking	Nation	1956 Olympic Points	1956 Est. Population	1956 Points per Million
1	Australia	278.50	9.43	29.53
2	Finland	98.50	4.28	23.01
3	Sweden	164.00	7.25	22.62
4	Hungary	220.50	9.85	22.39
5	New Zealand	26.00	2.21	11.76
6	Ireland	28.50	2.89	9.86
7	Trinidad*	7.00	.71	7.00
8	Denmark	29.00	4.43	6.55
9	Romania	108.00	17.49	6.17
10	Norway	21.00	3.47	5.40
11	Czechoslovakia	71.50	13.25	5.00
12	Iceland*	5.00	.16	6.05
13	Bulgaria	34.50	7.63	4.52
14	Bahamas	4.00	.12	4.00
15	Italy	185.00	49.40	3.74
16	{Great Britain	180.50	51.20	3.53
	{United States	593.00	167.94	3.53
18	U.S.S.R.	722.00	210.00	3.44
19	Canada	52.00	16.08	3.23
20	Germany	223.00	71.20	3.13
21	France	120.50	43.50	2.77
22	Poland	73.50	28.00	2.63
23	{Chile	17.00	6.91	2.46
	{Turkey	61.00	24.79	2.46
25	Iran	48.00	20.20	2.33
26	Uruguay	6.00	2.69	2.23
27	Austria	12.00	7.15	1.63
28	Japan	139.00	90.00	1.54
29	South Africa	24.00	16.91	1.42
30	Yugoslavia	22.00	17.80	1.24
31	Belgium	11.00	8.94	1.23
32	Korea	22.00	21.80	1.01
33	Switzerland	5.00	5.02	1.00
34	Argentina	18.50	19.47	.95
35	Mexico	17.00	30.54	.56
36	Greece	4.00	8.23	.49
37	Portugal	3.00	9.39	.32
38	Brazil	12.00	59.00	.20
39	Malaya	1.00	6.15	.16
40	Cuba	1.00	6.30	.16
41	{Nigeria	2.00	31.20	.06
	{Pakistan	5.00	83.60	.06
43	{India	10.00	376.00	.03
	{Spain	1.00	29.20	.03

*Points per million population cannot be calculated for countries under this amount other than crediting actual points as of population of one million.

UNOFFICIAL OLYMPIC RANKINGS

on basis of

Points Scored Per Million Population

1960 Ranking	Nation	1960 Olympic Points	1960 Population	1960 Points per Million
1	Hungary	168½	10.20	16.51
2	Australia	166-1/3	10.10	16.46
3	New Zealand	37	2.50	14.80
4	Denmark	51	4.57	11.16
5	Finland	42	4.45	9.44
6	Sweden	64½	7.44	8.67
7	Switzerland	38¾	5.5	7.05
8	Czechoslovakia	82½	13.90	5.93
9	Norway	20	3.61	5.54
10	Bulgaria	43	7.86	5.47
11	Italy	271	50.90	5.32
12	Poland	158¾	30.00	5.29
13	Romania	86½	19.23	4.49
14	Germany	319¼	74.00	4.31
15	U.S.S.R.	795½	221.8	3.60
16	Singapore	5	1.5	3.33
17	Netherlands	39¾	12.0	3.31
18	British W.I.	10	3.1	3.22
19	United States	565½	180.0	3.14
20	Turkey	85	27.39	3.10
21	Belgium	26	9.11	2.85
22	Great Britain	138¼	52.00	2.66
23	Austria	15	7.30	2.06
24	Iceland*	2	.18	2.0
25	Japan	152	94.00	1.62
26	South Africa	21½	14.6	1.47
27	Yugoslavia	25½	18.84	1.35
28	Ireland	4	3.00	1.33
29	Puerto Rico	3	2.4	1.25
30	France	52¾	45.0	1.18
31	Greece	10	8.93	1.12
32	Iran	22	22.00	1.00
33	Bahamas*	1	.13	1.00
34	Venezuela	6	6.6	0.91
35	Canada	16	17.8	0.90
36	Ghana	5	6.6	0.76
37	Luxembourg*	¾	.35	0.75
38	Iraq	4	6.5	0.61
39	Argentina	11½	21.20	0.54
40	U.A.R.	15½	30.0	0.51
41	Ethiopia	10	20.0	0.50
42	Portugal	5	10.19	0.49
43	Cuba	3	6.77	0.46
44	Republic of China	5	11.0	0.45

*Points per million population cannot be calculated under this amount other than crediting actual points as of population of one million.

1964

UNOFFICIAL OLYMPIC RANKINGS

on basis of

Points Scored Per Million Population

(Summer Games Only)

1964 Ranking	Nation	1964 Olympic Points	1964 Population	1964 Points per Million
1	Hungary	206.50	10.14	20.36
2	New Zealand	47.00	2.64	17.36
3	Trinidad*	13.00	0.95	13.83
4	Australia	147.25	11.36	12.96
5	Finland	48.50	4.61	10.52
6	Bahamas*	10.00	.134	10.00
7	Sweden	75.00	7.73	9.70
8	Denmark	45.00	4.72	9.64
9	Bulgaria	75.25	8.20	9.18
10	Czechoslovakia	119.00	14.15	8.42
11	Jamaica	12.00	1.77	6.78
12	Netherlands	76.75	12.29	6.25
13	Switzerland	33.00	5.39	6.12
14	Poland	178.25	31.49	5.66
15	Romania	103.50	19.02	5.44
16	Germany	366.00	77.13	4.75
17	Italy	215.00	51.57	4.17
18	Ireland	11.25	2.85	3.95
19	United States	690.08	195.69	3.53
20	Japan	299.00	97.96	3.05
21	U.S.S.R.	700.08	230.58	3.00
22	Belgium	26.58	9.46	2.81
23	Great Britain	149.50	54.37	2.75
24	Yugoslavia	41.75	19.51	2.14
25	Canada	40.00	19.60	2.04
26	France	99.25	48.92	2.03
27	Bermuda*	2.00	.046	2.00
28	Turkey	44.00	32.00	1.37
29	Austria	9.75	7.25	1.34
30	Uruguay	3.50	2.71	1.30
31	Puerto Rico	3.00	2.50	1.20
32	Cuba	8.50	7.63	1.12
33	Korea	27.33	28.50	0.96
34	Argentina	18.00	22.35	0.81
35	Tunisia	3.50	4.56	0.76
36	Ghana	5.75	7.74	0.74
37	Iran	17.33	23.42	0.74
38	Kenya	7.00	9.36	0.74
39	Ethiopia	13.00	22.59	0.57
40	Norway	2.00	3.72	0.54
41	Portugal	5.00	9.16	0.54
42	Ivory Coast	1.00	3.75	0.27
43	Republic of China	2.00	12.42	0.22
44	Venezuela	1.00	8.72	0.12

Other point scorers below the above: Brazil, Peru, Uganda, Nigeria, Spain, Chile, Colombia, Philippines, United Arab Republic, Pakistan, Mexico, Afghanistan, Burma, and India.

*Points per million population cannot be calculated under this amount other than crediting actual points as of population of one million.

1968

UNOFFICIAL OLYMPIC RANKINGS

on basis of

Points Scored Per Million Population

(Summer and Winter Games Combined)

1968 Ranking	Nation	1968 Olympic Points	1968 Population	1968 Points per Million Population*
1	Norway	156.66	4.0	39.0
2	Hungary	221.0	10.5	21.5
3	East Germany	348.0	17.5	20.0
4	Finland	88.18	4.75	18.55
5	Sweden	139.5	8.00	17.43
6	Austria	110.0	7.5	14.6
7	Australia	145.0	12.0	12.08
8	Czechoslovakia	152.0	14.5	10.5
9	Denmark	48.0	4.8	10.0
10	Mongolia	19.0	2.0	9.5
11	Switzerland	56.33	6.2	9.1
12	Bulgaria	72.0	8.5	8.45
13	Netherlands	107.8	12.8	8.4
14	New Zealand	20.0	2.75	7.2
15	Romania	122.5	19.75	6.2
16	Kenya	57.5	10.0	5.75
17	Trinidad	5.5	1.2	4.6
18	United States	896.83	202.0	4.44
19	Poland	145.33	32.5	4.4
20	France	218.25	50.7	4.3
21	West Germany	243.0	60.0	4.05
22	Jamaica	8.0	2.0	4.0
23	Canada	76.0	21.0	3.62
24	U.S.S.R.	776.0	238.0	3.26
25	Italy	162.0	54.0	3.0
26	Tunisia	14.0	4.7	3.0
27	Cuba	25.0	8.3	3.0
28	Yugoslavia	56.5	20.25	2.78
29	Great Britain	133.0	55.0	2.41
30	Japan	218.5	100.0	2.18
31	Bahamas	2.0	1.0	2.0
32	Mexico	70.0	46.0	1.52
33	Greece	13.0	9.0	1.44
34	Iran	38.0	26.5	1.43
35	Venezuela	10.0	9.8	1.02
36	Uganda	8.5	8.5	1.00

*About 15 more countries were Olympic point scorers but below 1 point per million population.

UNOFFICIAL OLYMPIC RANKINGS

on basis of

Points Scored per Million Population

(summer and winter games combined)

1972 Ranking	Nation	1972 Olympic Points	1972 Population	Points per Million Population
1	East Germany	621½	17,562,068	35.39
2	Norway	122	3,974,350	30.70
3	Finland	114	4,802,470	23.74
4	Hungary	232	10,552,500	21.99
5	Sweden	159½	8,314,800	19.18
6	Bulgaria	163	8,659,978	18.82
7	Switzerland	99	6,438,400	15.38
8	Australia	158	13,060,000	12.10
9	Netherlands	130	13,491,997	9.64
10	New Zealand	26	2,950,740	8.81
11	Cuba	61	8,823,000	6.91
12	Czechoslovakia	102½	14,874,000	6.89
13	West Germany	413	60,293,760	6.84
14	Austria	49	7,874,000	6.22
15	Romania	120½	20,909,000	5.76
16	Poland	192	33,868,800	5.67
17	Mongolia	7½	1,545,000	4.85
18	Kenya	59	12,292,700	4.80
19	United States*	800½	208,101,136	3.84
20	U.S.S.R.*	939	249,268,000	3.77
21	Denmark	17	5,030,000	3.38
22	Jamaica	6	1,934,200	3.10
23	Italy	167½	54,871,430	3.05
24	Japan	279½	107,069,600	2.61
25	Great Britain	131½	56,475,000	2.33
26	Libya	5	2,177,700	2.30
27	Canada	50	22,047,000	2.27
28	Yugoslavia	48	21,232,000	2.26
29	Belgium	23	10,470,000	2.20
30	France	112½	52,010,200	2.16
31	North Korea	28½	14,643,200	1.94
32	Uganda	15	10,763,500	1.39
33	Greece	12½	9,093,210	1.37
34	Puerto Rico	3	2,700,000	1.11
35	Tunisia	5	5,520,800	.91
36	Ghana	7½	9,859,200	.76
37	Iran	23½	31,476,000	.74
38	Spain	22½	34,879,500	.64
39	Colombia	12	23,068,200	.52
40	Ecuador	3	1,714,500	.44
41	Ethiopia	8	26,598,000	.30
42	Turkey	11	37,925,000	.29
43	Senegal	1	4,120,500	.24
44	South Korea	8	36,864,000	.22
45	Brazil	21½	103,400,000	.21
46	Argentina	5	27,791,000	.18
47	Mexico	7	54,027,000	.13
48	Nigeria	7	59,405,400	.12
49	Portugal	1	9,780,000	.10

Pakistan, Burma, and India scored some Olympic points, but not sufficient to include in this table.

*U.S. points in this table do not include the points for first or second in Basketball, although 10 points are included for first place for the U.S.S.R. Results have not yet been decided.

UNOFFICIAL OLYMPIC RANKINGS

on basis of

Points Scored Per Million Population

(summer and winter games combined)

1976 Ranking	Nation	1976 Olympic Points	1976/77 Population	Points per Million Population
1	East Germany	902½*	16.77 million	53.82
2	Finland	126	4.74	26.58
3	Bulgaria	175*	8.80	19.89
4	Hungary	168*	10.65	15.77
5	New Zealand	42	3.11	13.50
6	Cuba	107*	9.46	11.31
7	Switzerland	68	6.33	10.74
8	Norway	43	4.04	10.64
9	Sweden	85	8.26	10.29
10	Trinidad	11	1.10	10.00
11	Romania	190*	21.53	8.82
12	Jamaica	18	2.09	8.61
13	Austria	64	7.52	8.51
14	Lichtenstein	8	20,000	8.00
15	Mongolia	12	1.53	7.84
16	West Germany	385½	61.40	6.28
17	Czechoslovakia	93*	15.03	6.19
18	Poland	207*	34.70	5.97
19	Canada	124	23.32	5.32
20	U.S.S.R.	1,103½*	258.70	4.27
21	Denmark	21	5.09	4.13
22	Bermuda	4	1.0	4.0
23	Australia	53	14.07	3.77
24	Belgium	35	9.83	3.56
25	U.S.A.	714½	216.82	3.30
26	Holland	45	13.85	3.25
27	Yugoslavia*	60½	21.72	2.79
28	Italy	139½	56.45	2.47
29	Ireland	7	3.20	2.19
30	Great Britain	110½	55.85	1.98
31	Japan	196½	113.86	1.73
32	France	88½	53.08	1.67
33	Singapore	3½	2.31	1.52
34	Portugal	12	9.73	1.23
35	North Korea	20	16.65	1.20
36	Panama	2	1.77	1.13

N.B. All others less than 1 Olympic point per million population

"DOES MAN IMPROVE?"
THE IMPROVEMENT IN MODERN OLYMPIC RECORDS

Event	Record as of 1896	Record as of 1976	Record Holder	Date	Improvement
100-meter dash	12 seconds	9.9 seconds	Jim Hines, U.S.A.	1968	17.5%
400-meter run	54.2 seconds	43.8 seconds	Lee Evans, U.S.A.	1968	19.2%
800-meter run	2 min. 11 sec.	1 min. 43.5 sec.	A. Juantorena, Cuba	1976	21.0%
1500-meter run	4 min. 33.2 sec.	3 min. 34.9 sec.	Kipchoge Keino, Kenya	1968	21.3%
Marathon, 26 miles*	2 hrs. 55 min. 20 sec.	2 hrs. 9 min. 55 sec.	W. Cierpinski, E. Germany	1976	28.6%
High Jump	5 ft. 11¼ in.	7 ft. 4¼ in.	Dick Fosbury, U.S.A.	1968	23.9%
Pole Vault**	10 ft. 9¾ in.	18 ft. ½ in.	W. Nordwig, East Germany	1972	67.5%
Broad Jump (Long Jump)***	20 ft. 9¾ in.	29 ft. 2½ in.	Bob Beamon, U.S.A.	1968	40.3%
Hop, Step and Jump (Triple Jump)	45 ft. 0 in.	57 ft. ¾ in.	V. Saneyev, U.S.S.R.	1968	26.8%
Shot Put	36 ft. 2 in.	69 ft. 6 in.	W. Komar, Poland	1972	92.2%
Discus***	95 ft. 7½ in.	224 ft. 0 in.	Mac Wilkins, U.S.A.	1976	133.4%
Javelin	(1906) 175 ft. 6 in.	310 ft. 4 in.	M. Nemeth, Hungary	1976	76.7%

*Gives only general idea of improvement, as course is different at each Olympics.

**Ridiculous ruling against pole previously approved and used by U.S. world champion, with record of 18 ft. 2½ in., resulted in a reduced improvement record and 1972 performance.

***Only records of Ancient Olympics (in cubits) prior to 500 B.C. are available. Broad Jump ± 23 ft. Discus ± 150 ft.

Most experts agree that startling improvements are based on improved form, techniques, food, training methods, and especially footing (site). Pre 500 B.C. performances were on packed sand.

MODERN OLYMPIC GAMES
WINNERS AND RECORDS

ARCHERY (MEN)

1972—John Williams, U.S.A._____2528   1976— Darrell Pace, U.S.A._____2571*
World's Record: 1976—Darrell Pace, U.S.A., Montreal _____1268/1440
1980—

ARCHERY (WOMEN)

1972—Doreen Wilber, U.S.A._____2424   1976—Luann Ryon, U.S.A.,_____2499*
World's Record: 1974—Emma Gapchenko, U.S.S.R., Oxford, Ohio_____1235/1440
1980—

BOXING

LIGHT FLYWEIGHT

1968—Fran Rodriguez, Venezuela
1972—G. Gedeo, Hungary

1976—Jorge Hernandez, Cuba
1980—

FLYWEIGHT

1904—George V. Finnegan, U.S.A.
1920—Frank Genaro, U.S.A.
1924—Fidel La Barba, U.S.A.
1928—Anton Kocsis, Hungary
1932—Stephen Enekes, Hungary
1936—Will Kaiser, Germany
1948—Pascuel Perez, Argentina

1952—Nate Brooks, U.S.A.
1956—Terence Spinks, Gr. Britain
1960—G. Torck, Hungary
1964—Fernando Atzori, Italy
1968—Ricardo Delgado, Mexico
1972—G. Kostadinov, Bulgaria
1976—Leo Randolph, U.S.A.
1980—

BANTAMWEIGHT

1904—O. L. Kirk, U.S.A.
1908—H. Thomas, Gr. Britain
1920—Walker, So. Africa
1924—W. H. Smith, So. Africa
1928—Vittorio Tamagnini, Italy
1932—Horace Gwynne, Canada
1936—Ulderico Sergo, Italy
1948—T. Csik, Hungary

1952—Pentti Hamalainen, Finland
1956—Wolfgang Behrendt, Germany
1960—O. Grigoryev, U.S.S.R.
1964—Takao Sakurai, Japan
1968—Valery Sokolov, U.S.S.R.
1972—Orlando Martinez, Cuba
1976—Gu Yong Jo, North Korea
1980—

FEATHERWEIGHT

1904—O. L. Kirk, U.S.A.
1908—R. K. Gunn, Gr. Britain
1920—Fritsch, France
1924—Jack Fields, U.S.A.
1928—L. Van Klaveren, Netherlands
1932—Carmelo Robledo, Argentina
1936—Oscar Casanoras, Argentina
1948—Ernesto Formenti, Italy

1952—Jan Zachara, Czechoslovakia
1956—Vladimir Sefronov, U.S.S.R.
1960—F. Musso, Italy
1964—Stanislav Stepashkin, U.S.S.R.
1968—Antonio Roldan, Mexico
1972—Boris Kousnetsov, U.S.S.R.
1976—Angel Herrera, Cuba
1980—

LIGHTWEIGHT

1904—H. J. Spenger, U.S.A.
1908—F. Grace, Gr. Britain
1920—Samuel Mosberg, U.S.A.
1924—Harold Nielsen, Denmark
1928—Carlo Orlandi, Italy
1932—Lawrence Stevens, So. Africa
1936—Imre Harangi, Hungary
1948—Jerry Dreyer, So. Africa

1952—Aureliano Bolognesi, Italy
1956—Richard McTaggart, Gr. Britain
1960—K. Pazdzier, Poland
1964—Jozef Grudzein, Poland
1968—Ronnie Harris, U.S.A.
1972—Jan Szezepanski, Poland
1976—Howard Davis, U.S.A.
1980—

313

LIGHT WELTERWEIGHT

1952—Charles Adkins, U.S.A.
1956—Vladimir Engoibarian, U.S.S.R.
1960—B. Nemecek, Czechoslovakia
1964—Jerzy Kulej, Poland
1968—Jerzy Kulej, Poland
1972—Ray Seales, U.S.A.
1976—Ray Leonard, U.S.A.
1980—

WELTERWEIGHT

1904—Al Young, U.S.A.
1920—Schneider, Canada
1924—J. S. DeLarge, Belgium
1928—Edward Morgan, New Zealand
1932—Edward Flynn, U.S.A.
1936—Sten Suvio, Finland
1948—Julius Torma, Czechoslovakia
1952—Zygmunt Chychia, Poland
1956—Necolae Linca, Romania
1960—Giovanni Benvenuti, Italy
1964—Giovanni Benvenuti, Italy
1968—Manfred Wolke, East Germany
1972—Emilio Correa, Cuba
1976—Jochen Bachfeld, East Germany
1980—

LIGHT MIDDLEWEIGHT

1952—Laszlo Papp, Hungary
1956—Laszlo Papp, Hungary
1960—W. McClure, U.S.A.
1964—Marian Kasprzyk, Poland
1968—Boris Lagutin, U.S.S.R.
1972—Dieter Kottysch, West Germany
1976—Jerzy Rybicki, Poland
1980—

MIDDLEWEIGHT

1904—Charles Mayer, U.S.A.
1908—J. W. N. T. Douglas, Gr. Britain
1920—H. W. Mallin, Gr. Britain
1924—H. W. Mallin, Gr. Britain
1928—Piero Toscani, Italy
1932—Carmen Barth, U.S.A.
1936—Jean Despeaux, France
1948—Laszlo Papp, Hungary
1952—Floyd Patterson, U.S.A.
1956—Guennaddi Chatkov, U.S.S.R.
1960—E. Crook, U.S.A.
1964—Valery Popenchenko, U.S.S.R.
1968—Chris Finnegan, Gr. Britain
1972—V. Lemechev, U.S.S.R.
1976—Michael Spinks, U.S.A.
1980—

LIGHT HEAVYWEIGHT

1920—Edward Eagan, U.S.A.
1924—H. J. Mitchell, Gr. Britain
1928—Victor Avendano, Argentina
1932—David E. Carstens, So. Africa
1936—Roger Michelot, France
1948—George Hunter, So. Africa
1952—Norvel Lee, U.S.A.
1956—James Boyd, U.S.A.
1960—C. Clay, U.S.A.
1964—Cosimo Pinto, Italy
1968—Dan Rozniak, U.S.S.R.
1972—Mate Parlov, Yugoslavia
1976—Leon Spinks, U.S.A.
1980—

HEAVYWEIGHT

1904—Sam Berger, U.S.A.
1908—A. L. Oldham, Gr. Britain
1920—Rawson, Gr. Britain
1924—Otto Von Porath, Norway
1928—J. Rodriguez Jurado, Argentina
1932—Santiago A. Lovell, Argentina
1936—Herbert Runge, Germany
1948—Rafael Iglesias, Argentina
1952—Edward Sanders, U.S.A.
1956—Pete Rademacher, U.S.A.
1960—F. De Piccoli, Italy
1964—Joseph Frazier, U.S.A.
1968—George Foreman, U.S.A.
1972—T. Stevenson, Cuba
1976—T. Stevenson, Cuba
1980—

(UNOFFICIAL) TEAM CHAMPIONS

1904—United States
1908—Great Britain
1920—Great Britain
1924—United States
1928—Italy
1932—United States
1936—Germany
1948—Italy/South Africa
1952—United States
1956—U.S.S.R.
1980—
1960—Italy
1964—U.S.S.R.
1968—U.S.S.R.
1972—Cuba
1976—U.S.A.

---

*Olympic Record.

CANOEING (MEN)

KAYAK SINGLES 1,000 METERS

1936—Gregor Hradetzky, Austria
1948—Gert Fredriksson, Sweden
1952—Gert Fredriksson, Sweden
1956—Gert Fredriksson, Sweden
1960—F. Hansen, Denmark

1964—Rolf Peterson, Sweden
1968—Mihaly Hesz, Hungary
1972—A. Shaparenko, U.S.S.R.
1976—Rudiger Helm, East Germany
1980—

KAYAK SINGLES 10,000 METERS

1936—Ernst Krebs, Germany
1948—Gert Fredriksson, Sweden
1952—Thorvald Stromberg, Finland
1956—Gert Fredriksson, Sweden
1960—None

1964—None
1968—None
1972—None
1976—None

CANADIAN SINGLES 1,000 METERS

1936—Francis Amyot, Canada
1948—Josef Holecek, Czechoslovakia
1952—Josef Holecek, Czechoslovakia
1956—Leon Rottman, Romania
1960—J. Parti, Hungary

1964—Jurgen Eschert, Germany
1968—Tibor Tatai, Hungary
1972—Ivan Patzaichin, Romania
1976—Matija Ljubek, Yugoslavia
1980—

CANADIAN SINGLES 10,000 METERS

1948—F. Capek, Czechoslovakia
1952—Frank Havons, U.S.A.
1956—Leon Rottman, Romania

1960—None
1972—None
1976—None

KAYAK PAIRS 1,000 METERS

1936—Austria (Adolf Kainz, Alfons Dorfner)
1948—Sweden (H. Berglund, L. Klingstroem)
1952—Finland (K. Wires, Y. Hietanen)
1956—Germany (M. Scheur, M. Miltenberger)
1960—Sweden (G. Fredriksson, S. Sjodelius)

1964—Sweden (S. Sjodelius, G. Utterber)
1968—U.S.S.R. (Shaparenko, Morazov)
1972—U.S.S.R. (N. Gorbachev, Kratassyuk)
1976—U.S.S.R. (Nagorny, Romanovsky)
1980—

KAYAK PAIRS 10,000 METERS

1936—Germany (P. Wevers, Ludwig Lamden)
1948—Sweden (G. Akerlund, H. Wetterstroem)
1952—Finland (K. Wires, Y. Hietanen)
1956—Hungary (J. Uranyi, L. Fabian)

1960—None
1972—None
1976—None

CANADIAN PAIRS 1,000 METERS

1936—Czech. (V. Syrovatka, F. Jan Brzak)
1948—Czechoslovakia (J. Brzak, B. Kudrna)
1952—Denmark (B. Rasch, F. Haunstoft)
1956—Romania (A. Dumitru, S. Ismailciuc)
1960—U.S.S.R. (L. Geyshter, S. Makarenko)

1964—U.S.S.R. (A. Khimich, S. Oschepkov)
1968—Romania (Patzaichin, Covallov)
1972—U.S.S.R. (V. Chessyunas, Y. Lobanov)
1976—U.S.S.R. (Petrenko, Vinogradov)
1980—

CANADIAN PAIRS 10,000 METERS

1936—Czechoslovakia (V. Mottle, Z. Skrdlant)
1948—U.S.A. (S. Lysak, S. Macknowski)
1952—France (G. Turlier, J. Laudet)
1956—U.S.S.R. (P. Kharine, G. Botev)

1960—None
1972—None
1976—None

KAYAK FOURS

1968—Norway (Amundsen, Berger, Soby, Johansen)
1972—U.S.S.R. (Filatov, Stezenko, Morozov, Didenko)
1976—U.S.S.R. (Chuhray, Degtiarev, Filatov, Morozov)
1980—

315

1924—Canada	1956—U.S.S.R.	1968—Hungary
1936—Austria	1960—Hungary	1972—U.S.S.R.
1948—Sweden	1964—Sweden	1976—U.S.S.R.
1952—Finland		

Added events in men's canoeing added at end of active appendix

CANOEING (WOMEN)

KAYAK SINGLES 500 METERS

1948—K. Hoff, Denmark	1964—L. Khvedosink, U.S.S.R.
1952—Sylvia Saimo, Finland	1968—Ludmilla Pinaeva, U.S.S.R.
1956—Elisavota Dementieva, U.S.S.R.	1972—Y. Ryabchinskaya, U.S.S.R.
1960—A. Seredina, U.S.S.R.	1976—Carola Zirzow, East Germany
	1980—

KAYAK PAIRS 500 METERS

1960—U.S.S.R. (M. Shabina, A. Seredina)	1972—U.S.S.R. (L. Pinaeva, E. Kuryshko)
1964—W. Germany (R. Esser, A. Zimmermann)	1976— U.S.S.R. (Popova, Kreft)
1968—W. Germany (R. Esser, A. Zimmermann)	1980—

CYCLING

ROAD RACE (INDIVIDUAL)

1896—Konstantinidis, Greece	1948—J. Bayaert, France
1906—Vast and Bardonneau (tie), France	1952—Andrae Noyelle, Belgium
1912—R. Lewis, South Africa	1956—Ercole Baldini, Italy
1920—H. Stenquist, Sweden	1960—V. Kapitonov, U.S.S.R.
1924—A. Blanchonnet, France	1964—M. Zanin, Italy
1928—H. Hansen, Denmark	1968—P. Vianelli, Italy
1932—Attilio Pavesl, Italy	1972—H. Kuiper, Netherlands
1936—R. Charpentier, France	1976—B. Johansson, Sweden
	1980—

ROAD RACE (TEAM)

1912—Sweden	1936—France	1964—Netherlands
1920—France	1948—Belgium	1968—Netherlands
1924—France	1952—Belgium	1972—U.S.S.R.
1928—Denmark	1956—France	1976—U.S.S.R.
1932—Italy	1960—Italy	1980—

1,000-METER SCRATCH

1896—Emile Masson, France (2,000 meters)	1936—Toni Merkens, Germany
1900—Tallendier, France	1948—Mario Ghella, Italy (920 meters)
1906—Francesco Verri, Italy	1952—Enzo Sacchi, Italy
1908—Void, time limit exceeded	1956—Michel Rousseau, France
1920—Maurice Peeters, Netherlands	1960—S. Gaiardoni, Italy
1924—Lucien Michard, France	1964—G. Pattenella, Italy
1928—R. Beaufrand, France	1968—D. Morelon, France
1932—Jacobus van Edmond, Netherlands	1972—D. Morelon, France
	1976—Anton Tkac, Czechoslovakia
	1980—

1,000-METER TIME TRIAL

1928—W. Falck-Hansen, Denmark	1960—S. Gaiardoni, Italy
1932—E. L. Gray, Australia	1964—Patrick Sercu, Belgium
1936—Arie Gerrit van Vliet, Netherlands	1968—P. Trentin, France
1948—J. Dupont, France	1972—Niels Fredborg, Denmark
1952—Russell Mockridge, Australia	1976—Klaus-Jürgen Grunke, East Germany
1956—Leondro Faggin, Italy	1980—

2,000-METER TANDEM

1906—Great Britain (Matthews, Rushen)
1908—France (Schilles, Auffray)
1920—Great Britain (Ryan, Lance)
1924—France (Choury, Cugnot)
1928—Netherlands (Leene, van Dijk)
1932—France (Perrin, Chaillot)
1936—Germany (Ihbe, Lorenz)
1948—Italy (Teruzzi, Perona)
1952—Australia (Cox, Mockridge)
1956—Australia (Brown, Marchant)
1960—Italy (Beghetto, Bianchetto)
1964—Italy (A. Damiano, S. Bianchetto)
1968—France (D. Morelon, P. Trentin)
1972—U.S.S.R. (Y. Sements, I. Tselovalnikov)
1976—None
1980—

4,000-METER PURSUIT (INDIVIDUAL)

1964—J. Daler, Czechoslovakia
1968—D. Rebillard, France
1972—Knut Knudsen, Norway
1976—Gregor Braun, West Germany
1980—

4,000-METER PURSUIT (TEAM)

1908—Great Britain
  (1,980 yards)
1920—Italy
1924—Italy
1928—Italy
1932—Italy
1936—France
1948—France
1952—Italy
1956—Italy
1960—Italy
1964—Germany
1968—Denmark
1972—West Germany
1976—West Germany
1980—

(UNOFFICIAL) TEAM CHAMPIONS

1896—France
1900—France
1904—None
1906—Great Britain
1908—Great Britain
1912—Sweden
1920—Great Britain
1924—France
1928—Netherlands
1932—Italy
1936—France
1948—France
1952—Italy
1956—Italy
1960—Italy
1964—Italy
1968—France
1972—U.S.S.R.
1976—West Germany
1980—

EQUESTRIAN EVENTS

3-DAY EVENT (INDIVIDUAL)

1912—Lt. A. Nordlander, Sweden
1920—Lt. H. Morner, Sweden
1924—A. D. C. Van Der Voort Van Zijp,
  Netherlands
1928—Lt. C. F. Pahud de Mortanges,
  Netherlands
1932—Lt. C. F. Pahud de Mortanges,
  Netherlands
1936—Ludwig Stubbendorff, Germany
1948—Capt. B. Chevallier, France
1952—Hans von Blixen-Finecke, Sweden
1956—Lt. Petrus Kastenman, Sweden
1960—L. R. Morgan, Australia
1964—M. Checcoli, Italy
1968—J. J. Guyon, France
1972—Richard Meade, Great Britain
1976—Edmund Coffin, U.S.A.
1980—

3-DAY EVENT (TEAM)

1912—Sweden (Nordlander, Aldercreutz, Casparsson)
1920—Sweden (H. Morner, Lundstrom, von Braun)
1924—Netherlands (van Zijp, de Mortanges, G. P. De Kruyff)
1928—Netherlands (de Mortanges, G. P. De Kruyff, van Zijp)
1932—U.S.A. (Earl Thomson, Edwin Argo, Harry Chamberlin)
1936—Germany (Ludwig Stubbendorff, Rudolph Lippert, Konrad Freiherr von Wangenheim)
1948—U.S.A. (F. S. Henry, C. H. Anderson, Earl Thomson)
1952—Sweden (von Blixen-Finecke, Stahre, Frolen)
1956—Great Britain (Lt. Col. F. Weldon, Arthur Rook, Albert Hill)
1960—Australia (L. Morgan, N. Lavis, W. Roycroft)
1964—Italy (M. Checcoli, P. Angioni, G. Ravano)
1968—Great Britain (D. Allhusen, R. Meade, R. Jones)
1972—Great Britain (R. Meade, G. Watson, J. Parker)
1976—U.S.A. (Coffin, Plumb, Davidson, Tauskey)
1980—

317

DRESSAGE (INDIVIDUAL)

1912—Capt. C. Bonde, Sweden
1920—Capt. Lundblad, Sweden
1924—E. V. Linder, Sweden
1928—C. F. von Langen, Germany
1932—F. Lesage, France
1936—H. Pollay, Germany
1948—Capt. H. Moser, Switzerland

1952—Major Henri St. Cyr, Sweden
1956—Major Henri St. Cyr, Sweden
1960—S. Filatov, U.S.S.R.
1964—H. Chammartin, Switzerland
1968—Ivan Kozomov, U.S.S.R.
1972—L. Linsenhoff, West Germany
1976—C. Stueckelberger, Switzerland
1980—

DRESSAGE (TEAM)

1928—Germany (Von Langen, Linkenback, Von Lotzbeck)
1932—France (Lesage, Marion, Jousseaume)
1936—Germany (Pollay, Gerhard, Von Oppein-Bronikowski)
1948—France (Jousseaume, Paillard, Buret)
1952—Sweden (St. Cyr, G. Persson, G. Boltenstern)
1956—Sweden (St. Cyr, G. Persson, G. Boltenstern)
1960—None
1964—Germany (H. Boldt, R. Klimke, J. Neckermann)
1968—West Germany (R. Klimke, J. Neckermann, L. Linsenhoff)
1972—U.S.S.R. (E. Petushkova, I. Kizimov I. Kalita)
1976—West Germany (Boldt, Klimke, Grillo)
1980—

PRIX DES NATIONS (INDIVIDUAL)

1912—Capt. J. Cariou, France, 186 points
1920—Lt. Lequio, Italy, 2 faults
1924—Lt. Gemuseus, Switzerland, 6 faults
1928—F. Ventura, Czechoslovakia, no faults
1932—Takeichi Nishi, Japan, 8 faults
1936—Kurt Hasse, Germany, 4 faults
1948—Col. H. Mariles, Mexico, 6¼ faults

1952—Pierre d'Oriola, France, 8 faults
1956—Hans Winkler, Germany, 4 faults
1960—R. D'Inzeo, Italy, 12 faults
1964—Pierre d'Oriola, France, 9 faults
1968—W. Steinkrauss, U.S.A., 4 faults
1972—G. Mancinelli, Italy, 8 faults
1976—A. Schockemoehle, West Germany
1980—

PRIX DES NATIONS (TEAM)

1912—Sweden (Lewenhaupt, Kilman, von Rosen), 545 points
1920—Sweden (von Rosen, Koenig, Norling), 14 faults
1924—Sweden (Theining, Stahle, Lundstrom), 42.25 faults
1928—Spain (de los Truxillos, Morenes, Fernandez), 4 faults
1932—All teams participating disqualified
1936—Germany (v. Barnekow, Hasse, Brandt), 44 faults
1948—Mexico (H. Mariles, Uriza, Valdes), 34.25 faults
1952—Great Britain (D. N. Stewart, W. W. White, H. M. Llewellyn), 40.75 faults
1956—Germany (H. Winkler, A. Lutke-Westhues, F. Thiedemann), 40 faults
1960—Germany (A. Schocke Mohle, F. Thiedemann, H. Winkler), 46.5 faults
1964—Germany (H. Schridde, K. Jarasinski, H. Winkler), 68.5 faults
1968—Canada (T. Gayford, J. Day, J. Elder), 39.5 faults
1972—West Germany (F. Ligges, H. Steenken, G. Wiltfang, H. G. Winkler), 32 faults
1976—France (Parot, Roquet, Rozier, Roche), 40 faults
1980—

(UNOFFICIAL) TEAM CHAMPIONS

1912—Sweden
1920—Sweden
1924—Sweden
1928—Netherlands
1932—United States

1936—Germany
1948—United States
1952—Sweden
1956—Germany
1960—Australia

1964—Germany
1968—West Germany
1972—West Germany
1976—West Germany
1980—

FENCING (MEN)

FOIL (INDIVIDUAL)

1896—E. Gravelotte, France
1900—E. Coste, France
1904—Ramon Fonst, Cuba
1906—Dillon-Cavanagh, France
1912—Nedo Nadi, Italy
1920—Nedo Nadi, Italy
1924—Roger Ducret, France
1928—Lucien Gaudin, France
1932—Gustavo Marzi, Italy

1936—Giulio Gaudini, Italy
1948—Jean Buhan, France
1952—Christian d'Oriola, France
1956—Christian d'Oriola, France
1960—V. Zhdanovich, U.S.S.R.
1964—Egon Franke, Poland
1968—Ian Drimbu, Romania
1972—Witold Wevda, Poland
1980— 1976—Fabio Dal Zotto, Italy

318

FOIL (TEAM)

1904—Cuba	1936—Italy	1964—U.S.S.R.
1920—Italy	1948—France	1968—France
1924—France	1952—France	1972—Poland
1928—Italy	1956—Italy	1976—West Germany
1932—France	1960—U.S.S.R.	1980—

EPEE (INDIVIDUAL)

1896—E. Gravelotte, France	1936—Franco Riccardi, Italy
1900—Ramon Fonst, Cuba	1948—Luigi Cantone, Italy
1904—Ramon Fonst, Cuba	1952—Eduardo Mangiarotti, Italy
1906—Comte de la Falaise, France	1956—Carlo Pavesi, Italy
1908—G. Alibert, France	1960—G. Delfino, Italy
1912—Paul Anspach, Belgium	1964—Grigory Kriss, U.S.S.R.
1920—A. Massard, France	1968—Gyozo Kulcsa, Hungry
1924—C. Delporte, Belgium	1972—C. Fenyvesi, Hungary
1928—Lucien Gaudin, France	1976—A. Pusch, West Germany
1932—G. Cornaggia-Medici, Italy	1980—

EPEE (TEAM)

1906—France	1932—France	1964—Hungary
1908—France	1936—Italy	1968—Hungary
1912—Belgium	1948—France	1972—Hungary
1920—Italy	1952—Italy	1976—Sweden
1924—France	1956—Italy	1980—
1928—Italy	1960—Italy	

SABER (INDIVIDUAL)

1896—J. Georgiadis, Greece	1936—Endre Kabos, Hungary
1900—Comte de la Falaise, France	1948—Aladar Gerevich, Hungary
1904—M. de Diaz, Cuba	1952—P. Kovacs, Hungary
1906—J. Georgiadis, Greece	1956—Rudolf Karpati, Hungary
1908—E. Fuchs, Hungary	1960—Rudolf Karpati, Hungary
1912—E. Fuchs, Hungary	1964—Tibor Pezsa, Hungary
1920—Nedo Nadi, Italy	1968—J. Pawlowski, Poland
1924—Alexandre Posta, Hungary	1972—V. Sidiak, U.S.S.R.
1928—E. Tersctyanszky, Hungary	1976—V. Krovopuskov, U.S.S.R.
1932—George Piller, Hungary	1980—

SABER (TEAM)

1906—Germany	1932—Hungary	1964—U.S.S.R.
1908—Hungary	1936—Hungary	1968—U.S.S.R.
1912—Hungary	1948—Hungary	1972—Italy
1920—Italy	1952—Hungary	1976—U.S.S.R.
1924—Italy	1956—Hungary	1980—
1928—Hungary	1960—Hungary	

(UNOFFICIAL) TEAM CHAMPIONS

1896—France	1924—France	1960—U.S.S.R.
1900—France	1928—France	1964—U.S.S.R.
1904—Cuba	1932—Italy	1968—U.S.S.R.
1906—France	1936—Italy	1972—Hungary
1908—France	1948—Italy*	1976—U.S.S.R.
1912—Hungary	1952—Italy	1980—
1920—Italy	1956—Italy	

*French claim victory but 1 point behind according to usual scoring system.

FENCING (WOMEN)

FOIL (INDIVIDUAL)

1924—E. O. Osller, Denmark
1928—Helene Mayer, Germany
1932—Elen Preis, Austria
1936—Ilona Elek, Hungary
1948—Ilona Elek, Hungary
1952—Irene Camber, Italy

1956—Gillian Scheen, Great Britain
1960—A. Schmid, Germany
1964—Ujalki Rejto, Hungary
1968—E. Norikova, U.S.S.R.
1972—A. Ragno Lonzi, Italy
1976—B. Schwarczenberger, Hungary
1980—

FOIL (TEAM)

1960—U.S.S.R.
1964—Hungary

1968—U.S.S.R.
1972—U.S.S.R.

1976—U.S.S.R.
1980—

GYMNASTICS (MEN)

FLYING RINGS

1896—Mitropoulos, Greece
1904—Herman T. Glass, U.S.A.
1924—F. Martino, Italy
1928—L. Stukelj, Yugoslavia
1932—George Gulack, U.S.A.
1936—A. Hudec, Czechoslovakia
1948—K. Frei, Switzerland

1952—G. Chaguinian, U.S.S.R.
1956—Albert Azarian, U.S.S.R.
1960—Albert Azarian, U.S.S.R.
1964—Albert Azarian, U.S.S.R.
1968—A. Nagayama, Japan
1972—A. Nagayama, Japan
1976—N. Andrianov, U.S.S.R.
1980—

LONG-HORSE VAULTS

1896—Karl Schumann, Germany
1904—Anton Heida, U.S.A.
    George Eyser, U.S.A. (tie)
1924—Frank Kriz, U.S.A.
1928—E. Mack, Switzerland
1932—S. Guglielmetti, Italy
1936—K. Schwarzmann, Germany
1948—P. J. Aaltonen, Finland
1952—V. Tchoukarine, U.S.S.R.

1956—Helmuth Bantz, Germany
    Valentine Mouratov, U.S.S.R. (tie)
1960—B. Shaklin, U.S.S.R.
    Takashi Ono, Japan (tie)
1964—H. Yamashita, Japan
1968—M. Voronin, U.S.S.R.
1972—K. Koeste, East Germany
1976—N. Andrianov, U.S.S.R.
1980—

ALL-AROUND (INDIVIDUAL)

1900—Sandras, France
1904—Anton Heida, U.S.A.
1906—Payssee, France
1908—Alberto Braglia, Italy
1912—Alberto Braglia, Italy
1920—G. Zampori, Italy
1924—L. Stukely, Yugoslavia
1928—G. Melz, Switzerland
1932—Romeo Neri, Italy

1936—K. Schwarzmann, Germany
1948—V. Huhtanen, Finland
1952—V. Tchoukarine, U.S.S.R.
1956—V. Tchoukarine, U.S.S.R.
1960—B. Shaklin, U.S.S.R.
1964—Yukio Endo, Japan
1968—Sawao Kato, Japan
1972—Sawao Kato, Japan
1976—N. Andrianov, U.S.S.R.
1980—

ALL-AROUND (TEAM)

1896—Germany
1904—United States
1906—Norway
1908—Sweden
1920—Italy
1924—Italy

1928—Switzerland
1932—Italy
1936—Germany
1948—Finland
1952—U.S.S.R.
1956—U.S.S.R.

1960—Japan
1964—Japan
1968—Japan
1972—Japan
1976—Japan
1980—

SIDE HORSE

1896—Zutter, Switzerland
1904—Anton Heida, U.S.A.
1924—J. Wilhelm, Switzerland
1928—H. Hanggi, Switzerland
1932—Stephen Pelle, Hungary
1936—Konrad Frey, Germany
1948—P. J. Aaltonen, Finland
1952—V. Tchoukarine, U.S.S.R.

1956—Boris Chakhline, U.S.S.R.
1960—B. Shaklin, U.S.S.R.
    E. Ekman, Finland (tie)
1964—M. Cerar, Yugoslavia
1968—M. Cerar, Yugoslavia
1972—V. Klimenko, U.S.S.R.
1976—Zoltan Magyar, Hungary
1980—

HORIZONTAL BAR

1896—H. Weingartner, Germany
1904—Anton Heida, U.S.A.
    E. A. Hennig, U.S.A. (tie)
1924—L. Stukely, Yugoslavia
1928—George Miez, Switzerland
1932—Dallas Bixler, U.S.A.
1936—A. Saarvala, Finland
1948—Josef Stalder, Switzerland

1952—J. Gunthard, Switzerland
1956—Takashi Ono, Japan
1960—Takashi Ono, Japan
1964—M. Cerar, Yugoslavia
1968—M. Voronin, U.S.S.R.
1972—M. Tsukahara, Japan
1976—M. Tsukahara, Japan
1980—

PARALLEL BARS

1896—Alfred Flatow, Germany
1904—George Eyser, U.S.A.
1924—A. Guttinger, Switzerland
1928—L. Vacha, Czechoslovakia
1932—Romeo Neri, Italy
1936—Konrad Frey, Germany
1948—M. Reusch, Switzerland

1952—Hans Eugstar, Switzerland
1956—V. Tchoukarine, U.S.S.R.
1960—B. Shaklin, U.S.S.R.
1964—Yukio Endo, Japan
1968—A. Nakayama, Japan
1972—Sawao Kato, Japan
1976—Sawao Kato, Japan
1980—

FREE EXERCISES

1932—Stephen Pelle, Hungary
1936—George Meiz, Switzerland
1948—F. Putaki, Hungary
1952—Karl Thoresson, Sweden
1956—Valentine Mouratov, U.S.S.R.

1960—Nobuyuki Aihara, Japan
1964—Franco Menichelli, Italy
1968—Sawao Kato, Japan
1972—Sawao Kato, Japan
1976—N. Andrianov, U.S.S.R.
1980—

(UNOFFICIAL) TEAM CHAMPIONS

1896—Germany
1900—France
1904—United States
1906—France
1908—Italy
1912—Sweden
1920—Italy

1924—Italy
1928—Switzerland
1932—United States
1936—Germany
1948—Switzerland
1952—U.S.S.R.
1956—U.S.S.R.

1960—Japan
1964—Japan
1968—Japan
1972—Japan
1976—Japan
1980—

GYMNASTICS (WOMEN)

ALL-AROUND (INDIVIDUAL)

	Points		Points
1952—M. Gorokhovskaja, U.S.S.R.	76.78	1968—V. Caslavska, Czechoslovakia	78.2
1956—L. Latynina, U.S.S.R.	74.931	1972—L. Tourischeva, U.S.S.R.	77.025
1960—L. Latynina, U.S.S.R.	77.031	1976—N. Comaneci, Romania	79.275
1964—V. Caslavska, Czechoslovakia	77.56	1980—	

ALL-AROUND (TEAM)

	Points		Points
1928—Netherlands	316.75	1960—U.S.S.R.	382.320
1936—Germany	506.50	1964—U.S.S.R.	363.20
1948—Czechoslovakia	445.45	1968—U.S.S.R.	382.85
1952—U.S.S.R.	528.46	1972—U.S.S.R.	380.50
1956—U.S.S.R.	444.80	1976—U.S.S.R.	390.35
		1980—	

BEAM

	Points		Points
1952—N. Botcharova, U.S.S.R.	19.22	1968—N. Kuchinskaya, U.S.S.R.	19.60
1956—A. Keleti, Hungary	18.800	1972—O. Korbut, U.S.S.R.	19.4
1960—E. Bosakova, Czechoslovakia	19.283	1976—N. Comaneci, Romania	19.95
1964—V. Caslavska, Czechoslovakia	19.499	1980—	

FLOOR EXERCISE

	Points		Points
1952—A. Keleti, Hungary	19.36	1964—L. Latynina, U.S.S.R.	19.599
1956—A. Keleti, Hungary	18.732	1968—V. Caslavska, Czechoslovakia	19.675
L. Latynina, U.S.S.R. (tie)		1972—O. Korbut. U.S.S.R.	19.575
1960—L. Latynina, U.S.S.R.	19.583	1976—N. Kim, U.S.S.R.	19.850
		1980—	

LONG-HORSE VAULT

	Points		Points
1952—E. Kalinthouk, U.S.S.R.	19.20	1968—V. Caslavska, Czechoslovakia	19.55
1956—L. Latynina, U.S.S.R.	18.883	1972—K. Janz, East Germany	19.525
1960—M. Nikolaeva, U.S.S.R.	19.316	1976—N. Kim, U.S.S.R.	19.80
1964—V. Caslavska, Czechoslovakia	19.483	1980—	

PARALLEL BARS

	Points		Points
1952—Margit Korondi, Hungary	19.40	1968—V. Caslavska, Czechoslovakia	19.650
1956—A. Keleti, Hungary	18.966	1972—K. Janz, East Germany	19.675
1960—P. Astakhova, U.S.S.R.	19.616	1976—N. Comaneci, Romania	
1964—P. Astakhova, U.S.S.R.	19.332	1980—	

TEAM DRILL

	Points				
1952—Sweden	74.20	1960—None		1972—None	
1956—Hungary	75.2	1964—None		1976—None	

MODERN (MILITARY) PENTATHLON

INDIVIDUAL

1912—G. Lilliehook, Sweden	1952—Lars Hall, Sweden
1920—J. Dryssen, Sweden	1956—Lars Hall, Sweden
1924—O. Lindman, Sweden	1960—F. Nemeth, Hungary
1928—S. A. Thofelt, Sweden	1964—F. Torok, Hungary
1932—J. G. Oxenstierna, Sweden	1968—Bjorn Ferm, Sweden
1936—G. Handrick, Germany	1972—Andras Balczo, Hungary
1948—W. Grut, Sweden	1976—J. Pyciak-Peciak, Poland
	1980—

TEAM

1912—Sweden	1936—Germany	1964—U.S.S.R.
1920—Sweden	1948—Finland	1968—Hungary
1924—Sweden	1952*—Hungary	1972—U.S.S.R.
1928—Sweden	1956—U.S.S.R.	1976—Great Britain
1932—Sweden	1960—Hungary	1980—

ROWING AND SCULLING

SINGLE SCULLS

1900—H. Barralet, France	7:35.6	1948—Mervyn T. Wood, Australia	7:24.4
1904—Frank B. Greer, U.S.A.	—	1952—Yuri Tyukalov, U.S.S.R.	8:12.8
1908—H. T. Blackstaffe, Gr. Brit.	—	1956—Vyacheslav Ivanov, U.S.S.R.	8:02.5
1912—W. D. Kinnear, Gr. Brit.	7:47.6	1960—Vyacheslav Ivanov, U.S.S.R.	7:13.96
1920—John B. Kelly, U.S.A.	7:35	1964—Vyacheslav Ivanov, U.S.S.R.	8:22.51
1924—J. Beresford Jr., Gr. Brit.	7:49.2	1968—Jan Wienese, Netherlands	7:47.8
1928—Henry R. Pearce, Australia	7:11	1972—Yuri Malishev, U.S.S.R.	7:10.12
1932—Henry R. Pearce, Australia	7:44.4	1976—P. Karppinen, Finland	7:29.03
1936—Gustav Schaefer, Germany	8:21.5	1980—	

*Became official team affair with official scoring system.

DOUBLE SCULLS

1904—United States (Atlanta Boat
    Club)_____ ————
1920—John B. Kelly, Paul V.
    Costello, U.S.A._____ 7:09
1924—John B. Kelly, Paul V.
    Costello, U.S.A._____ 6:34
1928—Paul V. Costello, Charles J.
    McIlwaine, U.S.A._____ 6:41.4
1932—Kenneth Myers, W. E. Garrett
    Gilmore, U.S.A._____ 7:17.4
1936—J. Beresford, Leslie
    Southwood, Gr. Britain____ 7:20.8
1948—B. H. Bushnell, R. D. Burnell,
    Gr. Britain_____ 6:51.3

1952—T. Cappozza, E. Guerrero,
    Argentina_____ 7:32.2
1956—A. Berkoutov, T. Tivkalov,
    U.S.S.R._____ 7:24
1960—V. Kozak, P. Schmidt,
    Czechoslovakia_____ 6:47.50
1964—O Tyurin, B. Dubrovsky,
    U.S.S.R._____ 7:10.66
1968—Sass, Timoshinin, U.S.S.R.____ 6:51.82
1972—Timoshinin, Korshikov,
    U.S.S.R._____ 7:01.77
1976—F. Hansen, A. Hansen,
    Norway _____ 7:13.20

1980—

PAIR-OARED SHELL WITH COXSWAIN

1900—R. Klein, F. A. Brandt,
    Netherlands_____ 7:34.2
1906—Italy (1,600 meters) _____ ————
1908—Italy (1,000 meters) _____ ————
1920—M. Olgeni, G. Scatturin, Italy__ 7:56
1924—E. Candeveau, A. Felber, E.
    Lachapelle, Switzerland____ 8:39
1928—H. Schochlin, C. Schochlin, H.
    Bourquin, Switzerland_____ 7:42.6
1932—J. A. Schauers, C. Kieffer, E.
    Jennings, U.S.A._____ 8:25.8
1936—G. Gustmann, H. Adamski, D.
    Arend, Germany_____ 8:36.9
1948—F. Pedersen, T. Henriksen, C.
    Andersen, Denmark_____ 8:00.5

1952—R. Salles, G. Mercier, B.
    Malivoire, France_____ 8:28.6
1956—A. Ayrault, C. Findlay, K.
    Seiffert, U.S.A._____ 8:26.1
1960—B. Knubel, H. Runneberg, K.
    Zerta, Germany_____ 7:29.14
1964—E. Ferry, C. Findlay, K.
    Mitchell, U.S.A._____ 8:21.33
1968—Baron, Sambo, Cipolla, Italy__ 8:04.81
1972—Gunkel, Lucke, Neubert, East
    Germany_____ 7:17.25
1976—Jahrling, Ulrich, Spohr,
    East Germany_____ 7:58.99

1980—

PAIR-OARED SHELL WITHOUT COXSWAIN

1900—Van Crambuge, DeSonville,
    Belgium_____ ————
1904—United States, Sewanhaka
    Boat Club_____ 10:57
1908—J. Fenning, G. Thompson, Gr.
    Britain_____ 8:41
1920—E. Olgeni, G. Scatturin, Italy__ 7:56.0
1924—W. H. Rosingh, A. C. Beynen,
    Netherlands_____ 8:19.4
1928—K. Moeschter, B. Muller,
    Germany_____ 7:06.4
1932—Lewis Clive, H. R. Arthur
    Edwards, Gr. Britain_____ 8:00
1936—Willi Eichhorn, H. Strauss,
    Germany_____ 8:16.1

1948—J. H. T. Wilson, W. G. R. M.
    Laurie, Gr. Britain_____ 7:21.1
1952—Charles Logg Jr., Thomas
    Price, U.S.A._____ 8:20.7
1956—James Fifer, Duvall Hecht,
    U.S.A._____ 7:55.4
1960—V. Boreiko, O. Golovanov,
    U.S.S.R._____ 7:02.01
1964—G. Hungerford, R. C. Jackson,
    Canada_____ 7:32.94
1968—Lucke, Bothe, East Germany__ 7:26.56
1972—Brietzke, Mager, East
    Germany_____ 6:53.16
1976—J. Landvoigt, B. Land-
    voigt, East Germany_____ 7:23.31

1980—

4-OARED SHELL WITH COXSWAIN

1900—Germany_____ 5:59.0
1906—Italy_____ 7:05.6
1912—Germany_____ 6:59.4
1920—Switzerland_____ 6:54
1924—Switzerland_____ 7:18.4
1928—Italy_____ 6:47.8
1932—Germany_____ 7:19.2
1936—Germany_____ 7:16.2

1948—United States_____ 6:50.3
1952—Czechoslovakia_____ 7:33.4
1956—Italy_____ 7:19.4
1960—Germany_____ 6:39.12
1964—West Germany_____ 7:00.44
1968—New Zealand_____ 6:45.62
1972—West Germany_____ 6:31.85
1976—U.S.S.R. _____ 6.40.22

1980—

4-OARED SHELL WITHOUT COXSWAIN

1900—France	7:11.0		1952—Yugoslavia	7:16
1904—United States	9:53.8		1956—Canada	7:08.8
1908—Great Britain	8:34.0		1960—United States	6:26.26
1924—Great Britain	7:08.6		1964—Denmark	6:59.30
1928—Great Britain	6:36.0		1968—East Germany	6:39.18
1932—Great Britain	6:58.2		1972—East Germany	6:24.27
1936—Germany	7:01.8		1976—East Germany	6:37.42
1948—Italy	6:39		1980—	

8-OARED SHELL

1900—United States, Vespers Boat Club	6:07.8		1936—United States, University of Washington	6:25.4
1904—United States, Vespers Boat Club	———		1948—United States, University of California	5:56.7
1908—Great Britain, Leander Club	———		1952—United States, Navy	6:25.9
1912—Great Britain, Leander Club	6:15		1956—United States, Yale	6:35.2
1920—United States, Navy	6:02.6		1960—Germany	5:57.18
1924—United States, Yale	6:33.4		1964—United States	6:25.4
1928—United States, University of California	6:03.2		1968—West Germany	6:07.0
			1972—New Zealand	6:08.94
1932—United States, University of California	6:37.4		1976—East Germany	5:58.29
			1980—	

(UNOFFICIAL) TEAM CHAMPIONS

1900—France	1924—United States	1956—United States
1904—United States	1928—United States	1960—Germany
1906—Italy	1932—United States	1964—United States
1908—Great Britain	1936—Germany	1968—E. Germany
1912—Great Britain	1948—Italy	1972—E. Germany
1920—United States	1952—United States	1976—East Germany
	1980—	

SHOOTING

FREE RIFLE 50 METERS

1908—A. A. Carnell, Great Britain	1952—Anatoli Bogdanov, U.S.S.R.
1912—F. S. Hird, United States	1956—V. Borissov, U.S.S.R.
1920—L. Nusslein, United States	1960—H. Hammerer, Austria
1924—Charles deLisle, France	1964—G. L. Anderson, United States
1932—Bertil Ronnmark, Sweden	1968—G. L. Anderson, United States
1936—Willy Rogeberg, Norway	1972—L. Wigger, United States
1948—Arthur Cook, United States	1976—K. Smieszek, West Germany
	1980—

ANY TARGET PISTOL 50 METERS

1896—S. Paine, United States	1952—Huelet Benner, United States
1900—Roedern, Switzerland	1956—Pentti Limnosuvo, Finland
1906—G. Orphanidis, Greece	1960—A. Gustchin, U.S.S.R.
1912—A. P. Lane, United States	1964—V. Markhanen, Finland
1920—Karl Frederick, United States	1968—G. Kosykh, U.S.S.R.
1936—Torsten Ullman, Sweden	1972—R. Skanaker, Sweden
1948—Cam E. Vasquez, Peru	1976—U. Potteck, East Germany
	1980—

RUNNING DEER

1900—L. Debret, France	1952—John Larsen, Norway
1908—O. Swahn, Sweden	1956—V. Romanenko, U.S.S.R.
1912—Alfred G. A. Swahn, Sweden	1960—None
1920—O. Olsen, Norway	1964—None
1924—J. K. Boles, United States	1968—None

324

CLAY BIRD (TRAP)

1900—R. de Barbarin, France
1906—Gerald Merlin, Great Britain (single
      shot)
1908—W. H. Ewing, Canada
1912—James R. Graham, United States
1920—M. Arie, United States
1924—Jules Halasy, Hungary

1952—George Genereux, Canada
1956—Galliano Rossini, Italy
1960—I. Domitrescu, Romania
1964—E. Mattarelli, Italy
1968—J. Braithwaite, Great Britain
1972—A. Scalzone, Italy
1976—D. Haldeman, U.S.A.
1980—

CLAY BIRD (SKEET)

1968—Y. Petrov, U.S.S.R.
1972—K. Wirnhier, West Germany

1976—J. Panacek, Czechoslovakia
      E. Swinkels, Netherlands (Tie)
1980—

SILHOUETTE PISTOL

1952—Karoly Takacs, Hungary
1956—Stevan Petrescu, Romania
1960—W. McMillan, United States
1964—P. Linnosvuo, Finland

1968—J. Zapedski, Poland
1972—J. Zapedski, Poland
1976—N. Klaar, East Germany
1980—

SMALL-BORE RIFLE (ALL-AROUND)

1952—Erling Kongshaug, Norway
1956—Anatoli Bagdanov, U.S.S.R.
1960—V. Shamburkin, U.S.S.R.
1964—Lones Wigger, United States

1968—B. Klingner, West Germany
1972—J. Writer, United States
1976—L. Bassham, U.S.A.
1980—

SMALL-BORE RIFLE (PRONE)

1952—Josef Sarbu, Romania
1956—Gerald Quellette, Canada
1960—P. Kohnke, Germany
1964—L. Hammerl, Hungary

1968—Jan Kurka, Czechoslovakia
1972—Ho Jun Li, North Korea
1976—A. Gazov, U.S.S.R.
1980—

(UNOFFICIAL) TEAM CHAMPIONS

1896—Greece
1900—France
1904—None
1906—France
1908—Great Britain
1912—Sweden
1920—United States

1924—United States
1928—United States
1932—Italy
1936—Germany
1948—Sweden
1952—Norway
1956—U.S.S.R.

1960—U.S.S.R.
1964—United States
1968—U.S.S.R.
1972—United States
1976—East Germany
1980—

SLALOM (MEN)

CANADIAN SINGLES

1972—Reinhard Eiben, East Germany   1976— None

KAYAK SINGLES

1972—Siegbert Horn, East Germany   1976— None

CANADIAN PAIRS

1972—East Germany (W. Hofmann, D. Amend)   1976— None

SLALOM (WOMEN)

KAYAK SINGLES

1972—A. Bahmann, East Germany   1976— None

SWIMMING AND DIVING (MEN)

100-METER FREESTYLE

1896—Alfred Hajos, Hungary	1:22.2	1936—Ferenc Czik, Hungary	0:57.6
1900—Jarvis, Great Britain	1:16.4	1948—Walter Ris, U.S.A.	0:57.3
1904—Z. de Holomay, Hungary	1:02.8†	1952—Clarke Scholes, U.S.A.	0:57.4
1906—Charles Daniels, U.S.A.	1:13.4	1956—John Hendricks, Australia	0:55.4
1908—Charles Daniels, U.S.A.	1:05.6	1960—J. Devitt, Australia	0:55.2
1912—D. P. Kahanamoku, U.S.A.	1:03.4	1964—Don Schollander, U.S.A.	0:53.4
1920—D. P. Kahanamoku, U.S.A.	1:01.4	1968—Mike Welden, Australia	0:52.2
1924—John Weissmuller, U.S.A.	0:59.0	1972—Mark Spitz, U.S.A.	0:51.22
1928—John Weissmuller, U.S.A.	0:58.6	1976—Jim Montgomery, U.S.A.	0:49.99*
1932—Y. Miyazaki, Japan	0:58.2	1980—	

World's Record: 1976—Jim Montgomery, U.S.A., Montreal _____ 0.49.99

200-METER FREESTYLE

1968—Mike Welden, Australia	1:55.2	1976— Bruce Furniss, U.S.A.	1:50.29*
1972—Mark Spitz, U.S.A.	1:52.78	1980—	

World's Record: Bruce Furniss, U.S.A., Montreal _____ 1:50.29

400-METER FREESTYLE

1900—Jarvis, Great Britain	—	1936—Jack Medica, U.S.A.	4:44.5
1904—Charles Daniels, U.S.A.	6:16.2‡	1948—Bill Smith, U.S.A.	4:41
1906—Otto Sheff, Australia	6:23.8‡	1952—Jean Boiteux, France	4:30.7
1908—H. Taylor, Great Britain	5:36.8	1956—Murray Rose, Australia	4:27.3
1912—G. R. Hodgson, Canada	5:24.4	1960—Murray Rose, Australia	4:18.3
1920—Norman Ross, U.S.A.	5:26.8	1964—Don Schollander, U.S.A.	4:12.2
1924—John Weissmuller, U.S.A.	5:04.2	1968—M. Burton, U.S.A.	4:09
1928—Albert Zorilla, Argentina	5:01.6	1972—B. Cooper, Australia	4:00.27
1932—Clarence Crabbe, U.S.A.	4:48.4	1976—B. Goodell, U.S.A.	3:51.93*
		1980—	

World's Record: 1976—B. Goodell, U.S.A., Montreal _____ 3:51.93

1,500-METER FREESTYLE

1908—H. Taylor, Great Britain	22:48.4	1952—Ford Konno, U.S.A.	18:30
1912—G. R. Hodgson, Canada	22:00	1956—Murray Rose, Australia	17:58.9
1920—Norman Ross, U.S.A.	22:23.2	1960—J. Konrads, Australia	17:19.6
1924—A. M. Charlton, Australia	20:06.6	1964—R. Windle, Australia	17:01.7
1928—Arne Borg, Sweden	19:51.8	1968—Mike Burton, U.S.A.	16:38.9
1932—K. Kitamura, Japan	19:12.4	1972—Mike Burton, U.S.A.	15:52.58
1936—Norboru Terada, Japan	19:13.7	1976—B. Goodell, U.S.A.	15.02.40*
1948—Jimmy McLane, U.S.A.	19:18.5	1980—	

World's Record: B. Goodell, U.S.A., Montreal _____ 15.02.40

400-METER FREESTYLE RELAY

1964—United States (S. Clark, M. Austin, G. Ilman, D. Schollander)	3:33.2	1972—United States (Stamm, Bruce, Spitz, Heidenreich)	3:26.42*
1968—United States (Walsh, Zorn, Rerych, Spitz)	3:31.7	1976— None	

World's Record: 1972—U.S. National Team (Stamm, Bruce, Spitz, Heidenreich), Munich 3:26.42

---

*Olympic Record.
†100 yards.
‡440 yards.

800-METER FREESTYLE RELAY

1908—Great Britain	10:55.6	1952—United States	8:31.1
1912—Australia	10:11.6	1956—Australia	8:23.6
1920—United States	10:04.4	1960—United States	8:10.2
1924—United States	9:53.4	1964—United States	7:52.1
1928—United States	9:36.2	1968—United States	7:52.3
1932—Japan	8:58.4	1972—United States	7:35.78
1936—Japan	8:51.5	1976—United States	7:23.22*
1948—United States	8:46	1980—	

World's Record: 1976—U.S. National Team (Bruner, Furniss, Naber, Montgomery), Montreal 7:23.22

100-METER BREASTSTROKE

1968—D. McKenzie, U.S.A.	1:07.7	1976—J. Hencken, U.S.A.	1:03.11*
1972—N. Taguchi, Japan	1:04.94	1980—	

World's Record: 1976—J. Hencken, U.S.A., Montreal 1:03.11

200-METER BREASTSTROKE

1908—F. Holman, Great Britain	3:09.2	1952—John Davies, Australia	2:34.4
1912—Walter Bathe, Germany	3:01.8	1956—Masura Furukawa, Japan	2:34.7
1920—H. Malmroth, Sweden	3:04.4	1960—W. Mulliken, U.S.A.	2:37.4
1924—R. D. Skelton, U.S.A.	2:56.6	1964—Ian O'Brien, Australia	2:27.8
1928—Y. Tsuruta, Japan	2:48.8	1968—Felipe Munoz, Mexico	2:28.7
1932—Y. Tsuruta, Japan	2:45.4	1972—J. Hencken, U.S.A.	2:21.55
1936—Detsuo Hamuro, Japan	2:42.5	1976—David Wilkie, Great Britain	2:15.11*
1948—Joe Verdeur, U.S.A.	2:39.3	1980—	

World's Record: 1976—David Wilkie, Great Britain, Montreal ---------------- 2:15.11

200-METER MEDLEY

1968—C. Hickcox, United States	2:12.0	1976— None	
1972—G. Larsson, Sweden	2:07.17*		

World's Record: 1974—David Wilkie, Great Britain, Vienna 2:06.32

400-METER MEDLEY

1964—R. Roth, United States	4:45.4	1972—G. Larsson, Sweden	4:31.98
1968—C. Hickcox, United States	4:84.4	1976—R. Strachan, U.S.A.	4:23.68*
		1980—	

World's Record: 1976—R. Strachan, U.S.A., Montreal 4:23.68

400-METER MEDLEY RELAY

1960—United States	4:05.4	1972—United States	3:48.16
1964—United States	3:58.4	1976—United States	3:42.22*
1968—United States	3:54.9	1980—	

World's Record: 1976—U.S. National Team (Naber, Hencken, Vogel, Montgomery), Montreal 3:42.22

100-METER BACKSTROKE

1904—Walter Brack, Germany	1:16.8†	1948—Allen Stack, U.S.A.	1:06.4
1908—A. Bieberstein, Germany	1:24.6	1952—Y. Oyakawa, U.S.A.	1:05.4
1912—Harry Hebner, U.S.A.	1:21.2	1956—David Thiele, Australia	1:02.2
1920—Warren Kealoha, U.S.A.	1:15.2	1960—D. Thiele, Australia	1:01.9
1924—Warren Kealoha, U.S.A.	1:13.2	1964—None	
1928—George Kojac, U.S.A.	1:08.2	1968—R. Mathes, East Germany	0:58.7
1932—M. Kiyokawa, Japan	1:08.6	1972—R. Mathes, East Germany	0:56.58
1936—Adolph Kiefer, U.S.A.	1:05.9	1976—John Naber, U.S.A.	0:55.49*
		1980—	

World's Record: 1976—John Nabor, U.S.A., Montreal 0:55.49

---

*Olympic Record.
†100 yards.

327

200-METER BACKSTROKE

1964—Ted Graef, U.S.A.	2:10.3	1972—R. Mathes, East Germany	2:02.82
1968—R. Mathes, East Germany	2:09.6	1976—John Naber, U.S.A.	1:59.19*
		1980—	

World's Record: 1976—John Nabor, U.S.A., Montreal _____ 1:59.19

100-METER BUTTERFLY STROKE

1968—D. Russell, U.S.A.	0:55.9	1976—Matt Vogel, U.S.A.	0:54.35
1972—Mark Spitz, U.S.A.	0:54.27*	1980—	

World's Record: 1972—Mark Spitz, U.S.A., Munich _____ 0:54.27

200-METER BUTTERFLY STROKE

1956—Bill Yorzyk, U.S.A.	2:19.3	1968—Carl Robie, U.S.A.	2:08.7
1960—M. Troy, U.S.A.	2:12.8	1972—Mark Spitz, U.S.A.	2:00.70
1964—Kevin Berry, Australia	2:06.6	1976—Mike Bruner, U.S.A.	1:59.23*
		1980—	

World's Record: 1976—Mike Bruner, U.S.A., Montreal _____ 1:59.23

SPRINGBOARD DIVE

	Points		Points
1904—G. E. Sheldon, U.S.A.	12⅔	1948—Bruce Harlan, U.S.A.	163.64
1906—G. Walz, Germany	156	1952—David Browning, U.S.A.	205.29
1908—A. Zurner, Germany	85½	1956—Bob Clotworthy, U.S.A.	159.56
1912—Paul Gunther, Germany	6	1960—G. Tobian, U.S.A.	170.00
1920—L. E. Kuehn, U.S.A.	6	1964—K. Sitzberger, U.S.A.	159.90
1924—A. C. White, U.S.A.	7	1968—B. Wrightson, U.S.A.	170.15
1928—Pete Desjardins, U.S.A.	185.04	1972—V. Vasin, U.S.S.R.	594.09
1932—Michael Galitzen, U.S.A.	161.38	1976—Phil Boggs	619.05
1936—Dick Degener, U.S.A.	163.57	1980—	

PLATFORM DIVE

	Points		Points
1928—Pete Desjardins, U.S.A.	98.74	1960—R. Webster, U.S.A.	165.56
1932—Harold Smith, U.S.A.	124.80	1964—R. Webster, U.S.A.	148.58
1936—Marshall Wayne, U.S.A.	113.58	1968—K. Dibiasi, Italy	164.18
1948—Sammy Lee, U.S.A.	130.05	1972—K. Dibiasi, Italy	504.12
1952—Sammy Lee, U.S.A.	156.28	1976—K. Dibiasi, Italy	600.51
1956—Joaquin Capilla, Mexico	152.44	1980—	

WATER POLO

1900—Great Britain	1928—Germany	1960—Italy
1904—United States	1932—Hungary	1964—Hungary
1908—Great Britain	1936—Hungary	1968—Yugoslavia
1912—Great Britain	1948—Italy	1972—U.S.S.R.
1920—Great Britain	1952—Hungary	1976—Hungary
1924—France	1956—Hungary	1980—

(UNOFFICIAL) TEAM CHAMPIONS

1896—Greece	1924—United States	1960—United States
1900—Great Britain	1928—United States	1964—United States
1904—United States	1932—Japan	1968—United States
1906—Great Britain	1936—United States	1972—United States
1908—Great Britain	1948—United States	1976—United States
1912—Germany	1952—United States	1980—
1920—United States	1956—Australia	

---

*Olympic Record.

SWIMMING AND DIVING (WOMEN)

100-METER FREESTYLE

1912—Fanny Durack, Australia	1:22.2		1952—Katakin Szoke, Hungary	1:06.8
1920—Ethelda Bleibtrey, U.S.A.	1:13.6		1956—Dawn Fraser, Australia	1:02
1924—Ethel Lackie, U.S.A.	1:12.4		1960—Dawn Fraser, Australia	1:01.2
1928—Albina Osipowich, U.S.A.	1:11		1964—Dawn Fraser, Australia	0:59.5
1932—Helene Madison, U.S.A.	1:06.8		1968—Jan Henne, U.S.A.	1:00.0
1936—Rika Mastenbroek,			1972—S. Neilson, U.S.A.	0:58.59
Netherlands	1:05.9		1976—K. Ender, East Germany	0.55.65*
1948—Greta Andersen, Denmark	1:06.3		1980—	

World's Record: 1976—K. Ender, East Germany, Montreal 0:55.65

200-METER FREESTYLE

1968—Debbie Meyer, U.S.A.	2:10.5		1976—K. Ender, East Germany	1:59.26*
1972—S. Gould, Australia	2:03.56*		1980—	

World's Record: 1976—K. Ender, East Germany, Montreal 1:59.26

400-METER FREESTYLE

1924—Martha Norelius, U.S.A.	6:02.2		1956—Lorraine Crapp, Australia	4:56.6
1928—Martha Norelius, U.S.A.	5:42.8		1960—S. von Saltza, U.S.A.	4:50.6
1932—Helene Madison, U.S.A.	5:28.5		1964—V. Duenkel, U.S.A.	4:43.3
1936—Rika Mastenbroek,			1968—D. Meyer, U.S.A.	4:31.8
Netherlands	5:26.4		1972—S. Gould, Australia	4:19.04
1948—Ann Curtis, U.S.A.	5:17.8		1976—P. Thuemer, East Germany	4:09.89*
1952—Valerie Gyenge, Hungary	5:12.1		1980—	

World's Record: 1976—P. Thuemer, East Germany, Montreal 4:09.89

800-METER FREESTYLE

1968—Debbie Meyer, U.S.A.	9:24.0		1976—P. Thuemer, East Germany	8:37.14
1972—K. Rothhammer, U.S.A.	8:53.68		1980—	

World's Record: 1976—P. Thuemer, East Germany, Montreal 8:37.14

400-METER RELAY FREESTYLE

1912—Great Britain	5:52.8		1952—Hungary	4:24.4
1920—United States	5:11.6		1956—Australia	4:17.1
1924—United States	4:58.8		1960—United States	4:08.9
1928—United States	4:47.3		1964—United States	4:03.8
1932—United States	4:38		1968—United States	4:02.5
1936—Netherlands	4:36		1972—United States	3:55.19
1948—United States	4:29.2		1976—United States	3:44.82*
			1980—	

World's Record: 1976—U.S. National Team (Peyton, Boglioli, Sterkel,
Babashoff) 3:44.82

100-METER BREASTSTROKE

1968—D. Bjedov, Yugoslavia	1:15.8		1976—H. Anke, East Germany	1:11.16
1972—C. Carr, U.S.A.	1:13.58		1980—	

World's Record: (Semi-final heat) 1976—H. Anke, East Germany, Montreal 1:10.86

*Olympic Record.

329

200-METER BREASTSTROKE

1924—Lucy Morton, Great Britain	3:33.2		1960—A. Lansbrough, Great Britain	2:49.5	
1928—Hilde Schrader, Germany	3:12.3		1964—G. Prozumenschikova,		
1932—Clare Dennis, Australia	3:06.3		U.S.S.R.	2:46.4	
1936—Hideko Maehata, Japan	3:03.6		1968—S. Wichman, U.S.A.	2:44.4	
1948—Nel van Vliet, Netherlands	2:57.2		1972—B. Whitfield, Australia	2:41.71	
1952—Eva Szekeley, Hungary	2:51.7		1976—M. Koshevaia, U.S.S.R.	2:33.35*	
1956—Ursula Happe, Germany	2:53.1		1980—		

World's Record: 1976—M. Koshevaia, U.S.S.R., Montreal _____ 2:33.35

100-METER BACKSTROKE

1924—Sybil Bauer, U.S.A.	1:23.2	1956—Judy Grinham, Great Britain	1:12.9	
1928—Marie Braun, Netherlands	1:22	1960—L. Burke, U.S.A.	1:09.3	
1932—Eleanor Holm, U.S.A.	1:19.4	1964—C. Ferguson, U.S.A.	1:07.7	
1936—Dina Senff, Netherlands	1:18.9	1968—Kay Hall, U.S.A.	1:06.2	
1948—Karen Harup, Denmark	1:14.4	1972—M. Belote, U.S.A.	1:05.78	
1952—Joan Harrison, South Africa	1:14.3	1976—U. Richter, East Germany	1:01.83*	
		1980—		

World's Record: 1976—Ulrike Richter, East Germany, Montreal _____ 1:01.83

200-METER BACKSTROKE

1968—Pokey Watson, U.S.A.	2:24.8	1976— U. Richter, East Germany	2:13.43*
1972—M. Belote, U.S.A.	2:19.19	1980—	

World's Record: 1976—Ulrike Richter, East Germany, Montreal _____ 2:13.43

100-METER BUTTERFLY STROKE

1956—Shelley Mann, U.S.A.	1:11	1968—L. McClements, Australia	1:05.5
1960—C. Schuler, U.S.A.	1:09.5	1972—M. Aoki, Japan	1:03.34
1964—S. Stouder, U.S.A.	1:04.7	1976—K. Ender, East Germany	1:00.13*
		1980—	

World's Record: 1976—K. Ender, East Germany, Montreal _____ 1:00.13

200-METER BUTTERFLY STROKE

1972—K. Moe, U.S.A.	2:15.57	1976— A. Pollack, East Germany	2:11.41*
		1980—	

World's Record: 1976—A. Pollack, East Germany, Montreal _____ 2:11.41

200-METER MEDLEY

1968—Claudia Kolb, U.S.A.	2:24.7	1976—None	
1972—S. Gould, Australia	2:23.07*	1980—	

World's Record: 1974—U. Tauber, East Germany, Vienna _____ 2:18.97

400-METER MEDLEY

1964—Donna de Varona, U.S.A.	5:18.7	1972—Gail Neall, Australia	5:02.97
1968—Claudia Kolb, U.S.A.	5:08.6	1976—U. Tauber, East Germany	4:42.77*
		1980—	

World's Record: 1976—U. Tauber, East Germany, Montreal _____ 4:42.77

400-METER MEDLEY RELAY

1960—United States	4:41.1	1972—United States	4:20.75
1964—United States	4:33.9	1976—East Germany	4:07.95*
1968—United States	4:28.3	1980—	

World's Record: 1976—East German National Team (Richter, Anke, Ender, Pollack), Montreal _____ 4:07.95

---

*Olympic Record.

330

PLATFORM DIVE

	Points		Points
1928—E. B. Pinkston, U.S.A.	31.60	1960—I. Kramer, Germany	91.28
1932—D. Poynton, U.S.A.	40.26	1964—L. Bush, U.S.A.	99.80
1936—D. Poynton, U.S.A.	33.93	1968—M. Duchkova, Czechoslovakia	109.59
1948—Vicky Draves, U.S.A.	68.87	1972—U. Knape, Sweden	390.0
1952—P. McCormick, U.S.A.	79.37	1976—E. Vaytsekhovskaia,	
1956—P. McCormick, U.S.A.	84.85	U.S.S.R.	406.59
1980—			

SPRINGBOARD DIVE

	Points		Points
1920—A. Riggin, U.S.A.	9	1956—P. McCormick, U.S.A.	142.36
1924—E. Becker, U.S.A.	8	1960—I. Kramer, Germany	139.09
1928—Helen Meany, U.S.A.	76.62	1964—I. Kramer, Germany	145.00
1932—G. Coleman, U.S.A.	87.52	1968—Sue Gossick, U.S.A.	150.77
1936—M. Gestring, U.S.A.	89.27	1972—Micki King, U.S.A.	450.03
1948—Vicky Draves, U.S.A.	108.74	1976—J. Chandler, U.S.A.	506.19
1952—P. McCormick, U.S.A.	147.30	1980—	

TEAM GAMES

SOCCER

1900—Great Britain	1924—Uruguay	1956--U.S.S.R.
1904—Great Britain	1928—Uruguay	1960—Yugoslavia
1906—Denmark	1932—None	1964—Hungary
1908—Great Britain	1936—Italy	1968—Hungary
1912—Great Britain	1948—Sweden	1972—Poland
1920—Belgium	1952—Hungary	1976—East Germany
	1980—	

BASKETBALL

1904—United States (demonstration)	1960—United States
1936—United States	1964—United States
1948—United States	1968—United States
1952—United States	1972—U.S.S.R.
1956—United States	1976—United States
	1980—

FIELD HOCKEY

1908—Great Britain	1948—India	1968—Pakistan
1920—Great Britain	1952—India	1972—West Germany
1928—India	1956—India	1976—New Zealand
1932—India	1960—Pakistan	1980—
1936—India	1964—India	

HANDBALL (MEN)

1972—Yugoslavia	1976—U.S.S.R.
	1980—

HANDBALL (WOMEN)

1976—U.S.S.R.
1980—

VOLLEYBALL (MEN)

1964—U.S.S.R.	1972—Japan
1968—U.S.S.R.	1976—Poland
	1980—

VOLLEYBALL (WOMEN)

1964—Japan	1972—U.S.S.R.
1968—U.S.S.R.	1976—Japan
	1980—

*Olympic Record.

331

TRACK AND FIELD (MEN)

100-METER DASH

1896--Thomas E. Burke, U.S.A.____ 0:12	1936—Jesse Owens, U.S.A._____ 0:10.3
1900—F. W. Jarvis, U.S.A._____ 0:10.8	1948—Harrison Dillard, U.S.A.____ 0:10.3
1904—Archie Hahn, U.S.A._____ 0:11	1952—Lindy Remigino, U.S.A._____ 0:10.4
1906—Archie Hahn, U.S.A._____ 0:11.2	1956—Bobby Morrow, U.S.A._____ 0:10.5
1908—Reggie Walker, South Africa_ 0:10.8	1960—A. Hary, Germany_____ 0:10.2
1912—Ralph C. Craig, U.S.A._____ 0:10.8	1964—Bob Hayes, U.S.A._____ 0:10.0
1920—Charles W. Paddock, U.S.A._ 0:10.8	1968—Jim Hines, U.S.A._____ 0:09.9*
1924—H. Abrahams, Great Britain__ 0:10.6	1972—Valery Borzov, U.S.S.R.____ 0:10.14
1928—Percy Williams, Canada_____ 0:10.8	1976—Hasely Crawford,_____0:10.06
1932—Eddie Tolan, U.S.A._____ 0:10.3	Trinidad

1980—

World's Record: 1968—Jim Hines, U.S.A., Mexico City_____0:09.9

200-METER DASH

1900—J. W. B. Tewksbury, U.S.A.__ 0:22.2	1948—Melvin E. Patton, U.S.A.____ 0:21.1
1904—Archie Hahn, U.S.A._____ 0:21.6	1952—Andy Stanfield, U.S.A._____ 0:20.7
1908—Bobby Kerr, Canada_____ 0:22.4	1956—Bobby Morrow, U.S.A._____ 0:20.6
1912—Ralph C. Craig, U.S.A._____ 0:21.7	1960—L. Berruti, Italy_____ 0:20.5
1920—Allan Woodring, U.S.A._____ 0:22	1964—Henry Carr, U.S.A._____ 0:20.3
1924—Jackson V. Scholz, U.S.A.__ 0:21.6	1968—Tommie Smith, U.S.A._____ 0:19.8*
1928—Percy Williams, Canada_____ 0:21.8	1972—Valery Borzov, U.S.S.R.____ 0:20.0
1932—Eddie Tolan, U.S.A._____ 0:21.2	1976—Donald Quarrie, Jamaica -- 0:20.23
1936—Jesse Owens, U.S.A._____ 0:20.7	1980—

World's Record: 1968—Tommie Smith, U.S.A., Mexico City_____0:19.8

110-METER HURDLES

1896—Tom Curtis, U.S.A._____ 0:17.6	1936—Forrest Towns, U.S.A._____ 0:14.2
1900—Alvin Kraenzlein, U.S.A.____ 0:15.4	1948—William Porter, U.S.A._____ 0:13.9
1904—F. W. Schule, U.S.A._____ 0:16	1952—Harrison Dillard, U.S.A.____ 0:13.7
1906—R. G. Leavitt, U.S.A._____ 0:16.2	1956—Lee Calhoun, U.S.A._____ 0:13.5
1908—Forrest Smithson, U.S.A.____ 0:15	1960—Lee Calhoun, U.S.A._____ 0:13.8
1912—F. W. Kelly, U.S.A._____ 0:15.1	1964—Hayes Jones, U.S.A._____ 0:13.6
1920—Earl Thomson, Canada_____ 0:14.8	1968—W. Davenport, U.S.A._____ 0:13.3
1924—D. C. Kinsey, U.S.A._____ 0:15	1972—R. Milburn, U.S.A._____ 0:13.24*
1928—Sam Atkinson, South Africa_ 0:14.8	1976—Guy Drut, France -------- 0:13.30
1932—George Saling, U.S.A._____ 0:14.6	1980—

World's Record: 1973—Rodney Milburn, U.S.A., Zurich_____0:13.1

400-METER HURDLES

1900—J. W. B. Tewksbury, U.S.A.__ 0:57.6	1948—Roy Cochran, U.S.A._____ 0:51.1
1904—Harry Tillman, U.S.A._____ 0:53	1952—Charles Moore, Jr., U.S.A.__ 0:50.8
1908—Charles Bacon, U.S.A._____ 0:55	1956—Glenn Davis, U.S.A._____ 0:50.1
1920—Frank Loomis, U.S.A._____ 0:54	1960—Glenn Davis, U.S.A._____ 0:49.3
1924—F. Morgan Taylor, U.S.A.____ 0:52.6	1964—Rex Cawley, U.S.A._____ 0:49.6
1928—L. D. Burghley, Great Britain_ 0:53.4	1968—D. Hemery, Great Britain____ 0:48.1
1932—Robert Tisdall, Ireland_____ 0:51.8	1972—J. Akii-Bua, Uganda_____ 0:47.8
1936—Glenn Hardin, U.S.A._____ 0:52.4	1976—Edwin Moses, U.S.A_____ 0:47.64*

1980—

World's Record: 1976—Edwin Moses, U.S.A., Montreal_____ 0:47.64

*Olympic Record.

400-METER RUN

1896—Thomas E. Burke, U.S.A.	0:54.2	1932—William A. Carr, U.S.A.	0:46.2
1900—Macy Long, U.S.A.	0:49.4	1936—Archie Williams, U.S.A.	0:46.5
1904—Harry Hillman, U.S.A.	0:49.2	1948—Arthur Wint, Jamaica	0:46.2
1906—Paul Pilgrim, U.S.A.	0:53.2	1952—George Rhoden, Jamaica	0:45.9
1908—Wyndham Halswelle, Great		1956—Charley Jenkins, U.S.A.	0:46.7
Britain (walkover)	0:50	1960—O. Davis, U.S.A.	0:44.9
1912—Charles Reidpath, U.S.A.	0:48.2	1964—M. Larrabee, U.S.A.	0:45.1
1920—Bevil Rudd, South Africa	0:49.6	1968—Lee Evans, U.S.A.	0:43.8*
1924—Eric Liddell, Great Britain	0:47.6	1972—Vincent Mathews, U.S.A.	0:44.7
1928—Ray Barbuti, U.S.A.	0:47.8	1976— A Juantorena, Cuba	0:44.26
		1980—	

World's Record: 1968—Lee Evans, U.S.A., Mexico City..0:43.8

800-METER RUN

1896—E. H. Flack, Australia	2:11	1936—John Woodruff, U.S.A.	1:52.9
1900—A. E. Tysoe, Great Britain	2:01.4	1948—Mal Whitfield, U.S.A.	1:49.2
1904—Jim D. Lightbody, U.S.A.	1:56	1952—Mal Whitfield, U.S.A.	1:49.2
1906—Paul Pilgrim, U.S.A.	2:01.2	1956—Tom Courtney, U.S.A.	1:47.7
1908—Mel Sheppard, U.S.A.	1:52.8	1960—Peter Snell, New Zealand	1:46.3
1912—Ted Meredith, U.S.A.	1:51.9	1964—Peter Snell, New Zealand	1:45.1
1920—A. G. Hill, Great Britain	1:53.4	1968—Ralph Doubelle, Australia	1:44.3
1924—Douglas Lowe, Great Britain	1:52.4	1972—David Wottle, U.S.A.	1:45.9
1928—Douglas Lowe, Great Britain	1:51.8	1976—A. Juantorena, Cuba	1:43.50*
1932—Tom Hampson, Great Britain	1:49.8	1980—	

World's Record: 1976—A. Juantorena, Cuba, Montreal..1:43.50

1,500-METER RUN

1896—E. H. Flack, Australia	4:33.2	1936—J. Lovelock, New Zealand	3:47.8
1900—C. Bennett, Great Britain	4:06	1948—Henri Eriksson, Sweden	3:49.8
1904—Jim D. Lightbody, U.S.A.	4:05.4	1952—J. Barthel, Luxembourg	3:45.2
1906—Jim D. Lightbody, U.S.A.	4:12	1956—Ron Delany, Ireland	3:41.2
1908—Mel Sheppard, U.S.A.	4:03.4	1960—H. Elliot, Australia	3:35.6
1912—A. Jackson, Great Britain	3:56.8	1964—Peter Snell, New Zealand	3:38.1
1920—A. G. Hill, Great Britain	4:01.8	1968—K. Keino, Kenya	3:34.9*
1924—Paavo Nurmi, Finland	3:53.6	1972—P. Vasala, Finland	3:36.3
1928—Harry Larva, Finland	3:53.2	1976— John Walker, New	
1932—Luigi Beccali, Italy	3:51.1	Zealand	3:39.17
		1980—	

World's Record: 1974—Filbert Bayi, Tanzania, Christchurch, N.Z.........................3:32.2

5,000-METER RUN

1912—H. Kolehmainen, Finland	14:36.6	1952—E. Zatopek, Czechoslovakia	14:06.6
1920—J. Guillemont, France	14:55.6	1956—V. Kuts, U.S.S.R.	13:39.6
1924—Paavo Nurmi, Finland	14:31.2	1960—M. Halberg, New Zealand	13:43.4
1928—Willie Ritola, Finland	14:38	1964—Bob Schul, U.S.A.	13:48.8
1932—Lauri Lehtinen, Finland	14:30	1968—M. Gammoudi, Tunisia	14:05.0
1936—Gunnar Hoeckert, Finland	14:22.2	1972—Lasse Viren, Finland	13:26.4
1948—Gaston Reiff, Belgium	14:17.6	1976—Lasse Viren, Finland	13:24.76
		1980—	

* World's Record: 1978—Henry Rono, Kenya, Berkeley..............................13:08.4

10,000-METER RUN

1912—H. Kolehmainen, Finland	31:20.8	1952—E. Zatopek, Czechoslovakia	29:17
1920—Paavo Nurmi, Finland	31:45.8	1956—V. Kuts, U.S.S.R.	28:45.6
1924—Willie Ritola, Finland	30:23.2	1960—P. Bolotnikov, U.S.S.R.	28:32.2
1928—Paavo Nurmi, Finland	30:18.8	1964—Billy Mills, U.S.A.	28:24.4
1932—Janusz Kusocinski, Poland	30:11.4	1968—N. Temu, Kenya	29:27.4
1936—Ilmari Salminen, Finland	30:15	1972—Lasse Viren, Finland	27:38.4*
1948—E. Zatopek, Czechoslovakia	29:59.6	1976—Lasse Viren, Finland	27:40.38
		1980—	

World's Record: 1978—Henry Rono, Kenya, Vienna..............................27:22.47

*Olympic Record.

333

400-METER RELAY

1912—Great Britain	0:42.4	1952—United States	0:40.1
1920—United States	0:42.2	1956—United States	0:39.5
1924—United States	0:41	1960—Germany	0:39.5
1928—United States	0:41	1964—United States	0:39.0
1932—United States	0:40	1968—United States	0:38.2
1936—United States	0:39.8	1972—United States	0:38.19*
1948—United States	0:40.6	1976—United States	0:38.33

1980—

World's Record: 1972—U.S. National Team (Black, Taylor, Tinker, Hart), Munich........0:38.19

1,600-METER RELAY

1908—United States	3:27.2	1952—Jamaica	3:03.9
1912—United States	3:16.6	1956—United States	3:04.8
1920—Great Britain	3:22.2	1960—United States	3:02.2
1924—United States	3:16	1964—United States	3:00.07
1928—United States	3:14.2	1968—United States	2:56.1*
1932—United States	3:08.2	1972—Kenya	2:59.8
1936—Great Britain	3:09	1976—United States	2:59.52
1948—United States	3:10.4	1980—	

World's Record: 1968—U.S. National Team (Matthews, Freeman, James, Evans),
Mexico City...2:56.1

10,000-METER WALK

1912—G. H. Goulding, Canada	46:28.4	1948—J. Mikaelsson, Sweden	45:13.2
1920—Ugo Frigerio, Italy	48:06.2	1952—J. Mikaelsson, Sweden	45:02.8*
1924—Ugo Frigerio, Italy	47:49	1956—None	

World's Record: 1958—G. Pinichkin, U.S.S.R., Stalinabad....................................42:18.3

20,000-METER WALK†

1956—Leonid Spirine, U.S.S.R.	1:31:27.4	1968—V. Golubnichy, U.S.S.R.	1:33:58.4
1960—V. Golubnichy, U.S.S.R.	1:34:07.2	1972—Peter Frankel, E. Germany	1:26:42.4
1964—R. Mathews, Great Britain	1:29:34.0	1976—Daniel Bautista,	
		1980— Mexico	1:24:40.6*

World's Record: 1976—Daniel Bautista, Mexico, Montreal......................1:24:40.6

50,000-METER WALK

1932—T. W. Green, Great Britain	4:50:10	1964—A. Pamich, Italy	4:11:12.4
1936—H. Whitlock, Great Britain	4:30:41.4	1968—C. Hohne, East Germany	4:20:13.6
1948—J. Ljunggren, Sweden	4:41:52	1972—B. Kannenberg, West	
1952—G. Dordoni, Italy	4:28:07.8	Germany	3:56:11.6*
1956—N. Read, New Zealand	4:30:42.8	1976— None	
1960—D. Thompson, Great Britain	4:25:30.0		

World's Record: 1972—B. Kannenberg, West Germany, Munich......................3:56:11.6

3,000-METER STEEPLECHASE

1920—P. Hodge, Great Britain	10:02.4	1956—C. Brasher, Great Britain	8:41.2
1924—Willie Ritola, Finland	9:33.6	1960—Z. Krzyszkowiak, Poland	8:34.22
1928—Toivo Loukola, Finland	9:21.8	1964—G. Roelants, Belgium	8:30.8
1932—V. Iso-Hollo, Finland	10:33.4‡	1968—A. Biwott, Kenya	8:51.0
1936—V. Iso-Hollo, Finland	9:03.8	1972—K. Keino, Kenya	8:23.6
1948—T. Sjoestrand, Sweden	9:04.6	1976—A. Gärderud, Sweden	8:08.02*
1952—H. Ashenfelter, U.S.A.	8:45.4	1980—	

World's Record: 1976—Andrus Gärderud, Sweden, Montreal......................8:08.02

---

*Olympic Record.
†In 1956 10,000-meter walk replaced by 20,000-meter walk.
‡Ran extra lap by mistake.

RUNNING BROAD (LONG) JUMP

1896	Ellery Clark, United States	20 ft. 9¾ in.
1900	Alvin Kraenzlein, United States	23 ft. 6⅞ in.
1904	Myer Prinstein, United States	24 ft. 1 in.
1906	Myer Prinstein, United States	23 ft. 7½ in.
1908	Frank Irons, United States	24 ft. 6½ in.
1912	A. L. Gutterson, United States	24 ft. 11¼ in.
1920	William Petterssen, Sweden	23 ft. 5½ in.
1924	Dehart Hubbard, United States	24 ft. 5⅛ in.
1928	Edward B. Hamm, United States	25 ft. 4¾ in.
1932	Edward Gordon, United States	25 ft. ¾ in.
1936	Jesse Owens, United States	26 ft. 5⁵⁄₁₆ in.
1948	Willie Steele, United States	25 ft. 8 in.
1952	Jerome Biffle, United States	24 ft. 10.03 in.
1956	Gregory Bell, United States	25 ft. 8¼ in.
1960	Ralph Boston, United States	26 ft. 7¾ in.
1964	Lynn Davies, Great Britain	26 ft. 5½ in.
1968	Bob Beamon, United States	29 ft. 2½ in.*
1972	Randy Williams, United States	27 ft. ½ in.
1976	Arnie Robinson, United States	27 ft. 4¾ in.
1980		

World's Record: 1968—Bob Beamon, U.S.A., Mexico City............29 ft. 2½ in.

POLE VAULT

1896	William W. Hoyt, United States	10 ft. 9¾ in.
1900	I. K. Baxter, United States	10 ft. 9-9/10 in.
1904	C. E. Dvorak, United States	11 ft. 6 in.
1906	Gouder, France	11 ft. 6 in.
1908	A. C. Gilbert, E. T. Cook (tie), United States	12 ft. 2 in.
1912	H. J. Babcock, United States	12 ft. 11½ in.
1920	Frank Foss, United States	13 ft. 5 in.
1924	Lee Barnes, United States	12 ft. 11½ in.
1928	Sabin W. Carr, United States	13 ft. 9⅜ in.
1932	William Miller, United States	14 ft. 1⅞ in.
1936	Earle Meadows, United States	14 ft. 3¼ in.
1948	Guinn Smith, United States	14 ft. 1¼ in.
1952	Robert Richards, United States	14 ft. 11¼ in.
1956	Robert Richards, United States	14 ft. 11½ in.
1960	Don Bragg, United States	15 ft. 5⅛ in.
1964	Fred Hansen, United States	16 ft. 8¾ in.
1968	Bob Seagren, United States	17 ft. 8½ in.
1972	Wolfgang Nordwig, East Germany	18 ft. ½ in.*
1976	T. Slusarski, Poland	18 ft. ½ in.
1980		

World's Record: 1972—Bob Seagren, U.S.A., Eugene, Oregon...........18 ft. 5¾ in.†

RUNNING HOP STEP AND JUMP (TRIPLE JUMP)

1896	James B. Connolly, United States	45 ft.
1900	Myer Prinstein, United States	47 ft. 4¼ in.
1904	Myer Prinstein, United States	47 ft.
1906	P. O'Connor, Ireland	48 ft. 2 in.
1908	T. J. Ahearne, Great Britain	48 ft. 11¼ in.
1912	G. Lindblom, Sweden	48 ft. 5⅛ in.
1920	V. Tuulos, Finland	47 ft. 6⅞ in.
1924	A. W. Winter, Australia	50 ft. 11⅛ in.
1928	Mikio Oda, Japan	49 ft. 10¹³⁄₁₆ in.
1932	Chuhel Nambu, Japan	51 ft. 7 in.
1936	Naoto Tajima, Japan	52 ft. 5⅞ in.
1948	Arne Ahman, Sweden	50 ft. 6¼ in.
1952	Adhemar da Silva, Brazil	53 ft. 2½ in.
1956	Adhemar da Silva, Brazil	53 ft. 7½ in.
1960	J. Schmidt, Poland	55 ft. 1¾ in.
1964	J. Schmidt, Poland	55 ft. 3½ in.
1968	V. Saneyev, U.S.S.R.	57 ft. ¾ in.*
1972	V. Saneyev, U.S.S.R.	56 ft. 11 in.
1976	V. Saneyev, U.S.S.R.	56 ft. 8¾ in.
1980		

World's Record: 1972—V. Saneyev, U.S.S.R., Sukhumi, U.S.S.R.............57 ft. 2¾ in.

*Olympic Record.
†With standard pole barred at 1972 Olympics.

335

RUNNING HIGH JUMP

1896—Ellery Clark, United States	5 ft. 11¼ in.
1900—I. K. Baxter, United States	6 ft. 2-4/5 in.
1904—Sam Jones, United States	5 ft. 11 in.
1906—Con Leahy, Ireland	5 ft. 9⅞ in.
1908—H. F. Porter, United States	6 ft. 3 in.
1912—Alma Richards, United States	6 ft. 4 in.
1920—Dick Landon, United States	6 ft. 4¼ in.
1924—Harold Osborn, United States	6 ft. 5 15/16 in.
1928—Robert W. King, United States	6 ft. 4⅜ in.
1932—D. McNaughton, Canada	6 ft. 5⅝ in.
1936—Cornelius Johnson, United States	6 ft. 7 15/16 in.
1948—John Winter, Australia	6 ft. 6 in.
1952—Walter Davis, United States	6 ft. 8¼ in.
1956—Charlie Dumas, United States	6 ft. 11¼ in.
1960—R. Shavlakadze, U.S.S.R.	7 ft. 1 in.
1964—Valery Brumel, U.S.S.R.	7 ft. 1¾ in.
1968—Dick Fosbury, United States	7 ft. 4¼ in.*
1972—Yuri Tarmak, U.S.S.R.	7 ft. 3¾ in.
1976—J. Wzsola, Poland	7 ft. 4½ in.
1980—	

World's Record: 1973—Dwight Stones, U.S.A., Munich .... 7 ft. 6½ in.

16-LB. SHOT PUT

1896—Robert Garrett, United States	36 ft. 2 in.
1900—Richard Sheldon, United States	46 ft. 3⅛ in.
1904—Ralph Rose, United States	48 ft. 7 in.
1906—Martin Sheridan, United States	40 ft. 4-4/5 in.
1908—Ralph Rose, United States	46 ft. 7½ in.
1912—Pat McDonald, United States	50 ft. 4 in.
1920—Willie Porhola, Finland	48 ft. 7⅛ in.
1924—Clarence Houser, United States	49 ft. 2⅜ in.
1928—John Kuck, United States	52 ft. 11/16 in.
1932—Leo Sexton, United States	52 ft. 6 3/16 in.
1936—Hans Woellke, Germany	53 ft. 1 13/16 in.
1948—Wilbur Thompson, United States	56 ft. 2 in.
1952—Parry O'Brien, United States	57 ft. 1½ in.
1956—Parry O'Brien, United States	60 ft. 11 in.
1960—W. Nieder, United States	64 ft. 6¾ in.
1964—Dallas Long, United States	66 ft. 8½ in.
1968—Randy Matson, United States	67 ft. 4¾ in.
1972—W. Komar, Poland	69 ft. 6 in.*
1976—U. Beyer, East Germany	69 ft. ¾ in.
1980—	

World's Record: 1973—Allan D. Feverbach, U.S.A., San José, Calif. .... 71 ft. 7 in.

DISCUS THROW

1896—Robert Garrett, United States	95 ft. 7½ in.
1900—Rudolph Bauer, Hungary	118 ft. 2-9/10 in.
1904—Martin Sheridan, United States	128 ft. 10½ in.
1906—Martin Sheridan, United States	136 ft. ⅓ in.
1908—Martin Sheridan, United States	134 ft. 2 in.
1912—A. R. Taipale, Finland	148 ft. 3.9 in.
1920—E. Niklander, Finland	146 ft. 7¼ in.
1924—Clarence Houser, United States	151 ft. 5¼ in.
1928—Clarence Houser, United States	155 ft. 2-4/5 in.
1932—John Anderson, United States	162 ft. 4⅞ in.
1936—Kenneth Carpenter, United States	165 ft. 7 29/64 in.
1948—Adolfo Consolini, Italy	173 ft. 2 in.
1952—Simeon Iness, United States	180 ft. 6½ in.
1956—Al Oerter, United States	184 ft. 11 in.
1960—Al Oerter, United States	194 ft. 2 in.
1964—Al Oerter, United States	200 ft. 1½ in.
1968—Al Oerter, United States	212 ft. 6½ in.
1972—Ludrik Danek, Czechoslovakia	211 ft. 3 in.
1976—Mac Wilkins, United States	221 ft. 5½ in.
1980—	

World's Record: 1968—L. Jay Silvester, U.S.A., Reno, Nev. .... 224 ft. 5 in.
1972—Rickard Bruch, Sweden, Stockholm .... 224 ft. 5 in.

---

*Olympic Record.

1900—John Flanagan, United States		167 ft. 4 in.
1904—John Flanagan, United States		168 ft. 1 in.
1908—John Flanagan, United States		170 ft. 4¼ in.
1912—Matt McGrath, United States		177 ft. 7 in.
1920—Pat Ryan, United States		173 ft. 5⅝ in.
1924—Fred Tootel, United States		174 ft. 10⅛ in.
1928—Pat O'Callaghan, Ireland		168 ft. 7½ in.
1932—Pat O'Callaghan, Ireland		176 ft. 11⅛ in.
1936—Karl Hein, Germany		185 ft. 4³⁄₁₆ in.
1948—Imre Nemeth, Hungary		183 ft. 11½ in.
1952—Josef Csarmak, Hungary		197 ft. 11¾ in.
1956—Harold Connolly, United States		207 ft. 3½ in.
1960—V. Rudenkov, U.S.S.R.		220 ft. 1⅝ in.
1964—Romvald Klim, U.S.S.R.		228 ft. 10½ in.
1968—G. Zsivotzky, U.S.S.R.		240 ft. 8 in.
1972—A. Bondarchuk, U.S.S.R.		248 ft. 8 in.
1976—Juri Sedych, U.S.S.R.		254 ft. 4 in.*
1980—		

World's Record: 1976—Juri Sedych, U.S.S.R., Montreal ----- 254 ft. 4 in.

JAVELIN THROW

1906—E. Lemming, Sweden		175 ft. 6 in.
1908—E. Lemming, Sweden		178 ft. 7½ in.
1912—E. Lemming, Sweden		198 ft. 11¼ in.
1920—Jonni Myyra, Finland		215 ft. 9¼ in
1924—Jonni Myyra, Finland		206 ft. 6¾ in.
1928—E. H. Lundquist, Sweden		218 ft. 6⅛ in.
1932—Matti Jarvinen, Finland		238 ft. 7 in.
1936—Gerhard Stoeck, Germany		235 ft. 8¹³⁄₃₂ in.
1948—Kaji Rautavaara, Finland		228 ft. 10½ in.
1952—Cy Young, United States		242 ft. ¾ in.
1956—Egil Danielsen, Norway		281 ft. 2¼ in.
1960—V. Cyoulenko, U.S.S.R.		277 ft. 8¾ in.
1964—P. Nevala, Finland		271 ft. 2¼ in.
1968—J. Lusis, U.S.S.R.		295 ft. 7 in.
1972—K. Wolferman, West Germany		296 ft. 10 in.
1976—M. Nemeth, Hungary		310 ft. 4 in.*
1980—		

World's Record: 1976—M. Nemeth, Hungary, Montreal ----- 310 ft. 4 in.

DECATHLON†

	Points		Points
1912—H. Wieslander, Sweden	7,724.495‡	1952—Bob Mathias, U.S.A.	7,887
1920—H. Loveland, Norway	6,804.35	1956—Milton Campbell, U.S.A.	7,937
1924—H. Osborn, U.S.A.	7,710.775	1960—R. Johnson, U.S.A.	8,392
1928—Paavo Yrjola, Finland	8,053.29	1964—W. Holdorf, Germany	7,887
1932—James Bausch, U.S.A.	8,462.235	1968—Bill Toomey, U.S.A.	8,193
1936—Glenn Morris, U.S.A.	7,900	1972—N. Avilov, U.S.S.R.	8,454
1948—Bob Mathias, U.S.A.	7,139	1976—Bruce Jenner, U.S.A.	8,618
		1980—	

MARATHON

No World or Olympic Records, for while distance the same, course varies. Distance: 26 miles and 385 yards.

1896—Spiridion Loues, Greece	2:55:20	1932—Juan Zabala, Argentina 2:31:36
1900—Michel Teato, France	2:59:00	1936—Kitei Son, Japan 2:29:19.2
1904—T. J. Hicks, U.S.A.	3:28:53	1948—Delfo Cabrera, Argentina ... 2:34:51.6
1906—W. J. Sherring, Canada	2:51:23.6	1952—Emil Zatopek, Czech. 2:23:03.2
1908—John J. Hayes, U.S.A.	2:55:18	1956—Alain Mimoun, France 2:25:00
1912—K. K. McArthur, South Africa	2:36:54.8	1960—B. Abebe, Ethiopia 2:15:16.2
1920—H. Kolohmainen, Finland	2:32:35.8	1964—B. Abebe, Ethiopia 2:12:11.2
1924—A. C. Stenroos, Finland	2:41:22.6	1968—M. Wolde, Ethiopia 2:20:26.4
1928—El Ouafi, France	2:32:57	1972—Frank Shorter, U.S.A. 2:12:19.8
		1976—W. Cierpinski, East Germany 2:09:55.0

1980—

---

*Olympic Record.
†Scoring system changed several times.
‡Jim Thorpe, U.S.A., won but was later disqualified.

337

1896—United States	1924—United States	1960—United States
1900—United States	1928—United States	1964—United States
1904—United States	1932—United States	1968—United States
1906—United States	1936—United States	1972—United States
1908—United States	1948—United States	1976—United States
1912—United States	1952—United States	1980—
1920—United States	1956—United States	

TRACK AND FIELD (WOMEN)

100-METER DASH

1928—Elizabeth Robinson, U.S.A.	0:12.2	1956—Betty Cuthbert, Australia	0:11.5
1932—Stella Walsh, Poland	0:11.9	1960—Wilma Rudolf, U.S.A.	0:11.0†
1936—Helen Stephens, U.S.A.	0:11.5	1964—Wyomia Tyus, U.S.A.	0:11.4
1948—Fannie Blankers-Koen,		1968—Wyomia Tyus, U.S.A.	0:11.0*
Netherlands	0:11.9	1972—Renate Stecher, E. Germany	0:11.07
1952—M. Jackson, Australia	0:11.5	1976—A. Richter, West Germany	0:11.08
1980—			

World's Record: 1973—Renate Stecher, East Germany, Dresden 0:10.8

200-METER DASH

1948—Fannie Blankers-Koen,		1964—Edith MacGuire, U.S.A.	0:23.0
Netherlands	0:24.4	1968—I. Kirszenstein, Poland	0:22.5
1952—M. Jackson, Australia	0:23.7	1972—Renate Stecher, E. Germany	0:22.4*
1956—Betty Cuthbert, Australia	0:23.4	1976—B. Eckert, East Germany	0:22.37
1960—Wilma Rudolf, U.S.A.	0:23.2	1980—	

World's Record: 1973—Renate Stecher, East Germany, Dresden 0:22.1

80-METER HURDLES‡

1932—Mildred Didrikson, U.S.A.	0:11.7	1956—Shirley Strickland de La	
1936—Trebisonda Villa, Italy	0:11.7	Hunty, Australia	0:10.7
1948—Fannie Blankers-Koen,		1960—I. Press, U.S.S.R.	0:10.6
Netherlands	0:11.2	1964—K. Balzer, Germany	0:10.5
1952—Shirley Strickland de La		1968—M. Caird, Australia	0:10.3*
Hunty, Australia	0:10.9		

World's Record: 1965—I. Press, U.S.S.R., Tbilisi, U.S.S.R. 0:10.3
1968—M. Caird, Australia, Mexico City 0:10.3

100-METER HURDLES

1972—A. Ehrhardt, East Germany 0:12.59* 1976—J. Schaller, East
1980— Germany 0:12.77

World's Record: 1972—A. Ehrhardt, East Germany, Munich 0:12.59
1972—Pamela Ryan, Australia, Warsaw 0:12.59

400-METER RUN

1964—Betty Cuthbert, Australia	0:52.0	1972—M. Zehrt, East Germany	0:51.08
1968—Colette Besson, France	0:52.0	1976—I. Szewinska, Poland	0:49.29*
		1980—	

World's Record: 1976—Irene Szewinska, Poland, Montreal 0:49.29

800-METER RUN

1960—Shevcova-Lisenka, U.S.S.R.	2:04.3	1972—H. Falck, West Germany	1:58.6
1964—Anne Packer, Great Britain	2:01.15	1976—T. Kazankina, U.S.S.R.	1:54.94*
1968—M. Manning, U.S.A.	2:00.9	1980—	

World's Record: 1976—T. Kazankina, U.S.S.R., Montreal 1:54.94

1,500-METER RUN

1972—L. Bragina, U.S.S.R. 4:01.4* 1976—T. Kazankina, U.S.S.R. 4:05.48
1980—

World's Record: 1972—Ludmilla Bragina, U.S.S.R., Munich 4:01.4

*Olympic Record.
†Wind rules out world record.
‡In 1972 changed to 100 meters with hurdles 3 inches higher.

400-METER RELAY

1928—Canada	0:48.4	1960—United States	0:44.5
1932—United States	0:47	1964—Poland	0:43.6
1936—United States	0:46.9	1968—United States	0:42.8
1948—Netherlands	0:47.5	1972—West Germany	0:42.81
1952—United States	0:45.9	1976—East Germany	0:42.55*
1956—Australia	0:44.5	1980—	

World's Record: 1974—East German National Team (Maletzki, Stecher, Heinisch, Echert), Rome......................0:42.51

RUNNING BROAD JUMP

1948—Olga Gyarmati, Hungary	18 ft. 8½ in.
1952—Yvette Williams, New Zealand	20 ft. 5¾ in.
1956—Elzbieta Krzeskinska, Poland	20 ft. 9¾ in.
1960—V. Krepkina, U.S.S.R.	20 ft. 10¾ in.
1964—Mary Rand, Great Britain	22 ft. 2¼ in.
1968—V. Viscopoleanu, Romania	22 ft. 4½ in.*
1972—H. Rosendahl, West Germany	22 ft. 3 in.
1976—A. Voigt, East Germany	22 ft. ½ in.
1980—	

World's Record: 1970—H. Rosendahl, West Germany, Turin, Italy..................22 ft. 5¼ in.

RUNNING HIGH JUMP

1928—Ethel Catherwood, Canada	5 ft. 3 in.
1932—Jean Shiley, United States	5 ft. 5¼ in.
1936—Ibolya Csak, Hungary	5 ft. 3 in.
1948—Alice Coachman, United States	5 ft. 6⅛ in.
1952—Esther Brand, South Africa	5 ft. 5¾ in.
1956—Mildred McDaniel, United States	5 ft. 9¼ in.
1960—I. Balas, Romania	6 ft. ¾ in.
1964—I. Balas, Romania	6 ft. 2¾ in.
1968—M. Rezkova, Czechoslovakia	5 ft. 11¾ in.
1972—U. Mayforth, West Germany	6 ft. 3¼ in.*
1976—R. Ackermann, East Germany	6 ft. 4 in.
1980—	

World's Record: 1974—R. Witschas, East Germany, Rome..................6 ft. 5 in.

SHOT PUT

1948—Micheline Ostermeyer, France	45 ft. 1½ in.
1952—Galina Zybina, U.S.S.R.	50 ft. 1½ in.
1956—Tamara Tychkevitch, U.S.S.R.	54 ft. 5 in.
1960—T. Press, U.S.S.R.	56 ft. 9⅞ in.
1964—T. Press, U.S.S.R.	59 ft. 6¼ in.
1968—M. Gummell, East Germany	64 ft. 4 in.
1972—N. Chizhova, U.S.S.R.	69 ft. 0 in.
1976—I. Khristova, Bulgaria	69 ft. 5 in.*
1980—	

World's Record: 1973—N. Chizhova, U.S.S.R., Varna, Bulgaria..................70 ft. 4¼ in.

DISCUS THROW

1928—H. Konopacka, Poland	129 ft. 11⅞ in.
1932—Lillian Copeland, United States	133 ft. 2 in.
1936—Gisela Mauermayer, Germany	156 ft. 3³⁄₁₆ in.
1948—Micheline Ostermeyer, France	137 ft. 6½ in.
1952—Nina Romaschkova, U.S.S.R.	168 ft. 8½ in.
1956—Olga Fikotova, Czechoslovakia	176 ft. 1½ in.
1960—N. Ponomareva, U.S.S.R.	180 ft. 8¼ in.
1964—T. Press, U.S.S.R.	187 ft. 10¾ in.
1968—L. Manoliu, Romania	191 ft. 2½ in.
1972—Faina Melnik, U.S.S.R.	218 ft. 7 in.
1976—E. Schlaak, East Germany	226 ft. 4½ in.*
1980—	

World's Record: 1974—Faina Melnik, U.S.S.R., Prague..................229 ft. 4 in.

---

*Olympic Record.

JAVELIN THROW

1932—Mildred Didrikson, United States	143 ft. 4 in.
1936—Tilly Fleischer, Germany	148 ft. 2¾ in.
1948—H. Baume, Austria	149 ft. 6 in.
1952—Dana Zatopekova, Czechoslovakia	165 ft. 7 in.
1956—Inessa Iacunzem, U.S.S.R.	176 ft. 8 in.
1960—E. Ozolina, U.S.S.R.	183 ft. 8 in.
1964—M. Penes, Romania	198 ft. 7½ in.
1968—A. Nemeth, Hungary	198 ft. ½ in.
1972—Ruth Fuchs, East Germany	209 ft. 7 in.
1976—Ruth Fuchs, East Germany	216 ft. 4 in.*
1980—	

World's Record: 1974—Ruth Fuchs, East Germany, Rome............220 ft. 6 in.

PENTATHLON

	Points		Points
1964—I. Press, U.S.S.R.	5,246	1972—Mary Peters, Great Britain	4,801†
1968—I. Becker, West Germany	5,098	1976—S. Siegl, East Germany	4,745
		1980—	

WEIGHT LIFTING

FLYWEIGHT (115 lbs.)

1972—Z. Smalcerz, Poland	745 lbs.*	1976—A. Voronin, U.S.S.R.	534½ lbs.
		1980 —	

World's Record: 1972—Z. Smalcerz, Poland, Munich............745 lbs.

BANTAMWEIGHT (123 lbs.)

1948—Joe N. De Pietro, U.S.A.	677½ lbs.	1968—M. Nassiri, Iran	808½ lbs.
1952—Ivan Udodov, U.S.S.R.	694 lbs.	1972—Imre Foeldi, Hungary	833 lbs.*
1956—Charley Vinci, U.S.A.	753½ lbs.	1976—N. Nourikian,	
1960—Charley Vinci, U.S.A.	760 lbs.	Bulgaria	578½ lbs.
1964—Aleksei Vakhonin, U.S.S.R.	788.15 lbs.		

1980—

World's Record: 1972—Imre Foeldi, Hungary, Munich............833 lbs.

FEATHERWEIGHT (132 lbs.)

1920—E. de Haes, Belgium	484 lbs.	1956—Isaac Berger, U.S.A.	776½ lbs.
1924—M. Gabetti, Italy	885½ lbs.	1960—E. Minaev, U.S.S.R.	821 lbs.
1928—F. Andrysek, Austria	632½ lbs.	1964—Y. Miyake, Japan	875 lbs.
1932—R. Suvigny, France	632½ lbs.	1968—Y. Miyake, Japan	865 lbs.
1936—A. Terlazzo, U.S.A.	687½ lbs.	1972—N. Nourikian, Bulgaria	888 lbs.*
1948—M. S. J. Fayad, Egypt	732½ lbs.	1976—N. Kolenisnikov,	
1952—R. Chimishkyan, U.S.S.R.	743½ lbs.	U.S.S.R.	628 lbs.

1980—

World's Record: 1972—N. Nourikian, Bulgaria, Munich............888 lbs.

LIGHTWEIGHT (148½ lbs.)

1920—A. Neyland, Estonia	567.68 lbs.	1952—Tommy Kono, U.S.A.	798¾ lbs.
1924—E. Decottignies, France	968 lbs.	1956—Igor Rybak, U.S.S.R.	837½ lbs.
1928—K. Helbig, Germany	709½ lbs.	1960—N. Bushuev, U.S.S.R.	876 lbs.
H. Hass, Austria (tie)		1964—W. Baszanowski, Poland	951½ lbs.
1932—Rene Duverger, France	715 lbs.	1968—W. Baszanowski, Poland	962½ lbs.
1936—M. A. Mesbah, Egypt	753½ lbs.	1972—M. Kirzhinov, U.S.S.R.	1,014 lbs.*
1948—I. Shams, Egypt	793¼ lbs.	1976—P. Korol, U.S.S.R.	672 lbs.
		1980—	

World's Record: 1972—M. Kirzhinov, U.S.S.R., Munich............1,014 lbs.

*Olympic Record.
†New scoring system.

MIDDLEWEIGHT (165 lbs.)

1920—Gance, France	540.012 lbs.	1956—F. Bogdanovskii,			
1924—C. Galimberti, Italy	1,083½ lbs.		U.S.S.R.	925¾	lbs.
1928—F. Roger, France	738.01 lbs.	1960—A. Kurynov, U.S.S.R.		964¼	lbs.
1932—R. Ismayr, Germany	759 lbs.	1964—H. Zdrazila, Czech.		979	lbs.
1936—Khadr El Touni, Egypt	852½ lbs.	1968—V. Kurentsov, U.S.S.R.		1,045	lbs.
1948—F. I. Spellman, U.S.A.	859½ lbs.	1972—Y. Bikov, Bulgaria		1,069.23	lbs.*
1952—Peter George, U.S.A.	881½ lbs.	1976—Y. Mitkov, Bulgaria		738½	lbs.
		1980—			

World's Record: 1972—Y. Bikov, Bulgaria, Munich----------------------------------1,069.23 lbs.

LIGHT HEAVYWEIGHT (181½ lbs.)

1920—E. Cadine, France	639.334 lbs.	1956—Tommy Kono, U.S.A.		986¼	lbs.
1924—C. Rigoulot, France	1,105½ lbs.	1960—I. Palinski, Poland		975¼	lbs.
1928—E. S. Nosseir, Egypt	781 lbs.	1964—R. Plyukfeider, U.S.S.R.		1,045	lbs.
1932—L. Hostin, France	803 lbs.	1968—B. Selitsky, U.S.S.R.		1,067	lbs.
1936—L. Hostin, France	821 lbs.	1972—L. Jenssen, Norway		1,118	lbs.*
1948—Stan Stanczyk, U.S.A.	920 lbs.	1976—V. Shary, U.S.S.R.		804½	lbs.
1952—T. Lomakin, U.S.S.R.	920¼ lbs.	1980—			

World's Record: 1972—L. Jenssen, Norway, Munich----------------------------------1,118 lbs

MIDDLE HEAVYWEIGHT (198 lbs.)

1952—N. Schemansky, U.S.A.	980¾ lbs.	1968—K. Kangasniemi, Finland		1,138½	lbs.
1956—A. Voroblev, U.S.S.R.	1,019¼ lbs.	1972—A. Nikolov, Bulgaria		1,157	lbs.*
1960—A. Voroblev, U.S.S.R.	1,041¼ lbs.	1976—D. Rigert, U.S.S.R.		843	lbs.
1964—V. Golovanov, U.S.S.R.	1,072½ lbs.	1980—			

World's Record: 1972—A. Nikolov, Bulgaria, Munich----------------------------------1,157 lbs.

HEAVYWEIGHT (220 lbs.)

1920—F. Bottini, Italy	595.24 lbs.	1952—John Davis, U.S.A.		1,013¾	lbs.
1924—J. Tonani, Italy	1,138½ lbs.	1956—Paul Anderson, U.S.A.		1,102	lbs.
1928—J. Strassberger,		1960—Y. Vlasov, U.S.S.R.		1,184¼	lbs.
Germany	819½ lbs	1964—L. Zhabotinsky, U.S.S.R.		1,259½	lbs.
1932—J. Skobla, Czech.	836 lbs.	1968—L. Zhabotinsky, U.S.S.R.		1,259½	lbs.
1936—J. Manger, Germany	902 lbs.	1972—Yan Talts, U.S.S.R.		1,278	lbs.*
1948—John Davis, U.S.A.	997¼ lbs.	1976—Y. Zaitsev, U.S.S.R.		848½	lbs.
		1980—			

World's Record: 1967—L. Zhabotinsky, U.S.S.R., Yerevan, U.S.S.R.----------------------1,298 lbs

SUPER HEAVYWEIGHT (over 220 lbs.)

1972—V. Alexeev, U.S.S.R.	1,411 lbs.*	1976—V. Alexeev, U.S.S.R.	970	lbs.
		1980—		

World's Record: 1972—V. Alexeev, U.S.S.R., Munich----------------------------------1,411 lbs.

(UNOFFICIAL) TEAM CHAMPIONS

1920—France	1948—United States	1968—U.S.S.R.
1924—Italy	1952—United States	1972—Bulgaria
1928—Germany	1956—United States	1976—U.S.S.R.
1932—France	1960—U.S.S.R.	1980—
1936—Egypt	1964—U.S.S.R.	

N.B. change in 1976 called for addition of one less lift.

WRESTLING

Catch-as-Catch-Can or Freestyle

PAPERWEIGHT (105½ lbs.)

1972—R. Dmitriev, U.S.S.R.	1976—H. Issaev, Bulgaria
	1980—

FLYWEIGHT (114½ lbs.)

1904—R. Curry, United States (105 lbs.)	1964—S. A. Haydari, Iran
1948—V. L. Vitala, Finland	1968—S. Nakata, Japan
1952—Hassen Gemici, Turkey	1972—K. Kato, Japan
1956—M. Tsalkaimanidze, U.S.S.R.	1976—Y. Takada, Japan
1960—A. Bilek, Turkey	1980—

---

*Olympic Record.

341

BANTAMWEIGHT (125½ lbs.)

1904—G. N. Mehnert, United States (115 lbs.)	1952—Shohachi Ishii, Japan
1908 G. N. Mehnert, United States (119 lbs.)	1956 H. Dagistanli, Turkey
1924—Kustaa Pihlajamaki, Finland	1960—T. McCann, United States
1928—K. Makinen, Finland	1964 Y. Vetake, Japan
1932—Robert E. Pearce, United States	1968 Y. Vetake, Japan
1936—Odon Zombory, Hungary	1972 H. Yanagida, Japan
1948—Nassuh Akkam, Turkey	1976 V. Umin, U.S.S.R.
	1980—

FEATHERWEIGHT (136½ lbs.)

1896—Karl Schumann, Germany	1948 Gazanfer Bilge, Turkey
1904—I. Niflot, United States	1952 Bayram Sit, Turkey
1908—G. S. Dole, United States	1956 Shoze Sasabara, Japan
1920—Charles E. Ackerly, United States	1960 M.Daginstanlı, Turkey
1924—Robin Reed, United States	1964 O. Watanabe, Japan
1928—Allie Morrison, United States	1968 M. Kaneko, Japan
1932 Herman Pihlajamaki, Finand	1972 Z. Abdulbekov. U.S.S.R.
1936 Kustaa Pihlajamaki, Finland	1976 Y. Jung Mo, South Korea
	1980—

LIGHTWEIGHT (149½ lbs.)

1904—B. J. Bradshaw, United States	1952 Olle Anderberg, Sweden
1908—G. de Relwyskow, Great Britain	1956 E. Habibi, Iran
1920—Kalle Antilla, Finland	1960 S. Wilson, United States
1924—Russell Vis, United States	1964 E. Dimov, Bulgaria
1928—O. Kapp, Estonia	1968 A. Movahed, Iran
1932—Charles Pacome, France	1972—D. Gable, United States
1936—Karoly Karpati, Hungary	1976 P. Pinegin, U.S.S.R.
1948—Celal Atik, Turkey	1980—

WELTERWEIGHT (163 lbs.)

1904—O. F. Roehm, United States	1956—Mistro Ikeda, Japan
1924—Herman Gehri, Switzerland	1960 D. Blubaugh, United States
1928—A. J. Haavisto, Finland	1964 I. Ogan, Turkey
1932 Jack F. Van Bebber, United States	1968 M. Atalay, Turkey
1936—Frank Lewis, United States	1972—Wayne Wells, United States
1948—Yasar Dogu, Turkey	1976—I. Date, Japan
1952—William Smith, United States	1980—

MIDDLEWEIGHT (180 lbs.)

1904—Charles Erickson, United States	1952—David Gimarkuridze, U.S.S.R.
1908—S. V. Bacon, Great Britain	1956—Nikola Nikdov, Bulgaria
1920 E. Leino, Finland	960—H. Gungor, Turkey
1924 Fritz Haggmann, Switzerland	1964—P. Gardjev, Bulgaria
1928—E. Kyburg, Switzerland	1968—B. Gurevitch, U.S.S.R.
1932—Ivar Johansson, Sweden	1972—L. Tediashvili, U.S.S.R.
1936—Emile Poilvec, France	1976 J. Peterson, U.S.A.
1948—Glenn Brand, United States	1980—

LIGHT HEAVYWEIGHT (198 lbs.)

1920—Anders Larsson, Sweden	1956—Gholam Takhti, Iran
1924—John Spellman, United States	1960 I. Atli, Turkey
1928—T. S. Sjostedt, Sweden	1964—A. Medved, U.S.S.R.
1932—Peter J. Mehringer, United States	1968 A. Ayuk, Turkey
1936—Knut Fridell, Sweden	1972 B. Peterson, United States
1948—Henry Wittenberg, United States	1976 L. Tediashvili, U.S.S.R.
1952—Wiking Palm, Sweden	1980—

HEAVYWEIGHT (220 lbs.)

1904—B. Hansen, United States	1952—Arsen Mekokishvili, U.S.S.R.
1908—G. C. O'Kelly, Great Britain	1956—Hamid Kaplan, Turkey
1920—Roth, Switzerland	1960—W. Dietrich, Germany
1924—Harry Steele, United States	1964 A. Ivanitsky, U.S.S.R.
1928—Johan C. Richthoff, Sweden	1968—A. Medved, U.S.S.R.
1932—Johan C. Richthoff, Sweden	1972—I. Yarygin, U.S.S.R.
1936—Kristjan Palusalu, Estonia	1976—I. Yarygin, U.S.S.R.
1948—George Bobis, Hungary	1980—

1972—A. Medved, U.S.S.R. 1976—S. Andiev, U.S.S.R.
1980—

(UNOFFICIAL) TEAM CHAMPIONS

1904—United States	1932—United States	1960—Turkey
1908—Great Britain	1936—United States	1964—Japan
1920—United States	1948—Turkey	1968—U.S.S.R.
1924—United States	1952—U.S.S.R.	1972—U.S.S.R.
1928—Finland	1956—Turkey	1976—U.S.S.R.
	1980—	

Greco-Roman

PAPERWEIGHT (105½ lbs.)

1972—G. Berceanu, Romania 1976 —A. Shumakov, U.S.S.R.
1980—

FLYWEIGHT (114½ lbs.)

1948—Pietro Lombardi, Italy	1964—T. Hanahara, Japan
1952—Boris Gourevitch, U.S.S.R.	1968—Peter Kirov, Bulgaria
1956—Nikolai Solovlev, U.S.S.R.	1972 —P. Kirov, Bulgaria
1960—D. Pirvulescu, Romania	1976—V. Konstantinov, U.S.S.R.
	1980—

BANTAMWEIGHT (125½ lbs:)

1924—Edward Putsep, Estonia	1956—K. Vyropaev, U.S.S.R.
1928—K. Leucht, Germany	1960—O. Karavayev, U.S.S.R.
1932—Jakob Brendel, Germany	1964—M. Ichiguchi, Japan
1936—Martin Lorincz, Hungary	1968—J. Varga, Hungary
1948—K. R. Peterson, Sweden	1972—R. Kazakov, U.S.S.R.
1952—Imre Hodos, Hungary	1976—P. Ukkola, Finland
	1980—

FEATHERWEIGHT (136½ lbs.)

1906—Y. Raigalp, Finland	1952—Jakov Pounkine, U.S.S.R.
1912—Kalle Koskelo, Finland	1956—R. Makinen, Finland
1920—Friman, Finland	1960—M. Sille, Turkey
1924—Kalie Antilla, Finland	1964—I. Polyak, Hungary
1928—V. Wall, Estonia	1968—Roman Rurua, U.S.S.R.
1932—Giovanni Gozzi, Italy	1972 —G. Markov, Bulgaria
1936—Ysar Erkan, Turkey	1976 —K. Lipien, Poland
1948—M. Octav, Turkey	1980—

LIGHTWEIGHT (149½ lbs.)

1906—Watzi, Austria	1948—K. Freij, Sweden
1908—E. Poro, Italy	1952—Chasame Safine, U.S.S.R.
1912—E. E. Vare, Finland	1956—K. Lehtonen, Finland
1920—E. E. Vare, Finland	1960—A. Kordidze, U.S.S.R.
1924—Oskari Friman, Finland	1964—K. Ayvaz, Turkey
1928—L. Keresztes, Hungary	1968—M. Munemura, Japan
1932—Erik Malmberg, Sweden	1972—S. Khisamutchinov, U.S.S.R.
1936—Lauri Koskela, Finland	1976—S. Nalbandian, U.S.S.R.
	1980—

WELTERWEIGHT (163 lbs.)

1932—Ivar Johansson, Sweden	1960—Mithat Bayrak, Turkey
1936—Rodolf Svodberg, Sweden	1964—A. Kolesov, U.S.S.R.
1948—Gosta Anderson, Sweden	1968—R. Vespa, East Germany
1952—Mikios Szilvasi, Hungary	1972—V. Macha, Czechoslovakia
1956—Mithat Bayrak, Turkey	1976—A. Bykov, U.S.S.R.
	1980—

MIDDLEWEIGHT (180 lbs.)

1906—Weckman, Finland
1908—F. M. Martenson, Sweden
1912—C. E. Johansson, Sweden
1920—Westergren, Sweden
1924—Edward Westerlund, Finland
1928—Vaino Kokkinen, Finland
1932—Vaino Kokkinen, Finland
1936—Ivar Johansson, Sweden

1948—Axel Gronberg, Sweden
1952—Axel Gronberg, Sweden
1956—Vuivi Kartozia, U.S.S.R.
1960—D. Dobrew, Bulgaria
1964—B. Simic, Yugoslavia
1968—Lothar Metz, East Germany
1972—C. Hegedus. Hungary
1976—M. Petkovic, Yugoslavia
1980—

LIGHT HEAVYWEIGHT (198 lbs.)

1908—W. Weckman, Finland
1912—A. O. Ahlgren, Sweden
   J. Boling, Finland (tie)
1920—Claes Johansson, Sweden
1924—Karl Westergren, Sweden
1928—S. Moustafa, Egypt
1932—Rudolph Svensson, Sweden
1936—Axel Cardier, Sweden

1948—Karl Nilsson, Sweden
1952—Kolpo Grondahl, Finland
1956—V. Nikolaev, U.S.S.R.
1960—T. Kis, Turkey
1964—B. Alexanirov, Bulgaria
1968—Boyan Radev, Bulgaria
1972—V. Rezantsev, U.S.S.R.
1976—V. Rezantsev, U.S.S.R.
1980—

HEAVYWEIGHT (220 lbs.)

1896—Schumann, Germany
1906—J. Jensen, Denmark
1908—R. Welsz, Hungary
1912—U. Saarela, Finland
1920—Lindfors, Sweden
1924—Henri Deglane, France
1928—J. R. Svensson, Sweden
1932—Karl Westergren, Sweden
1936—Kristjan Palusalu, Estonia

1948—Armet Kirecci, Turkey
1952—Ionganes Kotkas, U.S.S.R.
1956—A. Parfenev, U.S.S.R.
1960—I. Bogdan, U.S.S.R.
1964—I. Kozma, Hungary
1968—I. Kozma, Hungary
1972—N. Martinescu Romania
1976—N.Balboshin, U.S.S.R.
1980—

SUPER HEAVYWEIGHT (over 220 lbs.)

1972—A. Roshin, U.S.S.R.

1976—A. Kolchinski, U.S.S.R.
1980—

(UNOFFICIAL) TEAM CHAMPIONS

1912—Finland
1920—Finland
1924—Finland
1928—Germany
1932—Sweden

1936—Sweden
1948—Sweden
1952—U.S.S.R.
1956—U.S.S.R.
1960—U.S.S.R.

1964—U.S.S.R.
1968—U.S.S.R.
1972—U.S.S.R.
1976—U.S.S.R.
1980—

Judo

LIGHTWEIGHT (137 lbs.)

1964—T. Nakatani, Japan
1972—T. Kawaguchi, Japan

1976— H. Rodriguez, Cuba
1980—

WELTERWEIGHT (154 lbs.)

1972—T. Nomura, Japan

1976—V. Nevzorov, U.S.S.R.
1980—

MIDDLEWEIGHT (176 lbs.)

1964—I. Okano, Japan
1972—S. Sekine, Japan

1976— I. Sonoda, Japan
1980—

LIGHT HEAVYWEIGHT (205 lbs.)

1972—S. Chochosvili, U.S.S.R.

1976— K. Ninomiya, Japan
1980—

HEAVYWEIGHT (over 205 lbs.)

1964—I. Inokuma, Japan   1976— S. Novikov, U.S.S.R.
1972—W. Ruska, Netherlands   1980—

OPEN CLASS

1964—A. Geesink, Netherlands   1976—H. Uemura, Japan
1972—W. Ruska, Netherlands   1980—

(UNOFFICIAL) TEAM CHAMPION

1964—Japan   1972—Japan   1976—Japan
1980—

YACHTING

STAR CLASS

1932—Jupiter, United States   1960—Tornado, U.S.S.R.
1936—Wannsee, Germany   1964—Gem, Bahamas
1948—Hilarius, United States   1968—United States
1952—Merope, Italy   1972—Australia
1956—Kathleen, United States   *1976—Tornado Class—Great Britain
1980—

DRAGON CLASS

1948—Pan, Norway   1964—White Lady, Denmark
1952—Pan, Norway   1968—Williwaw, United States
1956—Slaghoken II, Sweden   1972—Wyuana, Australia
1960—Nirefs, Greece   *1976—470 Class—West Germany
1980—
*Changes in nomenclature and classes.

SOLING CLASS

1972—U.S.A. (Melges, Allen, Bentsen)   1976— Denmark (Jensen, Bandolowski, Hansen)
1980—

TEMPEST CLASS

1972—U.S.S.R. (Mankin, Dyrdyra)   1976— Sweden (Albrechtson, Hansson)
1980—

MONOTYPE (Finn Dinghy)

1920—Van der Bresen, Netherlands   1952—P. Elvstrom, Denmark (Finn class)
1924—L. Huybrechts, Belgium   1956—P. Elvstrom, Denmark
1928—S. G. Thorell, Sweden   1960—P. Elvstrom, Denmark
1932—J. Lebrun, France   1964—W. Kuhweide, Germany
1936—D. Kagchelland, Netherlands   1968—V. Mankin, U.S.S.R.
1948—P. Elvstrom, Denmark   1972—S. Maury, France
    (Firefly class)   1976—J. Schumann, East Germany
1980—

SHARPIE CLASS (Flying Dutchman)

1900—Olle, Great Britain   1936—Italia, Italy
1908—Cobweb, Great Britain   1956—Jest, New Zealand (sharpie class)
1912—Taifun, Norway   1960—Sirene, Norway (Flying Dutchman)
1920—Sildra (new), Norway   1964—Pandora, New Zealand
    Irene (old), Norway   1968—Superdoccious, Great Britain
1924—Bera, Norway   1972—Superdoccious, Great Britain
1928—L'Aile VI, France   1976—J. and E. Diesch, West Germany
1932—Angelita, United States   1980—

(UNOFFICIAL) TEAM CHAMPIONS

1900—France   1924—Norway   1956—Sweden
1904—None   1928—Sweden   1960—Denmark
1906—None   1932—United States   1964—United States
1908—Great Britain   1936—Germany   1968—United States
1912—Sweden   1948—United States   1972—Australia
1920—Norway   1952—United States   1976—West Germany
1980—

WINTER GAMES

BIATHLON

INDIVIDUAL

1960—K. Lestander, Sweden_____ 1:33:21.6
1964—V. Melanin, U.S.S.R._____ 1:20:26.8
1968—M. Solberg, Norway_____ 1:13:45.9

1972—M. Solberg, Norway_____ 1:15:55.5
1976—N. Kruglov, U.S.S.R._____ 1:14:12.26
1980—

RELAY

1968—U.S.S.R._____ 3:13:02.4
1972—U.S.S.R._____ 1:51:44.92

1976—U.S.S.R. _____ 1:57:55.64
1980—

BOBSLEDDING

2-MAN

1932—United States_____ 8:14.74
1936—United States_____ 5:29.29
1948—Switzerland_____ 5:29.20
1952—Germany_____ 5:24.54
1956—Italy_____ 5:30.14

1960—None
1964—Great Britain_____ 4:21.9
1968—Italy_____ 4:41.54
1972—West Germany_____ 4:57.07
1976—East Germany _____ 3:44.42
1980—

4-MAN

1924—Switzerland_____ 5:45.54
1928—United States (5-man)_____ 3:20.5
1932—United States_____ 7:53.68
1936—Switzerland_____ 5:19.85
1948—United States_____ 5:20.1
1952—Germany_____ 5:07.84

1956—Switzerland_____ 4:10.44
1960—None
1964—Canada_____ 4:14.46
1968—Italy_____ 4:17.39
1972—Switzerland_____ 4:43.07
1976—East Germany _____ 3:40.43
1980—

ICE HOCKEY

1920—Canada
1924—Canada
1928—Canada
1932—Canada
1936—Great Britain

1948—Canada
1952—Canada
1956—U.S.S.R.
1960—United States
1964—U.S.S.R.

1968—U.S.S.R.
1972—U.S.S.R.
1976—U.S.S.R.
1980—

LUGE (TOBOGGANING)

INDIVIDUAL (MEN)

1964—T. Koehler, Germany_____ 3:26.77
1968—Manfred Schmid, Austria_____ 2:52.48

1972—W. Scheidel, E. Germany_____ 3:27.58
1976—D. Guenther, _____ 3:27.688
       East Germany
1980—

2-MAN

1964—Austria_____ 1:41.62
1968—East Germany_____ 1:35.85

1972—Italy, E. Germany (tie)_____ 1:28.35
1976—East Germany _____ 1:25.604
1980—

INDIVIDUAL (WOMEN)

1964—O. Enderlein, Germany_____ 3:24.67
1968—Erica Lechner, Italy_____ 2:28.66

1972—Anna Muller, E. Germany_____ 2:59.18
1976—M. Schumann, _____ 2:50.621
       East Germany
1980—

*Olympic Record.

FIGURE SKATING

SINGLES (MEN)

	Points
1908—Ulrich Salchow, Sweden	1,865.5
1920—Gillis Grafstrom, Sweden	2,575.25
1924—Gillis Grafstrom, Sweden	2,575.25
1928—Gillis Grafstrom, Sweden	2,698.25
1932—Karl Schafer, Austria	2,602
1936—Karl Schafer, Austria	2,959
1948—Richard Button, United States	191.177
1952—Richard Button, United States	192.256
1956—Hayes Jenkins, United States	166.4
1960—David Jenkins, United States	1,440.2
1964—Manfred Schnelldorfer, Germany	1,916.9
1968—Wolfgang Schwarz, Austria	1,904.1
1972—Ondrei Nepela. Czechoslovakia	2,739.1
1976—John Curry, Great Britain	192.74
1980—	

SINGLES (WOMEN)

	Points
1908—Madge Syers, Great Britain	
1920—Magda Julin, Sweden	
1924—Heima von Szabo-Plank, Austria	2,094.25
1928—Sonja Henie, Norway	2,452.25
1932—Sonja Henie, Norway	2,302.5
1936—Sonja Henie, Norway	2,971.4
1948—Barbara Ann Scott, Canada	163.077
1952—Jeannette Altwegg, Great Britain	161.756
1956—Tenley Albright, United States	169.6
1960—Carol Heiss, United States	1,409.1
1964—Sjoukje Dijkstra, Netherlands	2,018.5
1968—Peggy Fleming, United States	1,970.
1972—Beatrix Schuba, Austria	2,751.5
1976—Dorothy Hamill, United States	193.80
1980—	

PAIRS

	Points
1908—Ann Hubler, Heinrich Burger, Germany	
1920—Ludovika & Walter Jakobsson, Finland	
1924—H. Englemann, A. Berger, Austria	74.50
1928—Andree Joly, Pierre Brunet, France	100.50
1932—Andree & Pierre Brunet, France	76.7
1936—Maxie Herber, Ernst Baier, Germany	103.3
1948—Micheline Lannoy, Pierre Baugniet, Belgium	11.227
1952—Ria & Paul Falk, Germany	11.400
1956—Elizabeth Schwartz, Kurt Oppelt, Austria	14
1960—Barbara Wagner, Robert Paul, Canada	80.4
1964—Ludmila Belousova, Oleg Protopopov, U.S.S.R.	104.4
1968—Ludmila Belousova, Oleg Protopopov, U.S.S.R.	315.2
1972—Irina Rodnina, Alexei Ulanov, U.S.S.R.	420.4
1976—Irina Rodnina, Aleksandr Zaitsev, U.S.S.R.	140.54
1980—	

SPEED SKATING (MEN)

500 METERS

1924—Charles Jewtraw, U.S.A.	0:44	1956—Evgeny, Grishin, U.S.S.R.	0:40.2
1928—Clas Thunberg, Finland		1960—Evgeny Grishin, U.S.S.R.	0:40.2
Bernt Evensen, Norway (tie)	0:43.4	1964—Terry McDermott, U.S.A.	0:40.1
1932—John A. Shea, U.S.A.	0:43.4	1968—Erhard Keller, W. Germany	0:40.3
1936—Ivar Ballangrud, Norway	0:43.4	1972—Erhard Keller, W. Germany	0:39.44
1948—Finn Helgesen, Norway	0:43.1	1976—E. Kulikov, U.S.S.R.	0:39.17*
1952—Ken Henry, U.S.A.	0:43.2	1980—	

*Olympic Record.
**Added events listed on page

1,500 METERS

1924—Clas Thunberg, Finland..... 2:20.8	1960—E. Grishin, U.S.S.R.
1928—Clas Thunberg, Finland..... 2:21.1	R. Aas, Norway (tie)........ 2:10.4
1932—John A. Shea, U.S.A........ 2:57.5	1964—Ants Antson, U.S.S.R........ 2:10.3
1936—C. Mathisen, Norway........ 2:19.2	1968—Kees Verkerk, Netherlands.. 2:03.4
1948—Sverre Farstad, Norway..... 2:17.6	1972—Ard Schenk, Netherlands.... 2:02.96
1952—Hjalmar Andersen, Norway.. 2:20.4	1976—J.-E. Storholt, Norway..... 1:59.38*
1956—E. Grishin, U.S.S.R.	1980—
Y. Mikhailov, U.S.S.R. (tie).. 2:08.6	

5,000 METERS

1924—Clas Thunberg, Finland..... 8:39	1956—Boris Shilkow, U.S.S.R...... 7:48.7
1928—Ivar Ballangrud, Norway.... 8:50.5	1960—Viktor Kosichkin, U.S.S.R... 7:51.3
1932—Irving Jaffee, U.S.A........ 9:40.8	1964—Knut Johannesen, Norway... 7:38.4
1936—Ivar Ballangrud, Norway.... 8:19.6	1968—F. Anton Maier, Norway..... 7:22.4
1948—Reidar Liakiew, Norway..... 8:29.4	1972—Ard Schenk, Netherlands.... 7:23.61
1952—Hjalmar Andersen, Norway.. 8:10.6	1976—S. Stensen, Norway 7:24.48*
	1980—

10,000 METERS

1924—Julien Skutnabb, Finland....18:04.8	1956—Sigge Ericsson, Sweden.....16:35.9
1928—Irving Jaffee, U.S.A.........18:36.5†	1960—Knut Johannesen, Norway...15:46.6
1932—Irving Jaffee, U.S.A.........19:13.6	1964—Jonny Nilsson, Sweden.......15:50.1
1936—Ivar Ballangrud, Norway....17:24.3	1968—Johnny Hoeglin, Sweden.....15:23.6
1948—Ake Seyffarth, Sweden......17:26.3	1972—Ard Schenk, Netherlands....15:01.35
1952—H. Andersen, Norway........16:45.8	1976—P. Kleine, Netherlands 14:50.59*
	1980—

SPEED SKATING (WOMEN)

500 METERS

1960—H. Hasse, Germany.......... 0:45.9	1972—A. Henning, U.S.A........... 0:43.33
1964—L. Skoblikova, U.S.S.R...... 0:45.0	1976—S. Young, U.S.A. -------- 0:42.76*
1968—L. Titova, U.S.S.R.......... 0:46.1	1980—

1,000 METERS

1960—K. Guseva, U.S.S.R.......... 1:34.1	1972—M. Pflug, W. Germany....... 1:31.4
1964—L. Skoblikova, U.S.S.R...... 1:33.2	1976—T. Averina, U.S.S.R. 1:28.43*
1968—C. Geijssen, Netherlands... 1:32.6	1980—

1,500 METERS

1960—L. Skoblikova, U.S.S.R...... 2:25.2	1972—D. Holum, U.S.A............ 2:20.8
1964—L. Skoblikova, U.S.S.R...... 2:22.6	1976—G. Stepanskaya, U.S.S.R. .. 2:16.58*
1968—V. Mustonen, Finland....... 2:22.4	1980—

3,000 METERS

1960—L. Skoblikova, U.S.S.R...... 5:14.3	1972—S. Baas-Kaiser, Netherlands. 4:52.14
1964—L. Skoblikova, U.S.S.R...... 5:14.9	1976—T. Averina, U.S.S.R. 4:45.19*
1968—J. Schut, Netherlands....... 4:56.2	1980—

SKIING (MEN)

JUMPING—NORDIC (70 METERS)

	Points
1924—Jacob T. Thams, Norway	18.96
1928—Alfred Andersen, Norway	19.208
1932—Birger Ruud, Norway	228.1
1936—Birger Ruud, Norway	232.0
1948—Petter Hugsted, Norway	228.1
1952—Arnfinn Bergmann, Norway	226.0
1956—Antti Hyvarinen, Finland	227.0
1960—Helmut Recknagel, Germany	227.2
1964—Viekko Kankkonen, Finland	229.9
1968—Jiri Raska, Czechoslovakia	216.8
1972—Yukio Kasaya, Japan	244.2
1976—J. G. Aschenbach, East Germany	252.0
1980—	

*Olympic Record.
†Thawing of ice caused event to be canceled. Jaffee had best time.

JUMPING—NORDIC (90 METERS)

		Points
1964—Toralf Engan, Norway		230.7
1968—V. Beloussov, U.S.S.R.		231.3
1972—W. Fortuna, Poland		219.9
1976—K. Schnabl, Austria		234.8
1980—		

CROSS-COUNTRY (15-18 KILOMETERS)

1924—Thorleif Haug, Norway (18 km)	1:14:31
1928—Johann Grottumsbraaten, Norway (19,700 meters)	1:37:1
1932—Sven Utterstrom, Sweden (18,214 meters)	1:23:7
1936—Erik-Aug. Larsson, Sweden (18 km)	1:14:38
1948—M. Lundstrom, Sweden	1:13:50
1952—Hallgeir Brenden, Norway	1:01:34
1956—Hallgeir Brenden, Norway (15 km)	0:49:39.0
1960—Haakon Brusveen, Norway	0:51:55.5
1964—Eero Meantyranta, Finland	0:50:54.1
1968—Harold Groenninger, Norway	0:47:54.2
1972—S. A. Lundback, Sweden	0:45:28.24
1976—N. Bajukov, U.S.S.R.	0:43:58.47
1980—	

30 KILOMETERS

1956—Veikko Hakulinen, Finland	1:44:06
1960—Sixten Jernberg, Sweden	1:51:03.9
1964—Eero Meantyranta, Finland	1:30:50.7
1968—Franco Nones, Italy	1:35:39.2
1972—V. Vedenin, U.S.S.R.	1:36:31.15
1976—S. Saveliev, U.S.S.R.	1:30:29.38
1980—	

50 KILOMETERS

1924—Thorleif Haug, Norway	3:44:32
1928—P. Hedlund, Sweden	4:52:37
1932—Veli Saarinen, Finland	4:28:00
1936—Elis Viklund, Sweden	3:30:11
1948—Nils Karlsson, Sweden	3:47:48
1952—Veikko Hakulinen, Finland	3:33:33
1956—Sixten Jernberg, Sweden	2:50:27
1960—Kelevi Hamalainen, Finland	2:59:06.3
1964—Sixten Jernberg, Sweden	2:43:52.6
1968—Die Ellefsaeter, Norway	2:28:45.8
1972—Paal Tyldum, Norway	2:43:14.75
1976—I. Formo, Norway	2:37:30.05
1980—	

SLALOM—ALPINE

1948—Edi Reinalter, Switzerland	2:10.3
1952—Othmar Schneider, Austria	2:00.0
1956—Toni Sailer, Austria	3:14.7
1960—Ernst Hinterseer, Austria	2:08.9
1964—Joseph Stiegler, Austria	2:11.13
1968—Jean Claude Killy, France	2:39.73
1972—Francisco Ochoa, Spain	1:49.27
1976—P. Gros, Italy	2:03.29
1980—	

GIANT SLALOM—ALPINE

1952—Stein Eriksen, Norway	2:25.0
1956—Toni Sailer, Austria	3:00.1
1960—Roger Staub, Switzerland	1:48.3
1964—Francois Bonlieu, France	1:46.7
1968—Jean Claude Killy, France (2)	3:29.28
1972—Gustav Thoeni, Italy	3:09.62
1976—H. Hemmi, Switzerland	3:26.97
1980—	

DOWNHILL RACE—ALPINE

1948—Henri Oreiller, France	2:55.0
1952—Zeno Colo, Italy	2:30.8
1956—Toni Sailer, Austria	2:52.2
1960—Jean Vuarnet, France	2:06.0
1964—Egon Zimmerman, Austria	2:18.16
1968—Jean Claude Killy, France	1:59.85
1972—Bernhard Russi, Switzerland	1:51.43
1976—F. Klammer, Austria	1:45.73
1980—	

NORDIC COMBINED (15/18-KILOMETER RACE AND JUMP)*

		Points
1924—Thorleif Haug, Norway		18.906
1928—Johan Grottumsbraaten, Norway		17.833
1932—Johan Grottumsbraaten, Norway		446.00
1936—Oddbjorn Hagen, Norway		430.30
1948—Heikki Hasu, Finland		448.80
1952—Simon Slattwik, Norway		451.60
1956—Sverre Stenersen, Norway		445.00
1960—Georg Thoma, Germany		457.952
1964—Tormod Knutsen, Norway		469.28
1968—Franz Keller, West Germany		449.04
1972—Ulrich Wehling, East Germany		413.34
1976—Ulrich Wehling, East Germany		423.39
1980—		

40-KILOMETER RELAY

1936—Finland	2:41:33	1964—Sweden	2:18:34.6
1948—Sweden	2:32:08	1968—Norway	2:08:33.5
1952—Finland	2:20:16	1972—U.S.S.R.	2:04:47.94
1956—U.S.S.R.	2:15:30	1976—Finland	2:07:59.72
1960—Finland	2:18:45.6	1980—	

SKIING (WOMEN)

DOWNHILL RACE

1948—Hedi Schlunegger, Switzerland	2:28.3
1952—Trude Jochum-Beiser, Austria	1:47.1
1956—Madeleine Berthod, Switzerland	1:40.7
1960—Heidi Beibi, Germany	1:37.6
1964—Christl Haas, Austria	1:55.39
1968—Olga Pall, Austria	1:40.87
1972—Marie Therese Nadig, Switzerland	1:36.68
1976—R. Mittermaier, West Germany	1:46.16
1980—	

10-KILOMETER CROSS-COUNTRY—NORDIC

1952—L. Wideman, Finland	41:40
1956—L. Kozyreva, U.S.S.R.	38:11
1960—M. Gusakova, U.S.S.R.	39:46.6
1964—Claudia Boyarskikh, U.S.S.R.	40:24.3
1968—Toini Gustaffson, Sweden	36:46.5
1972—Galina Kulakova, U.S.S.R.	34:17.82
1976—R. Smetanina, U.S.S.R.	30:13.41
1980—	

SLALOM—ALPINE

1948—Gretchen Fraser, United States	1:57.2
1952—Andrea Mead Lawrence, United States	2:11.4
1956—Renne Colliard, Switzerland	1:52.3
1960—Anne Heggtveit, Canada	1:49.6
1964—Christine Goitschel, France	1:29.86
1968—Marielle Goitschel, France	1:25.86
1972—Barbara Cochran, United States	1:31.24
1976—R. Mittermaier, West Germany	1:30.54
1980—	

GIANT SLALOM—ALPINE

1952—Andrea Mead Lawrence, United States	2:06.8
1956—Ossi Reichert, Germany	1:56.5
1960—Yvonne Ruegg, Switzerland	1:39.9
1964—Marielle Goitschel, France	1:53.1
1968—Nancy Greene, Canada	1:51.97
1972—Marie Therese Nadig, Switzerland	1:29.90
1976—K. Kreiner, Canada	1:29.13
1980—	

*Changed from 18-kilometer cross-country to 15-kilometer cross-country in 1956.

350

3 x 5 KILOMETER RELAY

1956—Finland	1:09:01
1960—Sweden	1:04:21.4
1964—U.S.S.R.	0:59:20.2
1968—Norway	0:57:30.0
1972—U.S.S.R.	0:48:46.15
1976—U.S.S.R.	1:07:49.75
1980—	

5-KILOMETER CROSS-COUNTRY

1964—C. Boyarskiskh, U.S.S.R.	17:50.5	1972—G. Kulakova, U.S.S.R.	17:00.5
1968—T. Gustaffsson, Sweden	16:45.2	1976—H. Takalo, Finland	15:48.69
		1980—	

ADDED EVENTS IN 1976

CANOEING (MEN)

KAYAK SINGLES 500M

1976—Vasile Diba, Romania ____ 1:46.41*
1980—

KAYAK DOUBLES 500M

1976—East Germany, (Mattern, Olbricht) ____ 1:35.87*
1980—

CANADIAN SINGLES 500M

1976—Aleksandr Rogov, U.S.S.R. ____ 1:59.23*
1980—

CANADIAN DOUBLES 500M

1976—U.S.S.R., (Petrenko, Winogradov) ____ 1:45.81*
1980—

TRACK AND FIELD (WOMEN)

4 x 400M RELAY

1976—East Germany	3:19:23*
World's Record East German Team (Maletzki, Rhode, Streidt, Brehmer)	3:19.23
1980—	

WINTER SPORTS

ICE DANCING

1976—U.S.S.R. (L. Pakhomova, A. Gorshkov)	209.92
1980—	

SPEED SKATING (MEN) 1,000M

1976—P. Mueller, U.S.A.	1:19.32*
1980—	

DAILY SPORT SCHEDULE OF 1980 OLYMPIC GAMES

LAKE PLACID, NEW YORK

Sport	Feb 12	Feb 13	Feb 14	Feb 15	Feb 16	Feb 17	Feb 18	Feb 19	Feb 20	Feb 21	Feb 22	Feb 23	Feb 24
Opening Ceremony	×	×											
Alpine Ski (men)		×	×				×	×			×		
Alpine Ski (women)						×			×	×		×	
Biathlon				×	×			×			×	×	×
Bobsled					×	×		×	×			×	×
Cross Country (men)			×		×		×			×			
Cross Country (women)						×	×	×	×	×		×	
Figure Skating			×	×							×	×	×
Ice Hockey				×	×		×						×
Luge					×		×	×			×		
Ski Jumping													
Speed Skating (men)		×			×	×				×			
Speed Skating (women)			×	×	×				×				
Ceremonies			×	×	×	×	×	×	×	×	×	×	×

MOSCOW

Sport	Jul 19	Jul 20	Jul 21	Jul 22	Jul 23	Jul 24	Jul 25	Jul 26	Jul 27	Jul 28	Jul 29	Jul 30	Jul 31	Aug 1	Aug 2	Aug 3
Opening Ceremony	×															
Archery		×									×	×	×	×		
Athletics			×	×	×	×	×	×	×	×						
Basketball (men)		×	×	×		×	×	×	×	×	×					
Basketball (women)			×	×		×	×		×	×						

MOSCOW (Continued)

Sport	Jul 19	Jul 20	Jul 21	Jul 22	Jul 23	Jul 24	Jul 25	Jul 26	Jul 27	Jul 28	Jul 29	Jul 30	Jul 31	Aug 1	Aug 2	Aug 3
Boxing		×		×	×	×	×	×	×	×	×	×	×		×	
Canoe & Kayak						×						×	×	×	×	
Cycling (track)		×	×	×	×	×		×								
Cycling (road)										×						×
Equestrian							×	×	×	×		×	×	×	×	×
Fencing			×	×		×	×	×	×	×	×	×	×			
Field Hockey (men)			×	×	×	×		×	×	×	×	×	×	×		
Field Hockey (women)				×	×		×	×	×	×	×	×	×			
Football						×		×	×		×			×		
Gymnastics						×	×	×		×					×	
Handball (men)				×		×		×			×	×	×			
Handball (women)			×	×	×	×	×	×		×	×	×	×	×	×	
Judo			×	×	×	×	×									
Modern Pentathlon					×	×	×	×	×							
Rowing					×	×	×	×	×							
Shooting		×	×	×	×	×	×	×								
Swimming			×	×	×	×	×	×	×	×						
Diving						×	×	×	×	×	×	×				
Waterpolo		×	×	×	×	×	×	×	×	×	×	×	×	×	×	
Volleyball (men)		×	×	×	×	×	×	×	×	×	×	×	×	×	×	
Volleyball (women)					×	×	×	×	×	×	×	×				
Weightlifting						×	×	×	×	×	×	×	×	×		
Wrestling Free Style		×	×	×	×	×	×									
Wrestling Greco-Roman									×	×	×	×				
Yachting								×	×	×	×	×	×	×		
Closing Ceremony																×